FEMINIST JUDGMENTS: REWRITTEN TAX OPINIONS

Could a feminist perspective change the shape of the tax law? Most people understand that feminist reasoning has tremendous potential to affect, for example, the law of employment discrimination, sexual harassment, and reproductive rights. Few people may be aware, however, that feminist analysis can likewise transform tax law (as well as other statutory or code-based areas of the law). By highlighting the importance of perspective, background, and preconceptions on the reading and interpretation of statutes, *Feminist Judgments: Rewritten Tax Opinions* shows what a difference feminist analysis can make to statutory interpretation. This volume, part of the Feminist Judgments Series, brings together a group of scholars and lawyers to rewrite tax decisions in which a feminist emphasis would have changed the outcome or the court's reasoning. The volume includes cases that implicate gender on their face (such as medical expense deductions for fertility treatment or gender confirmation surgery and special tax benefits for married individuals) as well as cases without an obvious connection to gender (such as the tax treatment of tribal lands and the business expense deduction). This book thus opens the way for a discussion of how viewpoint is a key factor in all statutory interpretation cases.

Bridget J. Crawford is Professor of Law at the Elisabeth Haub School of Law at Pace University.

Anthony C. Infanti is Professor of Law at the University of Pittsburgh School of Law.

Feminist Judgments Series Editors

Bridget J. Crawford
Elisabeth Haub School of Law at Pace University

Kathryn M. Stanchi
Temple University Beasley School of Law

Linda L. Berger
University of Nevada, Las Vegas William S. Boyd School of Law

Advisory Panel for Feminist Judgments Series

Feminist Judgments: Rewritten Tax Opinions

Edited by

BRIDGET J. CRAWFORD
Pace University

ANTHONY C. INFANTI
University of Pittsburgh

CAMBRIDGE
UNIVERSITY PRESS

CAMBRIDGE
UNIVERSITY PRESS

University Printing House, Cambridge CB2 8BS, United Kingdom

One Liberty Plaza, 20th Floor, New York, NY 10006, USA

477 Williamstown Road, Port Melbourne, VIC 3207, Australia

314–321, 3rd Floor, Plot 3, Splendor Forum, Jasola District Centre, New Delhi – 110025, India

79 Anson Road, #06–04/06, Singapore 079906

Cambridge University Press is part of the University of Cambridge.

It furthers the University's mission by disseminating knowledge in the pursuit of
education, learning, and research at the highest international levels of excellence.

www.cambridge.org
Information on this title: www.cambridge.org/9781316510209
DOI: 10.1017/9781108225007

© Cambridge University Press 2017

First published 2017

Printed in the United States of America by Sheridan Books, Inc.

A catalogue record for this publication is available from the British Library.

Library of Congress Cataloging-in-Publication Data
NAMES: Crawford, Bridget J., editor. | Infanti, Anthony C., 1968– , editor.
TITLE: Feminist judgments : rewritten tax opinions / Bridget J. Crawford, Elisabeth Haub School
    of Law at Pace University; Anthony C. Infanti, University of Pittsburgh School of Law.
DESCRIPTION: Cambridge, United Kingdom ; New York, NY, USA : Cambridge University Press,
    2018. | Series: Feminist judgments series | Includes bibliographical references and index.
IDENTIFIERS: LCCN 2017025167 | ISBN 9781316510209 (hardback : alk. paper) |
    ISBN 9781316649596 (pbk. : alk. paper)
SUBJECTS: LCSH: Taxation–Law and legislation–United States–Cases. | Sex discrimination–Law
    and legislation–United States–Cases. | Feminist jurisprudence–United States.
CLASSIFICATION: LCC KF6289 .F46 2018 | DDC 343.7304–DC23 LC record available
    at https://lccn.loc.gov/2017025167

ISBN 978-1-316-51020-9 Hardback
ISBN 978-1-316-64959-6 Paperback

Contents

Advisory Panel for *Feminist Judgments: Rewritten Tax Opinions*

Alice G. Abreu, Professor of Law, Temple University Beasley School of Law

Patricia A. Cain, Professor of Law, Santa Clara University School of Law

Joseph M. Dodge, Professor of Law, Emeritus, Florida State University College of Law

Mary Louise Fellows, Everett Fraser Professor of Law, Emerita, University of Minnesota Law School

Wendy C. Gerzog, Professor of Law, Emerita, University of Baltimore School of Law

Steve R. Johnson, Dunbar Family Professor, Florida State University College of Law

Marjorie E. Kornhauser, John E. Koerner Professor of Law, Tulane University Law School

Ajay K. Mehrotra, Executive Director and Research Professor, American Bar Foundation, and Professor of Law, Northwestern University Pritzker School of Law

Beverly I. Moran, Professor of Law & Professor of Sociology, Vanderbilt University School of Law

Richard L. Schmalbeck, Simpson Thacher & Bartlett Professor of Law, Duke University School of Law

Nancy Staudt, Dean and Howard & Caroline Cayne Professor of Law, Washington University School of Law

Lawrence A. Zelenak, Pamela B. Gann Professor of Law, Duke University School of Law

Notes on Contributors

Nicole Appleberry is Clinical Assistant Professor of Law at the University of Michigan Law School.

Linda M. Beale is Professor of Law and Director of Graduate Studies at Wayne State University School of Law.

Jennifer E. Bird-Pollan is the James and Mary Lassiter Associate Professor of Law at the University of Kentucky College of Law.

David A. Brennen is Dean and Professor of Law at the University of Kentucky College of Law.

Patricia A. Cain is Professor of Law at Santa Clara University School of Law.

Grant Christensen is Assistant Professor of Law at the University of North Dakota School of Law.

Danshera Cords is Professor of Law at Albany Law School.

Bridget J. Crawford is Professor of Law at the Elisabeth Haub School of Law at Pace University.

David B. Cruz is Professor of Law at the University of Southern California Gould School of Law.

Michelle Lyon Drumbl is Clinical Professor of Law and Director of the Tax Clinic at Washington and Lee University School of Law.

Mary Louise Fellows is the Everett Fraser Professor of Law, Emerita at the University of Minnesota Law School.

Wendy C. Gerzog is Professor of Law, Emerita at the University of Baltimore School of Law.

Mary L. Heen is Professor of Law at the University of Richmond School of Law.

Anthony C. Infanti is Professor of Law at the University of Pittsburgh School of Law.

Nancy J. Knauer is the I. Herman Stern Professor of Law and Director of Law & Public Policy Programs at Temple Univerity Beasley School of Law.

Kathleen A. Lahey is a professor on the Faculty of Law, Queen's University.

Francine J. Lipman is the William S. Boyd Professor of Law at the University of Nevada, Las Vegas William S. Boyd School of Law.

Goldburn P. Maynard Jr. is Assistant Professor of Law at the University of Louisville Brandeis School of Law.

Ann M. Murphy is Professor of Law at Gonzaga University School of Law.

Katherine Pratt is Professor of Law and the Sayre Macneil Fellow at Loyola Law School Los Angeles.

Mildred Wigfall Robinson is the Henry L. and Grace Doherty Charitable Foundation Professor of Law at the University of Virginia School of Law.

Ruthann Robson is Professor of Law and University Distinguished Professor at the City University of New York School of Law.

Allison Anna Tait is Assistant Professor of Law at the University of Richmond School of Law.

Chloe Thompson is an attorney for the Snoqualmie Indian Tribe and Adjunct Professor at Seattle University School of Law.

Elaine Waterhouse Wilson is Associate Professor of Law at the West Virginia University College of Law.

Preface

Could a feminist perspective change the shape of the tax law? To begin to answer this question, we brought together a group of scholars and lawyers to rewrite, using feminist perspectives, significant tax cases from the United States Tax Court, federal Circuit Courts of Appeals, and the United States Supreme Court. Some of them implicate gender on their face – questions about the deductibility of fertility expenses or the use of gender in actuarial tables, for example – but others implicate gender less obviously, such as a case involving the ability of state and local governments to tax Indian land, or the ability of a businessman to take a deduction for the repayment of certain debts. This book challenges the belief that statutes are neutral. Most people understand that feminist reasoning has tremendous potential to affect, for example, the law of employment discrimination, sexual harassment, and reproductive rights. Few people may be aware, however, that feminist analysis can likewise transform tax law (as well as other statutory or code-based areas of the law). By highlighting the importance of perspective, background, and preconceptions on the reading and interpretation of statutes, *Feminist Judgments: Rewritten Tax Opinions* shows what a difference feminist analysis can make to statutory interpretation.

This volume, like all of the books in Cambridge University Press's Feminist Judgments Series, demonstrates that judges with feminist viewpoints could have changed the law, based on the precedent and law in effect at the time of the original decision. Or, even if the desired result could not be achieved under the current law, this volume shows how a powerful dissent can serve to draw attention to the fact that the tax law operates in many cases to the disadvantage of women, racial minorities, LGBT taxpayers, and other historically subordinated groups. Together, the opinions and commentaries in this volume illustrate the importance of diversity of perspectives on the bench so that judges do not approach their work with a uniform worldview influenced by the same set of preconceptions and privileges. For judges, lawyers, students, and members of the general public, reading these critical opinions helps expose the ways in which judges – and, in turn, the development of the law – are subtly influenced by preconceptions, existing power hierarchies, prevailing social norms, and "conventional" wisdom. This book argues that the tax law is not neutral, but rather is shaped by the society that produces and applies it. At the same time, this book holds out the hope that the tax system can be reformed to be an instrument of greater justice and equality for all people.

Acknowledgments

This book would not have been possible without the support of Cambridge University Press, which so enthusiastically endorsed a series of books following the publication of *Feminist Judgments: Rewritten Opinions of the United States Supreme Court* (2016). The larger U.S. Feminist Judgments project is intellectually indebted to the women who created the Women's Court of Canada and the UK Feminist Judgments Project, which inspired similar projects throughout the world.

We are grateful to Kathryn M. Stanchi and Linda Berger for their leadership and guidance. We wish to thank the members of our Advisory Panel, who embraced the project with enthusiasm and helped us think about the book's organization, limitations, and challenges. Our editor John Berger provided guidance and assistance throughout the publication process.

For research assistance, we thank Briana Alongi and Kyrie Lokhaiser. For administrative assistance, we thank Judy Jaeger and the staff in the University of Pittsburgh School of Law's Document Technology Center.

Each of us would like to thank the many colleagues, students, friends, and family members who have supported our work on this project. Bridget Crawford thanks Horace Anderson, Catharine MacKinnon, Vanessa Merton, Dan Renkin, Michelle Simon, and the members of the Women's Association of Law Students at the Elisabeth Haub School of Law at Pace University. Anthony Infanti thanks the University of Pittsburgh School of Law for its financial support of his work on this project and his family for their support and understanding during his many hours of work on this project. We both thank all of our contributors for their enthusiasm and many hours of work and dedication (and numerous rounds of editing!) that have brought this project to life.

Table of Cases

Table of Internal Revenue Code Sections

Table of Treasury Regulation Sections

PART I

Introduction and Overview

Introduction to the *Feminist Judgments*: *Rewritten Tax Opinions* Project

BRIDGET J. CRAWFORD AND ANTHONY C. INFANTI

How would judicial opinions change if the judges used feminist methods and perspectives when deciding cases? That is a question that various groups of scholars, working around the globe and mostly independently of each other, have taken up in a series of books of "shadow opinions" – literally rewritten judicial decisions – using precedents, authorities, theories, and approaches that were in existence at the time of the original decision to reach radically different outcomes and often using saliently different reasoning. This global sociolegal movement toward critical opinion writing originated when a group of lawyers and law professors who called themselves the Women's Court of Canada published a series of six decisions in 2008 in the *Canadian Journal of Women and the Law*. Inspired by that project, scholars have produced similar projects in the United Kingdom,[1] Australia,[2] the United States,[3] and Ireland.[4] Other projects well under way involve New Zealand law[5] and international law.[6] Nascent projects are under consideration in India and Scotland as well.

---

[1] *See* Feminist Judgments: From Theory to Practice (Rosemary Hunter et al. eds., 2010).

[2] *See* Australian Feminist Judgments: Righting and Rewriting Law (Heather Douglas et al. eds., 2015).

[3] *See* Feminist Judgments: Rewritten Opinions of the United States Supreme Court (Kathryn M. Stanchi, Linda L. Berger, & Bridget J. Crawford eds., 2016).

[4] *See* Northern/Irish Feminist Judgments: Judges' Troubles and the Gendered Politics of Identity (Máiréad Enright et al. eds., 2017).

[5] *See New Research Project to Look at New Zealand Judgments from a New Angle*, ADLS (Oct. 16, 2015), http://www.adls.org.nz/for-the-profession/news-and-opinion/2015/10/16/new-research-project-to-look-at-new-zealand-judgments-from-a-new-angle/ (describing Feminist Judgments Project Aotearoa).

[6] *See Feminist International Judgments Project: Women's Voices in International Law*, U. Leicester, http://www2.le.ac.uk/institution/researchimages/feminist-international-judgments-project-women2019s-voices-in-international-law (last visited Mar. 31, 2017) (describing Feminist International Judgments (Troy Lavers & Loveday Hodson eds., forthcoming)).

What all of these projects have in common is that they involve rewriting judicial opinions that, up until this point, have mostly, if not entirely, been grounded in questions of constitutional interpretation. The Women's Court of Canada, for example, focused attention on Section 15 (the equality clause) of the Canadian Charter of Rights and Freedoms (for a discussion of Section 15 in this volume, see Kathleen Lahey's contribution in Chapter 2). The U.S. project, *Feminist Judgments: Rewritten Opinions of the United States Supreme Court*, examined twenty-five key cases on gender ranging from 1873 to 2015, most of which involved the interpretation of constitutional rights.

This book approaches the question posed at the start of this chapter from a different perspective – that is, it concerns the rewriting of judicial opinions in an area of law that is largely governed by statute and in which constitutional arguments play a relatively small role. This book thus takes the sociolegal movement of critical opinion writing in a new, hitherto uncharted direction. The book is also – and quite appropriately in view of the tax system's key and keystone role in society – the first in a series of U.S.-based *Feminist Judgments* books to be published by Cambridge University Press. Future volumes in the series are expected to take up other areas of law and a variety of state and federal court decisions organized around different subject matters.

THE APPEAL OF CRITICAL OPINION WRITING

Critical opinion writing, as a form of scholarship, has tremendous appeal to us – and given the number of completed, ongoing, and nascent projects around the world, it obviously appeals to others in different countries and across a variety of areas of law, too. But why? For us, critical opinion writing is appealing because it represents a multidimensional and iterative challenge to preconceived notions about law's subjects and objects as well as about how law is created and interpreted and how it develops. Critical opinion writing challenges not only the law and the legal system to open its vistas but also represents particular challenges to those who write and rewrite judicial opinions and to those who read and consume those opinions.

Critical opinion writing challenges the rewriter – professors and practitioners who are mostly accustomed to analyzing, applying, and critiquing judicial opinions rather than writing them from the ground up – by forcing the critic/consumer to place herself in the shoes of the judge/opinion writer. With views colored by the path that history has taken since the original opinion was written but confined to sources available at the time the original opinion was drafted, the rewriter finds that she must wrestle with and resolve the issues and conundrums that judges routinely face. Thought must be given to achieving a just result in the case at hand while taking a broader view of how the case fits into the general framework and structures of the law so as not to prematurely stymie future legal development or foreclose it altogether. This move of placing the critic/consumer of judicial opinions into the role of the judge provides the opinion rewriter with a new lens for viewing and interpreting judicial opinions when she returns to her life as a critic/consumer of judicial opinions. This experience should provide the rewriter with a new appreciation for the difficulty of crafting good judicial opinions and increase her empathy for the role played by judges.

At the same time, critical opinion writing challenges judges themselves by highlighting the contingent nature of the opinions that they write and their role in the process of making law. Imagining an alternative path for the law – whether by directly displacing the majority opinion in a case or by laying the groundwork for taking a different path in the future through an imagined concurring or dissenting opinion – challenges the aura of neutrality and objectivity conveyed by the tone that judges generally use when writing their opinions, as well as the notion that it is not so much the person as the judicial office pronouncing judgment. The rewritten opinions thus pointedly show that, however nostalgic the analogy, deciding cases is about much more than being a baseball umpire who simply calls balls and strikes, as some have contended.[7] Through the act of producing work in the form of a judicial opinion (rather than the more typical law review article or essay critiquing an opinion), the opinion rewriter demonstrates that judges possess no monopoly on articulating what the law ought to be, much less on purporting to correctly interpret the law or to set the law on a path toward furthering the cause of justice and the flourishing of society. The commentaries provided alongside the rewritten opinions underscore this challenge by explaining just how the rewritten opinions differ from the originals and by imagining what a different path for sociolegal history might have looked like. Taken together, the opinions and commentaries in this volume also help make the case for ensuring that there is a diversity of backgrounds on the bench so that judges do not approach their work with a uniform worldview influenced by the same set of preconceptions and privilegings and can thus helpfully challenge and question each other's perspectives.

For those who read these rewritten opinions (and we hope that some sitting judges will be among the readers of this volume), critical opinion writing may help expose the ways in which judges – and, in turn, the development of the

---

[7] Bob Egelko, *Roberts Deftly Evades Attempts to Pin Him Down*, S.F. CHRON., Sept. 15, 2006, at A4.

law – are subtly influenced by preconceptions, endemic privilegings and power hierarchies, and prevailing social norms and "conventional" wisdom. Especially when compared with the original opinions, the rewritten opinions concretely demonstrate how opening oneself to different and differing viewpoints that bring to the surface and call into question how underlying subjective experiences and perspectives can influence the current interpretation and application of the law – as well as its future development – in ways that benefit society as a whole. Naturally, the commentaries included with each rewritten opinion in this volume facilitate this process, but, in the end, there is no substitute for comparing the original and rewritten opinions side by side and examining them for yourself. Whether you are a student of tax law, a practitioner, a judge, or merely an interested taxpayer, actively engaging in this process of questioning judicial decision-making can help sensitize readers of judicial decisions to the multiple (and sometimes insidious) influences on any decision-maker. For those judges among our readers, this process can go far toward ensuring that these influences do not inappropriately creep into their own opinion writing.

GOALS OF THE PROJECT

This volume, *Feminist Judgments: Rewritten Tax Opinions*, is unique primarily for two reasons. First, its focus is on an area of law that most people do not associate with feminism or gender equality. Second, as mentioned earlier, this volume focuses on an area of law that is largely controlled by statutes and in which constitutional arguments typically play a relatively small role. But just as the volume that gave rise to this series, *Feminist Judgments: Rewritten Opinions of the United States Supreme Court*, showed how feminist analysis can transform decisions of the nation's highest court, so too does this volume show how feminist analysis can transform tax law (as well as other statutory or code-based areas of the law) by highlighting the importance of perspective, background, and preconceptions on the reading and interpretation of statutes. As William Eskridge argues in *Dynamic Statutory Interpretation*, with the passage of time, the perspective of anyone interpreting a law "diverges from that of the statute as a result of changed circumstances which give rise to unanticipated problems, developments in law and the statute's evolution, and different political and ideological frameworks."[8] In Eskridge's view, statutes are just as much subject to interpretation as the common law and the

---

[8]   William N. Eskridge Jr., Dynamic Statutory Interpretation 11 (1994).

Constitution are – and understanding this fact is crucial to understanding how the modern regulatory state operates.[9] This book of rewritten tax opinions similarly stands on the foundational belief that statutes are susceptible to multiple interpretations, and who is doing the interpreting matters greatly.

Within the scholarly tax community, there historically has been great resistance to bringing noneconomic "perspectives" to bear in the analysis or interpretation of tax law (whether those perspectives are based on critical race theory, feminism, queer theory, or other "outsider" approaches to the law). Instead, "mainstream" scholars have traditionally viewed tax law as closely aligned with the "science" of economics. From this perspective, the core questions addressed by tax law cut across all lines of difference in society – save those of income or, for those working in the transfer tax area, wealth – and are thus unaffected by concerns relating to race, ethnicity, gender and gender identity/expression, sexual orientation, socioeconomic class, immigration status, and disability. For this reason, "mainstream" tax scholars resist the notion that these "social" concerns play any part in our "neutral" tax laws and greet the critical tax scholars who raise these concerns through work that draws attention to the differential or discriminatory impact of tax laws on traditionally subordinated groups either with hostility or, more commonly, a cold shoulder.

For scholars and laypeople alike, tax is considered to be an arcane and technical subject, but all can agree that taxes have a direct impact on the pocketbook. Taxes impact each of us in terms of how much of our salary we take home from work each pay period; how much we pay for items at the grocery store; how much it costs us to purchase and own a home (due to the deductibility of home mortgage interest and property taxes and transfer taxes levied at the time of purchase or sale); and how much it costs us to transfer to family and friends, either by gift or inheritance, the property that we accumulate during our lives – just to name a few examples. It is thus unsurprising that tax is often seen as linked more closely with economics than law. In keeping with this view, the dominant mode of analyzing tax law focuses on people as little more than the sum of their financial transactions. That is, "mainstream" tax analysis homogenizes taxpayers so that all lines of difference (save those of income or wealth) are fully erased or ignored. Obviously, this thinking leaves no room to conceive of the possibility of a feminist tax judgment. But what the dominant mode of analysis ignores – and what this volume highlights – is the fact that tax statutes are rarely determinative on their own. Approaching

---

[9] *Id.* at 1–2.

the critical tax project from a different vantage point, this volume shows that the context in which parties and courts operate influences the understanding, interpretation, and application of statutes.

METHODOLOGY

When *Feminist Judgments: Rewritten Opinions of the United States Supreme Court* was still in its editing phase, we recognized the potential for extending that book's methodology to our area of shared expertise – taxation. Our plans for this book began when we assembled a list of eight tax cases culled from our own knowledge and scholarship. We were interested in cases that implicated gender on their face (such as those involving medical expense deductions for certain fertility-related expenditures or gender confirmation surgery) as well as cases that require an understanding of the way that tax issues function in different historical, political, and economic settings (such as the state taxation of land set aside for American Indians). In composing our initial list of cases that might be ripe for feminist rewriting, we did not limit the cases to any particular court or jurisdiction, mostly because very few tax cases make it all the way to the Supreme Court and also because decisions issued by the U.S. Tax Court and other lower courts play a large role in the development and practice of tax law.

In order to benefit from the input of colleagues with different areas of tax expertise, we assembled a diverse and distinguished group of a dozen leading tax scholars as our Advisory Panel to help evaluate the cases on our list as especially deserving (or not) of feminist rewriting and to suggest other cases. This Advisory Panel consists of Alice G. Abreu, Patricia A. Cain, Joseph M. Dodge, Mary Louise Fellows, Wendy C. Gerzog, Steve R. Johnson, Marjorie E. Kornhauser, Ajay K. Mehrotra, Beverly I. Moran, Richard L. Schmalbeck, Nancy Staudt, and Lawrence A. Zelenak. We received much valuable feedback from the Advisory Panel and expanded the list of potential cases to twenty-four. We then issued a public call for authors, allowing prospective authors to indicate their preferences for rewriting an opinion or writing a commentary on any of the cases on the list of twenty-four. Prospective authors were further invited to suggest cases that were not on our list, too.

With the goal of choosing the most qualified and diverse authors, and taking into account the input of our Advisory Panel, we narrowed our selection to eleven cases. Eight of the cases came from the list of twenty-four; three were suggested by the intended authors. Most of the contributors to this volume are tax specialists (whether academics or practitioners), but some have nationally recognized expertise in a substantive specialty that underlies the tax law focus of the chosen case. We are proud that our contributors represent a range of expertise and experience. The authors include nationally recognized senior tax experts, well-known feminist scholars, specialists in other substantive areas of the law, junior scholars, a law dean, a practicing attorney, and colleagues whose primary teaching work occurs in the clinical setting. We sought diversity of gender, sexual orientation, race, perspective, expertise, and status in the academy, consistent with an active commitment to a volume that would represent many viewpoints and voices. In addition, we have included a chapter written by Canadian feminist tax scholar Kathleen Lahey immediately following this Introduction in order to provide an important comparative/international context for the rewritten opinions in this volume.

WHAT IS A FEMINIST JUDGMENT ANYWAY?

In our call for participation, we explicitly stated that we, as volume editors, conceive of feminism as a broad movement concerned with justice and equality, and that we welcomed proposals to rewrite cases in a way that brings into focus issues such as gender, race, ethnicity, socioeconomic class, disability, sexual orientation, national origin, and immigration status. In keeping with the stance taken in the compilation and editing of *Feminist Judgments: Rewritten Opinions of the United States Supreme Court*,[10] we did not instruct authors on what we believed to be a "feminist" interpretation of the cases or confine them to any certain method or process for completing their work. From our perspective, this book is squarely within the tradition of critical tax theory, scholarship that we have described as sharing one or more of the following goals: "(1) to uncover bias in the tax laws; (2) to explore and expose how the tax laws both reflect and construct social meaning; and (3) to educate nontax scholars and lawyers about the interconnectedness of taxation, social justice, and progressive political movements."[11] To be sure, feminism has been historically motivated by concern for equality for women, but the most effective and inclusive feminism takes into account the way that many intersecting identities can make the quest for justice more complex and elusive, given the structure of both the law itself as well as the meaning of equal protection as interpreted by twenty-first-century courts. We did and do welcome a diversity

[10] Kathryn M. Stanchi, Linda L. Berger, & Bridget J. Crawford, *Introduction* to FEMINIST JUDGMENTS, *supra* note 3, at 3.

[11] Anthony C. Infanti & Bridget J. Crawford, *Introduction* to CRITICAL TAX THEORY: AN INTRODUCTION, at xxi (Anthony C. Infanti & Bridget J. Crawford eds., 2009).

of viewpoints about feminism's goals and practices and how they manifest themselves in judicial opinions.

GUIDELINES FOR OPINIONS AND COMMENTARY

The purpose of *Feminist Judgments: Rewritten Tax Opinions* is to show (not describe) how certain tax cases could have been decided differently if the judges had brought to bear a more gender-sensitive viewpoint. Authors were free to draw on their own understandings and interpretations of feminist theories and methods, but they were limited to rewriting their opinions based on the law and facts in existence at the time of the original decision. This is a key feature of all of the books in the Feminist Judgments Series. One of the underlying claims of this particular volume is that statutory interpretation, like decisions on constitutional questions, is affected by judicial experiences, perspectives, and reasoning processes. Opinion authors were free to rewrite the majority opinion, or add a dissent or concurring opinion. Of the eleven feminist judgments in this book, seven are rewritten majority opinions, two are dissents, one is a dissent in part and concurrence in part, and one is a concurrence. Some authors enjoyed the exercise of re-envisioning the original opinion from the ground up, had they been on the deciding court. Other authors found it easier to react to a majority opinion with which they disagreed and therefore chose to write a dissent. Of the eleven rewritten cases in the book, six are Supreme Court decisions, one is a federal circuit court opinion, and four are Tax Court opinions.

What these feminist tax judgments collectively demonstrate is that incorporating feminist theories and methods into tax cases is consistent with judicial duties and accepted methods of interpretation. The cases combat the notion that tax law is a pseudoscientific subdiscipline of economics in which application of the law is foreordained by economic principles or precepts. Instead, the body of rewritten cases shows that tax law is a product of the larger political, social, and cultural context in which it operates. Rather than being dictated by the plain language of statutes or the abstract (and perhaps unknowable) "will" of Congress, tax law decisions are contingent on the interpretational context brought to bear by the judge and the parties. Seen in this light, it becomes clear that the history and development of tax law does not follow a linear path, but can take (and could have taken) a multiplicity of different paths.

From a practical perspective, opinion authors were limited to 10,000 words, regardless of whether they were writing reimagined majority opinions, dissents, or concurrences, as appropriate to the court. Commentators had the difficult task of explaining, in 4,000 words or less, what the original court decided, how the feminist judgment differs from the original judgment, and what practical impact the feminist judgment might have had. Each opinion and commentary went through at least three rounds of editing with us, and opinion writers and commentators also shared their thoughts with each other throughout the process. In fact, many pairs of opinion writers and commentators worked quite closely and cooperatively through the rounds of editing, with the commentary writers incorporating points in their commentaries at the request of the opinion writers, and with opinion writers receiving comments on their opinions from the commentary writers. The members of our Advisory Panel also graciously read and gave comments on draft opinions, ensuring that the authors received feedback from multiple sources. The ultimate decision to accept or reject feedback, however, remained with the authors. If we had been the authors or commentators, we might have taken a different tack or reached a different conclusion in several cases in the book. And in some cases, opinion writers and commentators saw issues differently. In any event, we did not press authors to reach the conclusions we ourselves would have reached or force concordance between opinion writers and commentators. Instead, we celebrate these multiple viewpoints as consistent with the richness and complexity of feminist thought.

ORGANIZATION OF CASES AND WRITING CONVENTIONS

The eleven cases in the book span the date range of 1903 to 2013. They implicate a wide range of issues including gender difference, the basic meaning of equality, medical expense deductions, marriage, divorce, trusts, income tax filing status, Indian rights, business deductions, and eligibility for tax-exempt status. We considered a variety of different organizational frameworks for the cases, attempting to group them by common themes or subject matter. Ultimately, however, because many of the cases involve multiple issues, it was difficult to settle on any one coherent organizing framework. For that reason, we decided to present the cases in chronological order. By presenting cases from oldest to most recent, we (hopefully) have eliminated any of our personal bias in the way we may view the cases and allow readers to develop their own sense of how the opinions relate to each other and how various courts' style, language, and reasoning have evolved over more than a century.

A few words are also in order regarding some of the conventions used in writing the opinions and commentary included in this volume. In the opinions, for the sake of clarity, we asked authors to refer to the Internal Revenue Service as either the "IRS" or "Commissioner" (rather than "petitioner" or "respondent"). We also asked the opinion writers to refer in the text of their opinions to the Internal Revenue Code for the first time as "Internal Revenue Code § 61"[12] without reference to a date (which will vary in each case depending upon the tax year or years at issue). After the first mention, opinion authors were permitted to either refer to the Internal Revenue Code as "Code § 61" or, where there are repeated references and it is clear from the context what they are referring to, simply as "§ 61." Similarly, we asked opinion authors to refer in the text of their opinions to the Treasury Regulations as "Treasury Regulations § 1.61-1" for the first time and, after the first mention, permitted them to refer to the regulations simply as "Reg. § 1.61-1." All citations in the opinions follow the "blue pages" rules in *The Bluebook* system of citation that are normally used by judges and practitioners.

In the commentary, again for the sake of clarity, we asked authors to refer to the Internal Revenue Service as the "IRS." We also asked the commentary writers to refer in the text of their commentaries to the Internal Revenue Code for the first time as "Code § 61" and, after the first mention and where it was clear from the context what they were referring to, permitted them to refer to the Internal Revenue Code simply as "§ 61." Similarly, we asked commentary authors to refer to the Treasury Regulations as "Reg. § 1.61-1." Readers should thus assume that all references in the commentary to "Code" and "Reg." refer to the Internal Revenue Code and Treasury Regulations, respectively. All citations in the commentaries follow the regular rules that are used by law reviews, according to *The Bluebook* system of citation.

FEMINIST THEORIES AND METHODS

A. *Formal Equality vs. Substantive Equality*

Out of the important sex discrimination cases brought before the Supreme Court in the 1970s emerged what might be called a "formal equality" approach to sex discrimination. *Reed v. Reed*,[13] decided in 1971, was the first time that the Supreme Court ruled that a law violated women's rights to equal protection under the Fourteenth Amendment. That case involved an Idaho statute that accorded an automatic preference for a male administrator of a decedent's estate, given two individuals equally related to the decedent. Then-attorney (now Justice) Ruth Bader Ginsburg wrote the brief on behalf of the *Reed* plaintiff, successfully arguing that the Idaho law was unconstitutional.

---

[12] Section 61, which contains the definition of gross income, is merely used here as an example.
[13] 404 U.S. 71 (1971) (rejecting legal preference for male administrator of decedent's estate as between two equally related individuals).

Unfortunately, she did not persuade the Court to apply to gender discrimination cases the strict scrutiny that applied in racial discrimination cases.[14] In *Frontiero v. Richardson*,[15] Ginsburg was *amicus curiae* for the plaintiff in a case that challenged the Air Force's automatic allocation of spousal benefits to married male service members, but required married female service members to show that their husbands were dependent on them before receiving a spousal benefit. Eight of the justices agreed that the Air Force's policy was unconstitutional, but they could not agree on the appropriate level of scrutiny under which to evaluate the law. Thereafter it became likely that gender discrimination claims always would be subject to "intermediate scrutiny," not strict scrutiny.

For many feminists, removing formal obstacles to women's participation in all aspects of political, social, and economic life was the primary goal. Yet others became dissatisfied with this formal equality approach, and instead sought substantive equality between women and men. The underlying rationale is that in cases where women and men are not equally situated (e.g., pregnancy), treating the sexes the same operates in fact as a form of discrimination against women, by denying them the care they need.[16] This problem is illustrated by the case of *Geduldig v. Aiello*, in which the Supreme Court found that the exclusion of pregnancy from the California state disability plan did not violate the Equal Protection Clause, on the grounds that the classification made by California was between "pregnant women and nonpregnant persons."[17]

The debate about formal equality versus substantive equality echoes clearly in two of the feminist judgments in this book. In her rewrite of the majority opinion in *Manufacturers Hanover Trust Co. v. United States*,[18] Mary Heen considers the use of gender-based mortality tables in calculating the value of reversionary interests for estate tax purposes. She rejects the use of gender-specific tables, seeking formal equal treatment for women and men. In contrast, in her dissent in *Clack v. Commissioner*,[19] Wendy Gerzog closely examines the problems created by a gender-neutral statute, in regards to the

---

[14] *See, e.g.*, Brown v. Bd. of Educ., 347 U.S. 483 (1954) (outlawing segregation in public schools).
[15] 411 U.S. 677 (1973).
[16] *See, e.g.*, Catharine A. MacKinnon, *Substantive Equality: A Perspective*, 96 Minn. L. Rev. 1, 6 (2011) ("But what about all those situations in which the sex inequality is real, so the sexes are situated unequally? The more pervasive the reality of sex inequality is, the fewer outliers will be permitted in reality, so the more that reality will look like a sex-based difference, mapping itself onto (the social idea of) sex as such, which it will be increasingly rational for law to ignore as it ascends the tiers of scrutiny.").
[17] 417 U.S. 484, 497 n.20 (1974). [18] 775 F.2d 459 (2d Cir. 1985). [19] 106 T.C. 131 (1996).

estate tax marital deduction for certain transfers. Gerzog concludes the opposite of Heen – that is, that gender neutrality in the estate tax marital deduction
is masquerading as *de facto* sexism. Thus, Gerzog is primarily concerned with
substantive (as opposed to formal) equality between men and women.

B. *Antisubordination/Dominance Feminism*

Another significant concern of some feminists is the way that law reinforces
power imbalances. Of differences between men and women, Catharine
MacKinnon writes:

> [A]n equality question is a question of the distribution of power. Gender is
> also a question of power, specifically of male supremacy and female
> subordination. The question of equality is at the root a question of hierarchy,
> which – as power succeeds in constructing social perception and social
> reality – derivatively becomes a categorical distinction, a difference."[20]

Power differences between races, classes, and along other lines also are
feminist concerns, as policies that are neutral on their face can reinforce
existing hierarchies and oppressions.[21]

The feminist judgment written by Danshera Cords in *Cheshire v.
Commissioner*[22] is a reimagined majority Tax Court opinion that grants innocent spouse relief where the original court did not. Cords's feminist judgment
is deeply informed by a feminist understanding of power dynamics in intimate
relationships. In this way, the *Cheshire* feminist judgment builds on the work
of feminist theorists like Catharine MacKinnon who expose the way that
power imbalances – particularly, but not exclusively, between men and
women – are built into human relationships and then become entrenched
in law and culture.[23] By putting the woman at the center of the analysis, Cords
reaches a different opinion about the wife's income tax liability for substantial
omissions by her husband.

In his rewrite of *United States v. Rickert*,[24] the oldest of the cases included
in this volume, Grant Christensen reaches the same result as the U.S.

---

[20] Catharine A. MacKinnon, *Difference and Dominance, in* Feminism Unmodified 40 (1987). In
     her early writings, Professor MacKinnon called this the "dominance approach," but she has
     explained that "it's as much about subordination as dominance." Emily Bazelon, *The Return of
     the Sex Wars*, N.Y. Times Mag., Sept. 10, 2015, at 56, *available at* http://www.nytimes
     .com/2015/09/13/magazine/the-return-of-the-sex-wars.html?_r=0.
[21] Ruth Colker, *Anti-Subordination Above All: Sex, Race, and Equal Protection*, 61 N.Y.U. L. Rev.
     1003, 1007–10 (1986).
[22] 115 T.C. 183 (2000), *aff'd*, 282 F.3d 326 (5th Cir. 2002).
[23] *See generally* MacKinnon, *supra* note 20, at 32–45.   [24] 188 U.S. 432 (1903).

Supreme Court did in its original opinion, denying a state's ability to tax improvements and personal property on Indian land that was held in trust by the U.S. government for individual Indian allottees. But Christensen importantly rejects the Supreme Court's paternalistic approach in doing so – an approach that was infused "with its racist and classist assumptions that Indians were uncivilized and incapable of managing their own affairs, and therefore had to be managed like children, or like women in those days, by privileged white men who knew better" (to borrow the words of Chloe Thompson in her excellent and eye-opening commentary on this rewritten opinion). Instead, Christensen honors and embraces the agency and autonomy of individual Indians and Indian tribes in ways that protect them from infringement by state and local governments. Rewriting a case without an obvious link to gender, Christensen (and Thompson in her accompanying commentary) also show how feminist reasoning and methods can apply outside of cases that directly implicate gender.

C. *Intersectionality, Antiessentialism, and Multiple Identities*

One important branch of feminist legal theory that emerged in the 1990s was a critical focus on "women" as a monolithic category, without recognition of differences of race, class, immigration status, sexuality, or other significant identity categories. Angela Harris, for example, writes against what she calls "gender essentialism" – "the notion that there is a monolithic 'women's experience' that can be described independently of other facets of experience like race, class and sexual orientation."[25] Kimberlé Crenshaw similarly critiques any feminism that ignores the fact that gender may represent only one axis of a woman's oppression, when in fact oppression may intersect along the axes of gender and race, for example.[26]

In his rewritten concurring opinion in *Bob Jones University v. United States*,[27] David Brennen demonstrates the power of intersectional analysis. *Bob Jones University* concerned the revocation of two educational organizations' tax-exempt status because they had adopted and enforced racially discriminatory policies (founded on what were presumed to be sincerely held religious beliefs) concerning interracial dating, interracial marriage, and the

---

[25] Angela P. Harris, *Race and Essentialism in Feminist Legal Theory*, 42 STAN. L. REV. 581, 585 (1990).
[26] Kimberlé Crenshaw, *Demarginalizing the Intersection of Race and Sex: A Black Feminist Critique of Antidiscrimination Doctrine, Feminist Theory and Antiracist Politics*, 1989 U. CHI. LEGAL F. 139.
[27] 461 U.S. 574 (1983).

"mixing of the races." The original U.S. Supreme Court opinion in *Bob Jones University* explored only the racially discriminatory aspect of these policies and affirmed the denial of tax-exempt status to the two organizations because the Court found there was an established public policy against racial discrimination in education. The original opinion left open the question of whether other forms of discrimination might similarly result in the revocation of tax-exempt status. Brennen's opinion begins to fill that gap by highlighting the differential impact of the schools' policies on African-American women's freedom of association – with attendant, and potentially harsh, economic consequences for them. Brennen makes the case that, at the time *Bob Jones University* was decided, there was already an established public policy against gender discrimination in education and that gender discrimination was thus an additional ground for denying tax-exempt status to these two schools. In his concurrence, Brennen shows how the harms of discrimination are compounded and can be "especially burdensome" when multiple axes of discrimination (here, race and gender) intersect.

D. *Autonomy and Agency*

An emphasis on the ability of women – and all people – to make decisions about their own bodies is an important feminist commitment. For some feminists, that manifests as a concern about the ability to control whether and when to become pregnant, or resistance to government interference with women's bodies through forced sterilization or forced caesarean sections.[28] It is also a fundamental methodological commitment of many feminists to engage in what Katharine Bartlett has called "feminist practical reasoning," which includes taking a broad approach to the facts of each particular case.[29] Two rewritten opinions in this book both accentuate the autonomy or agency of the taxpayer, in ways that the original opinions did not, and also provide a factually rich context for the cases. In his rewrite of *O'Donnabhain v. Commissioner*,[30] which concerned a transgender woman's ability to deduct costs related to her gender confirmation surgery as a medical expense, David Cruz takes great care to respect the taxpayer, Rhiannon O'Donnabhain, as a human being. Cruz puts the issue of respecting O'Donnabhain front and

---

[28] *See, e.g.,* Rosalind Pollack Petchesky, *Abortion and Woman's Choice: The State, Sexuality, and Reproductive Freedom, in* FEMINIST JURISPRUDENCE: CASES AND MATERIALS 413–16 (Cynthia Grant Bowman et al. eds., 4th ed. 2011).

[29] *See generally* Katharine T. Bartlett, *Feminist Legal Methods,* 103 HARV. L. REV. 829, 849–58 (1990).

[30] 134 T.C. 34 (2010), *acq.,* 2011-47 I.R.B.

center by not only using the correct gender and pronouns to refer to her but also by including an explanation of this move in the text of his decision, rather than relegating it to a footnote as the original majority Tax Court opinion did. Cruz further humanizes O'Donnabhain by generally referring to her by name rather than adopting typical Tax Court convention that would have dictated referring to her as either "petitioner" or "taxpayer." Moreover, Cruz demonstrates sensitivity to the larger implications of labeling O'Donnabhain as suffering from a "disease," despite the attraction of doing so as an expeditious means of giving her and others access to the tax deduction that might bring gender confirmation surgery within financial reach.

A similar approach can be found in Jennifer Bird-Pollan's rewrite of *Magdalin v. Commissioner.*[31] Bird-Pollan affirms reproductive autonomy by rejecting the prevailing approach of sharply circumscribing the ability to deduct medical expenses associated with assisted reproductive technology in a way that effectively limits the deduction to different-sex married couples suffering from fertility problems. Bird-Pollan instead extends the deduction to all taxpayers – gay or straight, married or unmarried – by embracing the notion that reproduction is a function of the bodies of both men *and* women, whether they are married or not. Bird-Pollan's opinion also opens the door to breaking down stereotypical gender roles in parenting by facilitating reproduction and parenting outside of the different-sex married couple.

E. *Women's Experiences and Intimate Relationships*

It is not surprising that much of feminist scholarship is devoted to women's experience.[32] And because women are, in the view of Robin West, "profoundly relational,"[33] one subject of feminist legal analysis is marriage as an organizing principle in private and public life. Regardless of one's position on women as more or less "relational" than men, though, marriage and women's legal status within marriage has long been a subject of feminist critique.[34]

---

[31] 96 T.C.M. (CCH) 491 (2008), *aff'd* 2010-1 U.S. Tax Cas. ¶ 50,150 (1st Cir. 2009).

[32] MARTHA CHAMALLAS, INTRODUCTION TO FEMINIST LEGAL THEORY 4–5 (3d ed. 2013) (describing feminist commitment to studying women's experiences as an outgrowth of the "consciousness-raising groups of the late 1960s and early 1970s, where women were encouraged to express their subjective responses to everyday life and discovered that 'the personal was political,' in the sense that their personal problems also had a political dimension").

[33] Robin L. West, *The Difference in Women's Hedonic Lives: A Phenomenological Critique of Feminist Legal Theory*, 15 WIS. WOMEN'S L.J. 149, 210 (2000).

[34] *See, e.g.*, DECLARATION OF SENTIMENTS (1848), *in* FEMINIST JURISPRUDENCE, *supra* note 28, at 3–6 (listing grievances of women gathered at first women's rights conference held in Seneca Falls, New York in 1848, including the fact that married women were treated as "civilly dead").

In this volume, the tax consequences of marriage – as well as the questions about the primacy of marriage in the administration of the tax system – are key considerations of several of the included feminist judgments.

In *United States v. Davis*,[35] Patricia Cain's feminist dissent takes on the Supreme Court's outdated view of marriage and takes a position that ultimately would become the law in 1984, recognizing that divorcing couples often have functioned as a single economic unit, not as arm's-length bargainers. In Ann Murphy's dissent in *Lucas v. Earl*,[36] she, too, takes on marriage, but in a slightly different way than Cain does. Murphy would force the tax law to recognize the validity of the income-splitting arrangement entered into by a married couple, emphasizing that the wife is an equal (if not superior) financial partner to the marriage.

Ruthann Robson approaches marriage from a different vantage point in her rewrite of the landmark decision in *United States v. Windsor*,[37] which overturned Section 3 of the federal Defense of Marriage Act (DOMA) and required the federal government to legally recognize same-sex marriage for the first time. In reaching the same decision as the majority in *Windsor*, Robson draws on the narrative feminist method by focusing on the lives and lived experiences of the lesbian couple at the center of the tax controversy (rather than approaching DOMA's impact on same-sex couples at a more general or abstract level). But even in the context of telling the extraordinary story of these two women's lives and affirming the legal recognition of their relationship, Robson actively resists and calls for the overturning of the entrenched privileging of marriage in tax law and the recognition of a wider array of human relationships.

These judgments relating to marriage are informed by a focus on women's experience and consideration of how the law reproduces patterns of dominance of men over women, two classic moves in feminist legal theory.[38] As Cain herself has previously written, "legal scholarship is not feminist unless it is grounded in women's experience."[39] The opinions in *Davis*, *Lucas*, and *Windsor* live up to that definition.

F. Uncovering Implicit Male Bias

Martha Chamallas has identified uncovering implicit bias and male norms in the law as one of the "opening moves" of feminist theory.[40] Chamallas is

---

[35] 370 U.S. 65 (1962).   [36] 281 U.S. 111 (1930).   [37] 133 S. Ct. 2675 (2013).

[38] CHAMALLAS, *supra* note 32, at 4–5, 11–12.

[39] Patricia A. Cain, *Feminist Legal Scholarship*, 77 IOWA L. REV. 19, 20 (1991).

[40] CHAMALLAS, *supra* note 32, at 8.

referring here to a commitment to uncovering the way that laws that appear neutral on their face are actually based on and embody male experiences or male ideals. Making this very move, the feminist judgment written by Mary Louise Fellows in *Welch v. Helvering*[41] revisits the classic question broached in every basic income tax course regarding what constitutes a deductible "ordinary and necessary" business expense. In that rewritten Supreme Court majority opinion, Fellows questions the extent to which one's conception of the business world is based on a male model of doing business.

Fellows's reimagined feminist majority opinion sharply departs from the approach taken in Justice Benjamin Cardozo's iconic original opinion by drawing upon feminist practical reasoning, a method also adopted by David Cruz in *O'Donnabhain* and Jennifer Bird-Pollan in *Magdalin*, as noted earlier.[42] Fellows refuses to approach the question of deductibility abstractly and instead takes a more contextualized approach to determining whether an expense is ordinary and necessary. She dives into the facts presented to the Court and demands more – to the point of not actually rendering a decision in the case before the Court but rather sending the case back to the lower court for further fact finding that will facilitate a more nuanced and individualized decision of the question. In providing guidance to the lower courts on remand, Fellows also breaks with convention in her opinion by drawing liberally from literature (in particular, Mary Shelley's *Frankenstein*) to support her dismantling of the public/private hierarchy that is implicit in the allowance of a deduction for business expenses and the general disallowance of deductions for personal expenses. Fellows also draws on outsider perspectives to inform her interpretation of the phrase "ordinary and necessary" in order to open the way to innovation in business at a time of severe economic crisis while simultaneously avoiding the reinforcement of, and provision of tangible financial support to, businessmen's already privileged lives (along lines not only of gender but also of race, class, etc.)

G. *Additional Resources*

In describing some of the feminist theories and methods that writers of these feminist judgments employ, we have detailed only a small number of the multiple perspectives, concerns, and methods that comprise the rich field that is feminist legal theory. We have not mentioned socialist feminism,[43]

---

[41] 290 U.S. 111 (1933).   [42] *See supra* note 29 and accompanying text.
[43] *See, e.g.,* Cynthia Grant Bowman, *Recovering Socialism for Feminist Legal Theory in the 21st Century,* 49 Conn. L. Rev. 117 (2016).

postmodern feminism,[44] third-wave feminism,[45] pragmatic feminism,[46] queer theory,[47] or cultural feminism,[48] to name just a few other perspectives. For those who want to learn more about feminist legal theory generally, we recommend Martha Chamallas's book, *Introduction of Feminist Legal Theory*.[49] For those curious about feminist legal theory as applied to feminist judgments in particular, the first two chapters of *Feminist Judgments: Rewritten Opinions of the United States Supreme Court* provide a great deal of background and context.[50]

CONCLUSION

The opinions and commentaries in this book reveal three important claims. First, tax law is political. Second, statutes are just as subject to interpretation as constitutional provisions. And third, incorporating feminist methods or theories into the interpretive process of judicial decision-making can lead to results that may (or may not) vary from a decision that does not incorporate that perspective. Yet, as the rewritten opinions in this volume make clear, a feminist lens almost always leads to different reasoning and emphasis in a judicial opinion. It is thus important that the judiciary includes individuals with a variety of perspectives, including feminist ones. As the contributors to this volume demonstrate, both men and women can have feminist perspectives. In that sense, this volume should not be reduced to an argument for more women on the bench – although gender diversity is most certainly a desired goal for other reasons – because a judiciary that looks more like all of the citizens that it serves will increase public confidence in the integrity of the system.[51]

---

[44] *See, e.g.,* Mary Jo Frug, A *Postmodern Feminist Legal Manifesto (An Unfinished Draft)*, 105 HARV. L. REV. 1045 (1992).

[45] *See, e.g.,* Bridget J. Crawford, *Toward a Third-Wave Feminist Legal Theory: Young Women, Pornography and the Praxis of Pleasure*, 14 MICH. J. GENDER & L. 99 (2007).

[46] *See, e.g.,* Margaret Jane Radin, *The Pragmatist and the Feminist*, 63 S. CAL. L. REV. 1699 (1990).

[47] *See, e.g.,* Patricia A. Cain, *Feminist Jurisprudence: Grounding the Theories*, 4 BERKELEY WOMEN'S L.J. 191 (1989); Diana Majury, *Refashioning the Unfashionable: Claiming Lesbian Identities in the Legal Context*, 7 CAN. J. WOMEN & L. 286 (1994).

[48] *See, e.g.,* NANCY CHODOROW, THE REPRODUCTION OF MOTHERING: PSYCHOANALYSIS AND THE SOCIOLOGY OF GENDER 57–76 (1978) (marking the beginning of gender difference as infancy).

[49] *See supra* note 32.   [50] *See supra* note 3.

[51] *See* SALLY J. KENNEY, GENDER AND JUSTICE: WHY WOMEN IN THE JUDICIARY REALLY MATTER 6 (2013).

By showing how perspective makes a difference in judicial decision-making in tax cases in particular, we hope to illustrate to students, fellow academics, lawyers, and judges that there are many areas where the selected mode of analysis – in this case, feminism – can be just as important as legislative history and statutory language to the outcome of the case. We imagine that this book might be a useful tool in law school courses that focus on statutory interpretation or substantive tax law. Beyond the classroom, we hope that the text makes a substantive and practical contribution to critical tax theory by demonstrating that a focus on historically subordinated groups makes a difference in outcome. As we have argued previously, "a complete study of tax law and policy requires an understanding of the historical, social, political, and cultural contexts in which the tax laws operate."[52] To that list, we add that a robust understanding of tax law also requires an understanding of the perspective of the deciding judges, and that a feminist perspective tends to lead to outcomes that take seriously the issues, concerns, and experiences of traditionally disempowered people, with an emphasis on achieving and furthering the cause of social justice.

For feminists without significant tax backgrounds, we invite you to read this book to understand just how important the tax system is in achieving a fairer, more equal, and more inclusive society. For tax experts without familiarity with feminist theory, we invite you to consider how fundamental principles like gender equality can be incorporated into almost any tax analysis. For those who are experts in both feminist legal theory and taxation, welcome home.

This volume represents a collaboration among more than thirty individuals. As an academic collaboration, the book is itself a feminist exercise in bringing multiple voices together to push the boundaries of our understanding and inspire new ways of thinking. We hope you are as stimulated by this book as we are. Enjoy!

---

[52] Infanti & Crawford, *supra* note 11, at xxii.

2

Feminist Judging for Substantive Gender Equality in Tax Law

Changing International and Comparative Constitutional Contexts

KATHLEEN A. LAHEY

INTRODUCTION

"#LawNeedsFeminismBecause the male perspective is still seen as objective."[1] And tax law needs feminist judging because as the importance of taxing for gender equality is increasingly recognized in international and constitutional law, despite early leadership in bringing gender equality to tax law, the United States has fallen behind many other democratic nations simply by failing to follow through on those early accomplishments. Women in the United States have actively engaged in combatting gender discrimination generally and in relation to tax laws for well over a century. Indeed, the use of the "individual" as the personal tax unit, even before women won national voting rights in the United States, recognized women's full legal personality in fiscal policies consistent with the enactment in the 1800s of married women's property laws. Since getting the vote, however, women in the United States have faced increasing levels of sexism in tax laws, as wealthy taxpayers succeeded in replacing individual taxation of married women with joint taxation at the same time that postwar labor policies in the 1940s began to undercut women's move toward economic equality and rolled back important public and industry-based childcare programs.

Virtually at the same time that this rollback began in the United States, however, constitutional and international laws in other regions began to give legal expression to the principle of substantive gender equality. The goal of this movement has been to dismantle the political economy of gender, which continues today to allocate unpaid work, good paid work, income, wealth,

---

[1] Florence Ashley Paré, Sisterhood, Not Cisterhood: *l'inclusion comme position politico-morale*, 5 CONTOURS: VOICES OF WOMEN IN LAW / VOIX DE FEMMES EN DROIT 1, 10 (2017).

public benefits, and political power unequally on the basis of sex/gender, marital status, and social stereotypes. This chapter is not just about what other jurisdictions are accomplishing through feminist judging in tax cases, however. It is also about how parallel and sometimes uneven legal gender equality developments have sustained transnational rights discourses that have enabled some judges in some tax cases to displace traditional stereotyped thinking about the sex/gender system with transformative analysis of fundamental tax policy issues affecting women. These transnational gender equality movements hopefully can help feminist tax judging in the United States further the goal of increasing women's economic equality.

This chapter first highlights some of the similarities and differences in how U.S. and Canadian tax and constitutional law have historically framed issues of gender, and concludes that one notable point of departure in feminist judging of key tax issues lies in the divergent responses to early ratification of the Convention on the Elimination of All Forms of Discrimination against Women (CEDAW) in the two countries.[2] Canada and the United States were some of the earliest signatories, but the United States then did not ratify CEDAW. In contrast, Canada signed and ratified CEDAW at a crucial moment in the evolution of Canada's Constitution – at the same time that it included wide-ranging constitutional gender equality guarantees in its new 1982 Charter of Rights and Freedoms that then helped transform Canadian attitudes toward all forms of equality, including gender equality.

Next, this chapter looks closely at how the first Supreme Court of Canada constitutional equality decisions under its new Charter effectively turned the United States' constitutional aversion to "affirmative action" inside out as Canadian judges rejected the U.S. approach to defining the scope of permissible state action when dealing with differential treatment of historically disadvantaged groups. This resulted in early Canadian rulings that made it easier for constitutionally recognized groups to show that their equality rights had been violated. One of the keys to bringing about this change was the inclusion of a uniform constitutional standard of justification of discriminatory laws, policies, and practices in the Canadian Charter that requires governments to prove by the preponderance of the evidence that such differential treatment can be "demonstrably justified in a free and democratic society."

The remainder of the discussion focuses on how new dimensions in feminist judging in tax and fiscal issues have been actuated in other parts of the world, and the central role CEDAW has played in making that possible.

---

[2]   United Nations Convention on the Elimination of All Forms of Discrimination against Women, Mar. 1, 1980, 1249 U.N.T.S. 13.

In Canada, one of the ultimate outcomes of Canada's ratification of CEDAW was constitutional restructuring of equality concepts that supported feminist elaborations of substantive gender equality principles in two Supreme Court of Canada gender tax cases in which both Justices Claire L'Heureux-Dubé and Beverley McLachlin (now Chief Justice) dissented from male majority decisions upholding tax provisions that uniquely disadvantaged women engaged in paid work while being responsible for the care of young children.[3] The *Thibaudeau* case concerned the negative impact on custodial mothers forced to pay income tax on child support payments for which their husbands received deductions, and the *Symes* case contested the denial of business deductions for childcare expenses. Internationally, CEDAW itself has opened up new venues for feminist judging in tax and fiscal matters: CEDAW compliance mechanisms have led to two CEDAW Committee rulings holding national governments accountable for violating women's equality rights in a wide range of economic, fiscal, and development policies, and to the identification of the elements of "taxing for gender equality" that are essential to promoting women's economic and social equality.

U.S. AND CANADIAN TAXATION OF WOMEN: PARALLELS AND DIVERGENCES

A. *United States*

Long before Canada received its first constitution from Britain in 1867, women in the United States clearly understood that unfair taxation exacerbates gendered legal, property, and economic inequalities. The 1848 Seneca Falls, New York *Declaration of Sentiments* summed up the combined impact of taxing employed single women who would be denied all property rights upon marriage: "After depriving her of all rights as a married woman, if single, and the owner of property, he has taxed her to support a government which recognizes her only when her property can be made profitable to it."[4]

Married women's property laws rectified some forms of economic gender discrimination in the United States in the late 1800s. Then in 1913, defying British income tax practices, the new national income tax law adopted the individual as the taxpayer. The use of the individual tax unit suggests that women had been recognized as having fiscal room of their own to parallel

---

[3] Symes v. Canada, [1993] 4 S.C.R. 695 (Can.); Thibaudeau v. Canada, [1995] 2 S.C.R. 627 (Can.).
[4] 1 ELIZABETH CADY STANTON ET AL., HISTORY OF WOMAN SUFFRAGE 71 (1887).

their new individual legal rights to hold title to their own income and property. However, that legal status was quickly turned to the advantage of high-income spouses who could use their lower-income spouses' independent fiscal space for income-splitting purposes, a convenient alternative to using corporate "persons" as tax shelters.[5]

The struggle for individual taxation of married women in the United States culminated at the end of World War II as full-scale income splitting between spouses came into effect under headlines like "Does It Really Pay for the Wife to Work?" and "It Pays to Get Married."[6] The introduction of earned income tax credits, women's increased access to postsecondary education, and growing numbers of women in positions of responsibility have not, however, closed long-standing gender income, wealth, and opportunity gaps in the United States.

B. *Canada*

The taxation of women in Canada paralleled U.S. developments at the outset. Married women's property laws and voting rights were enacted at similar times; women entered into paid work in unprecedented numbers during World War I; and, when the first Canadian income tax act was enacted, the tax unit was declared to be the individual. Canadian politicians did give in to political demands for special dependent spouse exemptions, but did not seriously consider joint taxation of spouses. Also in parallel, Canadian women entered into paid work in even greater numbers during World War II; received enhanced individual tax benefits to help make that paid work pay; and were driven by laws, employers, and social attitudes out of paid work at war's end. Some degree of income splitting envy surfaced in postwar Canada, but the financial sting of women's loss of paid work was reduced not by enacting spousal income splitting, but by providing mothers with cash allowances so that they could independently provide for their children's needs.

During the 1950s and 1960s, women in Canada had little involvement in tax politics, although one Quebec husband sought court approval of spousal income splitting for tax purposes on the basis of that province's civil code community of property doctrine.[7] Unlike the U.S. courts, the Supreme Court

---

[5] Kathleen A. Lahey, *The "Capture" of Women in Law and Fiscal Policy: Implications for the Tax/Benefit Unit, Gender Equality, and Feminist Ontologies, in* CHALLENGING GENDER INEQUALITY IN TAX POLICY MAKING: COMPARATIVE PERSPECTIVES 11, 22–23 (Kim Brooks et al. eds., 2011).

[6] U.S. NEWS & WORLD REP., Mar. 1957, at 154, 156; *id.*, Feb. 1951, at 17.

[7] Sura v. Minister of Nat'l Revenue, [1962] S.C.R. 65 (Can.).

of Canada found that women's actual control over community property did not give them real income interests. The U.S. court decisions that had reached the opposite conclusion had no influence in that case.

The report of the Canadian Royal Commission on Taxation in the 1960s, however, did offer the Canadian government another chance to adopt U.S.-style spousal income splitting. Echoing Justice Douglas's ringing endorsement of income splitting in 1945 – "I see no reason why that which is in fact an economic unit may not be treated as one in law"[8] – the Canadian commission stated unequivocally that "the family is today, as it has been for many centuries, the basic economic unit in society."[9] The Royal Commission on the Status of Women in Canada soon after made similar recommendations, although Dr. Elsie Gregory MacGill, a member of the commission, objected strenuously to any form of family unit taxation. Citing the economic and psychological importance of encouraging women's independence and self-reliance, MacGill emphasized that women are entitled to be treated as individuals in all matters, and that this principle should apply to tax law as elsewhere.[10]

U.S. AND CANADIAN CONSTITUTIONAL EQUALITY PROVISIONS: LINKS AND GAPS

Canada has remained relatively conservative politically but has been quite open to human rights concepts on the political level.[11] One key judicial event was the appeal of the "Persons" case[12] to the UK Privy Council, which resulted in the judicial declaration that women are "qualified persons" who can be appointed to the Senate within the meaning of the Canadian Constitution. The heart of this decision was the finding that the British had "planted in Canada a living tree capable of growth and expansion within its natural limits" when it enacted the Constitution of Canada. Applying that "living tree" image of the constitution to the interpretation of the word "persons," the Privy Council concluded that because women in Canada had already attained many of the political, legal, economic, educational, and social rights often

---

[8]   Fernandez v. Wiener, 326 U.S. 340, 365 (1945) (Douglas, J., concurring).

[9]   3 CAN. ROYAL COMM'N ON TAXATION, REPORT OF THE ROYAL COMMISSION ON TAXATION 122–24 (1966).

[10] REPORT OF THE ROYAL COMMISSION ON THE STATUS OF WOMEN 429 (1970).

[11] An excellent place to start studying these differences is the collection of essays in CHALLENGING TIMES: THE WOMEN'S MOVEMENT IN CANADA AND THE UNITED STATES (Constance Backhouse & David H. Flaherty eds., 1992).

[12] Edwards v. Attorney Gen. of Can., [1930] AC 124 (PC).

limited to men elsewhere in the world and in earlier times, women were in fact constitutionally qualified to be appointed to the Senate.

The language and reasoning in the "Persons" decision contrasts dramatically with the narrow formalist conclusion in U.S. constitutional law that "separate but substantially equal" accommodation in the form of separate railway cars for persons of different races did not violate the requirement of "absolute equality" in the Equal Protection Clause of the Fourteenth Amendment to the U.S. Constitution, on the basis that it calls only for political equality but not for factual social equality.[13]

On the other hand, the expansive consideration given all possible relevant social, economic, and political factors in the "Persons" case is remarkably similar to the record and reasoning used in the 1954 decision in *Brown v. Board of Education*,[14] which "reached beyond cold legalism to cope with the realities – the social, psychic, emotional, political, and moral effects of segregation."[15] This connection is important because, as the U.S. Supreme Court began to drift further from *Brown* in the search for new constitutional grounds for maintaining hierarchical and *de facto* segregationist practices, *Bakke v. University of California*[16] only very narrowly permitted race to be included as a diversity factor among a large number of other university admissions criteria.

A. CEDAW

Both the United States and Canada were among the first signatories to the United Nations treaty, the Convention on the Elimination of All Forms of Discrimination Against Women, in 1980. CEDAW contains the most expansive general and the most detailed specific gender equality provisions of any international agreement touching on gender issues. Its detailed provisions arose from the need to continuously particularize women's substantive social, economic, legal, and political human rights to counter persistent pressure to read narrowly women's human rights in earlier treaties, such as the 1948 Universal Declaration of Human Rights. The detailed and expansive reach of CEDAW also provides concrete guidelines on what gender equality should mean in a wide range of circumstances found in countries around the globe.

---

[13] Plessy v. Ferguson, 163 U.S. 537 (1896).   [14] 347 U.S. 483 (1954).
[15] RICHARD BARDOLPH, THE CIVIL RIGHTS RECORD: BLACK AMERICANS AND THE LAW, 1849–1970, at 427 (1970).
[16] 438 U.S. 265 (1978).

Despite the fact that 189 countries in the world have by now either ratified or acceded to CEDAW, the United States remains one of just six countries that, as of 2017, have not. The United States is the only highly developed, democratic, rich country in this group of six states. The other five are Iran, the Guardian Council of which vetoed the Iranian parliamentary ratification of CEDAW; Palau, which signed in 2011 and has not yet ratified; Somalia; Sudan; and Tonga. This has meant that the United States has been left out of the expansive discourses on gender equality that have grown rapidly with the implementation of CEDAW.

B. *The Canadian Charter of Rights*

CEDAW was from the outset highly influential in Canada because it was signed and ratified just as the federal government decided that it was time to "repatriate" the Canadian Constitution from the United Kingdom and to constitutionalize human rights in a new Canadian Charter of Rights and Freedoms. The text of the new Canadian Charter was inspired by a wide range of human rights documents, including CEDAW, and by testimony in hundreds of federal public consultations across Canada in which thousands of people explained why and how the new Charter should protect the equality rights of women; Aboriginal peoples; people with disabilities; members of ethnic and cultural groups; lesbian, gay, and transgender persons; low-income persons; and workers.[17]

At the same time, however, feminist lawyers, law students, and academics focused intently on suggestions that the Charter should draw heavily on U.S. constitutional language because of concerns with how easily the Fourteenth Amendment was being used at the time to block equality-promoting laws. The then-recent *Bakke* decision underscored the risk that U.S.-style constitutional language could override the dynamic reasoning in the "Persons" case, close the door on equality-promoting laws by treating "affirmative action" as constitutionally impermissible discrimination, and embed the formalism of *Plessy v. Ferguson* in the new constitution despite the contextualized analysis illustrated by the more recent *Brown v. Board of Education*.

There was ample basis to oppose adopting U.S. approaches to gender equality issues in a new Charter of Rights. In 1973, the Supreme Court of Canada held in *Lavell* that federal legislation denying Indian status to Indian women who married non-Indian men (while extending Indian status to

---

[17] CAN. DEP'T OF JUSTICE, TOWARD EQUALITY: THE RESPONSE TO THE REPORT OF THE PARLIAMENTARY COMMITTEE ON EQUALITY RIGHTS (1986).

non-Indian women who married Indian men) did not violate the 1960 federal Bill of Rights gender equality provision.[18] The court reasoned that there was no gender discrimination in such a rule because it treated all Indian women alike and treated all Indian men alike, but did not have to accord the same legal treatment to Indian women and men.[19] The court held that gender-based classifications in the Indian Act did not attract the same level of scrutiny in Canada as race-based classifications in the Indian Act had attracted in *Drybones,* in which the Supreme Court of Canada had applied the reasoning in *Brown v. Board of Education* to find that race-based Indian Act rules violated the Canadian Bill of Rights.[20] There was widespread concern that the majority had obviously relied on the *Plessy* separate but equal doctrine in applying a lower level of scrutiny to gender distinctions in *Lavell,* and would do so in a new Charter of Rights as well unless a new approach to defining constitutionally impermissible sex discrimination could be formulated.

Just as the draft text of the Canadian Charter of Rights was being prepared, the UN Human Rights Committee ruled in 1981 that this same provision of the Indian Act was discriminatory when another First Nations woman brought a complaint on the *Lavell* issue to that international human rights tribunal.[21] But this decision did little to allay fears that U.S.-style constitutional provisions could prevent judges from reading the Charter as merely calling for formal equality. The 1978 Supreme Court of Canada decision in the *Bliss* case,[22] also brought under the Canadian Bill of Rights, had echoed the reasoning of the U.S. Supreme Court in concluding that denying unemployed women pregnancy and childbirth benefits did not violate sex equality rights because the denial affected all "pregnant persons" "equally."[23] The court found the policy to be gender neutral and, thus, that it did not discriminate against women who happen to be pregnant on the basis of their sex: "Any inequality between the sexes in this area is not created by legislation but by nature . . . . If [the law] treats unemployed pregnant women differently from other unemployed persons, be they male or female, it is . . . because they are pregnant and not because they are women."[24]

---

[18] Attorney Gen. of Can. v. Lavell, [1974] S.C.R. 1349 (Can.).   [19] *Id.* at 1372–73.

[20] *Id.* at 1387–88 (citing The Queen v. Drybones, [1970] S.C.R. 282, 299–300 (Can.) (Hall, J., concurring)).

[21] Lovelace v. Canada, U.N. Doc. A/36/40, at 12 (July 30, 1981).

[22] Bliss v. Attorney Gen. of Can., [1979] 1 S.C.R. 183 (Can.).

[23] *Cf.* Geduldig v. Aiello, 417 U.S. 484, 497 n.20 (1974) (reaching a similar conclusion on the same facts: "The program divides potential recipients into two groups – pregnant women and nonpregnant persons. While the first group is exclusively female, the second includes members of both sexes. The fiscal and actuarial benefits of the program thus accrue to members of both sexes.").

[24] *Bliss,* [1979] 1 S.C.R. at 190–91.

The court relied on *Lavell* to reach that conclusion. The court refused to acknowledge that it was about excluding pregnant women from unemployment benefit programs. Framed as a case about the relevance of gender distinctions, the court concluded that when differences in legal rights are based on "a relevant distinction," the "right to equality before the law would not be offended."[25]

Unprecedented feminist legal activism in reaction to these cases focused on ensuring that the whole Charter would be drafted to promote gender and intersectional equalities, protect the constitutional status of the historic "Persons" case, preclude the valid classification approach to defining potential violations of equality rights represented by *Plessy*, and put the burden of justifying discriminatory distinctions in laws, policies, and practices onto governments seeking to enforce such rules.

This activism resulted in the inclusion of not one but three separate and independent gender equality guarantees in the 1982 amendments to the Canadian Constitution. The first guarantee is drafted to encompass equality rights generally and in relation to historically disadvantaged groups – including sex – and is made up of Sections 1, 15(1), and 15(2). Section 15(1) guarantees that "Every individual is equal before and under the law and has the right to the equal protection and equal benefit of the law without discrimination and, in particular, without discrimination based on race, national or ethnic origin, colour, religion, sex, age or mental or physical disability." Section 15(2) permits affirmative action by stipulating that Section 15(1) "does not preclude any law, program or activity that has as its object the amelioration of conditions of disadvantaged individuals or groups including those that are disadvantaged because of race, national or ethnic origin, colour, religion, sex, age or mental or physical disability." Only if violations of Section 15 are found does Section 1 come into effect, and it limits governmental justification of discrimination "only to such reasonable limits prescribed by law as can be demonstrably justified in a free and democratic society."[26]

These clauses are designed to require substantive impact analysis of contested laws to prevent courts from drawing formalistic distinctions between equality and equal protection of the law, legal burdens versus legal benefits, and other narrow literalist types of distinctions that have been used to read down the broad purposes of constitutional human rights guarantees and counter the *Plessy* and *Bakke* reasoning that ameliorative action is itself discriminatory.

The second equality guarantee, Section 28, was designed to constitutionalize the core principles established in the "Persons" case and to ensure that no

---

[25] *Id.* at 192.
[26] Constitution Act, 1982, *being* Schedule B to the Canada Act, 1982, c 11, §§ 1, 15(1)–(2) (U.K.).

other provision of the Charter, including even Section 1, can be used to excuse differential treatment of women and men in state action even if demonstrably justified: "Notwithstanding anything in this Charter, the rights and freedoms referred to in it are guaranteed equally to male and female persons."[27] The third equality guarantee, Section 35(4), recognizes and affirms "existing aboriginal and treaty rights of the aboriginal peoples of Canada" in the Constitution Act[28] and further provides that, "[n]otwithstanding any other provision of this Act, the aboriginal and treaty rights referred to in subsection (1) are guaranteed equally to male and female persons."[29]

These provisions came into effect in 1982, with the exception of Section 15, which came into effect in 1985 to encourage advance government compliance. National consultations, Charter compliance legislative and research projects, and government departments focused in detail on the entire range of specific equality issues that could be challenged under Sections 15, 28, and 35(4). These studies and testimony produced detailed analysis of gender discrimination in every area of federal, provincial, and territorial law, including in all tax laws and policies.

Before Canadian judges were asked to rule on the constitutionality of tax and tax benefit provisions of particular concern to women, early Charter cases gave feminist judges the opportunity to demonstrate how even brand new constitutional equality provisions must be applied in light of all the material, economic, and social realities of disadvantaged groups.

CANADIAN EQUALITY JUDGMENTS SURPASS U.S. EQUALITY DOCTRINE

Justices Bertha Wilson and Claire L'Heureux-Dubé were the first two women justices appointed to the Supreme Court of Canada, in 1985 and 1987. When hearing *Andrews v. Law Society of British Columbia* in 1989,[30] an impressively unified court decisively moved beyond U.S. Fourteenth Amendment equality doctrine. The *Andrews* case was a Charter challenge to law society rules that prohibited permanent residents from being admitted to the British Columbia bar. This "citizens only" rule was defended on the basis that Section 15 of the Charter should be understood as adopting the three-pronged standard of review applied to Fourteenth Amendment equal protection claims in the United States, and that excluding noncitizen permanent residents from the practice of law was justifiable and thus nondiscriminatory under the rational

---

[27] *Id.* § 28.   [28] *Id.* § 35(1).   [29] *Id.* § 35(4).
[30] Andrews v. Law Soc'y of B.C., [1989] 1 S.C.R. 143 (Can.).

basis standard. The court rejected this approach, holding that the citizens-only rule imposed a burden on permanent resident lawyers that was not demonstrably justifiable on the factual level required by Section 1 of the Charter.

As the case of first impression regarding Section 15, the court plumbed competing concepts of constitutional equality guarantees to produce an approach fully reflective of the multidimensional provisions of Section 15 itself. Thus, the majority in *Andrews* refused to read Section 15 as in any way parallel to the Fourteenth Amendment. Instead, it found that because Section 15 is a stand-alone equality rights clause, courts are obligated to determine first and independently whether a denial of equality rights has been established, and only then, when a violation of equality rights has been found, can it evaluate evidence justifying that breach.

Writing for the court on the application of Section 15(1), Justice McIntyre rejected the "similarly situated" approach to defining equality. In his view, such a mechanical Aristotelian concept of discrimination could not sufficiently guide courts in evaluating the qualitative impact of the law, benefit, or burden on complainants. Justice McIntyre found that the similarly situated approach advocated on behalf of the rule was in fact broad enough "to justify the Nuremberg laws"; that "the formalistic separate but equal doctrine of *Plessy*"[31] could again support decisions like those in *Bliss*[32] and *Lavell*;[33] and that formalistic recognition of separate equalities could also fail to recognize "systemic discrimination" that can arise when beliefs about certain groups are uncritically accepted even without intent to discriminate.[34]

Justice McIntyre concluded that Section 15 was framed in terms expansive and specific enough to prohibit as discrimination any distinction, whether intentional or not, but based on grounds relating to personal characteristics of the individual or group, which has the effect of imposing burdens, obligations, or disadvantages on such individual or group not imposed upon others, or which withholds or limits access to opportunities, benefits, and advantages available to other members of society.[35]

Although some decisions have since strayed from this comprehensive approach, the court has maintained this approach to the Charter equality guarantees since then.

OVERCOMING GENDER DISCRIMINATION IN CANADIAN SEX/GENDER EQUALITY CASES

Both Canadian and U.S. courts have been slow to fully protect women's rights to gender equality in relation to gender-specific issues such as women's

---

[31] *Id.* at 166.   [32] *Id.* at 167–68, 170.   [33] *Id.* at 170.   [34] *Id.* at 173–74.   [35] *Id.* at 174.

rights to abortion, birth control, pregnancy leave, job security after leave, or income replacement benefits during maternity leave. Biological gender differences combined with stereotyped thinking about gender roles have historically justified reluctance to frame complaints on such issues as gender equality rights protected under the Fourteenth Amendment. As a consequence, abortion rights in the United States have been most reliably protected as a matter of privacy doctrine derived from the due process guarantee in the Fourteenth Amendment and not as gender equality rights,[36] while pregnancy and maternity leave income replacement claims have been vulnerable to findings that they provide unjustifiable demands for discriminatory special treatment not available equally to men.[37] By the time Canadian Charter gender equality rights were litigated, the multifaceted *Brown v. Board of Education* analysis of the harms of group-based hierarchies and marginalization had not been readily translated by U.S. courts into recognition of the importance of ameliorating historical disadvantage and stereotyping when gender hierarchies and disadvantages have been involved. Thus, in the late 1980s, the view in Canada was that women were not protected from gender discrimination and other forms of disadvantaging treatment as fully as other groups in U.S. constitutional law.

In contrast, by the time Charter challenges were brought on issues specific to women's realities, including abortion, pregnancy, maternity, and economic issues, Canada's ratification of CEDAW had given more credibility to the seriousness of gender inequalities affecting Aboriginal women, single parents, women living in poverty, disabled women, immigrant women, and women in paid work. This was reinforced when now-Supreme Court Justice Rosalie Abella oversaw the Royal Commission on Equality in Employment, which documented how the realities of workplace discrimination against women, Aboriginal peoples, disabled persons, and visible minorities affects their incomes, life chances, and economic security, and how constitutional principles established in leading human rights cases such as *Brown* could be used to eradicate systemic discrimination experienced by historically disadvantaged groups. Based on extensive legal analysis, the Abella commission proposed legislative reforms not just to rights to equal pay, but to rights to equal education and training, ongoing monitoring and enforcement of equal pay

---

[36] Roe v. Wade, 410 U.S. 113 (1973); Doe v. Bolton, 410 U.S. 179 (1973).

[37] *Geduldig v. Aiello*, 417 U.S. 484 (1974), represents the extreme form of this approach. *California Federal Savings & Loan Ass'n v. Guerra*, 479 U.S. 272, 289 (1987), began to reduce the level of scrutiny of sex-based classifications in order to uphold state legislation requiring employers to provide maternity disability leave benefits even if similar benefits were not given to men.

for work of equal value, and provision of childcare resources for those who could not engage in paid work due to socially assigned care responsibilities.[38]

On the heels of the Abella report, the courts began hearing two types of gender equality cases: Charter challenges pertaining to gender equality issues, and appeals from human rights tribunal rulings on claims filed on the basis of sex discrimination. These rulings adopted the Abella report redefinition of "discrimination," which had moved away from the formalism of U.S. equal protection concepts to recognize the social construction of discriminatory attitudes and beliefs, the structural effects of historical disadvantage, and the nature of systemic discrimination that may or may not be intentional: "Discrimination ... means practices or attitudes that have, whether by design or impact, the effect of limiting an individual's or a group's right to the opportunities generally available because of attributed rather than actual characteristics."[39]

All of these institutional changes – ratification of CEDAW, the data and jurisprudential recommendations made in the Abella report, appointments of women judges to all levels, including to the Supreme Court of Canada – led to palpable changes in judicial approaches to gender equality issues in both constitutional and human rights cases. In a whole series of key early decisions, the Supreme Court of Canada decisively shifted the focus in gender equality cases away from formalistic and stereotyped justifications for women's factual inequalities, and instead showed how both Charter and human rights provisions can be used to invalidate or correct laws, policies, and practices that consciously or culturally perpetuate structural, systemic sex/gender disadvantages.[40]

Not surprisingly, tax and related fiscal laws, which are rife with group-based distinctions, produced hundreds of Charter challenges, many on the basis of discriminatory gender impact. The next section examines how the breakthrough decisions in earlier Charter gender equality cases were used in two key tax cases, and how they have fared.

CHARTER CHALLENGES TO GENDER
DISCRIMINATION IN TAX LAWS

With the support of growing numbers of women lawyers and gender experts, legal aid funding for Charter challenges, and women-led litigation groups,

---

[38] Rosalie Silberman Abella, Report of the Commission on Equality in Employment (1984).

[39] Can. Nat'l Ry. Co. v. Canada, [1987] 1 S.C.R. 1114, 1138–39 (Can.).

[40] Kathleen Mahoney, *Judicial Bias: The Ongoing Challenge*, 2015 J. Disp. Resol. 43, 50–54.

numerous cases seeking to redress sex/gender discrimination in tax law were among the hundreds of Charter challenges brought against both procedural and substantive provisions in Canadian income tax laws. Despite the emerging pro-equality Charter and the willingness of the Supreme Court to adopt a contextualized approach to gender equality claims in earlier nontax cases, feminist efforts to combat gender discrimination in income tax laws nonetheless failed absolutely.

In retrospect, the reason could not be more obvious: constitutional and human rights claims have almost never helped many taxpayers – let alone women – convince courts to correct the discriminatory features of tax laws. This has now been confirmed twice in Canada since the Charter came into effect. Detailed review of some 300 Charter challenges raised in Canadian income tax cases between 1985 and 1995 found that only two cases raising substantive equality issues under Section 15 of the Charter (as opposed to procedural issues) were successful, one of which was impliedly reversed by the negative Supreme Court decision in *Thibaudeau*.[41] A follow-up study of 134 Section 15 Charter challenges brought in income tax cases between 1996 and 2016 found that all those Section 15 claims failed; no appeals from any of these cases even reached the Supreme Court of Canada.[42] To say that raising gender equality challenges to discriminatory tax laws has been to date a "loser move" is an understatement.

Nonetheless, in the wake of the successful earlier Charter gender decisions, dissenting opinions written by Supreme Court Justices L'Heureux-Dubé and McLachlin (now Chief Justice) lay out how and why denial of business deductions for childcare expenses and compulsory taxation of child support payments to custodial mothers violate Section 15 of the Charter.[43] These two opinions provide valuable insights into how constitutional gender equality guarantees can be used to argue for tax and fiscal policies that promote substantive gender equality instead of undermining it.

In *Symes*, Justice L'Heureux-Dubé concluded that gender-neutral income tax rules permitting the deduction of expenses incurred for the purpose of

---

[41] [1995] 2 S.C.R. 627 (Can.). The other decision was more of a technical ruling. *See generally* Kathleen A. Lahey, *The Impact of the Canadian Charter of Rights and Freedoms on Income Tax Law and Policy, in* Charting the Consequences: The Impact of Charter Rights on Canadian Law and Politics 109 (David Schneiderman & Kate Sutherland eds., 1997).

[42] Kyle Gardiner, *Charter Equality Challenges to the Income Tax Act: The Unsuccessful Streak is Strong, 30 Years On,* ABlawg.ca (Sept. 2, 2016), http://ablawg.ca/2016/09/02/equality-challenges-to-tax-unsuccessful-30-years/.

[43] Symes v. Canada, [1993] 4 S.C.R. 695, 776 (Can.); Thibaudeau v. Canada, [1995] 2 S.C.R. 627, 641 (Can.).

earning income from business had to be interpreted in light of Charter substantive gender equality values to permit deduction of necessary childcare expenses, and that any interpretations that prohibited or limited the deduction of such childcare expenses violate Section 15 gender equality rights. In *Thibaudeau*, she concluded that income tax provisions that disparately impact women violate substantive guarantees of gender equality and must be remedied by reading them consistently with the purposes of Section 15, or if that is not possible, they must be struck as being inconsistent with women's substantive gender equality rights under the Charter. The *Symes* decision is discussed in depth in this section because of the originality and importance of the reasoning Justice L'Heureux-Dubé brought to bear on these issues.

A. Symes v. Canada: *Male Majority Denies Business Deductions for Childcare Expenses*

Elizabeth Symes, a partner in a law firm with two young children, deducted the salary she paid for full-time childcare as a business expense when filing her personal income tax returns. When Revenue Canada denied these business deductions and tried to limit her to the small amounts of childcare expenses that could be deducted for single parents and secondary earners under Section 63 of the Income Tax Act, she brought a Section 15 gender equality Charter challenge to establish her right to deduct the full amounts of her childcare expenses as business expenses.

Symes's position was simple: She was entitled by Section 18(1)(a) of the Income Tax Act to deduct all her childcare expenses in calculating the profit from her law practice because those expenses had all been "incurred for the purpose of gaining or earning income from business."[44] She further submitted that this provision and the prohibition in Section 18(1)(h) against deducting "personal or living expenses" as business expenses had to be interpreted consistently with Charter values of substantive gender equality, as must Section 63 of the Act, with the result that interpretations of these provisions as denying or limiting her deductions either breach Section 15 of the Charter or must be constitutionally corrected to permit those deductions.

When the *Symes* appeal came before the Supreme Court of Canada, Justice Iacobucci, writing for the five male members of the court, ruled that the childcare expenses were not deductible under Section 18(1)(a) of the Act because (1) they were traditionally considered to be "personal or living

---

[44] Income Tax Act, R.S.C. 1952, c 148, § 18(1)(a) (Can.).

expenses" under Section 18(1)(h) of the Act; (2) accountants responsible for certifying business deductions did not, at that time, recognize childcare expenses as business expenses; and/or (3) allowing Symes to deduct them as business expenses would undermine the purpose of Section 63 of the Act, which he characterized as a complete code regulating deductions for child-care expenses for all eligible taxpayers but for no others. He also found that none of these rules were ambiguous, and therefore that Charter gender equality values did not have to be invoked as an interpretive aid.

Justice L'Heureux-Dubé's dissenting opinion (with Justice McLachlin concurring in the dissent) spelled out the errors in the majority judgment in detail. She concluded first that Justice Iacobucci had erred in failing to interpret the business expense deduction provisions in light of the changing social and economic roles and needs of women as an historically disadvantaged class, and thus found his ruling to be inconsistent with Charter gender equality values guaranteed in Sections 15 and 28 of the Charter. Second, she concluded that ruling that Symes could not deduct any of her actual childcare business expenses except to the extent permitted by Section 63 of the Act constituted a violation of Section 15 of the Charter.

1. Charter Values: Childcare Services Are Crucial to Women's Economic Equality

Justice L'Heureux-Dubé grounded the Charter values issue in evidence that while women's roles as income earners had changed dramatically since the 1950s, they were still socially expected to take responsibility for the bulk of childcare in ways that men were not, a social attitude that thus disadvantages women in being able to earn business profits. She drew upon a wide range of research studies in the record as establishing the factual importance of child-care resources to women's economic engagement and empowerment. Citing evidence that women's labor force participation rates had grown from just 24 percent in 1951 to 56 percent in 1987, Justice L'Heureux-Dubé concluded that "for most Canadian families, the issue of child care is of crucial importance," and thus that courts are obligated by Section 15 of the Charter to "consider whether child care expenses can be accommodated within the definition of a business expense" by interpreting statutes through analysis that "recognizes the evolution of our societal structure ... in context, not in a vacuum."[45]

---

[45] *Symes*, [1993] 4 S.C.R. at 793 (L'Heureux-Dubé, J., dissenting).

Relying on Statistics Canada studies and the Abella report, Justice L'Heureux-Dubé concluded that even though Canadian law assigns the duty of care to both parents, the social science evidence made it clear that mothers factually still do virtually all the day-to-day care work as well as the work of planning care, and that as women have entered into professional and managerial positions, "having children" has been identified as "a major disruption in career patterns and as a problem for women."[46] She relied on studies of Canadian lawyers to point out that women lawyers spend almost twice as much time caring for children as male lawyers; that women lawyers are more than three times more likely to have to obtain paid childcare than male lawyers; and that a "majority of women reported loss of income due to child rearing whereas only a small minority of men did so."[47]

The weight of this evidence led Justice L'Heureux-Dubé to conclude: "The reality of Ms. Symes' business life necessarily includes childcare. The 1993 concept of business expense must include the reality of diverse business practices and needs of those who have not traditionally participated fully in the world of business."[48]

2. Many Routine Business Expenses Have Substantial "Personal" Attributes

Justice L'Heureux-Dubé then turned to the question of how male judges could be so certain that childcare expenses are "personal" expenses when so many expenditures that are unquestionably treated as being deductible business expenses also have substantial personal dimensions. Pointing out that male judges' perceptions of "objective facts" are shaped by their own unconscious frames of reference, Justice L'Heureux-Dubé gave the example of a case in which "driving a Rolls Royce has been held to be an incident of a professional business" giving rise to deductible business expenses "because some men believe expensive cars enhance their professional image." Noting that even though such expenditures may be "potentially personal," such expenses have been accepted "as a legitimate business expense and, as each reflects a real cost incurred by certain kinds of business people to produce income from business, a deduction has been allowed."[49] She also cited the Supreme Court's approval of Royal Trust Company's business deductions of golf club dues, initiation fees, greens fees, and restaurant bills paid on behalf of its executives because "the evidence proved conclusively that the practice of

---

[46] *Id.* at 829.   [47] *Id.* at 803.   [48] *Id.* at 802.   [49] *Id.* at 803.

paying the club dues resulted in business from which the appellant gained or produced income."[50] From this she concluded that the "real costs incurred by businesswomen with children are no less real, no less worthy of consideration, and no less incurred in order to gain or produce income from business."[51]

She also emphasized that even if business expenditures on "lavish entertainment and the wining and dining of clients and customers" are personally enjoyable, they are still "obviously business expenses rather than personal ones."[52] So too, she argued, "while the care of children may be personally rewarding, this 'choice' is a choice unlike any others" because it is "one from which all of society benefits, yet much of the burden remains on the shoulders of women."[53] Drawing the analogy to Justice Dickson's reasoning in one of the earlier Charter gender equality cases "[t]hat those who bear children and benefit society as a whole thereby should not be economically or socially disadvantaged seems to bespeak the obvious," she concluded that "it is unfair to impose all of the costs of pregnancy upon one half of the population."[54]

3. Businesses Are Permitted to Deduct Childcare Business Expenses

Justice L'Heureux-Dubé emphasized the inconsistency of denying Symes the right to deduct her own childcare costs as expenses of her own business operation, when Canada had already embarked on encouraging employers to provide tax-exempt childcare facilities or services to their employees and fully deduct the costs of such programs. Even when provision of such childcare facilities may be classified as giving rise to a taxable benefit to the employee, the costs of providing those facilities would still give rise to deductible expenses on the part of the employer. To deny the self-employed or small business owners the same right of deductibility disadvantages women-led businesses, which tend to be smaller and less profitable as compared with men's businesses, and intensifies preexisting gender disadvantages.

If businesses can deduct childcare expenses paid on behalf of their employees, then so too should self-employed business owners be able to deduct their own childcare expenses. If that were not permitted, then instead of being able to carry out their business activities on business premises, there is a significant risk that businesswomen would have to move their business premises to their homes. This can marginally increase total business profits, but it is not likely to enhance the profitability or durability of the business operation.[55]

---

[50] *Id.* at 796.   [51] *Id.* at 803.   [52] *Id.* at 803–04.   [53] *Id.* at 804.   [54] *Id.*

[55] There is surprisingly little empirical research on the structures, locations, financing, and profitability of women's self-employment, but a recent Australian study has documented these

4. Nondeductibility of Business Childcare Expenses Discriminates Against Women

All of these considerations led Justice L'Heureux-Dubé to conclude that not only are women's childcare expenses legitimate business expenses under Section 18(1)(a) of the Act, but that Section 63, which makes more limited childcare deductions available to a wider category of income earners, easily coexists with the business deductibility provision. This interpretation of gender-neutral statutory provisions in light of the changing social and economic realities of women's lives, she concluded, is consistent with the urgency of ensuring that such tax benefits do not exclude women simply because they had not claimed such business expenses in the past, particularly now that women's economic need for the right to deduct childcare as a business expense had begun to expand as they had greater opportunities to engage in professions and establish their own businesses. Reasoning that regardless of whether the case for deductibility is clear-cut or debatable,

> one must ... examine that ambiguity through the prism of the values enshrined in the Charter and, in particular in ss. 15 and 28. These sections encompass and embrace the importance and significance of equality between the sexes and the Act must be interpreted in a manner that does not run contrary to, but rather enhances, these principles.[56]

Summing up the Charter values interpretation issue, she concluded that to deny these deductions would permit gender inequality in the deductibility of business childcare expenses to continue, to the detriment of women as an already-disadvantaged class:

> When ensuring that laws conform with the imperatives of the Charter, it is important to consider whether a situation or law has different implications for men and women. To disallow childcare as a business expense clearly has a differential impact on women and we cannot simply pay lip service to equality and leave intact an interpretation which privileges businessmen, and which continues to deny the business needs of businesswomen with children.[57]

The interpretation of laws must change over time to remain consistent with an "altered and ever-changing societal context."[58]

---

points in detail. AUSTL. BUREAU OF STATISTICS, PROFILE OF AUSTRALIAN WOMEN IN BUSINESS, chs. 2–3 (2015).
[56] *Symes*, [1993] 4 S.C.R. at 819 (L'Heureux-Dubé, J., dissenting).   [57] *Id.*   [58] *Id.* at 793.

5. Charter Breach: The Majority Decision Violates
Section 15 of the Charter

In the second part of her opinion, Justice L'Heureux-Dubé concluded that the majority decision classifying Symes's childcare expenses as nondeductible "personal or living expenses" within the meaning of Section 18(1)(h), and thus as childcare expenses that could only be deducted to the extent permitted by Section 63 of the Act, produced a rule of law that unjustifiably discriminates against women on the basis of their sex and thus violates Section 15 of the Charter. Justice L'Heureux-Dubé characterized the purpose of the Section 15 gender equality guarantee as "the attainment of true substantive equality between men and women."[59] The closing paragraph of her dissent spells out just what a "true" substantive gender equality analysis would encompass in this situation:

> In the context of the Charter investigation in the case at hand, we must keep foremost in our minds the unequal cost of childcare that women have traditionally borne, the effect of such cost on the ability of women to participate in business or otherwise be gainfully employed and, finally, the impact of childcare on women's financial ability and independence. In my view, such a "contextual" approach is an attempt to attack the problem of privilege and to understand the diversity of people's experiences. When issues are examined in context, it becomes clear that some so-called "objective truths" may only be the reality of a select group in society and may, in fact, be completely inadequate to deal with the reality of other groups. As the Honourable Bertha Wilson comments ... :
>
>> Real lives, contemporary women's lives, should not only be taken seriously but should be regarded as primary in interpreting constitutional guarantees which impact directly or indirectly on women's equality. Experiences must not be "shoehorned" to fit within the constitutional guarantees; rather, the constitutional guarantees must be interpreted in a way that is responsive to women's reality.[60]

In this historic dissent, the feminist case for finding that the denial of business expense deductions for childcare expenses constitutes sex discrimination comes down to the utter failure to provide even a small tax benefit to ameliorate the long-standing traditional barriers to women's economic equality,

---

[59] *Id.* at 820.
[60] *Id.* at 826–27 (quoting Bertha Wilson, *Women, the Family, and the Constitutional Protection of Privacy*, 17 QUEEN'S L.J. 5, 13 (1992)).

chief among which is women's continuing cultural responsibility for childcare in the face of government refusals to fund childcare services for all, and men's unwillingness to adjust their own work hours and incomes to fill the gap. As Justice L'Heureux-Dubé summed it up, childcare expenses are completely necessary business expenses for many more women than for men: "[F]or most men, the responsibility of children does not impact on the number of hours they work, nor does it affect their ability to work . . . . [A] woman's ability even to participate in the workforce may be completely contingent on her ability to acquire childcare."[61]

B. *Feminist Judgments in* Thibaudeau

The second tax case to reach the Supreme Court of Canada took the position that compelling custodial mothers to include child support payments in their own income in order to give tax deductions to the parent paying the child support did not violate Charter sex equality rights because it was designed to confer a net tax benefit on the postdivorce "family unit."[62] The evidence before the Court was that due to their generally lower incomes, custodial mothers tend to receive more child support payments than men; that payor parents tend to get larger tax reductions for paying child support than the taxes paid on that support by the custodial parents; and that there was no mechanism by which those larger tax reductions might be shared with the custodial parent, whose ability to provide adequate support for self and children was thereby impaired.

Reasoning that the benefit unit of this tax provision was not individual custodial parents but was the "post-divorce family unit," the male majority of the Court concluded that, on balance, more such "units" received a net benefit from this scheme than suffered a detriment. They simply ignored the negative systemic impact of this system on custodial mothers within those units, because they insisted that the benefit unit was not the individual but was some version of the family. In their dissenting opinions, both feminist judges drew attention to the discriminatory impact of this insistence on impressing the structure of the family on couples who had gone to great length to legally separate themselves into unmarried individuals with their own households and who were no longer cohabiting.

In her dissenting opinion, Justice L'Heureux-Dubé pointed out that what matters is not the impact of a policy on an abstract "unit" as a whole, but how it affects "each member of the couple."[63] She concluded that this form of

---

[61] *Id.* at 800.   [62] Thibaudeau v. Canada, [1995] 2 S.C.R. 627 (Can.).
[63] *Id.* at 644 (L'Heureux-Dubé, J., dissenting).

income splitting violated the Charter gender equality guarantees because it provided an "upside-down subsidy" that literally gave generous tax benefits to the higher-income spouse as a reward for making child support payments, but financed them by shifting the financial burden of funding those tax benefits to the lower-income spouse – the one already responsible for the day-to-day care of the children and thus also likely to have less time and flexibility in obtaining well-paid work. She added that the benefit received by the higher-income spouse "will only be shared with the custodial spouse or with the children in the event that a conscious redistribution is made by the judge fixing the quantum of child support, or by the good graces of the payor,"[64] because the lower-income parent does not have recourse to the courts to ensure that the tax or cash benefits given to noncustodial parents are used for care of children – let alone for paid childcare to enable the lower-income partner to engage in paid work. Thus, this system intensifies the disadvantages already imposed on women's paid work by large gender wage gaps and lack of affordable paid childcare.

Justice McLachlin (as she was then) agreed that the whole system ran counter to Charter gender equality imperatives. Pointing out that Canadian society "strongly encourages women to attain financial self-sufficiency, and, in pursuit of that essential objective, to increase their income" after divorce, she emphasized that the taxation of child support payments actually undercut that goal: "The higher the income of the custodial parent, the ... more she will be penalized. ... Such a mechanism not only does not encourage women to attain financial self-sufficiency, it seems designed in some cases to discourage them from increasing their income."[65] Thus, she also concluded that giving the "choice" as to how such tax benefits are used to the higher-income spouse does not require the parent who receives them "to share the tax savings." Instead, the scheme "appears to benefit only the person on whom [it] is conferred" and "works to the disadvantage" of the other parent when, as in many cases, "the tax benefit is not passed on to the [other] parent or the children."[66]

TAXING FOR GENDER EQUALITY: DOMESTIC AND
INTERNATIONAL GENDER EQUALITY GUARANTEES

The breakthrough feminist judgments in *Symes* and *Thibaudeau* stand out from the universe of gender-related tax decisions in their direct demonstration of why two of the most damaging features of the political economy of gender as constructed under conditions of long-term gender inequality – women's

[64] *Id.* at 647.   [65] *Id.* at 712–13 (McLachlan, J., dissenting).   [66] *Id.* at 727.

disproportionate responsibilities for human and social reproduction under conditions of material, legal, and political inequalities, and the use of couples as the tax/benefit unit – have to be invalidated in every policy context that reinforces them, if there is any chance of eliminating all forms of gender discrimination. And these two sets of judgments demonstrate how to invalidate them using the emerging value structure and principles of substantive gender equality.

The first of these damaging features – failure of too many countries at all levels of development to facilitate gender-equal social sharing of human physical and social reproduction – is the core problem: By the end of most women's lives, it will have been their disproportionate responsibilities for unpaid work of all kinds, predominantly their unpaid human and social reproduction work, that will have deprived them of equal time, support, energy, and rights to attain economic self-sufficiency or even autonomy. Thus, on average, they will have far lower incomes and much less economic security than their male counterparts. By not even giving women some financial relief through tax deductions for their increasing use of paid care services to enable them to enter more fully into paid work, women face entrenched labor market discrimination in hiring, pay, job security, and benefits, and, on top of that, are also expected to meet their own needs and pay out of their lower average earnings the costs of those care services that enable them to increase their paid work time. And they are in competition with many other workers who have disproportionately greater access to unpaid services of spouses, mothers, daughters, sisters, and even friends to help them manage their family lives, as well as higher incomes with which to pay for care services not otherwise generously offered at no cost, plus tax benefits for the support of wives or dependent family members. The failure to permit women to use tax deductions or other fiscal benefits to reduce the costs they have to pay for care services out of their substantially lower average incomes, combined with the equally intransigent refusal to cancel the many unpaid work benefits and affirmative tax benefits given to men who support others – benefits that often increase in monetary value as men's higher incomes increase – ensures that the unpaid/paid work and income inequalities that define the political economy of women simply cannot change in any meaningful way.

The second of these two features of the political economy of gender is that, although the unitary concept of spouses as constituting a legal and social unit that subsumes women's productive capacities and well-being to the needs of the "unit" is gradually being replaced with recognition of women as autonomous rights-bearing individuals, the former concept remains deeply entrenched in tax laws. Thus, the absorption of women's fiscal space into the adult couple "unit" even after divorce by means of income-splitting tax laws ensures that women will be overtaxed even as they attempt to use their own fiscal space to become economically secure through paid work. In other words, the use of all manner of joint or couple-based tax measures during and after marriage adds an invisible but powerful tax law barrier to the attainment of substantive gender equality.

But now that feminist judges have carved out clear jurisprudential paths that can liberate women – and men – from these forms of legal economic discrimination, how, with feminist judges forming mainly minorities on top national courts, can they ensure that their opinions can ever become widely accepted enough to change women's social, economic, legal, political, and constitutional realities? Part of the answer, of course, is to get the word out about these feminist opinions, and to show how they can help promote substantive gender equality in every aspect of contemporary life. By rewriting incorrect decisions around the core insights and principles developed in these crucial feminist tax opinions, and by drawing on them in all aspects of fiscal policy analysis, minds can be changed, judicial decisions can be influenced, and women's and men's lives can also begin to change. There are other judicial processes forming internationally in treaty compliance mechanisms, however, of which the most important are those supported by CEDAW.

A. *While Waiting for CEDAW and the Beijing Platform for Action*

The United States is not the only country that is waiting for CEDAW. The failure of even the increasingly gender-equal Supreme Court of Canada to apply its own highly regarded gender equality constitutional guarantees to tax and other fiscal policies is painfully obvious.

But the good news is that implementation of CEDAW has gained momentum. The standard of substantive gender equality has been explicitly strengthened by adoption of the Beijing Platform for Action as a guide to implementing CEDAW; by the expansion of the compliance mechanisms used by the CEDAW Committee; by growing understanding that, as a core human right, gender equality should be adopted as a core normative standard by international financial, human rights, and development organizations; and by making taxing for gender equality an acknowledged global policy priority as new transnational normative standards have been adopted in relation to poverty, gender, economic, and environmental sustainability goals[67] as well as

---

[67] *See* U.N. Secretary-General, *Critical Milestones toward Coherent, Efficient and Inclusive Follow-up and Review at the Global Level*, U.N. Doc. A/70/684 (Jan. 15, 2016). The sustainable development goals came into effect on January 1, 2016. *See* Paris Agreement, Dec. 12, 2015, Entry into Force, U.N. Doc. C.N.735.2016.TREATIES-XXVII.7.d (Oct. 5, 2016).

in relation to revenue issues and financing for development.[68] These documents commit to mainstreaming gender equality and poverty reduction outcomes on a systemic basis, including specifically in relation to all revenue issues.[69] Implementing substantive gender equality rights generally – and more specifically in relation to long-standing discrimination in taxation, benefit, and other fiscal laws through national constitutional and human rights litigation – may have become blocked in countries like the United States and Canada, but expanding understanding of the importance of the issues has increased uptake at the transnational and international levels. Feminist judgments like those produced by Justices L'Heureux-Dubé and McLachlin in *Symes* and *Thibaudeau* may have been marginalized even as other important equality rights have gained recognition, but they are nonetheless now having transformative impact in the larger global community.

B. *The Beijing Platform for Action*

Ushering in the Beijing Platform for Action in 1995, Hillary Rodham Clinton famously opened the Fourth United Nations World Conference on Women by proclaiming, "Human rights are women's rights, and women's rights are human rights."[70] Although the U.S. Senate still has not ratified CEDAW, the world is increasingly taking up concepts of substantive gender equality inspired by the best of U.S. and Canadian constitutional jurisprudence,[71] but that are not widely applied in the United States and are still not applied to gender and tax issues in Canada.

---

[68] U.N. DEP'T OF ECON. & SOC. AFFAIRS, ADDIS ABABA ACTION AGENDA OF THE THIRD INTERNATIONAL CONFERENCE ON FINANCING FOR DEVELOPMENT (2015).

[69] U.N. Secretary-General, *Review and Appraisal of the Implementation of the Beijing Declaration and Platform for Action and the Outcomes of the Twenty-Third Special Session of the General Assembly* ¶ 247, U.N. Doc. E/CN.6/2015/3 (Dec. 15, 2014) (explicitly committing to gender-based analysis of all fiscal measures in their linkages to gender and their impact on women).

[70] Hillary Rodham Clinton, Remarks for the United Nations Fourth World Conference on Women (Sept. 5, 1995), http://www.un.org/esa/gopher-data/conf/fwcw/conf/gov/950905175653 .txt. Gender equality is built into the Universal Declaration of Human Rights (art. 2) and the International Covenant on Civil and Political Rights (art. 3), but neither document enumerates or enforces gender equality rights in the general and particularized way that CEDAW does.

[71] E.g., Brown v. Bd. of Educ., 347 U.S. 483, 491–94 (1954) (differentiating physically equal but racially segregated facilities from equality of outcomes); *see also* Sandra Fredman & Beth Goldblatt, *Gender Equality and Human Rights* (UN Women Discussion Paper No. 4, 2015) (bringing Supreme Court of Canada jurisprudence on substantive equality directly into analysis of how gender equality is to be construed in applying CEDAW and the Beijing Platform).

The Beijing Platform for Action[72] is a massive document containing over 360 detailed paragraphs spelling out exactly what issues and analytic methods are to be used by state signatories to assess and improve the gender impact of laws, policies, and practices. It contains separate sections on each of the subject matter areas covered by CEDAW, as well as extensive sections on governance mechanisms for implementing gender mainstreaming and gender impact analysis of all existing and proposed laws and government actions. It calls upon all governments and agencies to develop and implement gender equality action plans, and it is increasingly used as the standard against which periodic country reviews and Platform implementation carried out by the United Nations are evaluated.

The concept of gender mainstreaming places states under obligations to review all aspects of social, economic, political, workplace, cultural, and legal rules and activities for their gender impact, and to revise and monitor them until all gender inequalities are eradicated. Gender mainstreaming uses gender-based analysis and gender budgeting to evaluate the gender impact of laws, policies, and programs in substantive qualitative and quantitative terms, and gender budgeting tracks these effects from publication of the budget through to the completion of budget execution.[73] Nongovernmental and academic advocates and experts increasingly participate in all these processes to increase accountability.

C. *CEDAW Committee General Recommendations*

From time to time, the CEDAW Committee publishes general recommendations to provide guidance regarding the interpretation and application of CEDAW and the Beijing Platform. General Recommendation No. 25 confirms that "gender equality" includes the right to formal equality as well as the right to *de facto* equality, or equality of opportunity, resources, and outcomes.[74] Since this general recommendation was published, the United Nations has agreed to use the term "substantive equality" to encompass all

[72] U.N. Fourth World Conference on Women, *Report of the Fourth World Conference on Women*, U.N. Doc. A/CONF.177/20 (Oct. 17, 1995).

[73] For details of these methods, see Kathleen A. Lahey, *Women, Substantive Equality, and Fiscal Policy: Gender-Based Analysis of Taxes, Benefits, and Budgets*, 22 CAN. J. WOMEN & L. 27 (2010).

[74] U.N. Comm. on the Elimination of Discrimination Against Women, General Recommendation No. 25: Article 4, para.1, of the Convention (on Temporary Special Measures), at para. 8 (2004), http://tbinternet.ohchr.org/Treaties/CEDAW/Shared%20 Documents/1_Global/INT_CEDAW_GEC_3733_E.pdf.

aspects of gender equality called for by CEDAW. In 2015, the United Nations elaborated on the meaning of substantive gender equality when it stated that the wide and inclusive language used in Article 1 of CEDAW

> takes a first step toward advancing the notion of substantive equality in its comprehensive definition of "discrimination against women":
>
> *(it) shall mean any distinction, exclusion, or restriction made on the basis of sex which has the effect or purpose of impairing or nullifying the recognition, enjoyment, or exercise by women, irrespective of their marital status, on a basis of equality of men and women, of human rights and fundamental freedoms in the political, economic, social, cultural, civil, or any other field.*[75]

This understanding of substantive equality is intended to encompass older, narrower concepts of discrimination such as direct discrimination (discriminatory treatment) and indirect discrimination (discriminatory outcomes of gender-neutral laws), as well as purposive discrimination (deliberate or intentional discrimination) and discrimination in effect (without deliberate intent to produce a discriminatory outcome).

This development is particularly important because this expansive understanding of substantive equality displaces earlier terms such as "implicit," "explicit," and "gender bias" when talking about the gender impact of tax laws, and "equity" as the standard or goal instead of the term "equality."[76]

D. *CEDAW Optional Protocol*

In 2000, adoption of the CEDAW Optional Protocol gave the CEDAW Committee authorization to conduct inquiries and hearings into violations of CEDAW. The jurisprudence produced through these proceedings has grown rapidly, and, in 2014 and 2015, produced two decisions that demonstrate the power of CEDAW to prohibit gender discrimination in fiscal policy, order remedies for legislation that does not comport with CEDAW, and make far-reaching recommendations on how systemic discrimination against

---

[75] UN Women, Progress of the World's Women 2015–2016: Transforming Economies, Realizing Rights 36 (2015) (quoting Hanna Beate Schöpp-Schilling, *Reflections on a General Recommendation on Article 4(1) of the Convention on the Elimination of All Forms of Discrimination against Women, in* Temporary Special Measures: Accelerating De Facto Equality of Women Under Article 4(1) UN Convention on the Elimination of All Forms of Discrimination against Women 15 (Ineke Boerefijn et al. eds., 2003)).

[76] Alda Facio & Martha I. Morgan, *Equity or Equality for Women – Understanding CEDAW's Equality Principles*, 60 Ala. L. Rev. 1133 (2008) (explaining why "equity" as a legal concept cannot do much to eradicate sex discrimination).

Indigenous women and peoples is to be eliminated consistently with the Beijing Platform and with CEDAW general and country recommendations.

In the 2014 *Blok* decision, the Netherlands was found to have violated women's maternity leave rights by repealing maternity allowances for self-employed women.[77] The *Blok* decision applied the substantive equality test, found that countries are bound by CEDAW when ratifying it even if they do not enact domesticating legislation supporting suits under CEDAW, and ordered payment of monetary damages. The 2015 *Canadian Inquiry* decision, which arose from complaints brought on behalf of Indigenous women after decades of efforts to obtain improved living conditions and life opportunities for them and their communities, found violations of numerous specific provisions of CEDAW, held all levels of Canadian government accountable for these violations, and ordered all levels of government to take five pages of specific remedial steps, including numerous fiscal steps, to lift Indigenous women and communities from the depths of long-standing poverty and risks.[78]

E. *UN Special Rapporteur on Extreme Poverty: Taxing for Gender Equality*

After 2008, as the OECD and International Monetary Fund began to examine the connection between fiscal austerity policies, tax cuts, and growing levels of income inequalities,[79] the relationship between taxation and gender inequalities began to receive increased attention. While the bulk of the literature focused primarily on finding tax and fiscal policies that could synergistically promote income equality, economic growth, and gender equality,[80] a report on "taxing for gender equality" by the UN Special Rapporteur on Extreme Poverty and Human Rights recast these issues as issues of gender equality human rights.[81] This report analyzes how countless features of corporate and

---

[77] Blok v. Netherlands, Communication No. 36/2012, U.N. Doc. CEDAW/C/57/D/36/2012 (Mar. 24, 2014).

[78] Report of the Inquiry Concerning Canada, U.N. Doc. CEDAW/C/OP.8/CAN/1 (Mar. 30, 2015).

[79] *See, e.g.*, ORG. FOR ECON. COOPERATION & DEV., GROWING UNEQUAL? INCOME DISTRIBUTION AND POVERTY IN OECD COUNTRIES (2008).

[80] ORG. FOR ECON. COOPERATION & DEV., DIVIDED WE STAND: WHY INEQUALITY KEEPS RISING (2011); ORG. FOR ECON. COOPERATION & DEV., GENDER AND TAXATION: WHY CARE ABOUT TAXATION AND GENDER EQUALITY? (2010); Isabelle Joumard et al., *Less Income Inequality and More Growth – Are They Compatible? Part 3. Income Redistribution via Taxes and Transfers Across OECD Countries* (OECD Econ. Dep't Working Papers No. 926, 2012), http://dx.doi .org/10.1787/5k9h296b1zjf-en.

[81] Magdalena Sepúlveda Carmona, *Report of the Special Rapporteur on Extreme Poverty and Human Rights. Mission to Mozambique* (2014), *available at* http://ssrn.com/abstract=2502982.

personal income, value-added, excise, sales, and property taxes; fees and charges; and transfer laws systemically intensify women's economic disadvantages, perpetuate gender inequalities and poverty, and thus violate CEDAW. And even more crucially, the report concluded with detailed recommendations on systemic tax changes needed to attain and sustain gender equality in countries at all levels of development, and with particular attention on joint tax provisions like those litigated in *Thibaudeau*; lack of alleviation of women's heavy responsibilities for unpaid work of all kinds, including most care work; and the risks of high consumption tax rates on women and households living in poverty.

F. U.S. Cities Adopting CEDAW

While waiting for national ratification, CEDAW is making its way into the fabric of municipal governance policies in the United States. In 1998, San Francisco passed a CEDAW ordinance that literally integrated its provisions into its municipal code, and set up a Department on the Status of Women to manage compliance.[82] Some twenty-five cities have now followed suit, and another twenty-five are exploring this strategy.

CONCLUSION

Existing feminist tax judgments, even when written as dissenting opinions, provide invaluable starting points for envisioning what the material and social realities of substantive gender equality will look like in specific contexts. The opinions written by Justices L'Heureux-Dubé and McLachlin (as she then was) demonstrate that the first and biggest step in writing feminist tax judgments is to perceive how gender stereotypes and hierarchies shape the tendency to tolerate in tax laws arbitrary rules and concepts that fly in the face of obvious known facts about everyday realities, such as the pretense that a divorced couple operates as much like an "economic unit" as a couple raising their children together. Or the pretense that purchase of expensive cars or even planes has the "business purpose" of saving commuting or travel time in business, but that the purchase of childcare services for the "purpose" of saving thinking or working time from unpaid work is not qualitatively "businesslike" even when increased childcare services factually increase business profits and reduce risks of business losses.

---

[82] S.F. Cal., Municipal Code, ch. 12K, http://sfgov.org/dosw/cedaw-ordinance.

Not all feminist judging must be done by women, but feminist judging to be effective does have to begin by giving due weight to the realities of gendered existences. Even insisting on the basic fact that "pregnant persons" is not a gender-neutral or a legal category containing a mix of persons classified as legal males and legal females can provide the step out of abstract theoretical constructs and into the realities of gendered hierarchies, constraints, opportunities, and burdens that make it possible to come to judicial decisions that increase substantive equality between women and men.

One of the realities about the gender impact of feminist judging, however, is that its qualitative and conceptual impact will far outstrip its measurable gender effects in everyday life. True, Justices L'Heureux-Dubé's and McLachlin's dissents in *Thibaudeau* challenged the federal government in charge of the income tax laws requiring custodial parents to pay income tax on their child support payments to such an extent that the government repealed those rules and replaced them with child support guidelines reflecting fair allocations of after-tax incomes to both parents – a gigantic impact for one opinion. But the incremental impact of that change on a custodial parent's net after-tax income as compared with the previous system is statistically hard to measure and is just one of the many hundreds of specific tax provisions that impact women differently than men each and every day in every country in the world. So, it will be a monumentally slow process to replace existing tax/transfer systems with those that are fully structured around producing gender-equal outcomes.

But the potential for substantial gender impact is there, too. When governments are either ordered by their top courts or by the CEDAW Committee to implement adequate, flexible, and affordable childcare programs, the effect will undoubtedly be transformative for women presently locked into high levels of unpaid work as part of their daily lives and thus competing in quite unequal conditions for equal dignified after-tax incomes. Unfortunately, it is now 169 years since the insightful comments on the taxation of women in the Seneca Falls Declaration, and it has taken layers of legal institutional developments to get to where feminist judging is now – married women's property laws; voting rights; filing taxes as "individuals" but being taxed as part of an "economic unit"; getting women into the legal profession; getting women appointed to the bench; getting feminist perspectives legitimated in the academy and in scholarly publications; getting feminism into legal analysis; and then getting CEDAW signed and ratified; getting civil society engaged in using the periodic reporting, gender-based analysis tools, reporting cycles, and optional protocols to get more feminist judicial decisions produced at the international treaty level, etc.

Clearly the job is not done yet. But the gaps are now known, visible, and documented more fully every day. The 360 paragraphs of the Beijing Platform for Action can guide any policy process through a useful gender-based analysis. Even though Canada has been relatively more proactive in implementing gender equality than the United States – with CEDAW; has a more gender-equal constitution than many countries; has feminist judges at every level; and even, as of March 22, 2017, has its first-ever gender budget statement in the national budget, only 22 years after it originally promised to do so – women still face significant gender gaps in all aspects of their lives.

But by building on the best of actual feminist judgments and all those waiting to be written, progress is not just possible but inevitable. Women's knowledges grow exponentially each year as they grapple with evermore visible gender inequality machinery and learn how to use evermore effective gender equality machinery – even the deep complex machineries of tax law.

PART II

The Feminist Judgments

3

Commentary on *United States v. Rickert*

CHLOE THOMPSON

Nobody bothered to make Charles Crawford, Adam Little Thunder, Solomon Two Stars, Victor Renville, or their tribe, the Sisseton and Wahpeton Nation[1] (of the Dakota people), parties to *United States v. Rickert*. After all, they were Indians – "formerly untutored savages,"[2] "wards of the United States and under its guardianship and supervision," "in a condition of pupilage or dependency," "weak[] and helpless[]," "to be maintained as well as prepared for assuming the habits of a civilized life," under the "complete control" of the United States,[3] and, simply, "inferior."[4] The fact that they had important interests at stake was ignored by both the litigants and the courts, who cared only about the interests of the state, local, and federal governments. This commentary and the rewritten feminist version of *Rickert* that follows reject this racist and paternalistic framework, recognizing instead the agency of these individuals and the sovereignty of their tribal government.

BACKGROUND

Charles Renville Crawford lived an epic life.[5] As a young man, he traveled with an 1858 Dakota treaty delegation to Washington, DC.[6] By then, the once-vast Dakota homelands within Minnesota had been reduced to a ten-mile strip

---

[1] Now known as the Sisseton-Wahpeton Oyate. Also referred to herein as the Sisseton and Wahpeton Bands, which is what the United States then called them.
[2] United States v. Rickert, 106 F. 1, 6 (1901).
[3] United States v. Rickert, 188 U.S. 432, 433–44 (1903).
[4] *Id.* at 443 (quoting Choctaw Nation v. United States, 119 U.S. 1, 28 (1886)).
[5] This Commentary focuses on Crawford due to space considerations, but the other men lived similarly remarkable lives.
[6] Barbara T. Newcombe, *A Portion of the American People: The Sioux Sign a Treaty in Washington in 1858*, MINN. HIST., Fall 1976, at 82–96.

along each side of the Minnesota River, and the 1858 treaty further eliminated the northern strip.[7] Soon thereafter, scarcity of game on the diminished
reservation (to which increased white settlement nearby contributed), poor
harvests, and unpaid government annuities led to the U.S.-Dakota War of
1862. Crawford (like many Sisseton and Wahpeton) remained "friendly" to the
white settlers in the region during the war.[8] Nevertheless, after the war, he and
other Dakota, including elders, women, and children, were force-marched
approximately 110 miles, through November weather and aggressively hostile
towns, to Fort Snelling, where they were held for the winter in an internment
camp.[9] Hundreds of Dakota died during this period.[10]

As a consequence of the war, Congress passed legislation in 1863 unilaterally
abrogating all treaties with certain bands of Dakota, including the Sisseton and
Wahpeton,[11] and authorizing the removal of the Dakota from Minnesota.[12]
The Dakota lost what little land they had left in Minnesota, and were deprived
of past-due and future government annuity payments owed to them. They
became "homeless wanderers, frequently subject to intense sufferings from
want of subsistence and clothing to protect them from the rigors of a high
northern latitude."[13]

Crawford was instrumental in reestablishing a homeland for his people,
traveling again to Washington, DC with an 1867 treaty delegation.[14] The 1867
treaty[15] established the Lake Traverse Reservation where Crawford would
resettle, establish a farm, become a Presbyterian minister, raise a large family,
and live into his eighties.[16]

The 1867 treaty promised that the reservation would be "permanent" and
that the federal government would provide the Sisseton and Wahpeton with
items to promote their "agricultural improvement and civilization," which

---

7   2 INDIAN AFFAIRS: LAWS AND TREATIES, 785–89 (Charles J. Kappler ed., 1904), *available at*
    http://digital.library.okstate.edu/kappler/ [hereinafter INDIAN AFFAIRS].
8   THROUGH DAKOTA EYES: NARRATIVE ACCOUNTS OF THE MINNESOTA INDIAN WAR OF 1862, at
    112–19, 201–03, 259–60 (Gary Clayton Anderson & Alan R. Woolworth eds., 1988) [hereinafter
    DAKOTA EYES].
9   Waziyatawin Angela Wilson, *Decolonizing the 1862 Death Marches, in* IN THE FOOTSTEPS OF
    OUR ANCESTORS: THE DAKOTA COMMEMORATIVE MARCHES OF THE 21ST CENTURY 49–56
    (Waziyatawin Angela Wilson ed., 2006).
10 *Id.*; *Forced Marches and Imprisonment*, MINN. HIST. SOC'Y, http://www.usdakotawar.org/
    history/aftermath/forced-marches-imprisonment (last visited Dec. 16, 2016).
11 Act of Feb. 16, 1863, ch. 37, 12 Stat. 652.   12 Act of Mar. 3, 1863, ch. 119, 12 Stat. 819.
13 2 INDIAN AFFAIRS, *supra* note 7, at 956–59.   14 DAKOTA EYES, *supra* note 8, at 112.
15 *See supra* note 13.
16 DAKOTA EYES, *supra* note 8, at 112–13; 1900 and 1910 U.S. Census Records, *available at*
    www.ancestry.com (indicating that Crawford was married three times and had at least eleven
    children).

might include building materials and farming equipment. It also provided that the Sisseton and Wahpeton were authorized to adopt and enforce laws.[17] They accordingly adopted a constitution in 1884[18] and within months were actively exercising legislative, law enforcement, and judicial authority over the reservation.[19]

In 1887, Congress passed the General Allotment Act (GAA),[20] a paternalistic piece of legislation that would prove disastrous for Indian people. The GAA authorized the allotment of Indian lands to individual Indians. Any remaining land could then be sold, by agreement with a tribe. The United States would hold the allotments in trust for twenty-five years, subject to extension at presidential discretion. At the expiration of the trust period, clear fee title to the land would be conveyed to the Indian allottees. Finally, every Indian allottee would become a U.S. citizen.

Pursuant to the GAA, the United States and the Sisseton and Wahpeton Bands entered into an agreement on December 12, 1889.[21] The agreement provided for the cession of all unallotted lands at a price of $2.50 per acre (significantly more than the $1.25 to $1.50 per acre that the United States paid contemporaneously to several other tribes for their land[22]). Notably, that amount would be held by the United States and disbursed at its discretion for the "education and civilization" of the tribe and its members. The agreement also reflected one of the tribe's priorities – that before the land cession took effect, the United States would compensate them for the loss of their annuities. Finally, the agreement provided for the allotment of 160 acres to "each individual member ... including married women." This was unusual (and is interesting from a feminist perspective) in that it treated all members of the tribe equally, without regard to gender, marital status, or age.[23] On one hand, the tribe and its members impressively exercised their agency in obtaining certain concessions from the federal government. After all, in some cases, the government did not even bother entering into agreements with tribes and simply carried out allotment unilaterally. On the other hand, as in

---

[17] Albeit subject to the approval of their federal Indian agent.

[18] David E. Wilkins, Documents of Native American Political Development: 1500s to 1933, at 192–210 (2009).

[19] *Id.* (setting forth Indian Agent Benjamin Thompson's 1884 annual report describing, among other things, the organization and functioning of the Nation's government).

[20] Ch. 119, 24 Stat. 388 (1887) (codified as amended, with key portions repealed, at 25 U.S.C. § 331 *et seq.*).

[21] 1 Indian Affairs, *supra* note 7, at 428–32.

[22] DeCoteau v. Dist. Cty. Court for Tenth Judicial Dist., 420 U.S. 425, 441 (1975).

[23] Typically, married women did not receive allotments, and single adults and children received smaller allotments.

many cases, the agreement probably was not entirely voluntary – the tribe likely entered into the agreement under significant duress, with winter approaching and its members still deprived of their annuity payments and suffering from ill health and bad harvests.[24]

The agreement resulted in the loss of nearly 75 percent of the 918,000-acre reservation.[25] More land would subsequently be lost by passing into fee status and being sold, mortgaged and foreclosed upon, or seized for unpaid taxes.[26] Across the country, allotment had similarly disastrous consequences. As a result of allotment, over ninety million acres of Indian land were lost.[27] And serious jurisdictional and land-use problems were created.[28] Congress repudiated its failed policy in 1934, ending allotment and extending the trust period indefinitely – first for some,[29] and later for all,[30] Indian lands.

The experience of Crawford and his compatriots is but one example of the problems allotment caused. Between 1888 and 1892, the four men obtained allotments on the Lake Traverse Reservation. It appears they believed, and probably with good reason, given the citizenship provision of the GAA mentioned above, that this made them U.S. citizens.[31] By 1899–1900, they had made improvements to their allotments, consisting of houses, barns, fences, and other fixed permanent improvements.[32] They had also acquired personal property, including horses, livestock, wagons, and agricultural implements,

---

[24] *DeCoteau*, 420 U.S. at 431; WILKINS, *supra* note 18, at 193.
[25] *DeCoteau*, 420 U.S. at 433, 435 n.16.
[26] Indian Land Consolidation Act Amendments of 2000, Pub. L. No. 106-462, § 101, 114 Stat. 1991.
[27] *Id.*
[28] *Id.* In many areas, allotment created "checkerboard" reservations, interspersed with non-Indian-owned land, leading to jurisdictional issues. Another problem is fractionated ownership, which occurs when many descendants own land, making it difficult to reach agreement regarding any beneficial use of the land.
[29] The Indian Reorganization Act (IRA) ended allotment as of June 18, 1934. 25 U.S.C. § 5101 (Westlaw through Pub. L. No. 115-43). It also extended the trust period indefinitely, *id.* § 5102, for those tribes who did not reject the application of the IRA, which they had the option to do, *id.* § 5125.
[30] In 1990, Congress made the extension of the trust period generally applicable, regardless of whether a tribe had accepted or rejected the IRA. *Id.* § 5126. The Sisseton and Wahpeton rejected the IRA, but the trust period for their land was extended periodically by executive order in the meantime.
[31] *See* DeCoteau v. Dist. Cty. Court for Tenth Judicial Dist., 420 U.S. 425, 435 n.16 (1975) (quoting Renville's father in 1889: "We are now citizens . . . ."); 3 GEORGE W. KINGSBURY, HISTORY OF DAKOTA TERRITORY 668 (1915) (describing Two Stars being a delegate at the 1894 South Dakota Democratic Convention); 1900 Census records, *available at* www.ancestry.com (stating that Crawford and Renville are citizens).
[32] United States v. Rickert, 106 F. 1, 2–3 (1901).

some or all of which were apparently issued to them by the U.S. government,[33] presumably in partial fulfillment of its obligations under the 1867 treaty and 1889 agreement.

Then James A. Rickert, Treasurer of Roberts County, South Dakota,[34] entered the scene, assessing and taxing the improvements and personal property for tax years 1899 and 1900. Interestingly, from a feminist perspective, it appears that Rickert assessed the improvements and personal property of other Indian allottees as well, including some women,[35] but there is no indication that he attempted to tax them.[36] That may indicate that Rickert specifically targeted Crawford and the others. After all, Rickert's most vigorous argument was that they were "citizens of the state and qualified electors," and should accordingly bear their fair share of Roberts County's expenses.[37] Women could not vote at the time,[38] so they would not have fit that narrative well. Crawford and the others arguably did fit that narrative, however, perhaps better than some of the other male tribal members.[39] But whether they were singled out or not, surely Rickert's actions came as an unpleasant surprise to them.

Here, it is important to know that it had long been held that states lack jurisdiction in Indian country.[40] Moreover, as a condition of its entry into the Union, South Dakota disclaimed jurisdiction in Indian country, agreeing that land owned by any Indian or tribe would "remain under the absolute jurisdiction and control of the Congress of the United States."[41] Nevertheless, Rickert was poised to seize and sell the property in question when the United States intervened, seeking an injunction to restrain him.[42]

The U.S. Circuit Court for the District of South Dakota[43] denied the United States' motion for a temporary injunction,[44] finding that Crawford

---

[33] *Id.*   [34] Much of the Lake Traverse Reservation is located within Roberts County.

[35] Assessment records provided by Deb Wooley, Roberts County Treasurer, to the author.

[36] Email from Deb Wooley, Roberts County Treasurer, to Chloe Thompson, Assoc. Gen. Counsel, Port Madison Enters. (Sept. 28, 2016, 1:46 p.m.) (on file with author) (stating that the county's tax records only go back to 1904). There is no indication in the case file that Rickert sought to tax anyone besides Crawford, Little Thunder, Two Stars, and Renville.

[37] Brief for Appellee at 4–6, United States v. Rickert, 188 U.S. 432 (1903) (No. 216), *in* THE MAKING OF MODERN LAW: U.S. SUPREME COURT RECORDS AND BRIEFS, 1832–1978 [hereinafter MOML].

[38] S.D. CONST. of 1889, art. VII, § 1.

[39] Among other things, they were leaders in their tribe, most of them had some political/ diplomatic experience, they appear to have held themselves out as citizens, and, ironically, they appear to have been fulfilling the GAA's purposes relatively well.

[40] *E.g.*, United States v. Kagama, 118 U.S. 375 (1886); The Kansas Indians, 72 U.S. 737 (1866); Worcester v. Georgia, 31 U.S. 515, 561 (1832).

[41] S.D. CONST. of 1889, art. XXII.   [42] United States v. Rickert, 106 F. 1, 4 (1901).

[43] As it was then called.   [44] *Rickert*, 106 F. at 6.

and his compatriots were citizens, with all the accompanying rights and privileges, including a voice in the making of state tax law, which considered both the improvements and the personal property to be taxable. Therefore, Crawford and the others were obliged to pay Rickert's taxes. The court further held that the United States had no interest in the improvements and personal property and that equitable relief was not appropriate.

On appeal, the Eighth Circuit Court of Appeals submitted five certified questions to the U.S. Supreme Court, which can be paraphrased as follows: (1) was the allotted land taxable;[45] (2) were the permanent improvements thereon taxable; (3) was the personal property in question taxable; (4) did the United States have standing (or capacity, which was the term then used); and (5) did the United States have a remedy at law such that equitable relief was not appropriate?[46]

ORIGINAL OPINION

In the original *Rickert* opinion,[47] the Supreme Court held that none of the real or personal property in question was taxable by the state. The Court's reasoning included its findings that the allotments were held in trust by the United States; that state taxation of the improvements would defeat the purpose of the GAA, which contemplated that the Indians would improve and cultivate the allotted lands; and that state taxation of the personal property (which the Court held was the property of the United States) would defeat the United States' interest in inducing the Indians to "adopt the habits of civilized life." The Court then perfunctorily held that the United States had standing, and that only equitable relief would be adequate. The Court also briefly addressed Rickert's argument that Crawford and the others were citizens and should be treated the same as other citizens, but avoided reaching any conclusion regarding their citizenship status.

The Court devoted the majority of its discussion, though, to describing the inferiority and dependency of the Indians, which necessitated the protection and control of the United States. The core of the *Rickert* decision rests on the judicially created guardian-ward relationship between the federal government and Indians, with its racist and classist assumptions that Indians were

---

45   This was not actually at issue in the case, *id.*, and the case file does not indicate how it became a certified question, but the Eighth Circuit presumably anticipated future arguments on the issue and therefore added the issue on its own.

46   Certificate from the U.S. Circuit Court of Appeals for the Eighth Circuit, at 2–3, *in* MOML, *supra* note 37.

47   United States v. Rickert, 188 U.S. 432 (1903).

uncivilized and incapable of managing their own affairs, and therefore had to be managed like children, or like women in those days, by privileged white men who knew better.[48] *Rickert* contains no recognition of the existence of a tribal government with jurisdiction over the land, people, and property in question. Nor does it recognize that the individuals in question had any property rights, or might deserve a say in the matter. This treatment of the individual and collective Dakota has parallels to the treatment of women at the time (e.g., they could not vote, some were still subject to coverture, etc.).

Most scholars of federal Indian law would undoubtedly say the result in *Rickert* – that the state lacks the authority to tax Indian allotments and the improvements and personal property thereon – is correct. However, the reasoning behind it is decidedly paternalistic, and it contains language that is quite derogatory towards Indian people. Had it been different, *Rickert* could have established some bright lines that would have been empowering for tribes ever since.

FEMINIST JUDGMENT

The rewritten majority opinion of Professor Grant Christensen, writing as Justice Christensen, corrects the troublesome aspects of *Rickert* and establishes those bright lines. Christensen's opinion holds, as did the original opinion, that none of the real or personal property in question is subject to state taxation. But Christensen completely rewrites the reasoning of *Rickert*. Several feminist themes emerge from his rewrite.

One is his rejection of oppressive language. The most initially obvious problem with *Rickert* is its paternalistic and at times overtly racist language, which immediately jumps out at any modern reader.[49] Christensen, of course, eliminates that language.

Another is his rejection of the guardian-ward relationship (with all its inherent racism, classism, paternalism, and even gendered undertones) as the basis for the decision. Christensen instead recognizes the agency and interests of the tribe and its members throughout the opinion. This contrasts sharply with the original opinion, in which Crawford, his compatriots, and their tribe were virtually invisible and their interests were entirely ignored, in a way that parallels the historical legal invisibility of most women in the United States. Christensen, on the other hand, explicitly concludes that Crawford and the others were citizens, and also that they would have standing to sue with

---

[48] To be fair, tribes now sometimes use the associated trust relationship to their benefit.

[49] *See supra* notes 2–4 and accompanying text.

respect to any of the property interests in question, regardless of whether they were citizens or not. Indeed, with respect to the personal property, he holds that *only they* would have standing, in contrast with the original opinion's identification of only federal interests in all three types of property and its conclusion that the federal government owned the personal property. Likewise, in concluding that only equitable relief would be appropriate, Christensen points out that the men exercised agency in choosing their particular allotments, and that they may have done so for a variety of reasons, so simply relocating the men (again) would not be a suitable remedy. Additionally, Christensen's opinion appropriately recognizes the existence of a sovereign tribal government with an interest in the matter – the Sisseton and Wahpeton Nation, which was actively exercising authority over its territory at the time.[50] The original opinion, on the other hand, completely ignored the tribal government and seemed to assume that if the federal government did not have an interest (e.g., if the land passed into fee status), then the state would have jurisdiction.

Most importantly, Christensen's opinion reflects the feminist theme of equality – he recognizes the tribe as a governmental authority on at least equal footing with the state. He holds that the tribe has territorial jurisdiction, to the exclusion of the state, over all land set aside by the United States for, or owned or controlled by, the tribe or its members (i.e., Indian land). Several significant bright line rules flow from this holding.

First, the state has no authority over land as long as it remains Indian land, whether in trust or fee status. By contrast, the original opinion rested on the fact that the United States still held the land in trust, and the state had no authority to tax the United States. It was contemplated at the time, however, that allottees would eventually obtain a fee patent, at which point the land would presumably have become taxable by the state. By clarifying instead that land remains free from state jurisdiction so long as it is Indian land, Christensen's opinion might have directly prevented some of the land losses that occurred when property passed out of trust.[51] Absent state jurisdiction, that property could not have been seized by the state for unpaid taxes or mortgages.

Second, permanent improvements on Indian land are part of the land, regardless of any state tax law to the contrary. That would have protected improvements as long as the land remained Indian land, and would likely have prevented future litigation on the issue right up to the present day.[52]

---

[50] *See supra* notes 18–19 and accompanying text.
[51] Presumably, the potentially problematic Burke Act of 1906 would not exist.
[52] *E.g.*, Confederated tribes of the Chehalis Reservation v. Thurston Cty., 724 F.3d 1153 (9th Cir. 2013) (involving a county's attempt to tax a resort facility on tribal trust land).

Finally, Christensen reaffirms a bright-line, territorial view of tribal jurisdiction, à la *Worcester*.[53] By clarifying that tribal authority, to the exclusion of state authority, extends not only to Indian land and to property owned by Indians thereon, but also to all persons and activities thereon, Christensen's opinion would have had a profound impact on the subsequent development of federal Indian law and life in Indian country. With Christensen's *Rickert* as precedent, the Supreme Court might not have chipped away at tribal jurisdiction as it has in recent decades,[54] creating, among other things, jurisdictional gaps that have allowed non-Indian abusers of Native women and children to go unpunished.[55] And the Court might not have issued decisions in the 1970s and 1980s allowing state taxation of non-Indians in Indian country.[56] Those decisions have had the practical effect of impeding tribes from fully exercising their inherent sovereign authority to tax.[57] But with Christensen's reaffirmation of territorial jurisdiction, tribes could have been collecting those much-needed tax revenues ever since, and perhaps could have generated earlier and more economic development activity in Indian country, by being able to confidently offer tax incentives for businesses to locate on reservations, by attracting customers with favorable tax rates, and so on, like other governments do. In short, Christensen's opinion would have enhanced the recognition of tribes as governments on at least equal footing with states.

But equality is a funny thing in the field of federal Indian law, where even the right result sometimes means that people are not treated equally. No doubt from Rickert's perspective, it was unfair that the Dakota did not have to pay taxes when their non-Indian neighbors did. Yet, as in all Indian law cases, there are important historical and legal reasons for that, which cannot be ignored. That is why this commentary's look at *Rickert* does not begin with four Dakota men receiving tax bills in 1900. It begins with how they survived a war, lost everything, and ended up, probably with little more than the clothes on their backs, in the permanent homeland the United States promised them; how they reestablished a tribal government that actively exercised jurisdiction

---

[53] *See supra* note 40 and accompanying text.

[54] *E.g.*, Montana v. United States, 450 U.S. 544 (1981) (establishing a presumption against tribal civil regulatory jurisdiction over non-Indians on non-Indian-owned fee land within the reservation); Oliphant v. Suquamish, 435 U.S. 191 (1978) (holding that a tribe lacks criminal jurisdiction over non-Indians in its territory).

[55] Congress recently took a small step towards correcting this injustice. *See* 25 U.S.C. § 1304 (Westlaw through Pub. L. No. 115-43).

[56] *E.g.*, Washington v. Confederated tribes of the Colville Indian Reservation, 447 U.S. 134 (1980); Moe v. Salish & Kootenai tribes of Flathead Reservation, 425 U.S. 463 (1976).

[57] Though tribes may often retain their inherent authority to tax non-Indians in Indian country, state taxation of those individuals may mean that tribes cannot, as a practical matter, collect tribal taxes without putting themselves at a business disadvantage.

over that homeland; how they drove such a hard bargain for those allotments, even under desperate conditions; and how they paid so dearly for those improvements and that personal property, which were part of the consideration the United States agreed to pay for their land cessions and for the hardships they had endured. All of that is why the result in *Rickert* is correct, and why the following rewritten feminist version, which appropriately recognizes the sovereignty of the Sisseton and Wahpeton Nation and the agency and interests of its members, is even better.

UNITED STATES v. RICKERT, 188 U.S. 432 (1903)

JUSTICE GRANT CHRISTENSEN DELIVERED THE OPINION OF THE COURT

At its core, this case is about the tangled relationship between the United States, its constituent states, and the many sovereign Indian nations that exist within its borders. In many ways, the evolution of this relationship is unique and distinct from the interactions of peoples in Europe, and accordingly a common law respecting the various sovereignties that exist within the United States must develop *sui generis* from first principles articulated primarily by American courts and informed by the deep history of relations between these competing sovereigns.

Respecting this complicated relationship – whereby Indian nations that have never ratified the U.S. Constitution are situated alongside American states that trace their origin to the ratification of this nation's founding document – the Eighth Circuit Court of Appeals has asked us to clarify these first principles as they relate to taxation by the State of South Dakota of the land, structures, and personalty held by the members of a tribe with a treaty relationship with the United States located as an enclave within its borders.

The proper metes and bounds of those first principles are still evolving, but today we clarify that property is subject to either the sovereignty of the state in which it is situated or of an Indian tribe, but not both. The mutually exclusive nature of sovereignty requires compromise and cooperation where boundaries meet, but ultimately a state has no place regulating, adjudicating, administering, or enforcing its rules on land properly controlled by an Indian tribe.

The Attorney General of the United States instigated this present action against the defendant, James Rickert, as county treasurer and tax collector for Roberts County in South Dakota for the purpose of restraining him from seizing and selling the property of enrolled members of the Sisseton Band of

Sioux Indians: Charles R. Crawford, Adam Little Thunder, Solomon Two Stars, and Victor Renville. Each of the enrolled members of the Sisseton Band holds individual tracts of land under the Agreement of December 12, 1889, which was ratified by Congress in the Act of March 3, 1891, ch. 543, 26 Stat. 989, 1035. These allotted lands were distributed under the same terms and conditions laid out by Congress in the General Allotment Act of 1887, ch. 119, 24 Stat. 388, approved February 8, 1887. Under this scheme, land used collectively by the tribe was divided up among the members of the Sisseton Band of Sioux Indians. Under the General Allotment Act, the United States holds the real property in trust for a period of twenty-five years, at which point the fee title interest is to be turned over to the individual Indian. *Id.* § 5, 24 Stat. at 389. On their respective lands, the individual members of the Sisseton Band of Sioux Indians have erected structures and husbanded livestock in an effort to improve the land and create the basic infrastructure necessary to earn a living.

The State of South Dakota maintains that, because the individual tribal members now own specific tracts of land and those tracts lose any vestige of federal protection after twenty-five years, the state has the right to tax the buildings and structures affixed to the land as well as all personal property of the tribal members from the date the tribe's lands were allotted. If the individual tribal members refuse or are unable to pay the tax, South Dakota claims the right to seize the buildings, structures, and personalty and sell the same in order to satisfy the unpaid tax assessments. South Dakota maintains that it has the right to seize and sell the property irrespective of any tribal or federal protections that may continue to exist. It argues that Indian land, once allotted, is considered part of the state and thus subject to South Dakota's scheme for taxation. Moreover, South Dakota claims the right to determine what property is real property and what property is personal property for the purposes of taxation under state law, and it has maintained that buildings and structures affixed to land constitute personal property.

In 1899, and again in 1900, in his official capacity as county treasurer and tax collector, Rickert assessed against the individual Indian allottees a tax upon the value of the improvements made to the land itself including the construction of homes and farm buildings. He also issued a tax assessment on the value of the personal property kept on the land including the value of livestock, wagons, farm implements, and other personal property held by the Indian allottees. Having not received payment of the assessment, Rickert attempted to seize (1) the homes and buildings attached to the real property and (2) the tribal members' individual personalty. Rickert further attempted to force a sale of these assets in order to pay the assessed taxes. The Eighth Circuit Court of

Appeals, in anticipation of future arguments made by the State of South Dakota, has also asked this Court whether South Dakota may tax (3) the allotments themselves, which constitute real property.

The United States, acting through its attorney, sought an immediate injunction against the above collection actions taken and intended by Rickert. The U.S. Attorney argued that any asset seizure and sale of real or personal property located on lands subject to the General Allotment Act might cloud the title of the United States, which currently holds the land in trust, and open the United States up to claims for compensation from the individual Indians.

The U.S. Circuit Court for South Dakota held that "South Dakota has the right to tax all property within her jurisdiction ... unless some paramount law of the United States prohibits the state from taxing." *United States v. Rickert*, 106 F. 1, 5 (1901). The court further held that under the law of South Dakota "personal property shall, for the purpose of taxation, be construed to include ... all improvements made by persons upon the lands held by them under the laws of the United States." *Id.* at 6. Having thus concluded that improvements to land as well as livestock and other personal property were ordinarily taxable under the laws of South Dakota, the circuit court had to determine whether any law of the United States prohibited the exercise of South Dakota's power to tax. That court ultimately denied the motion for a temporary injunction, concluding that: "Other citizens of South Dakota are obligated to pay taxes upon improvements made upon lands of this character, and I can see nothing in law or policy of the United States or the state that would exempt these citizens ... from the same burden." *Id.* The circuit court accordingly denied the motion of the United States for an injunction. The United States appealed the decision to the Eighth Circuit Court of Appeals.

This case comes to us not on a writ of certiorari but through a series of questions certified by the judges of the United States Court of Appeals for the Eighth Circuit. Courts of Appeal are permitted to certify questions directly to the Supreme Court. Act of Mar. 3, 1891, ch. 517, § 6, 26 Stat. 826, 828 ("[T]he circuit court of appeals at any time may certify to the Supreme Court of the United States any questions or propositions of law concerning which it desires the instruction of that court for its proper decision.") This certification procedure is limited to those questions of sufficient "gravity and importance" that their answers require the attention of the Supreme Court. *In re Lau Ow Bew*, 141 U.S. 583, 587 (1891). Questions involving Indian law are unique to American jurisprudence and often present questions to appellate courts that cannot easily be answered without additional clarification of the status of tribal land or the division of powers between tribes, the federal government, and the states. *See United States v. Union Pac. Ry. Co.*, 168 U.S. 505 (1897);

United States v. Le Bris, 121 U.S. 278 (1887); *United States v. Rodgers*, 45 U.S. 567 (1846). Precisely because the relationship between states and Indian tribes is complicated and unique, the Eighth Circuit sought clarification from this Court of the appropriate first principles upon which to base its review of the appeal by the United States. The certified questions present issues of first impression for this Court, but whose answers follow from the clear understanding of tribes as sovereign political entities that exist on par with the several states. The questions certified are:

I. Has the United States such an interest in this controversy or in its subjects as entitles it to maintain this suit?

II. Has the United States a remedy at law so prompt and efficacious that it is deprived of all relief in equity?

III. Were the lands held by the allottees, Charles R. Crawford and the other Indians named in the bill, subject to assessment and taxation by the taxing authorities of Roberts County, South Dakota?

IV. Were the permanent improvements, such as houses and other structures upon the lands held by allotment by Charles R. Crawford and the other Indians named in the bill, subject to assessment and taxation by the taxing officers of Roberts County as personal property in 1899 and 1900?

V. Was the personal property, consisting of cattle, horses, and other property of like character, which had been issued to these Indians by the United States, and which they were using upon their allotments, liable to assessments and taxation by the officers of Roberts County in 1899 and 1900?

We will address each of the certified questions separately below.

I

As a threshold matter, we are asked to decide whether the United States may maintain this lawsuit. Our precedents dictate that the interest of the U.S. federal government, and not solely the interest of a third party, is required in order for the United States to properly appear as a party in litigation. *United States v. San Jacinto Tin Co.*, 125 U.S. 273, 285 (1888) ("[T]he right of the government of the United States to institute such a suit depends upon the same general principles which would authorize a private citizen to apply to a court of justice for relief ... the government must show that, like the private individual, it has such an interest in the relief sought as entitles it to move in the matter."). *San Jacinto* was clear that when the United States appears to contest a question regarding its property, "[i]f it be a question of property a case must be made in which the court can afford a remedy in regard to that property." *Id.* When the United States cannot show that it has a unique interest in the case, or when the remedy that can be provided by the Court cannot protect or ameliorate the United States' interest, then the United States lacks the capacity to sue and the case must be dismissed. When "the fact is manifest that the suit has actually been brought for the benefit of some third person, and that no obligation to the general public exists which requires the United States to bring it, then the suit must fail." *Id.* at 286. Our precedent requires us to necessarily determine what is the interest of the United States here alleged and to then consider whether there exists a remedy within the remit of this Court to issue that would satisfy the articulated interest of the United States.

While the United States maintains a property interest in individual allotments subject to the agreement made under the auspices of the Dawes Act, that property interest is limited to the prohibition of the sale of real property for the twenty-five-year period after the implementation of the agreement. The "United States does and will hold the land thus allotted, for the period of twenty-five years, in trust for the sole use and benefit of the Indian to whom such allotment shall have been made ... and that at the expiration of said period the United States will convey the same by patent to said Indian." General Allotment Act of 1887, ch. 119, § 5, 24 Stat. 388, 389. The United States has never held the full fee simple interest in the real property at issue despite its former status as public land. *See Johnson v. M'Intosh*, 21 U.S. 543, 587 (1823). After the Agreement of December 12, 1889, the limited interest in the real property held by the United States prior to allotment was further time restricted by the requirements of the Dawes Act. General Allotment Act § 5, 24 Stat. at 389.

The interest of the United States is limited to the real property itself and does not extend to the personal property of the individual members of the Sisseton tribe located on their respective allotments. *M'Intosh*, 21 U.S. at 587. While the United States may hold the fee title interest to the land, "the land thus allotted" in trust, there is nothing in federal law that contemplates that the United States has an interest in the personal property of the allottees. General Allotment Act § 5, 24 Stat. at 389. All legal interests, other than the merest fee interest, the right to acquire the land, have belonged and continue to belong entirely to the individual Indian allottees, including but not limited to the right to use, to occupy, to be upon, to modify, to profit from, to improve, and to husband upon the land, until those rights have been alienated by the Sisseton Band or the allottees themselves. *See M'Intosh*, 21 U.S. at 586–87.

It thus follows that while the United States has the capacity to seek an injunction against one of its constituent states to prohibit seizure and sale of tribal lands or the buildings and structures affixed to the land, it lacks the capacity to extend that injunction to the seizure and sale of personal property located on those lands. While the twenty-five-year probationary period created by the Dawes Act is tolled, General Allotment Act § 5, 24 Stat. at 389, the United States retains an actionable interest in the real property, and anything attached to it, now held in trust. The United States could reasonably be expected to be sued by the individual allottees if it permitted the land or the buildings and structures to be seized and sold. The power of the United States to prevent the diminution of its interests in real property is nonnegotiable. The Constitution vests in Congress the power to "dispose of and make all needful rules and regulations respecting the territory or other property belonging to the United States." *Wis. Cent. Ry. Co. v. Price Cty.*, 133 U.S. 496, 504 (1890). Accordingly, whatever interest the United States retains in the individual allotments prior to returning a patent directly to the individual allottees may clearly not be seized or sold by the State of South Dakota.

However, as it pertains to the personal property, the United States has no interest in the personal property found upon the allottees' lands that is distinct from the interest the individual allottees themselves claim to have regarding their personal property. Without a unique interest in the personal property distinct from the interest of the allottees themselves, this Court's precedent suggests that the United States lacks the capacity to bring an injunction on behalf of the individual allottees regarding the seizure or sale of their personal property.

We remain mindful that this Court disfavors the creation of a right without a suitable remedy. *See Eldridge v. Trezevant*, 160 U.S. 452 (1896) (holding that an individual has the right to seek an injunction against the state to secure the individual's right to his property). For reasons that are developed at length on the subsequent certified questions, the State of South Dakota has no jurisdiction to assess a tax against the personal property of the individual allottees. Since the United States lacks the capacity to prevent the seizure of the allottees' personal property, we risk a construction of the law that the allottees have a right not to have their personal property taxed or seized but lack a remedy to prevent that seizure. To ensure the clear title to and security of their property from seizure or sale, we now hold that the Indian allottees themselves have the capacity to seek an injunction directly from the circuit court.

The capacity of individual Indians to file suit on their own behalf has traditionally been severely circumscribed by this Court's deference to congressional findings that individual Indians are dependent upon the United States to exercise their political rights. *United States v. Kagama*, 118 U.S. 375, 384 (1886). In part, this holding has been based on the principle that individual Indians may owe an allegiance to their tribal nation that exceeds their allegiance to the United States. *Elk v. Wilkins*, 112 U.S. 94, 99 (1884). Almost two decades later, this Court now questions whether the deference to congressional findings in *Kagama* or the presumption in *Wilkins* that Indians born in the United States have not "surrendered themselves" to the jurisdiction of the United States remain tenable. *Id.* However, we need not decide today whether all Indians born in the United States are citizens in accordance with the Fourteenth Amendment's citizenship clause and thus endowed with the capacity to sue because all parties and the lower court concur that the individual Indian allottees present in this case are uncontestably citizens. *United States v. Rickert*, 106 F. 1, 14 (1901) (These allottees are "full citizens of the United States, and owners of property."). We agree with the U.S. Circuit Court for South Dakota that members of the Sisseton Band are certainly citizens of the United States. Their rights are no different from those rights enjoyed by any other citizen of the United States. Moreover, as allottees, they have an express right to enter the federal courts for the purpose of protecting the property associated with their respective allotments:

> That all persons who are in whole or in part of Indian blood or descent who are entitled to an allotment of land under any law of Congress, or who claim to be so entitled to land under any allotment Act, or under any grant made by Congress, or who claim to have been unlawfully denied or excluded from any allotment or any parcel of land to which they claim to be lawfully entitled by virtue of any Act of Congress, may commence and prosecute or defend any action, suit, or proceeding in relation to their right thereto in the proper circuit court of the United States; and said circuit courts are hereby given jurisdiction to try and determine any action, suit, or proceeding arising within their respective jurisdictions involving the right of any person, in whole or in part of Indian blood or descent, to any allotment of land under any law or treaty.

Act of Feb. 6, 1901, ch. 217, 31 Stat. 760.

Congress has clearly instructed the judiciary that, at least for the purposes of protecting an individual Indian's right to protect an allotment, the federal courts are to be open to Indians for all claims in a manner indistinguishable from claims made by any citizen. As the tribal members here are both allottees and citizens there can be no argument that they possess sufficient agency to themselves contest the taxation of their property by South Dakota. As will be discussed in greater detail in Part IV, *infra*, buildings and structures are part of the land itself, affording the individual members of the Sisseton Band the ability to challenge any taxation by South Dakota in a federal court. Any Indian wishing to protect allotted property from assessment, seizure, or sale by a state tax authority has the right to seek an injunction in federal court.

Therefore, as to the first question certified to us by the Eighth Circuit Court of Appeals, we hold that the United States retains its capacity to sue only to the extent that the land it holds in trust is subject to seizure and/or sale. However, the individual allottees retain the broad capacity to sue to protect *any* property interest, real or personal, related to their allotment. The exceptionally broad language used by Congress clearly contemplates that the jurisdiction of the federal Circuit Court of South Dakota is open to Indian allottees in order to protect *any* property interest surrounding their allotment.

II

As established in Part I, the United States does not have a defensible interest in the personal property of the allottees; however, during the twenty-five-year protection period provided by the General Allotment Act, the United States does have a limited interest in the real property and the buildings and structures affixed to the land now titled in the name of the individual Indian allottees. Accordingly, it becomes necessary to answer the second certified question regarding whether the United States has a remedy at law so prompt and efficacious that it is deprived of all relief in equity, including if an injunction against the seizure and sale of this property to satisfy an alleged tax debt by the State of South Dakota is sustained. We now hold that no remedy at law short of an injunction has the ability to protect the rights of either the United States or the individual allottees in the land, buildings, and structures that constitute the allotments.

The harm created by the seizure and sale of real property held by Indian allottees, whether or not held in trust by the United States, is incapable of remedy through monetary or other equitable relief. The tracts of land held by the allottees are specifically selected by each individual from among all the lands that constituted the Band's reservation. General Allotment Act of 1887, ch. 119, § 2, 24 Stat. 388, 388. Congress recognized that individual tribal members may have a specific connection to the lands that they have selected as part of their allotment and that these individuals may have already worked to improve that land or even have selected the property for its religious or cultural value. *Id.* §§ 2, 5, 24 Stat. at 387, 390. Because the tracts selected by individual tribal members are not fungible, if the United States were to lose a future anticipated action brought by the individual allottees for the loss of their specifically selected allotments, providing different public land of comparable value would not ameliorate the harms inflicted upon those tribal members. *Id.* It therefore becomes necessary for the United States to preserve the exact tracts of land selected by the allottees, with the attached structures and buildings, for as long as the United States maintains a limited interest in the property. For these reasons, and for further reasons articulated below, only an injunction avoids legal harm to the United States.

The United States has legally promised as a condition of the Agreement of December 12, 1889, to hold land allotted to individual members of the Sisseton Band in trust for a period of twenty-five years. *Id.* § 5, 24 Stat. at 389. The loss of this land, currently protected by the federal government, would open the United States up to claims of breach of trust from every individual allottee. *See* Act of Feb. 6, 1901, ch. 217, 31 Stat. 760.

It is manifest that no proceedings in law can be sufficiently prompt and efficacious as to protect the rights of the United States from future legal action. Should the allotted lands be seized and sold prior to a favorable determination for the government after proceeding in law, the available remedies would be insufficient to cure the generated harm (i.e., a requirement that the person who purchased the land from the county tax assessor return the allotted lands to the original Indian allottees). If the land were seized and sold, the obligation of the United States to hold the land in trust on behalf of the individual members of the Sisseton Band in accord with the Agreement of December 12, 1889, could only be satisfied by the return of the land selected by the individuals to their care. Should the state seize and sell the lands, the government's ability to uphold its obligation would be indefinitely frustrated. Because only a court in equity can evaluate the importance of the land and its structures to the individual allottees and take into account the cultural and religious values the specific allotted tracts protect, an injunction is not only appropriate but required.

This Court has not previously squarely addressed whether a state has the authority to levy taxes on Indian allotments. Nonetheless, our precedents weigh strongly against state taxation of land held by the United States. *Van Brocklin v. Tennessee*, 117 U.S. 151, 155 (1886). This prohibition against state taxation applies to any property in which the United States maintains a legal interest, even if it no longer holds the fee simple absolute. *Coosaw Mining Co. v. South Carolina*, 144 U.S. 550, 566 (1892); *Ry. Co. v. McShane*, 89 U.S. 444, 464 (1874). In *McShane*, we held that land promised to a railroad, where the railroad had in fact further sold or mortgaged part of the land, was still not taxable by Nebraska county assessors because the patent had not formally been issued to the railroad by the United States and therefore the United States retained an ultimate legal interest. *McShane*, 89 U.S. at 464. In *Coosaw*, we held that when property is under the protection of a sovereign government, no equitable compensation can correct for the loss of the land or the usufructuary rights that run with it and inure to the public. *Coosaw*, 144 U.S. at 566–67. Here, as long as the United States holds an interest in the land held by the Indian allottees, and could further be sued by the allottees for permitting the loss of the usufructuary rights attendant to the land, the United States may demand an injunction from the circuit court.

No amount of money awarded by a court would be sufficient to compensate the United States for the loss of its interest in the individual Indian allotments, nor could any amount of money fully compensate for the loss of the usufructuary rights enjoyed by members of Sisseton Band and protected by the United States in the Agreement of December 12, 1889. Thus, no remedy at law would be as sufficiently prompt and efficacious as a permanent injunction regarding the seizure and/or sale of the allotments. Given our precedents, the United States is likely to prevail on the merits should South Dakota attempt to seize the real property. The only way the United States can meet its obligations under the Agreement with the Sisseton Band is to seek an injunction to prevent the loss of the property. Should the United States have the capacity to maintain the suit against South Dakota, it is not only appropriate, but necessary, that the United States be permitted to seek an injunction against the county tax assessor.

III

Determining whether the State of South Dakota's regulatory authority[1] reaches unto the lands set aside for the Sisseton Band of Sioux Indians by the Agreement of December 12, 1889, requires a return to first principles of the relationship between the states and Indian tribes. Indian tribes are sovereign, and the sovereignty they manifest is at least as great as the sovereignty of any state. Because tribes maintain a government-to-government relationship with

---

[1] The certified question in this case pertains to the authority of South Dakota to tax the real property, buildings, and possessions of Indian people on allotted lands. For reasons explained in detail in this section, South Dakota lacks the authority to tax. However, for the purpose of providing guidance to the circuit courts, it is equally clear that not only the jurisdiction to tax but all state regulatory jurisdiction is improper on these lands. Instead, the tribe and the United States share concurrent regulatory authority to the complete exclusion of the State of South Dakota. That includes the right to levy any tax, to pass laws of general applicability, to regulate questions of land use, to determine labor rights, to build and police roads and rights of way, etc.

the United States stronger, perhaps, even than the contractual bond between the states of the Union, the traditional lands held in trust for them by the United States or held in fee by tribal members or the tribal government, are lands protected by the sovereignty of the tribe. Just like the Sisseton Band cannot assess taxes against land held by South Dakotans in Pierre, the State of South Dakota does not have the authority to levy or enforce a tax against lands allotted to members of the Sisseton Band or controlled by the tribe. These obligations are mutual and reciprocal. Neither the tribe nor the state has the authority to tax the property (real or personal) of the other. *See United States v. Kagama*, 118 U.S. 375, 384 (1886) ("[Indian tribes] owe no allegiance to the States, and receive from them no protection.").

The Constitution expressly contemplates that the sovereign status of an Indian tribe is akin to that of a state or foreign nation. The Commerce Clause, U.S. Const. art. I, § 8, cl. 3, gives Congress the power to regulate commerce "with foreign nations, and among the several states, and with the Indian tribes." Furthermore, the Treaty Clause gives treaties with tribes the same status as "the supreme law of the land" as treaties made with foreign governments. *Id.* art. IV. Together, these provisions give Indian tribes a constitutional status, one that requires the federal government of the United States to deal with Indian tribes in a manner befitting a government-to-government relationship, as one sovereign meeting another on an equal footing.

> The constitution, by declaring treaties already made, as well as those to be made, to be the supreme law of the land, has adopted and sanctioned the previous treaties with the Indian nations, and consequently admits their rank among those powers who are capable of making treaties .... We have applied them to Indians, as we have applied them to the other nations of the earth. They are applied to all in the same sense.

Worcester v. Georgia, 31 U.S. 515, 559–60 (1832). Just last year, this Court reaffirmed the constitutional independence of Indian tribes: "[T]his government had 'admitted, by the most solemn sanction, the existence of the Indians as a separate and distinct people, and as being invested with rights which constitute them a state, or separate community.'" *Cherokee Nation v. Hitchcock*, 187 U.S. 294, 305 (1902). There can be no doubt that Indian tribes embody a sovereignty with which the United States maintains relations and against which no state has the right to interfere. *Id.*

As a consequence of this constitutional status as a separate sovereign, Indian tribes and their members are clearly distinct from the sister states of the Union. "The treaties and laws of the United States contemplate the Indian territory as completely separated from that of the states; and provide that all intercourse with them shall be carried on exclusively by the government of the union." *Worcester*, 31 U.S. at 557. That exclusivity is expressly directed at the states. The Constitution creates a direct relationship between the tribe and the United States, one from which the states are excluded. For over a century the courts have enforced this separation between Indian tribes and states. tribes "owe no allegiance to the States, and receive from them no protection. Because of the local ill feeling, the people of the States where they are found are often their deadliest enemies." *Kagama*, 118 U.S. at 384. Against the danger of state usurpation of tribal land and resources the judiciary stands as barrier, determined to enforce these first principles of exclusivity. Property can be controlled by the tribe or by the state but not by both.

Judicial protection of tribal independence from state action dates back to this Court's decision in *Worcester v. Georgia*. There the State of Georgia wanted to extend civil and criminal authority over the Cherokee nation and over "all persons whatever" within Indian lands. *Worcester*, 31 U.S. at 548. This Court relied on early precedent to establish that the right of Indians to the land remains until those rights have been extinguished by a decision of the Indians themselves. "[T]he Indians are acknowledged to have an unquestionable, and, heretofore, unquestioned right to the lands they occupy, until that right shall be extinguished by a voluntary cession to our government." *Cherokee Nation v. Georgia*, 30 U.S. 1, 17 (1831). Accordingly, in *Worcester* we reasoned that Indian tribes are independent from states and act independently to govern the ownership, use, title, management, and protection of their lands. "The Indian nations had always been considered as distinct, independent political communities, retaining their original natural rights, as the undisputed possessors of the soil, from time immemorial." *Worcester*, 31 U.S. at 559. Against this independence, the State of South Dakota cannot infringe. In the same manner and for the same reasons that Georgia was unable to extend its regulatory authority to require persons on Cherokee lands to hold a license from the state, South Dakota tax assessors cannot require persons on Sisseton lands to pay taxes to the state.

For almost a century, our precedents have thus established that states cannot interfere with the ownership of Indian land. "It has never been contended, that the Indian title amounted to nothing. Their right of possession has never been questioned." *Johnson v. M'Intosh*, 21 U.S. 543, 603 (1823). Because Indian land is thus located "outside" of the state in which the lands are situated, the laws of the state have no force on lands controlled by Indians.

The [Indian] nation, then, is a distinct community occupying its own territory, with boundaries accurately described, in which the laws of [the state] can have no force, and which the citizens of [the state] have no right to enter, but with the assent of the [Indians] themselves, or in conformity with treaties, and with the acts of congress.

Worcester, 31 U.S. at 561. Despite being tempted to waver from this proposition at times, *see Utah & N. Ry. Co. v. Fisher*, 116 U.S. 28 (1885), we now reaffirm this territorial principle of jurisdiction articulated by Chief Justice Marshall: "[T]he laws of [the state] can have no force" on land controlled by Indians or set aside for them by the United States. *Worcester*, 31 U.S. at 561.

Land owned by individual Indians through the allotment process is entitled to the same protections from state interference as land owned by the tribe itself. *Ward v. Race Horse*, 163 U.S. 504, 515 (1894). When the United States has recognized land as being traditionally used by the tribe and its members, the sovereignty of the tribe rather than the interest of the state governs its use and regulation. *Id.*

Applying this precedent to the certified question, it is clear that the State of South Dakota has no authority to assess a tax on, or, consequently, to collect the tax by seizing or selling property that is currently controlled by an Indian tribe or one of its members. Returning to first principles, states and Indian tribes are coequal in their control of their respective citizens and lands. For as long as the individual allottees maintain a political relationship with the Sisseton Band, the State of South Dakota has no authority whatsoever to attempt to control or restrict activity upon or tax their land.

To be clear, the decision today does not rest upon the unique position of the Sisseton Band in South Dakota or upon any unique treaty agreement or relationship between the Band and the United States. Our first principles make clear that no state may extend its jurisdiction, to tax or otherwise, over land held by an Indian tribe or its members. The right of the tribe to regulate this land preexists the creation of any state and may be limited only with both the tribe's consent and the expressed approval of the United States. We reiterate: Land may be taxed by either the tribe or the state but not both. For as long as the land is owned or controlled by the Band or its members, the State of South Dakota lacks the authority to regulate the land.

IV

It follows from the answer to the preceding question that if the State of South Dakota lacks the authority to tax the real property held by Indian allottees, it should likewise lack the authority to tax buildings or structures permanently affixed to the real property. The improvements to which the certified question refers were of a permanent kind, contemplating houses, barns, silos, and other permanently attached structures that had essentially become a part of the land itself. That permanent fixtures become part and parcel of the land, and that the taxation of the fixture is governed by the taxation of the real property to which it is attached, are not controversial propositions. From taxation to mortgage, from foreclosure to bankruptcy, the rule is that the law that controls the real property governs also fixtures so sufficiently attached. *See, e.g., Rogers v. Prattville Mfg. Co.*, 81 Ala. 483, 483 (1886); *Union Compress Co. v. State*, 64 Ark. 136, 138 (1897); *Fratt v. Whittier*, 58 Cal. 126, 128–29 (Cal. 1881); *Ott v. Specht & Spahn*, 13 Del. 61, 70 (1887); *Atl. Gulf & R.R. Co. v. Allen*, 15 Fla. 637, 655 (1876). Accordingly, because South Dakota may not seize or sell the real property, it may not seize or sell the fixtures upon that property. The Sisseton Band, not the State of South Dakota, has the exclusive right to regulate any property owned or controlled by the Band or its members.

Counsel for South Dakota suggests that, because a formal patent will issue from the United States to the allottee at the end of the twenty-five-year period contemplated in the Agreement of December 12, 1889, the seizure and sale of fixtures attached to the land would not interfere with the underlying interest of the United States nor would it prevent the patent from being issued free of any assessment or encumbrance. South Dakota's argument fails for three reasons. First, as clarified in Part III of this opinion, South Dakota maintains no sovereign interest in regulating the affairs of Indian allotments and accordingly has no authority to assess, seize, or sell any asset located on Indian lands.

Second, the Dawes Act clearly contemplates that land held by Indian allottees would be improved during the period it was held in trust. Thus, the United States maintains an interest in more than just the land but also in the fixtures so constructed. Against either the interest of the Sisseton Band or the United States, South Dakota has no authority to impose its tax. This conclusion is consistent with the purposes of the Dawes Act. If South Dakota were able to seize and sell the buildings and structures located upon the allotments, the United States would open itself up to claims brought by tribal members for the loss of those fixtures. In order to satisfy the growing number of judgments against the United States for its failure to protect said fixtures, Congress would ever be increasing the appropriation to satisfy judgments under the Act. Such a consequence was surely never intended by Congress. It therefore cannot be fairly argued that the Dawes Act protects only the real property, but it must also protect the buildings and structures attached to the land. Such a construction prohibits the regulation by South Dakota and allows either the United States or the individual tribal members to protect, in court, their interest against seizure by the state in the Circuit Court of South Dakota.

Third, even if the above reasons were deemed insufficient, South Dakota has disclaimed any right to assess the property of individual Indians and enshrined that disclaimer in its Constitution:

> Second. That we, the people inhabiting the state of South Dakota, do agree and declare that we forever disclaim all right and title to the unappropriated public lands lying within the boundary of South Dakota, and to all lands lying within said limits owned or held by any Indian or Indian tribes . . . that no taxes shall be imposed by the state of South Dakota on lands or property therein belonging to or which may hereafter be purchased by the United States . . . . But nothing herein shall preclude the state of South Dakota from taxing as other lands are taxed any lands owned or held by any Indian who has severed his tribal relation and has obtained from the United States, or from any person a title thereto by patent or other grant save and except such lands as have been or may be granted to any Indian or Indians under any act of Congress containing a provision exempting the lands thus granted from taxation.

S.D. Const. art. 22, § 2. South Dakota went on to make this provision "irrevocable without the consent of the United States and the people of the State of South Dakota." *Id.* Such a disclaimer of any rights to Indian land, whether owned by the tribe or controlled by individual Indians was imposed upon South Dakota as a condition of statehood. Act of Feb. 22, 1889, ch. 180, § 4, 25 Stat. 676, 677. Thus, having joined the United States and accepted the stipulation that it cannot assess the land of Indian tribes or tribal members living within its border, South Dakota cannot now claim to have the authority to levy the assessment against Charles R. Crawford and other similarly situated Indians.

V

The answer to this final question, regarding the ability of South Dakota to tax the personal property of tribal members, follows from the answers to the third and fourth certified questions. Since South Dakota lacks the authority to assess tax on property owned by Indians on traditional tribal lands, it follows that the state similarly lacks the authority to assess the personal property of Indians located on those lands. Some of the personalty at issue here was provided to the tribal members by the United States under the fulfillment of its responsibility to the Sisseton Band; yet, as we clarified in the first certified question, the personal property of the allottees now belongs solely to the tribal members themselves. Regardless of its provenance, the United States has no interest whatsoever in the personalty and therefore lacks the capacity to maintain an action against the state; however, the tribal members do have the capacity to challenge the taxation of their personal property. To provide guidance to the circuit court regarding these anticipated challenges, we now make clear that the state cannot tax the personal property of anyone located on land owned or controlled by the Sisseton Band or its citizens.

From the first principles of Indian law, and the division of powers between the tribe and the state, there emerges the maxim that the personal property of the individual allottee may be subject to taxation and regulation by either the tribe or the state but not both. This is not language of ambivalence, but an affirmative requirement that any tax assessor must determine that personal property is not located on tribal land or land held by tribal members before levying a tax obligation. The tribe or tribal members have the capacity to challenge the decision of an assessor in federal court.

Since at least 1832 it has been clear that the appropriate sovereign to make rules for the governance of personalty is the sovereign with control over the real property upon which the personalty is located at the time the tax is assessed; it is a question of territorial incorporation. *Worcester v. Georgia*, 31 U.S. 515 (1832). The determinative characteristic is based upon the location of the property; for a state has no authority to regulate or assess property located on Indian land. *Id.* Because the personal property of these individual tribal members is located on their allotments, the Sisseton Band, and not the State of South Dakota, has the authority to regulate or tax the personal property of the individual allottees present here.

Answers certified.

4

Commentary on *Lucas v. Earl*

FRANCINE J. LIPMAN

BACKGROUND

At the dawn of the twentieth century in America, there was no income tax. The Supreme Court of the United States had recently ruled in *Pollock v. Farmers' Loan & Trust Co.* that a tax on rental income was unconstitutional.[1] In a controversial 5-4 decision, the *Pollock* Court determined that this income tax was a direct tax requiring apportionment among the states, based on population. Because Congress had not apportioned this direct tax, it was void under the Constitution. Moreover, because the Court determined the tax legislation was not severable, the entire Revenue Act of 1894 was deemed unconstitutional.

After *Pollock*, Congress would have had to apportion any income tax on rents, dividends, and interest. Rather than pursue that strategy to fund the Spanish-American War, Congress instead enacted a legacy tax in 1898 on large estates and devises. Legacy tax rates ranged from 0.75 percent to 15 percent, depending on the size of the gross estate and the relationship of legatees to the decedent. Devises to a surviving spouse were excluded from the legacy tax.

Against this backdrop, in 1901, Guy Chaffee Earl (G. C. Earl), a forty-year-old experienced lawyer, and Ella Jane Earl née Ford (E. F. Earl), a thirty-nine-year-old trained landscape and coastal scenery artist, were prospering in their marriage and busy raising four young children. The Earl children were named to honor the family's rich roots, especially E. F. Earl's parents Jerome and Martha (née Hayes) Ford. In 1901, the Earl household included Martha Ford Earl, the oldest child at ten; Guy Chaffee Jr. and "Ellie" Hayes, a set of seven-year-old twins; and Alice, a toddler.[2]

---

[1]   157 U.S. 429 (1895).
[2]   Family Tree of Guy Chaffee Earl and Ella Jane Ford, *Earl Family Tree*, TEACHMATH.NET (last visited Apr. 3, 2017).

In addition to four children, after thirteen years of marriage the Earls had accumulated considerable community property assets. E. F. Earl also had substantial personal wealth in her separate property valued at $30,000. Because G. C. Earl "was not very well," they decided to enter into an agreement "which would simplify their affairs in case he died during her lifetime."[3] The agreement would also ensure that if circumstances rendered E. F. Earl a surviving spouse with four young children, she would seamlessly be in full control of all of their assets without a protracted and costly probate.[4] The resulting written agreement treated all of their property that "either of us now has or may hereafter receive or acquire (of any and every kind) in any way, either by earnings (including salaries, fees, etc.) or any rights by contract or otherwise" and "all proceeds, issues and profits of any and all such property" as "received, held, taken and owned" as joint tenants with rights of survivorship.[5] Under California law, the agreement converted any community or separately held property into jointly held property that would pass by operation of law to the surviving spouse. Fortunately, both Earls lived and prospered together many more years in Northern California, with G. C. Earl passing away in 1935 at the age of seventy-four. E. F. Earl, the Earl children, and many grandchildren survived G. C.'s death. E. F. Earl lived until shortly after she celebrated her eighty-third birthday.

After the end of the Spanish-American War, Congress terminated the legacy tax, amended the Constitution, and enacted a progressive income tax. By February 1913, Congress and the requisite number of state legislatures had ratified the Sixteenth Amendment authorizing an income tax, whether or not apportioned. In October of the same year, Congress passed a progressive income tax on higher-income individuals. Under the Revenue Act of 1913, individual taxpayers, whether or not married, were required to file income tax returns reporting their separate income. In 1918, Congress allowed married taxpayers to elect to file a joint return combining their income, gains, and losses, but progressive and high income tax rates (up to 65 percent to fund World War I) made this option expensive for higher-income couples. To mitigate the cost of progressive income tax rates and to take advantage of doubling the benefits of the lower-rate brackets, couples residing in community property states sought to split their income by reporting one-half of their community income on their individual income tax returns.

In February 1921, U.S. Attorney General Alexander Palmer issued an opinion that the laws of all seven community property states other than

---

[3] Earl v. Comm'r, 10 B.T.A. 723, 723 (1928).   [4] *Id.*   [5] *Id.*

California vested a present interest in labor and property income in both spouses so taxpayers could properly split their income for income tax reporting purposes.[6] Attorney General Palmer opined that California community property laws vested ownership of all community income in husbands.[7] California wives had "mere expectancies of income" that vested in surviving wives at the time of their husbands' deaths.[8] Accordingly, married men in California were required to report their own income, as well as their wives' income, on their individual income tax returns. Thus, married Californians were treated differently than any other Americans, because common law married residents were required to include only their separate income on their individual income tax returns.

The Internal Revenue Service enforced the Attorney General's position even before the official opinion was issued, including with respect to the 1918 income tax returns filed by California residents Reuel D. and Sadie M. Robbins. Mr. and Mrs. Robbins each reported one-half of Mr. Robbins's earned income as well as their community income on their individual income tax returns. The government assessed a $6,788 tax deficiency, allocating all of the income to Mr. Robbins. Mr. and Mrs. Robbins paid the deficiency and sued for a refund in district court.[9]

Judge Partridge, of the U.S. District Court for the Northern District of California, wrote the *Robbins* opinion acknowledging the importance of this "test case" that he expected would be appealed directly to the Supreme Court of the United States. Judge Partridge also noted that overruling the IRS could potentially burden federal coffers with more than $77 million in refunds to California taxpayers. Judge Partridge reviewed and compared community property laws and relevant case law. He then reasoned that, in substance, California women had much more than a "mere expectancy" in community property income. Judge Partridge found

> that the whole income can be taxed to the husband only if it is that husband's income, to apply the distinction, as the Supreme Court said in *Eisner v. Macomber*, "according to truth and substance, without regard to form." And the truth and substance is that only one-half of the income really belongs to the husband; the other half, in law and right and justice [belongs] to the wife.[10]

As predicted, the case was appealed directly to the Supreme Court. In January, 1926, Justice Holmes wrote the Court's opinion that held for the government.[11]

---

[6] Community Property – Income and Estate Taxes, 32 Op. Att'y Gen. 435 (1921).   [7] *Id.*
[8] *Id.*   [9] Robbins v. United States, 5 F.2d 690 (N.D. Cal. 1925) (citations omitted).
[10] *Id.* (quoting Eisner v. Macomber, 252 U.S. 189, 206 (1919)).
[11] United States v. Robbins, 269 U.S. 315 (1926).

Following what Justice Holmes described as long-settled California state law that a wife had a mere expectancy interest in community income while her husband was alive, the Court denied the allocation of income equally between Mr. and Mrs. Robbins. Ironically, Mr. Robbins had died in 1919, the year after the couple allocated more than a mere expectancy of income to Mrs. Robbins on her tax return. In 1927, legislators amended California community property laws to provide equal, present vested interests in community property to married couples.[12]

In 1928, the Board of Tax Appeals (BTA), citing the Supreme Court's decision in *Robbins*, held that G. C. and E. F. Earl could not split between them and report separately G. C. Earl's 1920 and 1921 earned income. Despite the Earls' 1901 written agreement characterizing their property and income as jointly owned, the BTA agreed with the IRS that G. C. Earl was the proper taxpayer for his earned income. G. C. Earl appealed the decision to the U.S. Court of Appeals for the Ninth Circuit. The Ninth Circuit reversed the BTA, respecting the validity of the Earls' agreement to split their income under California law. The Ninth Circuit found that the income was jointly held immediately upon being earned by Mr. Earl and, therefore, should be allocated and taxed consistently.[13] The government petitioned the Supreme Court of the United States to hear the case, noting the serious fiscal risk to the federal government from the Ninth Circuit's determination that income could be divided between taxpayers by agreement effectively undermining progressive taxation. In October 1929, the Supreme Court agreed to hear the case.

ORIGINAL OPINION

In 1930, Justice Holmes delivered the unanimous, albeit short, opinion agreeing with the IRS and the BTA and reversing the Ninth Circuit's decision. The Court acknowledged without question the validity of the Earls' agreement under California law. Justice Holmes specifically noted that, technically speaking, G. C. Earl's salary and fees became the Earls' joint property. Justice Holmes recognized the "very forcible argument" that the statute sought to tax those beneficially receiving the income. However, the Court "hesitated" with the claim that one-half of G. C. Earl's income immediately became his wife's, given that it was only G. C. Earl who performed or even could perform the personal services. Justice Holmes quickly dismissed this concern,

---

[12] CAL. CIV. CODE § 161a (1927).   [13] Earl v. Comm'r, 30 F.2d 898, 899 (9th Cir. 1929).

stating that this case would not be decided by "attenuated subtleties" but rather on statutory construction.[14]

The Court determined that under the statute, the government had broad authority. It had the ability to:

> tax salaries to those who earned them and provide that the tax could not be escaped by anticipatory arrangements and contracts however skillfully devised to prevent the salary when paid from vesting even for a second in the man who earned it. That seems to us the import of the statute before us and we think that no distinction can be taken according to the motives leading to the arrangement by which the fruits are attributed to a different tree from that on which they grew.[15]

Thus, Justice Holmes planted a deeply rooted metaphor embodying a foundational judicial limit on "anticipatory assignment of income" for purposes of federal income tax.

FEMINIST JUDGMENT

Ann M. Murphy's dissent methodically presents and discusses the rich statutory and case law history underlying California community property laws. After carefully describing the historical foundation and evolution of these laws and the lower courts' struggles with interpreting them, Professor Murphy, writing as Justice Ann M. Murphy, applies California law to the Earls' written agreement. As the majority and lower courts conclude, Murphy agrees that the contract is valid and enforceable under California law. However, Murphy's feminist dissent departs from the majority in its determination that G. C. Earl's income was properly divided equally between G. C. and E. F. Earl. Murphy explains that because federal tax law follows state law for determinations regarding ownership of property, G. C. Earl's income was joint property when earned and the Earls' tax returns were accurate as filed.

The juxtaposition of Murphy's precise description of the chronological evolution of California community property rights against Justice Holmes's conclusory deference to the government's discriminatory position is the embodiment of feminist practical reasoning. Murphy's detailed explanations, thorough research, and well-supported analysis lay out the "intricacies of each specific factual context,"[16] while Holmes's opinion affirmatively states that he

---

[14] *Lucas v. Earl*, 281 U.S. 111, 114 (1930).   [15] *Id.* at 114–15.
[16] *See* Katharine T. Bartlett, *Feminist Legal Methods*, 103 HARV. L. REV. 829, 830 (1990).

would not decide the case with "attenuated subtleties."[17] Murphy carefully explains that California community property laws are derived from predecessor Spanish and Mexican laws that treat marriage as a partnership. Murphy notes the fundamental presumption of equality of the partners in the partnership stating that "[p]roperty acquired during a marriage is acquired through the joint efforts of both the husband and the wife." She further supports this position through a brief narrative description of the debate over this specific issue at the California Constitutional Convention. Murphy humanizes the legal history by specifically naming an engaged delegate, Henry A. Tefft. She recounts Tefft's empathic plea for equality for California spouses. Murphy tells the story of how Tefft urged others to be sympathetic to long-time California residents, and quotes him as saying that "the rights of the wife are as necessary to be cared for as those of the husband." This strategic logic and feminist storytelling uses respected, contemporary leaders to deliver supporting arguments and fortify her reasoning.

By comparison, Holmes's opinion is devoid of legislative history, definitions, or context. The original opinion acknowledges the Earls' contract as valid, but without explanation, the original opinion discounts its substance as a skillful device to prevent vesting of salary "in the man who earned it."[18] Holmes defers to the government with little analysis and few authorities. As Murphy lays out in her opinion, the majority states that the issue is a matter of statutory construction and not attenuated subtleties. Nevertheless, Holmes decides the case without any traditional statutory construction analysis and rejects an admittedly valid and enforceable anticipatory assignment of income.

Feminist tax law scholar Edward J. McCaffrey in his groundbreaking book *Taxing Women* notes that while on the one hand Justice Holmes accepts the Earls' contract as unquestionably valid and enforceable, Holmes also questions it because it is in the "private domain" between husband and wife.[19] Because of this context, Holmes "could barely conceive of any substantive reality to these manipulative forms."[20] McCaffrey describes Holmes as so firmly believing that Congress could tax the man who solely contracted and earned his salary, and ignore the private husband-wife agreement, that he decides the central issue of the case "almost by silent inference."[21]

Murphy's description of the agreement between the Earls embodies feminist themes when she highlights that E. F. Earl was the only party who had meaningful extant financial assets to provide consideration for the marital

---

[17] *Lucas*, 281 U.S. at 114. [18] *Id.* at 115.
[19] EDWARD J. MCCAFFREY, TAXING WOMEN 39 (1997). [20] *Id.* [21] *Id.* at 38–40.

agreement. E. F. Earl had $30,000 of separate property, relative to G. C. Earl's zero dollars of separate property. Murphy's discussion thus affirms the substance of the Earls' agreement and strengthens the claim that E. F. Earl had derivative rights under the contract. After all, she was agreeing to recharacterize as jointly held property significantly more (almost $1 million, using today's dollars) than G. C. Earl. The focus on E. F. Earl's superior financial bargaining power counters the stereotypical narrative that husbands provide the bulk of the consideration in community property arrangements.

The research of Reva Siegel and Carolyn Jones demonstrates that at least through the 1940s, judges in the early twentieth century were skeptical that wives could be legitimate financial partners in a marriage or that they contributed meaningfully to assets acquired during marriage.[22] Interspousal contracts and transactions like the Earls' were suspect as shams without substance and labelled as "bedchamber transactions" to call into question their authenticity.[23] Consistent with this skeptical approach, the majority in *Lucas v. Earl* acknowledges that the agreement is valid and enforceable under California law, but then rejects the same agreement as authoritative for federal income tax purposes. Murphy's highlighting of E. F. Earl's considerable financial contribution relative to her spouse is a proactive assertion that undercuts any concerns about the legitimacy of the substance of the Earls' agreement.

While Justice Holmes's renowned concluding metaphor that "fruit cannot be attributed to a different tree" is memorable, it is not particularly instructive. Patricia A. Cain and others have described the metaphor as a poor substitute for sound legal analysis; and vulnerable to misapplication.[24] Cain notes that Holmes's metaphor does not clarify that earnings will be taxed to the earner or the owner of the income, or the person who has control over the income. Holmes merely concludes that G. C. Earl's income must be taxed to him. Holmes never used his fruit and tree metaphor again, although he had the opportunity in several subsequent assignment of income cases.[25] Perhaps Holmes himself came to doubt the metaphor's usefulness.

The same year as *Earl*, in a unanimous opinion written by Justice Owen Roberts, the Supreme Court of the United States decided *Poe v. Seaborn*[26]

---

[22] See Reva B. Siegel, *The Modernization of Marital Status Law: Adjudicating Wives' Rights to Earnings, 1860–1930*, 82 GEO. L.J. 2127 (1994); Carolyn C. Jones, *Split Income and Separate Spheres: Tax Law and Gender Roles in the 1940s*, 6 LAW & HIST. REV. 259 (1988).

[23] Boris Bittker, *Federal Income Taxation and the Family*, 27 STAN. L. REV. 1389 (1975).

[24] Patricia A. Cain, *The Story of Earl: How Echoes (and Metaphors) from the Past Continue to Shape the Assignment of Income Doctrine*, in TAX STORIES: AN IN-DEPTH LOOK AT TEN LEADING FEDERAL INCOME TAX CASES 306–07 (Paul L. Caron ed., 2003).

[25] Id. at 307–08.   [26] 282 U.S. 101 (1930).

and three companion cases.[27] These cases held that married women in the community property states of Washington, Arizona, Louisiana, and Texas had vested property rights in community property and should be taxed on their one-half of community property income. In *Poe*, the Court found that under the federal statute, net income should be taxed to individuals based upon ownership determinations under state law (in that case, Washington), not control.[28] The Court found that wives and husbands in the community property states reviewed, as compared to common law states, were owners of one-half of the community income and should be taxed for federal purposes accordingly.[29] Given progressive income tax rates, higher-income married individuals in community property versus common law states across America generally benefited financially from income splitting.

The Court's decisions in *Poe* and its progeny provided that married couples subject to community property statutes were required to split their income for federal tax purposes. Alternatively, under the Court's decision in *Earl*, married couples in common law states could not split their earned income by contract to mitigate the costs of progressive taxation. Therefore, married couples with the same amount of earned income living in different states (common law versus community property law) had different tax results. Taxing similarly situated taxpayers differently based upon state of residence violates traditional norms of equity and uniformity. After almost two decades and several failed attempts, Congress corrected this different tax treatment with joint filing for married couples. The Revenue Act of 1948 provided income splitting for all married couples through mandatory joint filing and new married tax rates.[30] Married couples paid the same tax liability as two single taxpayers earning one-half of the total family income.

Implicit in this revised tax structure is a secondary-earner bias, that effectively increases the tax burden for secondary earners (most typically wives) and decreases the tax burden for primary earners (most typically husbands). This increased tax burden marginalizes secondary earners (most typically wives) by more heavily taxing their work outside of the household. Feminist scholars critique joint filing and its consequent corollaries as undermining a woman's

---

[27] Goodell v. Koch, 282 U.S. 118 (1930) (Arizona); Hopkins v. Bacon, 282 U.S. 122 (1930) (Texas); Bender v. Pfaff, 282 U.S. 127 (1930) (Louisiana). In early 1931, the Court extended income splitting to California spouses for post-1927 community property income. United States v. Malcolm, 282 U.S. 792 (1931).

[28] *Poe*, 282 U.S. at 110.   [29] *Id.* at 110–13.

[30] Revenue Act of 1948, Pub. L. No. 80-471, 62 Stat. 110, 114–16.

autonomy and inhibiting her fundamental right to work;[31] joint filing "produces a powerful structure against wives."[32]

Married joint filing has been described by critical tax scholars as subsidizing a sexist,[33] classist,[34] racist,[35] and homophobic[36] status quo. The tax subsidy benefiting certain married couples generally benefits couples that follow a traditional pattern where one spouse works outside the home and the other does not. Demographic studies support the empirical claim that these "traditional" arrangements are most likely to involve white, different-sex spouses in which the man is the high income-earner and the woman is taking care of their children and managing the household.[37] The subsidy commonly is called a "marriage bonus." It also has been described in sexist terms as "Uncle Sam's dowry" and monetized as the cash value of a wife.[38] The subsidy results from a decrease in a married couple's aggregate tax liability from married filing jointly status as compared to two separate individual tax returns. As many tax scholars have demonstrated, women working outside of the household, whether married or single, are often penalized with the burden of higher effective tax rates under the joint filing system with a notably gendered "marriage penalty."[39]

An ancillary result of joint filing is joint and several income tax liabilities for married couples. Tax law scholars including Richard Beck and Amy Christian have demonstrated that this burden not only disproportionately harms women in application, enforcement, and collection of tax liabilities, but coupled with

---

[31] Grace Blumberg, *Sexism in the Code: A Comparative Study of Income Taxation of Working Wives and Mothers*, 21 BUFF. L. REV. 49 (1971); Marjorie E. Kornhauser, *The Rhetoric of the Anti-Progressive Income Tax Movement*, 86 MICH. L. REV. 465 (1987); Edward J. McCaffrey, *Taxation and the Family: A Fresh Look at Behavioral Gender Biases in the Code*, 40 UCLA L. REV. 983 (1993).

[32] Amy C. Christian, *Joint and Several Liability and the Joint Return: Its Implications for Women*, 66 U. CIN. L. REV. 535, 537 (1998).

[33] Jones, *supra* note 22.

[34] Dorothy A. Brown, *The Marriage Bonus/Penalty in Black and White*, 65 U. CIN. L. REV. 787 (1997).

[35] *Id.*; *see also* Dorothy A. Brown, *Race and Class Matters in Tax Policy*, 107 COLUM. L. REV. 790 (2007).

[36] Anthony C. Infanti, *The Internal Revenue Code as Sodomy Statute*, 44 SANTA CLARA L. REV. 763 (2004); *see also* Patricia A. Cain, *Same-Sex Couples and the Federal Tax Laws*, 1 J.L. & SEXUALITY 97 (1991); Nancy J. Knauer, *Heteronormativity and Federal Tax Policy*, 101 W. VA. L. REV. 129 (1998).

[37] Brown, *supra* note 34; Marjorie E. Kornhauser, *Love, Money, and the IRS: Family, Income-Sharing, and the Joint Income Tax Return*, 45 HASTINGS L.J. 63 (1993).

[38] Ludwig S. Hellborn, *Uncle Sam's Dowry*, 44 PROC. ANN. CONF. ON TAX'N UNDER AUSPICES NAT'L TAX ASS'N, 310, 310–15 (1951).

[39] Stephanie Hunter McMahon, *To Have and to Hold: What Does Love (of Money) Have to Do with Joint Tax Filing?*, 11 NEV. L.J. 718, 720 n.10 (2011).

joint filing, creates gendered biases in the structure of the tax system.[40] Professor Christian demonstrates in her scholarship that the tax system's structural biases reinforce and exacerbate economic inequality between women and men.[41]

If Murphy's well-reasoned and supported dissent had been included with the majority's decision in *Lucas v. Earl* in 1930, it might have convinced Congress or the Court to overrule *Earl* at a subsequent date. This development would have afforded married couples in common law states the opportunity to enter into contracts to split their income, putting them on par with community property states. As a result, Congress might not have burdened the tax system with mandatory joint filing. Individual tax return filing could have continued and women and other minorities would no longer be penalized by joint filing and its attendant consequences. Tax liabilities would be emancipated from marital tax filing issues that bind, hinder, and compromise women's independence and distinct life choices.

LUCAS v. EARL, 281 U.S. 111 (1930)

JUSTICE ANN M. MURPHY, DISSENTING

Believing that Mr. Earl (G. C. Earl) and Mrs. Earl, his wife (E. F. Earl), entered into a valid contract under California law to convert his earnings to the joint property of himself and E. F. Earl, with the absence of any tax avoidance motive, I dissent.

The contract between G. C. Earl and E. F. Earl, residents of California, was executed on June 1, 1901 in Oakland, California. The terms of the contract are as follows:

It is agreed and understood between us that any property either of us now has or may hereafter acquire (of any and every kind) in any way, either by earnings (including salaries, fees, etc.) or any rights by contract or otherwise during the existence of our marriage, or which we or either of us may receive by gift, bequest, devise, or inheritance, and all the proceeds, issues, and profits of any and all such property shall be treated and considered and hereby is declared to be received, held, taken, and owned by us as joint tenants and not otherwise with the right of survivorship.

(signed) Guy C. Earl
Ella F. Earl

---

[40] Richard C.E. Beck, *The Innocent Spouse Problem: Joint and Several Liability for Income Taxes Should Be Repealed,* 43 VAND. L. REV. 317 (1990).

[41] Christian, *supra* note 32; *see also* Edward J. McCaffrey, *Slouching towards Equality: Gender Discrimination, Market Efficiency, and Social Change,* 103 YALE L.J. 595, 602–03 (1993).

Earl v. Comm'r, 10 B.T.A. 723, 723 (1928). The contract was valid under California law and was in effect from the date of the execution of the contract through the dates in issue in this case, calendar years 1920 and 1921. *Id.*

The Commissioner of Internal Revenue determined that salary earned by G. C. Earl in 1920 and 1921 was taxable to him only and the salary was not taxable one-half to G. C. Earl and one-half to E. F. Earl. The Board of Tax Appeals agreed. The Ninth Circuit Court of Appeals, viewing the contract above as binding on G. C. Earl and E. F. Earl, determined that only one-half of G. C. Earl's salary was taxable to him. We granted certiorari.

California became the thirty-first state to enter the Union on September 9, 1850. The Constitution of the State of California, passed in 1849, provided the following with respect to ownership of property by a wife:

> All property, both real and personal, of the wife, owned or claimed by marriage, and that acquired afterwards by gift, devise, or descent, *shall be her separate property*; and laws shall be passed more clearly defining the rights of the wife, in relation as well to her separate property, as to that held in common with her husband. Laws shall also be passed providing for the registration of the wife's separate property.

Cal. Const. of 1849, art. XI, § 14 (emphasis added). The law of community property, which had been the law of the Mexican Province of California, became the law of California "through Article XI, Subdivision 14, of the first Constitution of California (1849) and the act of Apr. 17, 1850, defining the rights of husband and wife." Walter Loewy, *The Spanish Community of Acquests and Gains and Its Adoption and Modification by the State of California*, 1 Calif. L. Rev. 32 (1912). California adopted the Common Law of England on April 13, 1850, but four days later it passed the "Act defining the Rights of Husband and Wife" to incorporate "the community property [law] borrowed from civil and Spanish law . . . ." William B. Bosley, *Married Women's Rights in Community Property Under the Law of California*, 10 Yale L.F. 236 (1901). Section 2 of that Act provides the following: "All the property acquired after the marriage by either husband or wife, except such as may be acquired by gift, bequest, devise, or descent, shall be common property." Loewy, *supra*, at 32. California looked to the civil and Spanish law for "the reasons which induced its adoption, and the rules and principles which govern its operation and effect." *Packard v. Arellanes*, 17 Cal. 525, 537 (1861).

The Spanish and Mexican laws, upon which California law is based, treat a husband and wife's relationship as a partnership. Property acquired during a marriage is acquired through the joint efforts of both the husband and the wife. The question of whether to retain the community property rules for husbands and wives was debated vigorously at the California Constitutional Convention. *See, e.g.,* F. Ross Browne, *Report of the Debates in the Convention of California, on the Formation of the State Constitution, in September and October, 1849* (1850). The community property law prevailed because it had been the law of the land in California for centuries. *Id.*

The Spanish-American colonies were governed by the Spanish laws called the *Recopilación de leyes de los Reynos de las Indias* (Compiled Laws of the Kingdoms of the Indies). Lowey, *supra,* at 36. This law continued to be recognized in Mexico (including the then-territory of California) when Mexico gained its independence in 1821. Due to its prevalence for years, it is not surprising that community property continued as the law for property ownership between a husband and wife after California became a state. Henry A. Tefft, one of the delegates at the Constitutional Convention in California, urged his fellow delegates to be sympathetic to the native Californians who had always lived under community property law. He further added that "the rights of the wife are as necessary to be cared for as those of the husband." Browne, *supra,* at 258 (quoting Henry Tefft).

After the Convention, there commenced an ongoing difference of opinion between the California legislature's view of community property and the California courts' view of this ownership status. There was even an internal inconsistency within the California court system and within the California legislature.

It was initially unclear how and in what capacity a wife held the community property. Initially, the California Supreme Court determined that the wife's interest in the community property was "present, definite, and certain." *Beard v. Knox,* 5 Cal. 252, 256 (1855). Later, the California Supreme Court stated the interest was a "mere expectancy." *Van Maren v. Johnson,* 15 Cal. 308, 311 (1860). In a seeming reversal of *Van Maren,* the California Supreme Court held in 1870 that, although the wife's interest was a mere expectancy, it was vested in her. *De Godey v. Godey,* 39 Cal. 157, 164 (1870). This twisting of the contrary terms (expectancy versus vested) appeared to be an attempt to protect the wife from the acts of an improvident husband. *Id.* at 157. In *De Godey,* the California Supreme Court held that the husband was unable to deprive the wife of her share of the community property via his will, and he could not "alienate it for the mere purpose of divesting her of her claims to it." *Id.* at 164. Later, in 1896 the California Supreme Court reversed its stance again and held that the legal title to community property was vested in the husband and "he has the absolute dominion and control of it." *In re Estate of Burdick,* 112 Cal. 387, 393 (1896). Further, the Court held that the wife had no interest whatsoever in the property until the dissolution of the community, and even then, only in whatever interest remained. *Id.*

The California legislature passed laws providing for increasingly expansive property rights for the wife. First, in 1852 and 1853, statutes were enacted to permit wives to establish businesses in California. Women were allowed to register as sole traders, and many did during the California gold rush from 1848 to 1858. *See* Theodore H. Hittell, An Act to Authorize Married Women to Transact Business in Their Own Names as Sole Traders, in *The General Laws of the State of California: From 1850 to 1864, Inclusive,* at 1024–25 (1872) (passed April 12, 1852 and amended April 8, 1862); *see also* 2 *Advertisements in the Marin County Journal* 3 n.31 (1862). In 1854, the legislature passed An Act to Authorize Married Women to Convey Real Estate Held by Them in Their Own Name, *The Statutes of California, Passed at the Sixth Session of the Legislature,* ch. 17 (1855). Finally, in 1891, by Section 172 of the Civil Code, a wife's written consent was required for her husband to transfer community property.

Despite the broad language of the legislative enactments, the California Supreme Court continued to interpret the law to limit the wife's ownership. In 1916, the Court reiterated its view that ownership of community property was wholly in the husband. *Spreckels v. Spreckels,* 172 Cal. 775 (1916) ("[I]n view of the long-settled doctrine that the entire estate therein is in the husband during the marriage relation ... it is not to be supposed that the legislature would have made a change of so radical a character ... ."). This undoubtedly led to the addition of California Civil Code Section 172a in 1917, which provides that a wife must consent to any instrument by which community property is conveyed, encumbered, or leased for a period exceeding one year.

Despite the holding in *Spreckels,* the "foundation" of the premise that the husband is the owner of all of the community property was weak. *See* Case Comment, *Community Property: Effect of the 1917 Amendment to Civil Code Section 172a,* 12 Calif. L. Rev. 124 (1924). The California Supreme Court even took judicial notice that "[i]t has become the universal custom with purchasers of real property to insist on her [the wife's] signature to all contracts relating thereto." *Robbins v. United States,* 5 F.2d 690, 704 (1925). Suffice it to say that the views on community property were wide-ranging and conflicting.

At the time he signed the contract with E. F. Earl, G. C. Earl was an attorney and officer of the Great Western Power Company. He surely understood the differing interpretations of the status of community property in California – interpretations that had started from the premise of Spanish community property law. This premise was that property acquired during a marriage is treated as property acquired via a partnership. With this knowledge, he and E. F. Earl entered into the above-referenced contract.

G. C. Earl and E. F. Earl married in 1888. During the marriage, they accumulated "considerable property, consisting of cash, bonds, lands, and other property." *Earl*, 10 B.T.A. at 723. All of this property, without the contract, was community property under the law of California. Prior to entering into the contract in 1901, E. F. Earl also owned $30,000 of her own separate property. G. C. Earl did not have any of his own separate property. Therefore, E. F. Earl provided the majority of the consideration for the 1901 contract. By agreeing to put all of her separate property and any future property into joint ownership, they made a decision to change the character of their property, both the property they currently owned and property to be acquired. This arrangement was not made in order to avoid tax. Indeed, as pointed out by the Board of Tax Appeals, the arrangement was made in order to facilitate financial matters in the event G. C. Earl died. He was ill and by putting property in joint ownership with right of survivorship, E. F. Earl would have the easiest path to providing for her family. The family finances would be in her name and she would not need to appear in a court to facilitate the transfer of funds. It is instructive that, as of the same date, "joint bank accounts were made." *Id.* at 724. The Earls were concerned about G. C. Earl's health and E. F. Earl's ability to carry on to support the family.

In the *Packard* case, the California Supreme Court stated that "the wife has no voice in the management of these affairs, nor has she any vested or tangible interest in the community property." 17 Cal. at 538. G. C. Earl and E. F. Earl chose to avoid this result and instead hold their property jointly. This is a valid California contract, as noted by the Ninth Circuit Court of Appeals (citing Section 161 of the Civil Code of California). Married women in California have the right to hold property and to transact business in their own names. *See* An Act to Authorize Married Women to Transact Business in Their Own Name as Sole Traders, in *The Statutes of California, Passed at the Third Session of the Legislature*, ch. 42 (1852). In 1920, the first tax year in issue in this case, women gained the right to vote in federal elections. *See* U.S. Const. amend. XIX (ratified 1920) (California ratification November 1, 1919). Women are now recognized as having rights to property and rights to suffrage.

Although the Commissioner urges us to find a special third class of property – under which the attorney's fees earned by Mr. Earl were for an instant community property and then joint property – that is clearly not what was contractually agreed. There is no California law treating property in this way. The contract provided that the parties agreed to treat all earnings as jointly held. G. C. Earl and E. F. Earl clearly decided against the community property treatment for their property. As stated by the Ninth Circuit, "the intention clearly expressed is that the earnings should be received, taken, and held from the very beginning as the joint property of both." *Earl v. Comm'r*, 30 F.2d 898, 899 (1929). G. C. and E. F. Earl were essentially using the contract to reflect the partnership and egalitarian theory of ownership of property during their marriage, as it had been under the Spanish territory of California law. The contract is not ambiguous. The contract should be interpreted for both property law and income tax purposes as it is written and in no other way.

I do not find the Commissioner's argument (that this contract was made to evade tax) in any way persuasive. As the Commissioner well knows, the income tax was declared unconstitutional five years prior to the date of the contract in this case. *Pollock v. Farmers' Loan & Trust Co.*, 157 U.S. 429 (1895). At the time that G. C. Earl and E. F. Earl contracted, there was no federal income tax. The tax statutes at issue in this case are the Revenue Acts of 1918 and 1921, passed well after the time this valid and bargained-for contract took effect. In its petition for certiorari, the Commissioner indicated that the principal question in this case is whether the tax acts of Congress may be *evaded* by an agreement sharing compensation. Pet. for Writ of Cert. 9. It could not reasonably be suggested that G. C. Earl and E. F. Earl intended to evade a tax that did not exist.

Although the majority states that this case "turns on the import and reasonable construction of the taxing act," 281 U.S. at 114, in fact, the majority treats this scenario as an "anticipatory arrangement[]" devised to avoid tax. *Id.* at 115. It is indeed difficult to see how G. C. Earl and E. F. Earl entered into this contract to avoid a tax. There was no income tax in 1901. As stated by the Ninth Circuit, this was a valid contract under California law, and the parties to the contract simply changed the character of their property from separate and community property to joint property. *Id.* Certainly one could imagine a contract of this type being executed after the tax acts took effect, in which case the majority's characterization might be correct. *Id.* In that case, one could interpret the contract as being one meant to avoid tax. These are not the facts with which we are presented, and I therefore dissent.

5

Commentary on *Welch v. Helvering*

NICOLE APPLEBERRY

BACKGROUND

The United States of America's first income taxes, adopted in 1862 and 1863 to help fund the Civil War, expired in 1872. Revived in 1894 only to be determined unconstitutional by the Supreme Court in *Pollock v. Farmers' Loan & Trust Co.*,[1] our income tax scheme finally achieved its permanent place in our hearts and minds with the culmination of the Sixteenth Amendment's four-year ratification process and, shortly thereafter, the passage of the Revenue Act of 1913.

Thus, when Thomas Welch was considering how to continue his father's business while fresh on the heels of his own voluntary bankruptcy and just two years into the involuntary bankruptcy of the company he owned with his father (whose discharge was still a few years out), our income tax system was a mere "tween." Welch and his trio of banker advisors could not have felt any reasonable certainty about the tax result of his proposed payments of E. L. Welch Company debts, unless favorable treatment was presumed from the general sense of entitlement that tends to accrue with class, gender, racial, and other privileges.

That just twenty years after the passage of the Revenue Act of 1913, the Supreme Court already had twelve cases to cite in *Welch* as it attempted to distinguish between business expenses that were "ordinary" (and thus currently deductible) and those that were "not ordinary" (and thus either disallowed entirely or capitalized) is a testament both to the vagueness of the nascent rule and the significant need for its explication. Over the ensuing decades, this distinction has been hotly contested, and courts used the foggy "ordinary and necessary" business expense deduction test to disallow current

---

[1]   157 U.S. 429, *aff'd on rehearing*, 158 U.S. 601 (1895).

deductions for expenses they found offensive in a variety ways – more personal than business, against public policy, for lobbying or other political activities, or unreasonable in amount. Many of these deductions are now explicitly forbidden by the Code.[2]

ORIGINAL OPINION

Justice Cardozo's original *Welch*[3] opinion disposed of the matter in a scant 1,700 words, setting forth few of the facts and little of the context presented in the feminist judgment of Professor Mary Louise Fellows, writing as Justice Fellows.[4] The Cardozo opinion started with the base assumption that expenses are "necessary" if they are "appropriate and helpful" for the taxpayer's business, and deferred to the taxpayer's perspective on this point, stating that "we should be slow to override his judgment."[5] This prong of the "ordinary and necessary" test was thus disposed of within a whopping two sentences.

From that point on, the Court labored to define "ordinary" expenses. It provided at least one step toward a standard that could actually be applied in real life: "Ordinary in this context does not mean that the payments must be habitual or normal in the sense that the same taxpayer will have to make them often . . . ."[6] Rather, the Court established that we should look to "norms of conduct" in "the life of the group, the community, of which [the individual] is part."[7] In the context of business expense deductions, that has come to mean expenses that would be ordinary within a particular taxpayer's industry.

From there, the Court seemed flummoxed by the task of developing additional factors to illuminate the test. Indeed, it stated that "[m]any cases in the federal courts deal with phases of the problem presented in the case at bar. To attempt to harmonize them would be a futile task."[8] Facing this futility, the Court declined to itself set forth a clear test, stating instead: "Here . . . the decisive distinctions are those of degree and not kind. The standard set up by the statute is not a rule of law; it is rather a way of life. Life in all its fullness must supply the answer to the riddle."[9]

Facing such a riddle, the Court deferred to the Internal Revenue Service's interpretation, stating that its "ruling has the support of a presumption of

---

[2]   E.g., I.R.C. §§ 162(c), (e)–(g), 280A (Westlaw through Pub. L. No. 115-43).
[3]   Welch v. Helvering, 290 U.S. 111 (1933).
[4]   Fellows's research included the briefs and transcript of record as well as an essay by Joel S. Newman, *The Story of* Welch: *The Use (and Misuse) of the "Ordinary and Necessary" Test for Deducting Business Expenses, in* TAX STORIES 197, 199–200 (Paul Caron ed., 2d ed. 2009).
[5]   *Welch*, 290 U.S. at 113.   [6]   *Id.* at 114.   [7]   *Id.*   [8]   *Id.* at 116.   [9]   *Id.* at 114–15.

correctness, and the petitioner has the burden of proving it to be wrong."[10] In this case, following the IRS's lead meant a determination that it is "extraordinary" to pay off another's debts.[11] And when it is done for business purposes like Welch's, the Court found it most like payments for "[r]eputation and learning," and so most like purchasing a capital asset like good will, and hence ineligible for the ordinary and necessary business expense deduction.[12]

FEMINIST JUDGMENT

Fellows declines to grab hold of the presumptive tails of the would-be authoritative elephants in front of her, picks up the gauntlet presented by the cryptic statute and unhelpful case law, and herself crafts guidance that, had it been provided in 1933, would have changed the course of tax history. It certainly would have been of significantly greater utility to future taxpayers attempting to determine the tax consequences of their actions. As there was an insufficient record to determine the precise result of the application of her test, she remands the case for further proceedings consistent with her opinion.

Fellows's feminist re-visioning[13] of the *Welch* opinion makes a purposeful choice to avoid the original's reflexive abdication of power to the already powerful. She defers to no one and nothing: for the "necessary" prong, not business people, not administrative agencies, and not the weight of preexisting legal rights and responsibilities.

She addresses Welch's request, and the original Court's willingness, to rubber stamp the "necessity" of the expenses, purportedly out of respect for his business judgment. As Fellows points out, this was a man who personally chose – and whose company was forced into – bankruptcy,[14] leaving creditors short $300,000 – the equivalent of well over $4 million in 2016 dollars.[15] Perhaps his business judgment was not worthy of such respect, and as she notes, too much deference to a taxpayer's "naked assertion" of the necessity of his expenses "impairs this country's progressive tax system

[10] *Id.* at 115. [11] *Id.* at 114. [12] *Id.* at 115.

[13] Tip of the nib, as feminist author Alison Bechdel would say, to Mary Daly, a radical feminist author who signaled her reconceptualization of common words with hyphens and slashes. *See, e.g.,* MARY DALY ET AL., WEBSTERS' FIRST NEW INTERGALACTIC WICKEDARY OF THE ENGLISH LANGUAGE (1987); MARY DALY, GYN/ECOLOGY: THE METAETHICS OF RADICAL FEMINISM (1978).

[14] Fellows does also acknowledge the challenges of the dramatically changing agricultural market after World War I, and the "turbulent economic situation ... since the stock market crash of 1929" (although the bankruptcies in question occurred in the 1920s, before the crash).

[15] $4,225,491.23, as calculated on www.usinflationcalculator.com (as of Sept. 16, 2016).

while it reinforces unwarranted cultural norms that accord a privileged place to well-heeled commercial interests."

Fellows also declines to follow the IRS's lead in elevating the relevance of Welch's legal rights and responsibilities. The IRS had taken the position that because Welch was not required to pay the company's debts, his doing so could not be considered "necessary." The original opinion did not adopt this reasoning (instead simply accepting the taxpayer's assertions of necessity). Fellows does not either, but for different reasons. A quintessential aspect of the American spirit is a robust individualism that abhors any restraint on our personal liberty. In that context, only the barest minimum of appropriate behavior is likely to be required by law. In most arenas, we prefer to encourage or discourage activity rather than mandate it. So, Fellows finds it inappropriate to deny deductions for all but legally required expenses. She aspires to recognize and reward behavior by the taxpayer that was more ethical than was strictly legally required.

Throughout her opinion, Fellows takes on the responsibility of considering the practical, personal, historical, and sociological in her quest to "shape a fair and just federal income tax system." Taking a broader, more contextualized view is arguably political, if not necessarily feminist. But while fairness is not exclusively a feminist concern, it is *a* feminist concern, and *truly* examining "life in all its fullness," including the perspectives and experiences of those who have been marginalized, is a feminist technique.[16]

From this more holistic perspective, Fellows recognizes the specifically feminist progress heralded by the passage of the Nineteenth Amendment, granting women the right to vote, and the associated sociological changes she anticipated would come, including "diminished ... boundaries between the private and public spheres and undermined social stratifications." She foresees an economic and political world improved by the incorporation of women, allowing us to move beyond the historical positioning of women as the embodiment of all that is private, altruistic, connective, and operating in the domestic sphere, and the valorizing of men as the embodiment of all that is public, acquisitive, competitive, and operating in the business sphere.

In a bravely atypical move even in current day jurisprudence, Fellows uses the characters, scenes, and themes of a novel, Mary Shelley's *Frankenstein; or, The Modern Prometheus*, to explicate the dangers and heartbreak of this gendered schism and to promote, instead, a "marketplace that embraces an ethos of caring." While literature is by no means inherently feminine or

---

[16] See the concept of "feminist practical reasoning," as explicated by Katharine T. Bartlett in *Feminist Legal Methods*, 103 HARV. L. REV. 829, 849 (1990).

feminist, its use in this manner is traditionally eschewed in court opinions, which keep a tight focus on the strict application of established law to the facts presented by the parties. Invoking fiction for insight and inspiration can be construed as a feminist move. Our dominant philosophical paradigm labels certain beings and activities as "feminine" (including women, the "domestic" arts, fiction that centers on human relationships, and emotions) and certain beings and activities as "masculine" (including men, the "serious" arts, fiction that centers on anything *but* relationships, and logic). The former is generally subordinated to the latter, more nuanced characterizations are treated with suspicion, and there are negative consequences for outright transgressions. The first printing of Mary Shelley's novel was published anonymously, with a preface by her husband. It was common for female writers of the time to publish anonymously or under male names in order to have any hope of being taken seriously. This may have been Ms. Shelley's intent as well. For Fellows to infuse the strictly "logical," facts-and-law based realm of court opinions[17] with fiction that has been revealed to be created by a woman is absolutely feminist. And to integrate the masculine and feminine spheres (in analytical writing) to prove a point about the integration of the masculine and feminine spheres (in economics, politics, and tax law) is delicious.

So, self-liberated to strike out on her own, what course does Fellows set? Her first step is to open an inquiry into an aspect entirely ignored by the original Court: the tax positions taken by the E. L. Welch Company with regard to these debts. She recognizes that to truly understand the transactions, it cannot be ignored that the taxpayer and his father owned the E. L. Welch Company together – after all, it was this connection that prompted Welch's personal payment of the corporation's debts. Pairing this more comprehensive understanding with a feminist orientation in favor of justice, Fellows determines that as a threshold matter, it would be fundamentally unfair to allow the taxpayer the benefit of deductions to which the company would not have been entitled, had it paid off its own debts.[18] The record did not reflect what the corporation would have been entitled to, so this question becomes the first to be answered by the lower court on remand. Only if Welch is requesting tax treatment to which the E. L. Welch Corporation would have been entitled does the inquiry proceed further.

---

[17] I suspect most if not all writers of legal opinions feel that their product is grounded in the purest of deductive reasoning (even where they also have personal feelings about the subjects at hand, and where others disagree about their logic).

[18] Fellows thanks Professor Charlotte Crane of Northwestern University School of Law for her insights about how a deduction for Welch's payments of E. L. Welch Company's debt might have duplicated the deductions already enjoyed by E. L. Welch Company.

Fellows next enters the weeds of the "ordinary and necessary" test, focusing the bulk of her discussion on the "necessary" prong. This gives it an independent vitality it has not had since the original *Welch* opinion. Rather than a simple "does the taxpayer assert it was necessary" test (as requested by Welch) or "was the taxpayer required to make the payments" test (as requested by the IRS), Fellows poses a series of questions to more thoroughly explore the actual business necessity of the payments. She wishes the lower court had examined the quality of Welch's "business training, experience, and other entrepreneurial qualifications" to assess the level of "skepticism" appropriate for his bald statement that the expenses were necessary. She directs the lower court to look closely at the payees' check endorsements disclaiming any connection between the payments and their present and future business relations with Welch. Fellows also highlights Welch's acknowledgement that the payments were made to "personal friends and customers," raising the possibility that they were more personal than business related, while still supporting, if otherwise appropriate, "the importance of ongoing relationships in the marketplace built on trust and fair dealing . . . [and] a tax rule that encourages and valorizes those conducting trades and businesses who act collaboratively with, rather than in opposition to, their customers, creditors, workers, and even their competitors."

Here it should be noted that the more robust factual investigation could reveal interesting details about the payments that were made. While the corporation was still going through the bankruptcy process, the taxpayer made payments to corporate creditors – possibly to only the creditors chosen by him, in amounts chosen by him, not necessarily according to the bankruptcy plan. Furthermore, a significant portion were made after the corporation was discharged from bankruptcy, with the vast majority of the debt left unpaid – and once again it seems probable the payments were made to corporate creditors chosen by him, in amounts chosen by him, not necessarily allocated as if the funds had been available in the bankruptcy. Whether intentional or not, Welch's payments may have subverted the bankruptcy plan in favor of enhanced payments to his favorite cronies in the grain business old boys' club. The taxpayer was a very wealthy man, making a significant amount of money at a relatively young age: adjusted for inflation to 2016 dollars, he earned $431,843.10 in 1925, $285,107.36 in 1926, $306,182.44 in 1927, and $368,710.17 in 1928.[19] While potentially not strictly necessary, the payments he made allowed him to maintain the social and economic privilege he held in the community, which it is doubtful a woman or other person not already benefited by nepotism, class, and race would have been able to access.

---

[19] As calculated by www.usinflationcalculator.com (as of Sept. 16, 2016).

Fellows also raises an eyebrow at the assertion that the taxpayer truly had to and was able to rebuild his reputation with these payments, given that he kept an exceedingly generous portion of his income for himself – perhaps far more than he would if he really had to maximize payments to the corporate creditors to keep his business afloat.

As previously mentioned, Fellows also uses *Frankenstein* to question the segregation of public and private, male and female, competition and collaboration, and business and personal consumption. She notes that expenses made in the public/business sphere (such as expensive features of luxury offices for executives, which are unnecessary for them to do their jobs) are routinely accepted as "necessary" business expenses, which "reinforces the elite status of some employees over others, and undercuts the progressivity of the income tax system." A well-known 1993 Supreme Court of Canada dissenting opinion made the corollary point, that with the increased presence of women in the businesses world, childcare that allows them to work should not be seen as a private consumption choice, but as a deductible business expense. In doing so, Justice L'Heureux-Dubé notes the importance of the context men and women generally operate within:

> [I]t is important to look closely at the dichotomy of business as opposed to personal expenses. If we survey the experience of many men, it is apparent why it may seem intuitively obvious to some of them that child care is clearly within the personal realm .... In fact, the evidence before the Court indicates that ... very few men ... made any work-related decisions on the basis of child-raising responsibilities. For women, business and family life are not so distinct and, in many ways, any such distinction is completely unreal, since a woman's ability to even participate in the work force may be completely contingent on her ability to acquire child care.[20]

Likewise, Fellows is advocating for a more integrated, holistic perspective in her *Welch* opinion. If hers had been the opinion actually issued in 1933, the ensuing eight decades would have looked very different, as the necessity of business expenses would be much more closely tailored to their actual business necessity and less tied to norms that perpetuate the privilege that accrues to historic insiders.[21]

Next, Fellows turns to her version of the "ordinary" prong of the test (historically the only prong with any "juice"). Here, she once again declines

---

[20] Symes v. Canada, [1993] 4 S.C.R. 695, 800 (Can.) (L'Heureux-Dubé, J., dissenting). My thanks to Anthony Infanti for directing me to this opinion.

[21] Namely wealthy white men who do not have the temerity to visibly differ from the elite in some other way, such as by being gay, having a disability, adhering to a nondominant religion, holding nondominant political beliefs, etc.

to follow the original opinion's deference to business judgment, as reflected in usual business practices. She sees common business practices as, at least potentially, "pernicious" ruts, particularly "now that women are gaining greater opportunities for economic success in the United States." Why encourage "the adversarial and noncollaborative traditions prevailing in the current marketplace" instead of "allow[ing] for evolving commercial norms" that would hopefully "introduce ... the virtues of prudence, fairness, and cooperation into ... business dealings"? Instead, Fellows sets forth a novel and yet logical definition of "ordinary": "an expenditure incurred ... with the reasonable expectation that it will increase income or reduce costs." She therefore remands this issue as well, asking the lower court to investigate whether Welch's payments "allowed him to avoid other costs, such as ... higher interest rate[s] or an additional loan requirement."

This test might seem nearly duplicative of the "necessary" prong, perhaps a softened version as it allows for advantageous as well as required business activity. However, it carries its own weight in the next step of her analysis: the determination of whether an otherwise "ordinary and necessary" expense relating to a durable asset is a current expenditure that repairs it, and therefore is immediately deductible, or represents the cost of acquiring or improving such an asset, and therefore must be capitalized. Here, Fellows once again harkens back to her *Frankenstein* analogy to suggest what would have resulted in a seismic shift in the course of tax law: an acknowledgment of, and financial support for, the integration of humanity (the domestic sphere, its "human capital" inhabitants, and their morality) into the business world (where gladiators are more typically rewarded). She refrains from advocating for the most extreme application of this principle, the deductibility of "human capital expenditures ... such as food and shelter," and once again presents a more nuanced, less segregated, less all-or-nothing possibility for the lower court to analyze on remand. In this stage, her more sophisticated, feminist approach allows for the possibility that the taxpayer's payments could, factually, either be immediately deductible payments to repair his reputation or capitalized payments to replace or substantially improve it.

Throughout her opinion, Fellows provides nuanced guidance that is feminist in its methodology and priorities. At first glance the more humane approach to business practices might be seen as coming with the trade-off of a more complicated regime, because Fellows encourages a more comprehensive, deeply factual analysis and reinvigorates the "necessary" prong of the "ordinary and necessary" business expense deduction test, which historically has been collapsed into the test's "ordinary" prong. However, the original opinion's treatment of the "necessary" prong was so poorly explicated that

Fellows's more thorough and thoughtful approach ultimately provides far clearer precedent that would (or should) have been welcome to the confused and clamoring masses in these interceding decades. It also allows for and encourages the evolution in business and society that was already underfoot and has proceeded apace ever since: the integration of women, formerly assigned the "private" and "personal" sectors, into the "public" and "business" spheres traditionally reserved for men. This has, in turn, exposed the unnecessary and even destructive nature of seeing the world through the limiting prism of such dichotomies. Our tax regime has not fully caught up; Fellows's judgment would have allowed it to adjust fluidly to our developing societal norms.

WELCH v. HELVERING, 290 U.S. 111 (1933)

JUSTICE MARY LOUISE FELLOWS DELIVERED
THE OPINION OF THE COURT

This case raises the question of whether a taxpayer can deduct from income amounts paid to the creditors of a now bankrupt closely held corporation, in which the taxpayer owned a minority interest.

I

In 1906, E. L. Welch, the father of the taxpayer, Thomas Welch, started a business in Minnesota under the name of E. L. Welch Company. The largest part of the business was handling grain on commission. At some unspecified time, the taxpayer joined his father's business. The record shows that, by the year 1922, the taxpayer at the age of thirty-four was serving as secretary and owned less than 1 percent of the shares of the corporation. His father, who was president, owned the rest.[1] The taxpayer took responsibility for traveling to rural areas for the purpose of maintaining relations with current customers and making contact with prospective ones. In addition to managing cash sales, trades, and futures contracts, he handled all grain arriving into Minneapolis and attended to its grading and loading. The taxpayer's father retained exclusive responsibility for the financial aspects of the business.

We take judicial notice that, after World War I, agricultural prices dropped dramatically, the railroad companies used their dominance in the market to

---

[1] At the time that the corporation was adjudicated bankrupt, its value was $50,000. The taxpayer held shares valued at $1,000 at that time and his father owned the remaining shares.

set high rates for storing and shipping grain, and farmers established coopera-tives so that they might be able to have more market power in setting prices for their products and costs of operation. The taxpayer and his father apparently were unable to adjust to the changing economic environment and the corpor-ation failed. E. L. Welch Company was adjudged an involuntary bankrupt on March 23, 1922, and was discharged from bankruptcy on July 6, 1926. Shortly after the corporation went into involuntary bankruptcy, the taxpayer on August 5, 1922, was adjudged a voluntary bankrupt and was discharged from bank-ruptcy on October 25, 1922.

During the years in controversy, 1924 to 1928 inclusively, the taxpayer continued in the grain commission business. He entered into a contract with Kellogg Company under which he purchased grain on its behalf in return for commissions. He conducted his business during this time in the same territory where he had carried on business for E. L. Welch Company. In his work for Kellogg Company he had some customers who previously had done business with E. L. Welch Company.

The taxpayer testified that he had asked three bankers for advice about how best to proceed regarding his own bankruptcy. They all were of the opinion that, if he made up the losses to the corporation's creditors, he could have future success in his business. He proceeded to make payments to the corporation's creditors. When asked whether he was able to build up a large business "largely because [he] . . . acted square with these creditors," he responded: "Yes, sir, to a certain extent." Tr. of R. 31. He then was asked the motive for the payments. He testified that he made the payments "to reestablish my credit for one thing, reestablish my business, and, further, it was a matter of a moral obligation." *Id.*

Before 1926, during which time the E. L. Welch Company's debts had not yet been discharged, the taxpayer took what he called an "assignment of certain claims" from the corporation and paid them. *Id.* at 30. The record leaves some ambiguity as to whether the taxpayer assumed personal liability for those assigned claims. The creditors he paid in 1924 included shippers, futures traders, and banks. He also paid creditors who had provided goods and services, such as water and printing, to the corporation. Except for those creditors with claims of less than $25, he paid no creditor in full. He paid the creditors by check and each check had the following endorsement:

> The payee of this check by the endorsement thereof accepts and agrees to apply the same on its claim against E. L. Welch Company according to the terms of the letter of transmittal. This has nothing to do with the present or future business relations with the maker of the check and is not to be considered as acknowledging any existing claim or renewing any barred claim against him.

Id. at 29–30. In 1925, the taxpayer again took assignment of claims from the corporation and paid by check, with the same endorsement as quoted above, $100 each to many of the same creditors he had paid in 1924. He did not take any assignment of claims from the corporation for the balance owed these creditors. In 1926, 1927, and 1928, with E. L. Welch Company's debts now discharged, the taxpayer took no further assignment of claims. During those three years, he continued to make payments by check, with the same endorsement as quoted above, to previous creditors of E. L. Welch Company. The claims of the corporation's creditors who received payments from the taxpayer amounted to about $300,000. The taxpayer paid a total amount of a little more than $47,000 to those creditors over the five years at issue. Those who received payments included nearly all the corporation's bank creditors and persons who the taxpayer has described as "personal friends and customers . . . of long standing." *Id.* at 31.

By his own description, the taxpayer "has paid out all his earnings except necessary living expenses to such customers." *Id.* at 5. As indicated below, he paid an average of about 40 percent of his gross income to creditors from 1924 through the year 1928.

Taxable Year	Gross Income (unadjusted for any payments to creditors)	Payments to Creditors
1924	$18,028.20	$3,975.97
1925	$31,377.04	$11,968.20
1926	$20,952.20	$12,615.95
1927	$22,119.61	$7,379.72
1928	$26,177.56	$11,068.25
Total	$118,654.64	$47,044.09

On the advice of a tax expert, for 1924, 1925, and 1926 the taxpayer excluded from his reported income all payments made to creditors of E. L. Welch Company. On his 1927 and 1928 income tax returns, he reported his total commissions and treated the payments to the creditors as a deduction.

The Commissioner of Internal Revenue ruled that these payments were neither excludable nor deductible from income as "ordinary and necessary" business expenditures. This Court views the exclusion of income in 1924, 1925, and 1926 on the taxpayer's tax returns as the equivalent of a deduction. We make no distinction in the analysis that follows between the taxpayer's tax treatment of his payments to E. L. Welch Company's creditors in the earlier

years as compared to his treatment of those payments in the later years. The
Commissioner argues that the payments of corporate debts by the taxpayer are
voluntary and gratuitous and do not qualify as "necessary." The Commissioner
alternatively argues that the payments represent capital expenditures and
should not be allowable as an immediate deduction. The Board of Tax
Appeals sustained the action of the Commissioner, adopting his reasoning.
Welch v. Comm'r, 25 B.T.A. 117 (1932). The Court of Appeals for the Eighth
Circuit affirmed on the ground that the expenditures are "very extraordinary
payments, and not expenses of the business at all." *Welch v. Comm'r*, 63 F.2d
976, 977 (8th Cir. 1933). The parties agree that the question of whether a
taxpayer can deduct an expenditure depends on our interpretation of the
statutory rule providing that "[i]n computing net income there shall be allowed
as deductions ... all the ordinary and necessary expenses paid or incurred
during the taxable year in carrying on any trade or business." Revenue Act of
1924, ch. 234, § 214, 43 Stat. 253, 269; Revenue Act of 1926, ch. 27, § 214, 44
Stat. 9, 26; Revenue Act of 1928, ch. 852, § 23, 45 Stat. 791, 799.

II

In one respect, we could resolve this case by acceding to the Commissioner's
interpretation of the applicable statutory provision and judgment that the
payments in controversy are not deductible. Deference to the Commissioner
would substantially reduce litigation in the federal courts and also reduce the
administrative costs of the income tax system as a whole. Nevertheless, these
so-called economic efficiency arguments should not deter us from consideration of other strongly held jurisprudential values.

The federal income tax has been and will remain the product of political
compromises based on geographical regions, economic sectors, and progressive and conservative ideologies. On the one side have been those politicians,
primarily representing merchants, farmers, artisans, and workers, who promote
a redistributional agenda, endorsing a tax system that attacks concentrations of
wealth and advocating for equitable sharing of the obligations of the federal
government. *See, e.g.,* 50 Cong. Rec. 332, 337, 413 (1913); 65 Cong. Rec. 2440,
3332 (1924). On the other side have been politicians, primarily representing
professionals, corporations, wealthy land owners, and others in the investor
class, who advance a business agenda, fearing that significant taxes on those
who have found pecuniary success will stifle economic growth to the detriment of everyone. *See, e.g.,* 50 Cong. Rec. 342, 415, 417 (1913); 65 Cong.
Rec. 2448, 2504 (1924). Given the far-reaching nature of the statutory scheme
and its relatively recent enactment, this Court refuses to abdicate statutory

interpretation responsibility to the executive branch of government. The Commissioner's expertise concerning the technical aspects of statutory interpretation shall not override our obligation to situate the federal income tax historically and culturally as we consider the specific facts of the case before us.

Any progressive income tax system must monetize taxpayers' complicated lives as it ranks taxpayers from the most to the least wealthy. Taking into account a myriad of taxpayers' daily social interactions, the tax system determines what constitutes income, what constitutes a deduction, and how each item should be valued. To date, this Court has not emphasized the cultural and moral issues at stake when we have decided constitutional and statutory interpretation issues pertaining to the income tax. *See, e.g., Eisner v. Macomber,* 252 U.S. 1 (1920). The facts of this case have heightened our appreciation of how much the federal income tax has and will continue to reflect this nation's values. The imperative to shape a fair and just federal income tax system rests on this Court's ability to recognize the multitude of ways the income tax influences cultural norms and institutions.

The parties center their arguments on the meaning of the language "ordinary and necessary," which is found in the statute authorizing deductions from income for expenditures "incurred during the taxable year in carrying on any trade or business." Both parties agree that the statute requires that an expenditure must meet both criteria. We recognize at the outset that the phrase "ordinary and necessary" does not lend itself to precise and unambiguous rules. Before addressing the parties' respective arguments regarding the appropriate interpretation of "ordinary and necessary," we find the need to raise a tax fairness concern.

III

Neither the taxpayer nor the Commissioner has addressed the question of how E. L. Welch Company's tax treatment of its debt should implicate, if at all, the deductibility of the taxpayer's payments to that corporation's creditors. The tax fairness concern we are raising necessarily starts with a consideration of the potential tax consequences to E. L. Welch Company resulting from its acquisition and nonpayment of debt. This Court has held that the mere procurement of debt does not result in income. *Bowers v. Kerbaugh-Empire Co.,* 271 U.S. 170, 175 (1926). The increase in a debtor's assets from the funds borrowed is offset by the increase in a debtor's liabilities and, therefore, does not result in any gain to the debtor. In turn, the tax law does not treat a debtor's subsequent repayment of a debt in full as a taxable event, because the debtor's decrease in assets is offset by the debtor's decrease in liabilities.

E. L. Welch Company acquired debt in two ways. The first was by its borrowing funds. The corporation likely used those funds to make business-related expenditures. Those expenditures presumably led either to current deductions from income or to a tax basis, determined by reference to the amount of borrowed funds the corporation invested in the durable assets it acquired. These tax attributes could have reduced, either immediately or over time, E. L. Welch Company's taxable income. The second way that E. L. Welch Company borrowed is when it acquired goods and services. Vendors provided the corporation goods and services, such as water and printing, on credit. If E. L. Welch Company reported its income on an accrual accounting basis, it could have deducted the amount charged for those goods and services against income in the year the vendors provided them rather than in a subsequent year when it paid the vendors. *Cf. United States v. Anderson*, 269 U.S. 422 (1926). Thus, regardless of how the corporation acquired debt, it had the ability to use that debt to reduce its tax liability. Moreover, upon its assignment of claims or discharge of its debt in bankruptcy, E. L. Welch Company, based on lower court cases, likely reported no income from the reduction of its liabilities unless that debt relief resulted in its gaining solvency. *See, e.g., E. B. Higley & Co. v. Comm'r*, 25 B.T.A. 127 (1932).

This Court refrains from addressing the question of whether a debtor has taxable income upon the assignment or discharge of debt if the debtor remains insolvent subsequent to the assignment or discharge of that debt. We defer judgment on that issue until such time as a case or controversy before this Court directly raises it. The case before us today presents the question of whether E. L. Welch Company's tax treatment of its debt should affect the tax characterization of the taxpayer's payments to E. L. Welch Company's creditors. We appreciate why the Commissioner and the taxpayer have assumed that the tax consequences surrounding E. L. Welch Company's debt have no pertinence to the proper tax treatment of the taxpayer's payment of the corporation's debt. Their approach parallels that of the statute, which, in general, treats each individual or legal entity as a separate taxpayer.

Yet, to ignore the tax advantages that E. L. Welch Company may have enjoyed as a result of the debt it had incurred and left unpaid raises serious tax fairness issues. The taxpayer claims a deduction for payments to those same creditors, reasoning that they were made for the purpose of advancing his own business interests. If the corporation had met its obligations and repaid its own creditors, the tax law would not have allowed the corporation to take a deduction for those repayments. That E. L. Welch Company may not have had to recognize income upon the assignment or discharge of its debt further weakens the taxpayer's argument that he should be allowed to deduct his payments to the corporation's creditors. His reasoning that tails both he and E. L. Welch Company win and heads the government loses has no place in a self-assessment tax system and we condemn it. Antagonistic and aggressive business practices may have a place within U.S. commerce, but it should never become the norm when taxpayers engage with their government.

When the taxpayer decided to improve his chances for a successful new business venture by settling some of E. L. Welch Company's debt, he blurred the lines between himself and E. L. Welch Company. In contrast to the taxpayer's tacit position that E. L. Welch Company's tax treatment of its debt is not pertinent to this Court's determination of his tax liability, the taxpayer argues that we should acknowledge that the corporation's failure to repay its debts negatively affected taxpayer's business prospects. A fair and just federal income tax system requires this Court to place a taxpayer's reporting positions into context and take account of a taxpayer's familial, professional, and financial relationships. We reject the parties' rigid and constrained analyses that make E. L. Welch Company's tax treatment of its debt irrelevant. To do so would leave the federal income tax system vulnerable to sophisticated financial maneuvers that weaken the income tax law. This Court leaves open the possibility that, under some circumstances, a deduction for a payment of another person's debt may be appropriate. We remand the case for the lower court to examine E. L. Welch Company's tax treatment of its debt. The lower court should deny the taxpayer a deduction for his payments to the creditors of E. L. Welch Company to the extent that the corporation, as a result of its debt, previously had reduced or otherwise avoided tax liability. If the lower court finds that E. L. Welch Company's tax treatment of its debt does not preclude the taxpayer from taking a deduction for payments made to the corporation's creditors, then the lower court must consider whether those payments qualify as "ordinary and necessary."

IV

The taxpayer argues for a definition of "necessary" that relies exclusively on the judgment of the businessman-taxpayer.

> [B]usiness men should have a free hand to adopt such means as will result in increased business and increased income ... and ... the Government should not exercise a supervisory power over the methods adopted, or determine after the event whether the course adopted was wise or unwise, advisable or unadvisable, prudent or imprudent, so long as no law is violated. It is the taxpayer, whose investment is at stake, who should determine ways and means and not the Government.

Pet'r's Br. 10. The taxpayer concedes that he must show that the expenditure meets the objective standard of "reasonably helpful in a business way." *Id.* at 18.

In contrast, the Commissioner argues "necessary" means "essential, needful, requisite, or indispensable." Resp't's Br. 6. Taxpayers cannot deduct expenditures that meet only an "expedient or convenient" standard. *Id.* at 7. The Commissioner reinforces this aspect of his argument by pointing out that the "claims upon which the payments were made were not the obligations of the [taxpayer] . . . and their payment was voluntary and gratuitous and therefore not deductible." *Id.* at 6. While acknowledging that the payments "may have some incidental effect upon his business, the Commissioner finds that the relationship between them and the business is too indirect. *Id.* at 10. The Commissioner's definition of "necessary" relies on an administrative regulation, which requires that the expenditures "directly connect[] with or pertain[] to the taxpayer's trade or business." Treas. Reg. 65, art. 101; *see* Resp't's Br. 8. The Commissioner strengthens the importance of the regulations by reminding us that Congress's repeated reenactment of the statutory provision "constitutes an approval and adoption of [its administrative] construction." Resp't's Br. 8. The Commissioner concludes its argument by stressing to this Court that "[d]eductions are a matter of legislative grace." *Id.*

We find both parties' dogmatic approaches unhelpful. Each seeks to claim superior judgment over the other. The taxpayer does so by asserting the primacy of his business acumen; the Commissioner does so under the auspices of strict statutory construction, regulatory authority, and legalities based on contract law. They have reduced the issue of what constitutes a "necessary" expenditure into a playground fight in which one boy in a pick-up game argues that the baseball he hit was fair while the other boy out in the field yells foul. Neither gives any ground to the other as each claims to have exceptional eyesight and discernment. While the playground dispute entails only one game on one day, the parties' respective interpretations of the term "necessary" jeopardize the current and future fairness and effectiveness of the tax system.

We find that Mary Shelley's Gothic novel, *Frankenstein; or, The Modern Prometheus* (1818, 1831), provides us an analytical framework by which this Court can infuse fair, honorable, and altruistic values into our statutory interpretation of the term "necessary." We do not pretend that Mary Shelley intended to say anything about U.S. businessmen, the marketplace, or taxation. Nevertheless, this rich and compelling text, influenced by Enlightenment writers, nineteenth-century theorists, and Shelley's own understanding of Western civilization's imperialistic and violent history leading to genocide and slavery, has much to teach us about commerce, personal and familial relationships, and cultural norms.

Shelley portrays Dr. Victor Frankenstein in his workshop as an isolated man consumed by his goal to achieve unprecedented glory. His prideful ambition to create life unrestrained by ethical considerations or a web of social and familial relationships clarifies the dangers of the taxpayer's claim for exclusive expertise in the business arena. Shelley's depiction of the creature exposes the harms resulting from uncontrolled efforts to pursue profits. Even as the creature repulses Frankenstein and others, Shelley consistently shows her sympathy toward him, especially when she has the creature narrate poignant moments of his own social deprivation. He describes his life in the hovel where he has taken refuge. His shelter shares a wall with a family's cottage. Through a crack in an otherwise blocked window, he witnesses an elderly father who is blind, his son, and his son's wife lovingly care for and learn from each other. He models his own conduct after theirs by furtively collecting wood for the family fire. As he learns their language and becomes literate, the pain of the creature's outcast status intensifies. For example, he finds a close parallel between himself and Adam's lonely existence in Eden in his reading of John Milton's *Paradise Lost*.

This Court draws a correspondence between Shelley's creature and marketplace successes inspired by individual avarice and selfishness. By allowing the creature to study and mimic fruitful domestic harmony, Shelley allows us to imagine the potential of a marketplace that embraces an ethos of caring. Her moving tale underscores this Court's responsibility to promote a marketplace, and, in turn, an income tax, that esteems prudence, fairness, and ethical conduct. Shelley reminds us that we must challenge taxpayers' arguments that depend on conventional understandings of commerce and an entitlement to deference based solely on business experience. She further admonishes us not to follow the Commissioner's lead and divorce profit-making activities from a taxpayer's ethical and moral responsibilities.

A

The taxpayer asserts the solipsistic argument that he, as well as other businessmen, should be the preeminent arbiters of what constitutes a "necessary" expenditure. The taxpayer presumably would not allow the judgment of his own business associates and workers to be beyond scrutiny. Yet, he asks this Court to adopt a rule that makes expenditures by a businessman virtually unassailable. We acknowledge that the taxpayer has precedent on his side. A number of lower courts have embraced a broad definition of "necessary," checked only by a good faith standard that the expenditures facilitate business generally. *E.g., A. Harris & Co. v. Lucas*, 48 F.2d 187 (5th Cir. 1931); *Am. Rolling Mill Co. v. Comm'r*, 41 F.2d 314 (6th Cir. 1930); *Corning Glass Works v. Lucas*, 37 F.2d 793 (D.C. Cir. 1929). With the benefit of Shelley's cautionary tale, we reject this interpretation of "necessary." The Commissioner and the lower courts must deny deductions for expenditures that taxpayers justify by the naked assertion that the expenditures are "reasonably calculated to further their general business interest." *Corning Glass Works*, 37 F.2d at 170. To do otherwise, places those in the business class in a unique position, as compared to any other class of taxpayers. They would have virtually unchecked authority to decide for themselves what constitutes a deductible expenditure. The taxpayer's interpretation of the term "necessary" impairs this country's progressive tax system while it reinforces unwarranted cultural norms that accord a privileged place to well-heeled commercial interests. We direct that the lower court on remand not defer, without inquiry, to the taxpayer's business acumen and instead consider the following evidentiary factors when deciding the question of whether the taxpayer's payments to E. L. Welch Company's creditors meet the requirement of "necessary."

The lower court should examine the facts surrounding the check endorsement, to which the taxpayer required each of E. L. Welch Company's creditors accede as a condition of their receiving payment from him. The endorsement states in part that the payment "has nothing to do with the present or future business relations with the maker of the check." Without further explanation by the taxpayer, the endorsement would seem to contradict his claim that the payments were "necessary" because they made possible his success in his new business venture. Another part of the taxpayer's testimony adds to our suspicion about whether his payments to E. L. Welch Company's creditors contributed to his financial achievements. His attorney asked him whether his payments led to his business success. Tr. of R. 31. His response tellingly was not an unqualified yes. Instead it was, "Yes, sir, to a certain extent." *Id.*

The omissions in the record should increase the lower court's skepticism about the taxpayer's claim for deference based on his status as a businessman. Other than that he worked in his father's corporation, the record fails to describe the taxpayer's business training, experience, and other entrepreneurial qualifications. Apparently, from his point of view, the fact that he had declared voluntary bankruptcy and that E. L. Welch Company was adjudged involuntarily bankrupt neither detracted from nor required any explanation to support his claim for deference to his business judgment. We appreciate that business ventures come with risks, and sometimes with substantial risks. Given the turbulent economic situation facing workers, investors, and incorporated and unincorporated businesses since the stock market crash of 1929, we are reluctant to judge a bankrupt enterprise too harshly. Nevertheless, the taxpayer's business setbacks reveal the potential threat to the integrity of the income tax law if the lower court were to rely on his business judgment to determine if the payments of E. L. Welch Company's debt qualify as "necessary" under the statute.

The broader context in which the taxpayer made the payments to E. L. Welch Company's creditors raises further questions about the factual basis for the conclusion that the payments to the creditors of E. L. Welch Company qualify as "necessary." The evidence indicates that the taxpayer's business and private life intersected in complex ways with regard to the payments. The taxpayer has testified that he made payments to "personal friends and customers . . . of long standing in the business." Tr. of R. 31. This apparent admission of multifaceted reasons for his paying the debts of the now bankrupt E. L. Welch Company makes his claim that he made the payments largely based on his business judgment less trustworthy.

The taxpayer also has stated that his payments to E. L. Welch Company's creditors reflected his commitment to rebuild his reputation as he entered into his new business venture. With unpaid debt in the hundreds of thousands, he paid disappointed creditors about $47,000 out of the income he earned in the years 1924 through 1928, while retaining $72,000, which he deemed "necessary" for his own "living expenses." *Id.* at 5. The record fails to reveal his personal and familial situation that would explain this level of household expenditures. We take note that, in 1928, nearly 66 percent of taxpayers filing tax returns had less net income than the taxpayer. Bureau of Internal Revenue, U.S. Treasury Dep't, *Statistics of Income for 1928: Compiled from Income Tax Returns and Including Statistics from Estate Tax Returns* (1930). This statistic should lead the lower court to look warily at the taxpayer's stated commitment to do right by the E. L. Welch Company's creditors.

With Shelley's Dr. Frankenstein in mind, this Court directs the lower court to avoid turning the taxpayer into a marketplace hero. We have set out a number of factual, legal, and policy reasons why this Court declines to defer to the taxpayer's business judgment and embrace his definition of "necessary." Our distrust in the taxpayer's understanding of the statutory requirement of "necessary" equals our doubts about the Commissioner's interpretation of that term.

B

The Commissioner has a two-pronged argument: (1) the taxpayer had no legal obligation to make the payments and (2) the payments had only an incidental, rather than a direct, effect upon his business. When the Commissioner focuses exclusively on legal duty, rather than moral and social obligations, he essentially embraces a business environment defined by avaricious, predatory, selfish, and noncollaborative conduct. The Commissioner's approach turns business activities into, at best, the equivalent of sport with strict, unbending rules. At worst, he associates commerce with conflict under which a businessman shuns compromise and cooperation and seeks financial triumph over his counterparts. To interpret "necessary" so narrowly valorizes business norms based on rights and obligations and rejects arrangements based on acknowledged interdependency and accommodation of each other's commercial needs. The Commissioner's distinction between direct and incidental expenditures heightens, rather than mitigates, the risk that the income tax law insufficiently accounts for, let alone encourages, virtuous conduct in the marketplace. We recognize that Congress in its enactments and the Commissioner through implementation of the income tax statute must assure that taxpayers deduct only income-producing expenditures and do not deduct expenditures for personal consumption and gifts. Our concern is that the Commissioner's analysis inadequately achieves those goals.

The analytical framework derived from Shelley's novel reveals why the Commissioner's two-pronged approach is too lenient. It fails to include a third prong that examines common business expenditures containing consumptive components. Seldom do we observe the Commissioner limit a deduction for an expenditure that mixes business and consumption, such as rental costs for a business executive's luxury office. By failing to adopt an approach that denies or at least limits the amount of a deduction for this type of expenditure, the Commissioner valorizes individual business owners and corporations over labor, strengthens taxpayers' claims regarding their business acumen, reinforces the elite status of some employees over others, and undercuts the progressivity of the income tax system. *Frankenstein* demonstrates the degree to which conventional understandings of the private sphere of the home and the public sphere of the marketplace have captured the Commissioner and lower courts. With the marketplace primarily viewed as the domain for men to act out their greed and aggression and earn respect by their doing so, the Commissioner has failed to assure that his rulings and regulations protect tax progressivity and weaken unproductive social hierarchies.

This Court, again with the help of Shelley's tale, has come to appreciate why the Commissioner's two-pronged approach also is too strict. The Commissioner's interpretation of "necessary" establishes a nearly impenetrable boundary between the domestic sphere and the marketplace. Shelley depicts the creature in his hovel observing the domestic activities in the cottage.

She contrasts that with Frankenstein in his workshop obsessed with the arrogant dream that he alone could fabricate a new form of life. The creature's hovel separated by a wall from the cottage can be understood, in our reading of the novel, as a liminal space in which the creature observes and values the power and productivity of the domestic sphere. At the risk of extending our unusual interpretation of Shelley's text too far, we view the creature in the hovel as the equivalent of the income tax law. Rather than locating the income tax law exclusively within the income-producing marketplace, our statutory interpretation of "necessary" embraces the productive and collaborative nature of the domestic sphere. This Court's approach has the further benefit of the tax law encouraging marketplace actors to accord higher regard to those who conduct themselves ethically and fairly than to those who achieve significant financial success through sharp practices.

The Commissioner, with his challenge to the taxpayer's deductions for payments to E. L. Welch Company's creditors, marks those expenditures as outside marketplace norms. He essentially equates business and profit-making with all that goes on in Frankenstein's isolated workshop and rejects the productive and collaborative nature of the domestic sphere. The Commissioner's analysis leads to his ignoring the values to which the creature aspires from his vantage point in the hovel. Shelley's *Frankenstein* serves as a lesson to this Court that traditional commercial conduct and understandings obscure how the income tax law and its implementation can harden the distinctions between the private and public spheres. Even if we are overdetermining the significance of the liminal features of the hovel, Shelley's cautionary novel still leads us to interpret the income tax law in a manner that does not exacerbate the inequalities those spheres hold in place. The tax law should not embody the privileged status enjoyed by men over women or promote the prestige enjoyed by corporate managers, business owners, and investors at the expense of employees, tradespeople, and other laborers.

Our reading of *Frankenstein* has its roots in one of the most significant political developments of this century. The political activism of the suffragist movement and the enactment of the Nineteenth Amendment in 1920, giving women the right to vote, have diminished the boundaries between the private and public spheres and undermined social stratifications. This movement and its success lead us to challenge our preconceived notions of business and business conduct. Women's suffrage has the potential to transform the political world and the U.S. economy. One now can envision women playing major roles at the local, state, and federal levels of government and exerting considerable influence on lawmaking, including the income tax. Their new-found standing creates new opportunities for women in the economic arena as well.

Some women and men may continue to embrace greed and participate wholeheartedly in the battle for money and economic power. Others, however, may resist the notion of business as a blood sport and look to incorporate the virtues typically associated with the domestic sphere into the marketplace. The economic crisis this country currently faces directs all of us to reconsider our outdated conceptions of business and businessmen. With women having more opportunity to provide political and economic leadership during this difficult period in U.S. history, the rigid distinctions between the home and the marketplace likely will dissipate, allowing all of us to reimagine commerce.

In the face of this defining moment in U.S. history, we conclude that our analysis of the income tax law can no longer rely on customary criteria to determine what constitutes personal consumption and what constitutes profit-making expenditures. The income tax and its implementation must evolve to accommodate the major cultural changes that have occurred and still lie ahead. With Shelley's *Frankenstein* as our guide, we reject the taxpayer's claim of privilege based on his business acumen. We also decline to accept the Commissioner's implicit argument that we should constrain "necessary" to mean norms equating the marketplace to a battleground. Instead, this Court defines "necessary" to mean prudent and fair business conduct that enhances, or at least does not weaken, tax progressivity.

We recognize that the lower court on remand may benefit from more guidance when it applies this definition. Without intending to presuppose what the evidence will show on remand, this Court uses a few examples below to assist the lower court in its determination of whether the taxpayer's payments to E. L. Welch Company's creditors meet the requirement of "necessary." These examples assume that the lower court has found that E. L. Welch Company's tax treatment of its debt does not preclude the taxpayer's deduction of payments made to the corporation's creditors. If the lower court finds that the taxpayer did not significantly constrain his living expenses or make other meaningful financial sacrifices during the time he made payments to E. L. Welch Company's creditors, the taxpayer's assertions that he made the payments as a matter of moral obligation and to reestablish his credit and business reputation carry less credibility. Findings of this type, in the absence of countervailing evidence, should lead the lower court to find that the payments fail to meet the "necessary" requirement. If the lower court finds that taxpayer made a payment to a creditor of E. L. Welch Company with whom the taxpayer had a long-term friendship to the exclusion of those creditors with whom he had primarily a business relationship, that payment, in the absence of countervailing evidence, should not qualify as "necessary." In contrast, if the lower court finds that taxpayer made a payment to a creditor of E. L. Welch Company with whom the taxpayer had, subsequent to his and the corporation's bankruptcies, obtained further credit or other assistance to his business, then that payment, in the absence of countervailing evidence, should qualify as "necessary." This finding rejects legal obligation as a talisman and acknowledges the importance of ongoing relationships in the marketplace built on trust and fair dealing. It also establishes a tax rule that encourages and valorizes those conducting trades and businesses who act collaboratively with, rather than in opposition to, their customers, creditors, workers, and even their competitors. This Court recognizes that our definition of "necessary" provides more opportunities for business taxpayers to reduce their tax liabilities as compared to employee taxpayers. In that respect, our characterization of the "necessary" requirement parallels the ones set forth by the taxpayer and the Commissioner. This Court's interpretation of "necessary" has the advantage of promoting cultural norms of fairness and rejecting unwarranted regard for conventional business practices.

V

A determination of the proper treatment of the taxpayer's payments to E. L. Welch Company's creditors requires this Court to match its robust definition of "necessary" with a correspondingly dynamic definition of "ordinary." The Commissioner interprets "ordinary" to mean "common, usual, often recurring." Resp't's Br. 6. In the context of the U.S. marketplace marked by greed, selfishness, and disharmony over the last several decades, the language of "common" and "usual" discourages taxpayers from establishing alternative approaches to commerce. That limitation seems especially pernicious now that women are gaining greater opportunities for economic success in the United States. The Commissioner's limited view of "ordinary" holds considerable risk to the economy and the commonweal in general. Under his definition, taxpayers – women as well as men – would have no incentives to introduce, through their expenditures, the virtues of prudence, fairness, and cooperation into their business dealings. This Court refuses to adopt the Commissioner's approach to the "ordinary" requirement. Instead, we interpret "ordinary" to mean an expenditure incurred by a taxpayer with the reasonable expectation that it will increase income or reduce costs. We embrace this characterization of "ordinary" because it supports alternatives to the adversarial and noncollaborative traditions prevailing in the current marketplace and allows for evolving commercial norms.

By tying the requirement of "ordinary" to a taxpayer's particular business situation and relating an expenditure to that taxpayer's profit-making strategy, this Court underscores the importance of the context under which a tax issue arises and minimizes the tax law's interference with innovative commercial practices. For example, our definition of "ordinary" would give the Commissioner authority to challenge expenditures, such as the previously mentioned rental costs for an executive's luxury office. Although these pricey rentals may be common and usual, a taxpayer may have a difficult time showing that a less expensive space would reduce the income that the taxpayer could earn or increase that taxpayer's other costs. Without presuming the outcome on remand, we can contrast the example of the rental costs for a luxury office to the taxpayer's payment to a creditor of E. L. Welch Company. It could qualify as "ordinary" if the taxpayer is able to show that the payment allowed him to avoid other costs, such as a higher interest rate or an additional loan requirement. The example of rental costs for an executive's luxury office demonstrates how this Court's definition of "ordinary" contests long-encrusted business norms. The example of a payment to another person's creditor establishes how our definition can accommodate prudent and fair business practices.

The term "ordinary" performs yet a second function in the determination of a taxpayer's annual income tax liability. The requirement of "ordinary" in the statute precludes an immediate deduction for expenditures related to the acquisition of a durable asset, even if it otherwise qualifies as "ordinary and necessary" as we have defined both terms above. The taxpayer argues that his payments are more appropriately in the nature of a current expenditure, such as advertising. Pet'r's Br. 9. The Commissioner argues that, if the taxpayer's payments of E. L. Welch Company's debt qualify as business related because they enhanced or restored his reputation, they are in the nature of the acquisition of a durable asset, such as goodwill. Resp't's Br. 10. The advertising/goodwill dispute between the parties reflects the well-recognized distinction between an expenditure that repairs a durable asset rather than replaces or improves that asset so as to increase its value and prolong its useful life. A taxpayer can immediately deduct the former type of expenditures, but must capitalize the latter type. *Ill. Merch. Tr. Co. v. Comm'r*, 4 B.T.A. 103, 106 (1926), *acq.*, 1926 V-2 C.B. 2.

The capitalization issue surrounding the taxpayer's payments to E. L. Welch Company's creditors obscures a more far-reaching question about human capital. Once again Shelley's nineteenth-century novel provides us important insights and demonstrates the inadequacies of the conventional tax analysis found in the parties' briefs. Frankenstein may have provided the sinews to replicate a human, but the creature attains humanity through his observations of life inside the cottage and the books he reads. Shelley turns him into a sympathetic figure by allowing him to acquire human capital. He learns how to be empathetic, generous, and attentive to the needs of others. This aspect of her tale leads us to conclude that human capital must have a consequential role in the interpretation of the income tax law, including the interpretation of the terms "necessary," "ordinary," and "durable asset."

Past applications of the income tax statute and accompanying regulations essentially have relegated human capital to the domestic sphere. The law has treated expenditures, such as university tuition, as personal consumption. With the apparent assumption that any expenditure having to do with human capital is *prima facie* nondeductible, the Commissioner concludes that the expenditures having to do with the taxpayer's reputation only indirectly related to his business. For practical and administrative reasons, the tax law must consign to the domestic sphere many human capital expenditures incurred by taxpayers, such as food and shelter. Nevertheless, this Court holds that expenditures incurred to enhance a taxpayer's reputation can, under certain circumstances, relate to the taxpayer's trade or business. By this holding, we intend to retrieve some expenditures for human capital from the domestic sphere and recognize them as part of the marketplace. In particular, we intend to treat as business related those expenditures incurred by a taxpayer to maintain, acquire, or reestablish an honest and forthright business reputation. In so doing, we institute a tax rule that supports and encourages ethical and fair marketplace practices.

An analysis of human capital in which the more sizeable the investment in human capital, the less likely it will be deductible, at first may seem counter-intuitive. The inability to deduct the investment initially arises from the fact that the larger the investment, the more likely the law will characterize that investment as an acquisition or a replacement of a durable asset. The law could mitigate that result if Congress were to change course and allow for amortization of intangible assets in general. If it did that, then taxpayers who make significant investments in their business reputations, for example, could deduct their investments over a number of years. This Court necessarily leaves the question of amortization of intangible assets for the Congress to address. The inability of the taxpayer, under current law, to amortize a significant investment in his reputation does not mean that this Court should not recognize the possibility that his payments to E. L. Welch Company's credit-ors could represent a repair, rather than a replacement, of his reputation and, thereby, qualify as immediately deductible.

The parties' briefs inadequately address the question of the proper role of human capital in the measurement of the taxpayer's taxable income. We remand this issue to the lower court to determine whether one or more of the payments to E. L. Welch Company's creditors improved the taxpayer's business reputation; and, if so, whether any of those payments were in the nature of a repair, as opposed to a replacement or a substantial improvement, of his reputation. The lower court should reach the questions surrounding human capital only if it has determined that the taxpayer's payments to E. L. Welch Company's creditors are otherwise deductible based on the guidance we have set forth above. If the lower court finds that a payment repaired the taxpayer's reputation, then the taxpayer can deduct it. If the lower court finds that a payment replaced or substantially improved his reputation, then the taxpayer must capitalize that expenditure.

The decree should be *reversed*. The case is remanded for further proceedings consistent with this opinion.

6

Commentary on *United States v. Davis*

LINDA M. BEALE

BACKGROUND

In *United States v. Davis*, decided June 4, 1962, the Supreme Court of the United States considered the appropriate treatment of a transfer of appreciated stock (and the deductibility of Mr. Davis's payment of his former wife's legal expenses in connection with the property transfer) on the joint income tax return of Thomas Davis and his new wife.[1] Mr. Davis transferred the stock to his former wife in satisfaction of any claims she might have against him, pursuant to a settlement agreement entered into prior to their divorce.[2] The Court agreed to take the case because of a conflict in the lower courts regarding the proper treatment of intramarital transfers for relinquishment of rights. The U.S. Tax Court (at that time, the Board of Tax Appeals) had concluded in two cases decided in 1940 and 1941 that such transfers were not taxable because the value of the wife's marital rights was indeterminable,[3] but the U.S. Courts of Appeals for the Third and Second Circuits, respectively, had reversed because "gain could be measured on the assumption that the relinquished marital rights were equal in value to the property transferred."[4] The Tax Court had followed the appellate decisions in subsequent cases,[5] but was reversed by the Sixth Circuit under the same logic originally applied by the Board of Tax Appeals in the earlier cases.[6] The Sixth Circuit's opinion came after the Court of Claims' 1954 foundational *Philadelphia Park Amusement Co.* case that determined that the fair market value of consideration

---

[1] 370 U.S. 65 (1962), *rev'g in part & aff'g in part*, 287 F.2d 168 (Ct. Cl. 1961).   [2] *Id.*
[3] Halliwell v. Comm'r, 44 B.T.A. 740 (1941); Mesta v. Comm'r, 42 B.T.A. 933 (1940).
[4] *Davis*, 370 U.S. at 68 (citing Comm'r v. Halliwell, 131 F.2d 642 (2d Cir. 1942), and Comm'r v. Mesta, 123 F.2d 986 (3d Cir. 1941)).
[5] *Id.* at 67–68 (citing a group of cases from 1947 through 1958).
[6] *Id.* at 68 (citing Comm'r v. Marshman, 279 F.2d 27 (1960)).

of indeterminate value is the value of the property for which it is exchanged in an arm's-length transaction.[7] The *Davis* case presented the Supreme Court the opportunity to decide the matter in the divorce context. The Justices reached a unanimous conclusion that the marital transfer was taxable as an exchange of valuable property for the release of an independent legal obligation.

ORIGINAL OPINION

The Court's unanimous decision in *Davis*, written by Justice Clark, is quite short. It briefly sets out a bare minimum of facts of the Davis's 1955 divorce under a separation agreement and voluntary property settlement. Those facts are worth expanding upon.

Thomas and Alice Davis were married in 1941. Thomas Davis was a high-ranking officer in E. I. DuPont de Nemours & Co. who was awarded stock in the company over his career as a bonus in connection with his employment.[8] After fourteen years of marriage resulted in a parting of the ways, the couple's property settlement agreed on a "division of their property,"[9] providing (among other things) for a transfer from the husband to the wife of one thousand shares of appreciated DuPont stock in "full settlement and satisfaction of any and all claims and rights against the husband whatsoever (including but not by way of limitation, dower and all rights under the laws of testacy and intestacy)."[10] In 1955, Davis transferred the first half of the stock having a basis of $74,775 and a value of $82,250.[11]

The couple lived in Delaware, a common law property state. A division of marital property under a divorce decree in a community property state was considered a division of jointly owned property, but it was not so considered in common law jurisdictions. Indeed, Delaware law gave Davis's former wife nothing other than an inchoate interest in the stock.[12]

Davis, who also remarried in 1955, filed a joint tax return for 1955 with his new wife, Grace.[13] He excluded the gain from the transfer of stock to his former wife, while also deducting various attorney's fees, including his

---

[7]   Philadelphia Park Amusement Co. v. United States, 126 F. Supp. 184 (Ct. Cl. 1954).

[8]   Karen B. Brown, *The Story of* Davis: *Transfers of Property Pursuant to Divorce, in* TAX STORIES 171, 172 (Paul L. Caron ed., 2d ed. 2009).

[9]   *Id.* (quoting the property settlement as incorporated into the January 5, 1955 divorce decree). The settlement is also quoted in Brief for Petitioner at 8, *Davis*, 370 U.S. 65 (Nos. 190, 268).

[10] *Davis*, 370 U.S. at 67.   [11] *Id.*

[12] "[T]he inchoate rights granted a wife in her husband's property by the Delaware law do not even remotely reach the dignity of co-ownership." *Id.* at 70.

[13] *Id.* at 66 n.1.

payment of his former wife's legal expenses for tax services related to the property settlement. The Internal Revenue Service assessed a deficiency, which Davis paid, on the basis of a capital gain of $3,737 (half the gain was deductible) and the disallowance of a portion of the claimed deduction for attorney's fees. Davis then sued in the U.S. Court of Claims (restructured in 1982 as the U.S. Court of Federal Claims), where he argued that the division of property between the spouses was nontaxable and that the transfer was not in satisfaction of his obligation to support his former wife. The Court of Claims rejected applicability of the *Philadelphia Park* case in the marital context, holding that the gain was not taxable because of the indeterminacy of the value of the relinquishment of his wife's rights. It allowed deduction only of fees relating to tax advice to Mr. Davis.

In line with the times, the Justices seemed oblivious to any gender equity issues at stake in their decision when they unanimously reversed the Court of Claims to conclude the transfer was taxable as an exchange of valuable property (the appreciated stock) for the release of the husband's independent legal obligation (the wife's dower and all rights under the laws of testacy and intestacy). The Justices reflected the patronizing view of women still prevalent at the time when they merely mentioned Davis's new wife in a footnote as a party to the proceedings.[14] Their language in discussing the former wife's property interests, and basis in the property acquired, was similarly dismissive and patronizing. Their consideration of the long-term policy implications for divorcing wives in a variety of financial circumstances was nonexistent.

There is no dispute in the case that Congress intends appreciation on stock to be taxed. The question is when the tax should be assessed in the marital context – when the husband transfers it to the wife, or when the wife later disposes of the stock. The government essentially argued that the marital context did not matter: the husband should be taxed by analogy with other transfers of property for release of independent legal obligations. The taxpayer's main argument was that the transaction between husband and former wife should be treated as a voluntary division of property between co-owners and not as a taxable exchange. He argued that this would appropriately equalize treatment of spouses' property divisions in common law states with the settled law for such divisions in community property states, avoiding a state-based property differentiation that should have no relevance for tax purposes.[15]

---

[14] The Court's opinion discusses the tax consequences for Thomas Davis as "the taxpayer" and merely notes in a footnote that his new wife, Grace Ethel Davis, was also a party to the proceeding because a joint return was filed in 1955. *Id.*

[15] *Id.* at 69–70.

Instead of taking the opportunity to recognize the basic equality rights of
married women wherever they might live, the Justices justified their decision with reliance on the legalistic niceties of Delaware law, in a short two
paragraphs that roamed close to old notions of coverture.

> The wife has no interest – passive or active – over the management or
> disposition of her husband's personal property. Her rights are not descend-
> able, and she must survive him to share in his intestate estate. Upon dissolu-
> tion of the marriage she shares in the property only to such extent as the court
> deems "reasonable." What is "reasonable" might be ascertained independ-
> ently of the extent of the husband's property by such criteria as the wife's
> financial condition, her needs in relation to her accustomed station in life,
> her age and health, the number of children and their ages, and the earning
> capacity of the husband.
> ... Delaware seems only to place a burden on the husband's property
> rather than to make the wife a part owner thereof. ... [T]he rights of
> succession ... do not differ significantly from the husband's obligations of
> support and alimony. They all partake more of a personal liability of the
> husband than a property interest of the wife.[16]

The Justices' response hardly took into account the argument for equal treatment of spouses in common law and community property states. It noted that
the Court has "not ignored" the jurisdictional differences in other cases (citing
Poe v. Seaborn[17]) and that Congress has alleviated the differential treatment
in some cases but not others. Further, it suggested that the "long-standing
administrative practice" in this area and "settled state of law in the lower
courts" that differed only on the question of whether the gain is indeterminable (and not on whether the transfer was a taxable event) created a "unanimity of views" relied on by taxpayers that supported taxability as a reasonable
interpretation of the statute.[18]

In reversing the Court of Claims' decision that the amount realized by
Davis was indeterminable, the Justices assumed that the settlement discussions ending the marriage were arm's length and therefore subject to the
Philadelphia Park holding.[19] Almost as an aside, they acknowledged the
emotional conflict impinging on decisions in the context of marital dissolu-
tions, suggesting that such facts may "weaken" the arm's-length assumption, but then they simply dismissed that consideration because of the
decision that the transaction was taxable.[20] They appended a concern about
uncertainty as to the wife's basis in the transferred property if the event were

---

[16] *Id.* at 70 (citations omitted). This language directly follows the sentence quoted *supra* note 12.
[17] 282 U.S. 101 (1930).   [18] *Davis*, 370 U.S. at 71.   [19] *Id.* at 72.   [20] *Id.*

not taxable, suggesting that "she might suffer inordinately" if she had to counter a government assessment.[21]

The Supreme Court affirmed the Court of Claims' holding on attorney's fees with little discussion.

FEMINIST PERSPECTIVES ON *DAVIS*

For many feminists, the *Davis* opinion and the congressional override via the enactment of Code § 1041 two decades later represent a quagmire of issues concerning the appropriate governmental position on the basic unit of taxation, the prioritization of marriage, and the role of family in determining tax policy. This unsettled feminist view of marriage stems in part from the long history of patriarchy and the legal concept of coverture in which women's property and very being were treated as absorbed by the male marital partner.[22] Yet whenever special provisions protect members of a marital union from taxation while subjecting singles to greater tax liabilities, the government has thrown its weight in favor of legalized marital unions. If the government does not provide similar tax benefits to domestic partnerships between unmarried couples or even less traditional living arrangements such as extended families, it has given its imprimatur to marital relations over other kinds of common living arrangements among people. Feminists who favor strictly egalitarian treatment for women and men and/or consider governmental pressure to form legally sanctioned marital unions a limitation on women's power to shape their lives and relationships may well find the original *Davis* rule that transfers in connection with a divorce are taxable less troubling than the § 1041 solution of nontaxability two decades later. The § 1041 result, for example, can be problematic because the property transferor, who in many cases has more power in the relationship and more property, receives a tax deferral while shifting the tax liability in respect of appreciation that occurred while the transferor held the property to the transferee, who may be in a more vulnerable position – especially if she sells quickly because of need. The American Law Institute had essentially proposed the § 1041 solution in 1954.[23]

---

[21] *Id.* at 73.

[22] *See, e.g.*, Erez Aloni, *Commentary on* Obergefell v. Hodges, *in* FEMINIST JUDGMENTS: REWRITTEN OPINIONS OF THE UNITED STATES SUPREME COURT 527, 529 (Kathryn M. Stanchi, Linda L. Berger & Bridget J. Crawford eds., 2016) (referencing Paula Ettelbrick, *Since When Is Marriage a Path to Liberation?*, OUT/LOOK, Fall 1989, at 14, and Erez Aloni, *Registering Relationships*, 87 TUL. L. REV. 573, 619–21 (2013)).

[23] FED. INCOME TAX STATUTE § X257 (AM. LAW INST., Draft Feb. 1954). The comments suggest that the change is appropriate because "marital settlements, in a sense, are involuntary

A 1963 commentary reflecting the implicit bias favoring the husband proposed similar legislation:

> By deferring the collection of the capital gains tax . . . the tax will be imposed at a time when the wife has the cash proceeds from the sale. In any case, such a method would prevent the taxing of the husband at the very moment when he is seriously depleting his estate and receiving in return *the release of the wife's marital rights which is worth nothing to anyone except himself.*[24]

In spite of these problems with the § 1041 solution, most feminists strongly object to the Justices' language and rationales in reaching the *Davis* holding, which seemed "out of touch with the realities of modern marital relations."[25]

In their failure to focus on the real-life mechanisms of divorce settlements, coupled with their patronizing disregard of the current wife and similarly patronizing treatment of the former wife and the emotional conflicts inherent in a marital breakup, the Justices revealed their insulation from the expectations and complexities of marriage and divorce. Whereas many spouses likely consider transfers within the family and even on divorce as gifts, the Justices relegated the taxpayer's arguments from that perspective to another dismissive footnote that labeled gift treatment "unrealistic" and stated flatly that a "negotiated settlement" (even in the marital context) cannot be a "gift in any sense of the term."[26]

The critiques of *Davis* are extensive, often focusing on complexity and the potential for whipsaw of the IRS.[27] One comment noted the inconsistency with Code § 267's approach and suggested that "the Court indulged in some analytically weak reasoning which may lead to an inequitable and inconsistent tax consequence" when it assumed arm's-length negotiations in divorce.[28] States attempted to avoid the *Davis* result by creating special characterizations of marital property rights.[29] The divorce context was complicated by the

---

exchanges" and it will be "much simpler" to avoid valuation until a later disposition, though they acknowledge the tax impact on the wife. *Id.* at 367–68.

[24] Note, *Federal Taxation: Tax Consequences of Divorce Property Settlements*, 1963 DUKE L.J. 365, 373 n.41 [hereinafter *Federal Taxation*] (emphasis added).

[25] Ajay K. Mehrotra, *Teaching Tax Stories*, 55 J. LEGAL EDUC. 116, 120 (2005) (describing Brown's criticism of the Court, in Brown, *supra* note 8).

[26] *Davis*, 370 U.S. at 69 n.6.

[27] *See, e.g.*, Paula J. Rice, *The Overruling of the* Davis *Case by the Enactment of Section 1041*, 4 BOS. U. J. TAX L. 123, 123–26, 123 n.5 & 125–26 nn.17–19 (1986) (citing various negative commentaries).

[28] *Federal Taxation*, *supra* note 24, at 368–70.

[29] *See, e.g.*, Leon Gabinet, *Section 1041: The High Price of Quick Fix Reform in Taxation of Interspousal Transfers*, 5 AM. J. TAX POL'Y 13, 14 & n.10 (1986) (noting statutory provisions in Oregon, Illinois, Minnesota, Kansas, Missouri, and North Carolina).

Farid-Es-Sultaneh case decided a decade and a half earlier, in which the Court determined that a wife had a cost basis in shares received pursuant to an antenuptual agreement in a transfer from her husband-to-be in relinquishment of marital property rights in her husband's estate.[30]

The various concerns led Congress in 1984 to enact Code § 1041 to make transfers between spouses and incident to divorce nontaxable events and give the recipient spouse a carryover basis in the property so transferred.[31] Congress explained that its decision was to correct the problems of whipsaw and uncertainty caused by the *Davis* decision while "mak[ing] the tax laws as unintrusive as possible with respect to relations between spouses."[32] The enactment provided a consistent rule across varying state jurisdictions and removed the oddity in the *Davis* opinion that the transferor spouse had a taxable transaction while the transferee spouse paid no tax on the exchange but received a stepped-up basis in the transferred property.

THE CAIN DISSENT AS A FEMINIST JUDGMENT

The feminist opinion of Professor Patricia A. Cain, writing as Justice Cain, does not resolve the feminist angst regarding appropriate treatment of various living arrangements as single taxable units, though that feminist concern underlies the initial discussion noting that wives are not "strangers" and that court decisions should recognize "the normal consequences of family solidarity." The Cain dissent on the treatment of the transfer of property also utilizes feminist theory in various ways to reject the dismissive and patronizing views projected by the Justices in the original opinion in support of Cain's position that the transfer should not be subject to tax.

Cain's dissent first argues against the systemic nature of women's inequality by looking to the realities of women's life experience of modern marriages (even in the 1960s) as partnerships between two individuals, a concept that is vastly different from the legal concept of coverture because it presumes that women can and do exercise autonomy and choice in their lives.[33] Cain accords here with the school of thought sometimes labeled "liberal feminism,"

---

[30] Farid-Es-Sultaneh v. Comm'r, 160 F.2d 812 (2d Cir. 1947).
[31] Deficit Reduction Act of 1984, Pub. L. No. 98-369, § 421, 98 Stat. 494, 793.
[32] STAFF OF JOINT COMM. ON TAXATION, 98TH CONG., GENERAL EXPLANATION OF THE REVENUE PROVISIONS OF THE DEFICIT REDUCTION ACT OF 1984, at 711 (Comm. Print 1984).
[33] *See* Patricia A. Cain, *Feminist Legal Scholarship*, 77 IOWA L. REV. 19, 20 (1971) (indicating that "analysis is formed by a distinctly feminist point of view ... shaped by an understanding of women's life experiences").

which argues that women should be treated as making, and allowed under law to make, choices in the same way as men.[34] Unlike the opinion of the Court that looked to a final "arm's-length" negotiation between the spouses over property, Cain thus focuses on the marriage in its entirety, a partnership that began in 1941 (a fact not mentioned in the Court's opinion) in a gendered world in which husbands worked and held title to most property while wives were assumed to work at home. She challenges the reader to understand the interplay between equality (a partnership between man and woman, something in this sense not unlike business partnerships or joint tenancies that are not generally subject to taxation upon dissolution) and difference (the actual differences among people, as well as the societally structured gendered roles for men and women).[35] This emphasis on the importance of relationships also borrows from communitarian feminists the theory that women are most empowered when they can function as members of communities with networks of relationships.

Second, Cain's dissent explodes the purportedly objective view the Court takes of the laws of different states, which lies at the root of the Court's justification (based on Delaware's laws on wives' property interests) for its dismissive treatment of the equality argument. Labelling this as "nonsense," Cain's dissent points out the "truth" and "reality" of community property wives' rights – including lack of management power and fewer rights than common law wives have in jointly owned common law property – in spite of the courts' legal fiction that community property wives are sufficiently vested to be treated as co-owners in the divorce context. This follows a strong feminist tradition of revealing the flaws in purportedly objective reasoning that often rests in society's implicit male bias.[36]

Finally, Cain's dissent deals with the impact of the Court's decision on women generally – not just Alice Davis, but divorcing wives in all the range of circumstances in which they find themselves at the moment of divorce, in spite of the affection that spurred the marriage at the outset. This final argument can perhaps be understood best in terms of feminists in the critical

---

[34] *See, e.g.*, Martha Chamallas, Introduction to Feminist Legal Theory 24–25 (1999) (discussing equality theorists).

[35] *See* Martha Minow, Making All the Difference: Inclusion, Exclusion, and American Law (1990) (developing a relational approach showing that neutral strategies purporting to disregard differences and special treatment explicitly acknowledging differences can both reinforce difference's stigma).

[36] *See, e.g.*, Catharine A. MacKinnon, *Difference and Dominance: On Sex Discrimination, in* Feminism Unmodified: Discourses on Life and Law 32, 36 (1987).

legal scholarship movement who argue for empowerment of women.[37] This approach asks the courts (again) to recognize the real-life experiences of women and directly consider which tax policy is the best to pursue, taking the full context of marriage, divorce, the history of disadvantage from coverture, and the empowerment struggle of women into account. This forces the court to acknowledge the potential for future harm to women if husbands offer less property in settlements because of the *Davis* rule. It also provides a basis for considering the transfer a gift, as the partners themselves may consider it because of their long-term committed relationship and the complex motives operative in divorce.

Cain concurs in the majority's decision regarding Mr. Davis's payment of his former wife's attorney's fees. Affirming that husband and wife are separate taxpayers, Cain agrees that his payments on her behalf are not deductible to him.

If there had been a feminist-oriented dissent such as Cain's on the taxation of the property transfer in the original *Davis* case, it might have led Congress to view the negotiations around dissolution of long-term marital relationships as something quite distinct from commercial, arm's-length negotiations. It likely would have led Congress to respond more quickly to the emerging view, evidenced in the American Law Institute's 1954 proposal, that transactions between spouses should not be taxable events. More importantly, it might have hastened recognition of the continuing subordinated position of wives in both community property and common law property states and helped to ignite a movement for courts making these kinds of decisions to consider more broadly the implicitly biased perspective that disregards wives' experiences, relationships, and interests in equal treatment with their spouses.

UNITED STATES v. DAVIS, 370 U.S. 65 (1962)

JUSTICE PATRICIA A. CAIN, DISSENTING
IN PART AND CONCURRING IN PART

My brethren have concluded that marital partners who are dissolving their relationship should be treated as legal strangers who are negotiating over

---

[37] *See, e.g.*, Frances Olsen, *Statutory Rape: A Feminist Critique of Rights Analysis*, 63 TEX. L. REV. 387 (1984) (providing a critique of statutory rape closely aligned with Catharine MacKinnon's antisubordination perspective revealing the falsity of the supposed objectivity of the law).

whatever ownership rights they might have in property that was acquired during their marital relationship. Whatever their agreement is, whether founded in honor to their private agreements or love for each other or in a desire to end what has become a burdensome relationship, the majority treats their agreement the same as any commercial agreement between a seller and a buyer at arm's length, where no such emotions are involved. And that is correct. If A transfers appreciated property to B in settlement of a debt owed to B, then yes, A will realize and recognize a gain on that transfer.

But in the case of divorcing spouses, the two parties are not really at arm's length. As we noted in *Helvering v. Clifford*, the wife should not be treated as a "complete stranger," and we should not "obscure the normal consequences of family solidarity." 309 U.S. 331, 336–37 (1940). If husband and wife cannot be treated as independent partners during the marriage, I see no reason to treat them as such when they divorce. Because I think the majority's view of this transaction denies the reality of the situation in which these two taxpayers experienced this transaction, I dissent.

Simone de Beauvoir, the feminist author of *The Second Sex*, described marriage as an "honorable career." Simone de Beauvoir, *The Second Sex* 327 (H.M. Parshley ed. & trans., 1953). She was, of course, referring to the woman in the marriage. Men have careers outside of marriage. Beauvoir's view of more modern marriages was that they were "a union freely entered into by the consent of two independent persons" who have reciprocal obligations to each other. *Id.* at 414. She also observed: "To 'catch' a husband is an art, to 'hold' him is a job – and one in which great competence is called for." *Id.* at 453. While Beauvoir's view of marriage clearly painted the husband as the meaningful existential actor, it included notions of agency by the wife and a certain amount of interdependence.

Today we should view marriage as a partnership. Two individuals come together. They make pledges to each other in which they promise to engage in joint efforts to establish a better life for both of them. Together. But together as two legal individuals and not as one legal entity in which only the husband could be a legal actor. That was coverture, and by 1962 we should be well beyond coverture, the old English system of marital property rights where the wife did not exist. *See, e.g.,* 1 William Blackstone, *Commentaries on the Laws of England* 442 (3d ed. 1768) (1753). Unfortunately, however, vestiges of coverture can be found in the tone of the majority opinion in this case.

Today, in 1962, wives should be, in the eyes of the law, equal partners with their husbands. To treat Mrs. Davis as an equal partner from the beginning of the marriage and through to the end of the marriage would accord her the same autonomy that we give to business partners who strike a bargain to work together on a project. Our tax laws do not tax those partners when they form their partnership and we do not generally tax them when they dissolve their partnership.

Instead, the majority seems to treat the two spouses as legal strangers, while at the same time denying the wife her just position in the marital partnership. Justice Clark's opinion suggests that the two spouses were negotiating at the time of divorce, and it is that negotiation that makes the transaction a taxable one, akin to a bargained-for exchange at a rummage sale. 370 U.S. at 69–71. This characterization totally ignores the beginning of the partnership. That is when the relevant bargain takes place. And both spouses should be viewed as equal bargainers at that moment of beginning (although history often tells us that the pernicious promise of romantic love may often weaken the woman in this initial bargain). *See, e.g.,* Beauvoir, *supra,* at 608 (quoting Lord Byron as saying, "Man's love is of man's life a thing apart; 'Tis woman's whole existence'"). Indeed, Beauvoir argues throughout her book *The Second Sex* that because women's options are limited, they are often more willing to compromise, believing that is their only option in the love relationship. *See* Beauvoir, *supra, passim.* Nonetheless, the law should recognize both spouses as equal bargainers in the beginning. Each had the ability to say yes or no to the formation of the partnership.

So, let us take a closer look at this initial bargain, the ensuing marriage, and dissolution. There are relevant facts here that the majority opinion simply ignores. That is because the majority focuses only on the moment of dissolution, ignoring context and history.

The marriage of Mr. and Mrs. Davis began in 1941. What were the promises and expectations then? In the best of times two people would promise to do their best to support and protect each other. But, of course, in 1941 each spouse, at least in families similar to the Davis family, would have been assigned a uniquely gendered role in carrying out that promise. Husbands would work in the marketplace. Wives would stay home and have babies, care for them, and provide basic support for husbands. As a result of these gendered roles, husbands would typically hold title to all the property acquired during the marriage. Despite the fact that any property acquired may be attributed to the efforts of both spouses, the wife typically would not have been recognized as a legal owner of the acquired property. She might have equitable claims against the property since her wifely efforts would have contributed to the family wealth. And she might have statutory claims as well, such as dower and support. This case requires us to think long and hard about the nature of these claims.

For Mrs. Davis, the required wifely tasks were likely to be greater than those of many wives married to working men. Mr. Davis quickly rose to high ranks in the Du Pont Company. A wife in such a position is often expected to entertain business associates and arrange social functions that would help smooth a husband's rise to the top. All of these tasks would be performed as part of the initial partnership agreement.

Over ten years later, the partnership began to fall apart. At that time, Mrs. Davis began to plan her departure. She consulted an attorney. The partnership had to be dissolved. But she believed that she should be entitled to her fair share of the original bargain. And her attorney agreed.

And so the departure was negotiated. Her husband owed her an obligation of support. They entered into a separate agreement to resolve conflicts over that obligation. But Mrs. Davis also claimed property rights in the property that had accrued to the couple during the marriage.

So what were those property rights? Applying the common law rules of Delaware, since those are the rules that apply to this Delaware couple, those rights appear to be somewhat minimal. Mrs. Davis had the right to support during her lifetime and a dower right in all real estate acquired by her husband, a right typically enforced at the death of the husband. True dower is a holdover from the common law of coverture. At common law, a widow was entitled to a life estate in one-third of the properties held by her husband. She was not thought to be entitled to more than a life estate, because the purpose of dower was to provide for her support after her husband's death. What her dower rights might be at divorce appears to be a more complicated question and varies from state to state.

Common law property states in this country have been moving away from the pure dower concept, especially as to rights at divorce. Some common law property states give divorce judges the power to divide property equitably at divorce. Apparently, Kansas was the first to do so in 1889. *See* 2 Irwin Taylor, *General Statutes of Kansas: 1889*, at 1568 (1889). Numerous other states followed suit. These differences among the states in marital property rights at divorce may create different tax rules at divorce under the reasoning of the majority opinion.

It is undisputed that, if the Davis couple had lived in a community property state, the property division would have been viewed as a nontaxable event in which Mrs. Davis was simply receiving her share of the community property. *See Comm'r v. Mills*, 183 F.2d 32 (9th Cir. 1950), *aff'g* 12 T.C. 468 (1949); *Walz v. Comm'r*, 32 B.T.A. 718 (1935) (nontaxable division of community but taxable exchange to extent husband transferred separate property to wife in exchange for her community property interest in other property). It is undisputed that, if the two spouses had entered into a business partnership and later dissolved that partnership, the dissolution would not have been a taxable event. *See Crawford v. Comm'r*, 39 B.T.A. 521 (1939). It is undisputed that if the two spouses had owned property as joint tenants or tenants in common and partitioned the property to give 50 percent to each spouse, the partition would not have been a taxable event. *See* Rev. Rul. 55-77, 1955-1 C.B. 339. And, finally, and perhaps more surprisingly, it is undisputed that if the taxpayer had been a corporation transferring appreciated property to satisfy a stockholder's claim, the transfer would not have triggered a tax liability. *See Gen. Utils. & Operating Co. v. Helvering*, 296 U.S. 200 (1935). In all of these cases, there is a transfer of appreciated property, but the transfer is not a *realization* event to the transferor.

I believe the Davis couple should be covered by these rules. Their agreement to split up the property acquired during marriage under state law principles that require the nontitled spouse to receive her "fair" share are similar to the split of community property or the partition of jointly owned property. The transaction is also akin to the dissolution of a business partnership. Mrs. Davis had rights in the property, determined under state law. The majority explains that her rights were inchoate, not sufficiently vested. But they were rights in property and they accrued during the marriage. Mr. Davis was required under state law to give her the property to which she was entitled.

There are no clear statutory rules governing transfers between spouses at time of divorce. Applying general principles of tax law, different lower courts have come up with different answers. If the property is jointly owned, either as community property or as a cotenancy, then the rule seems to be that there is no "realization event" and therefore no gain to be reported. Each spouse walks away with his or her share of the property, with its historical cost basis, and gain will only be recognized when the property is sold. *See Walz*, 32 B.T.A. 718. The rules are less clear when the transaction resembles the Davis transaction (e.g., a release of rights in exchange for a transfer of appreciated property that had been solely in the husband's name). Some lower courts have ruled that this is not a taxable "sale" by the husband. *See Comm'r v. Marshman*, 279 F.2d 27 (6th Cir.), *cert. denied*, 364 U.S. 918 (1960); *see also Davis v. United States*, 287 F.2d 168 (Ct. Cl. 1961). The reasoning in these decisions, however, is not that the transaction was a nontaxable division of property. Rather those courts claimed that the gain could not be calculated because there was no way to measure the "amount realized" by the husband on the transaction because the wife's rights could not be valued. Other lower courts ruled that such transactions were taxable exchanges and that the husband should be taxed on the realized gain. *See Comm'r v. Halliwell*, 131

F.2d 642 (2d Cir. 1942), *cert. denied,* 319 U.S. 741 (1943); *Comm'r v. Mesta,* 123 F.2d 986 (3d Cir. 1941), *cert. denied,* 316 U.S. 695 (1942).

The majority looks to the details of state property law to determine whether the *Walz* analysis or the *Halliwell* and *Mesta* analysis should apply. Justice Clark explains that whereas community property spouses are equally vested in their community property, common law property spouses are not. This is nonsense. Here, in 1962, even community property wives do not have management power over community property. *See Fernandez v. Wiener,* 326 U.S. 340, 363 (1945) (Douglas, J., concurring) (pointing out that it was constitutional to include all the community assets in the taxable estate of the husband because community property wives were not really vested in community assets).

The truth is that community property wives in 1962 have fewer rights over their community property than wives in common law property states have over jointly owned separate property. Yes, in *Poe v. Seaborn,* 282 U.S. 101 (1930), we did adopt the legal fiction that community property spouses equally owned community income and community property. But the reality is that the wife's ownership interest in community property was then, and still is, illusory. For example, in all community property states, it is the husband who has full management and control of the community property. He is viewed as acting as an agent of the wife, but, even so, he could sell the property or gift it away without her consent. She may have a claim that he acted in "fraud of her rights," but that is hardly the same as being an equal co-owner. *See* William M. Simmons, *The Interest of a Wife in California Community Property,* 22 Calif. L. Rev. 404 (1934) (discussing the complicated California history of a wife's right to challenge gifts of community property made by the husband).

Despite the reality that community property wives are not vested in community assets, courts in tax cases continue to apply the legal fiction that they are sufficiently vested when community assets are split at divorce. *See Walz,* 32 B.T.A. at 719. Applying this view, the wife is seen as taking what she already owned (albeit in a different form of ownership; i.e., as her separate property rather than as her community interest in the property). As such, the transfer is not a taxable event. *Id.*

If the Court is willing to apply a legal fiction to community property wives allowing them to receive transfers of appreciated property at divorce that do not impose tax burdens on their transferring husbands, then the Court should treat common law property wives the same. Mrs. Davis was in reality as much a partner with Mr. Davis as Mrs. Walz was with Mr. Walz. *See id.*

Wives in common law property states have been too long disadvantaged by the legacy of coverture, a system we inherited from England in which wives were not recognized as separate legal individuals. *See* Blackstone, *supra*, at 442. In this country, feminists began chipping away at the limitations of coverture as early as the nineteenth century. The first married women's property act was passed in Mississippi in 1839. T. J. Fox Alden & J. A. Van Hoesen, *Digest of the Laws of Mississippi* 920 (1839). Today, in every state wives can own property in their own names. *See, e.g.*, Act of Mar. 10, 1843, ch. 293, 1843 Md. Laws; Act No. 66, 1844 Mich. Pub. Acts 77–78; Law of Apr. 7, 1848, ch. 200, 1848 N.Y. Laws 307–08. Oregon even enshrined the right in its constitution. *See* Or. Const. of 1857, art. XV, § 5.

In common law jurisdictions, much of the property acquired during marriage is titled jointly between husband and wife, sometimes with rights of survivorship in order to avoid probate, or as tenants by the entirety to gain protection from creditors. In such cases, both spouses have present and equal vested rights in the property. By contrast, this is not true of most community property states. For example, despite the California legislature's 1927 enactment of a statute providing that husbands and wives were equally vested in community property, subsequent cases proved the statute a legal fiction, holding that the husband remained vested in the entire management and control of the community property. *See Hannah v. Swift*, 61 F.2d 307 (9th Cir. 1932). Today, in California, the husband remains the sole manager of community property. Cal. Civ. Code § 172 (West 1954). Sole management of the community assets by the husband remains the rule in other community property states (e.g., Texas and Louisiana). *See, e.g.*, La. Civ. Code Ann. art. 2404 (1870). And, as one early Louisiana opinion on this matter said: "The wife's title, during the existence of the community, is inchoate. ... The title remains in the meantime in the husband, as head and master of the community." *Jacob v. Falgoust*, 150 La. 21, 24 (1922). And yet courts continue to treat these community spouses as equally vested when analyzing tax consequences.

Common law property states have strengthened the claims of wives in additional ways. For example, some states (e.g., New York) have changed their dower rules so that widows can now receive more than a life estate in one-third of her husband's property, which is what she was entitled to under traditional dower rules. In such states, a widow is now entitled to a forced share of her husband's property, which she will own in fee simple absolute rather than as a legal life estate. *See, e.g.*, Act of Apr. 1, 1929, ch. 229, § 4, 1929 N.Y. Laws 499, 500–02. That change has not occurred in Delaware, however. That leaves wives like Mrs. Davis still disadvantaged by the legacy of coverture.

This Court should not continue that disadvantage by adding a tax cost to a Delaware property settlement that will likely disadvantage future wives like Mrs. Davis.

The reason this tax cost is likely to disadvantage wives is that in the future, husbands who are considering the transfer of appreciated property to settle their wives' claims to property will be advised by tax counsel of the effect of our opinion in this case. The rational husband in the position of Mr. Davis will likely respond by deciding to transfer less in value to his wife. There is a trade-off. The wife will get less in value but she will take the appreciated property with a higher basis (i.e., fair market value at the time of the transfer). That will produce no, or at least less, taxable gain when she is forced to sell.

But the practical result is that husbands like Mr. Davis will pay high rates of tax on the gain because they are typically high-income individuals. If the gain is a long-term capital gain, as it was in this case, then the maximum rate is only 25 percent. *See* I.R.C. § 1201; Stanley Surrey, *Definitional Problems in Capital Gains Taxation*, 69 Harv. L. Rev. 985 (1956). And all of the gain is recognized in the year of the transfer by the husband. Wives who are like Mrs. Davis, who have no other income, and who are selling the property in order to support themselves may pay little or no taxes on the sales. Only half of the gain is included in the tax base. *See* I.R.C. § 1201. And if she is at the lowest marginal tax bracket of 20 percent that would produce a tax at the rate of 10 percent. *See id.* § 1(a). And the sales can be spread out over a number of years to create sufficient annual support.

If the property transferred is not a capital asset (e.g., inventory or self-created art) then the high-income husband may be in the bracket of 91 percent. *Id.* The divorced wife with no other income, by contrast, may be at the lowest brackets (e.g., 20 percent or 22 percent). *Id.* These are practical considerations or consequences which the majority does not take into account.

There are additional practical consequences to this decision that the majority ignores. Facts matter. Context matters. The Commissioner found it easy to calculate the gain in this case because the property transferred was publicly traded stock. But this opinion is not limited to transfers of publicly traded stock. Suppose the wife wants the family home and the husband transfers it to her, together with furnishings (antiques that may have appreciated) and art (which also may have appreciated). To compute taxable gain in such cases will require appraisals, thereby adding an additional transaction cost to the dissolution of the marriage.

Nor am I as ready as my colleagues are to dismiss the claim that, at least in part, this transfer may have been a gift under the income tax statutes. Of course, if it were a gift, the transfer would be excluded from the wife's income and the transaction would not be treated as a sale or exchange to either party. While I prefer to justify nontaxation of these sorts of transactions as a non-realization splitting up of property rights, I do think the gift argument bears some scrutiny, and, perhaps, serves as a bolster to my conclusion that the transaction should not be taxed.

The majority cites to three gift tax cases that found that a transfer to a wife in exchange for a release of her marital rights constituted a taxable gift under the gift tax rules. *See Merrill v. Fahs*, 324 U.S. 308 (1945); *Comm'r v. Wemyss*, 324 U.S. 303 (1945); *Harris v. Comm'r*, 340 U.S. 106 (1950). A transfer is taxable as a gift for gift tax purposes if the transferor did not receive consideration in "money or money's worth." And we have consistently held that a release of marital rights is not consideration in "money or money's worth" for purposes of the gift tax, primarily because Congress decided first that such a release did not constitute consideration in "money or money's worth" under the estate tax. *See Merrill*, 342 U.S. at 315; *Wemyss*, 324 U.S. at 304; *Harris*, 340 U.S. at 107.

And I agree with the majority that just because a transfer is treated as a gift for gift tax purposes, it does not follow that the transfer is a gift for income tax purposes. The rule for income tax purposes is different from the rule for gift tax purposes. We decided two years ago in *Commissioner v. Duberstein*, 363 U.S. 278 (1960), that the test for whether or not a transfer is a gift under the income tax depends on the transferor's intent. If the transfer was made out of "detached and disinterested generosity" or "out of affection, respect, admiration, charity or like impulses" then the transfer is a gift under Code § 102. *Id.* at 285. There was no mention of money or money's worth in that opinion. It is astounding that the majority does not even mention *Duberstein*, an income tax case that defined gifts under § 102, and instead summarily concludes that the transfer to Mrs. Davis was "not a gift in any sense of the word." *See* 370 U.S. at 67 n.6. Perhaps this means that the majority believes that the rancor that typically accompanies a divorce could not possibly be associated with "affection, respect, admiration, charity or like impulses." *Robertson v. United States*, 343 U.S. 711, 714 (1952) (cited in *Duberstein*, 363 U.S. at 285). But in a ten-year marriage, surely there was some affection and love (charity). And surely any of us who have been involved in a long-term, committed relationship like marriage knows that there is a thin line between love and hate. The transfer at the end of the relationship in this case came about as a result of initial motives of affection and love. But for that one-time affection and love, the transfer would not exist. One might call this the "origin of the claim." By focusing solely on the moment of the transfer, the majority ignores the totality of the relationship. The failure to engage with this complex issue of motive in the case of divorce transfers moves this Court into an arena of objective and abstract reasoning devoid of sympathy, empathy, or understanding about what is really going on.

Divorce is a difficult enough transaction. Adding tax costs to this transaction will simply multiply the pain. I think this is a disastrous decision. I hope that Congress will not let it stand.

I do concur with the result that the majority reached concerning the nondeductibility by Mr. Davis of the attorney's fees he paid to his wife's attorney. Attorney's fees are not generally deductible, unless they fit within a specific Code section, such as § 162, authorizing the deductibility of trade or business expenses. Mr. Davis claimed he was entitled to those deductions under Code § 212(3), which authorizes a deduction "in connection with the determination, collection, or refund of any tax." He claimed a $5,000 deduction for tax advice relevant to the divorce. He paid half of that amount to his own attorney and half to his wife's attorney. While the statute itself is not explicit in requiring that the tax advice be for the taxpayer who made the payment, it is implicit. It is a general rule of tax law that if Taxpayer A pays Taxpayer B's deductible expenses, the payment is not deductible by Taxpayer A. Again, with a reference to coverture: Mr. Davis is a separate taxpayer from Mrs. Davis, especially once they are divorced. Any payment he makes for tax advice to her is not deductible by him. He claims that he paid the fee because of his obligation to provide family support. If that is true, then the payment is a "support" payment and its tax consequences should be determined under different rules from § 212(3). Whatever the payment is, it is not a payment for tax advice to Mr. Davis. As a result, it cannot be deducted by him on the authority of § 212(3).

Finally, I wish to make a brief comment about why I think cases like this are so difficult for our Supreme Court. We are a Court of national jurisdiction. We primarily hear cases involving federal constitutional issues and cases involving the construction of federal statutes. The Internal Revenue Code is a federal statute, and it is right that we should be the final arbiter of its meaning. But given the absence of federal principles of family law, family property law, or even of property law rights, it is difficult for a Court such as ours to maintain consistency in deciding cases that are strongly affected by the laws of the different states. In many cases, there is no way to avoid this lack of uniformity. Rights to property under state law often do matter for tax purposes. But I think we should minimize these geographical distinctions whenever possible. And I think the taxation of marital property settlements is one such arena. That is because I believe the core nature of a marriage is similar from state to state, even though marital property rights may differ.

The difference between Mrs. Davis and Mrs. Walz at time of divorce is really not that different. *See Walz,* 32 B.T.A. at 718–20. True, under state law the spouses may be entitled to different amounts under a property settlement. But the inherent nature of the property settlement is essentially the same, whether it occurs in a community property state or a common law property state. We have experienced this form of geographical discrimination before. After we decided in *Poe v. Seaborn*, 282 U.S. 101, that community property spouses could split their combined community income and each report only half on the single tax return that was in effect in those years, we faced eighteen years of taxpayers in the common law property states struggling to obtain the same income-splitting benefit that community property spouses enjoyed. In 1948, Congress erased the difference in the tax burden between community property spouses and common law property spouses when it passed the Revenue Act of 1948. That equalization of burden seems right. Congress could now decide to equalize the divorce tax burden by lessening the difference between the *Walz* taxpayers and the *Davis* taxpayers of the world (i.e., by remedying *Seaborn*-like problems that this opinion is likely to produce). It did so in 1948 to cure geographical discrimination in the tax burden. It is time to do so again.

I concur with respect to Part IV of the majority opinion relating to the attorney's fees. Otherwise, I dissent.

7

Commentary on *Bob Jones University v. United States*

ELAINE WATERHOUSE WILSON

BACKGROUND

What is charitable?

The question colors many areas of the law, including the federal tax code. Code § 501(c)(3) exempts from federal income taxation certain religious, charitable, and educational organizations. The Treasury Regulations define "charitable" as used in its "generally accepted legal sense."[1] As a result, the tax law understanding of charity encompasses the common law tradition of "charitable" from other disciplines.[2] This makes tax law's interpretation of charity malleable over time. Therein lie its weakness and its strength: the definition of "charitable" evolves with community standards.[3]

In *Bob Jones University v. United States*,[4] the Supreme Court struggled to define "charitable" in the context of the tax-exempt status of racially discriminatory private schools. Ultimately, the Court confirmed that an organization is not charitable – and consequently not tax-exempt – if it violates public policy. Specifically, the Court held that racially discriminatory schools are not charitable under § 501(c)(3) because "there can be no doubt" that racial discrimination in education "is contrary to a fundamental public policy."[5]

Despite this broad holding, the IRS has rarely used *Bob Jones* as a precedent to deny tax-exempt status.[6] *Bob Jones* has been invoked only against

---

[1] Treas. Reg. § 1.501(c)(3)-1(d)(2) (as amended in 2014).
[2] *See, e.g.*, Evans v. Abney, 396 U.S. 435 (1970).
[3] *See, e.g.*, Slee v. Comm'r, 42 F.2d 184 (2d Cir. 1930).   [4] 461 U.S. 574 (1983).
[5] *Id.* at 592.
[6] Justice Powell expressed concern that "there ... [is] little to circumscribe the ... almost unfettered power of the Commissioner." *Id.* at 611.

organizations that support racial discrimination or engage in criminal behavior.[7] Even though *United States v. Virginia* found an Equal Protection Clause violation in some all-male admission policies,[8] *Bob Jones* has never been applied to gender discrimination. Considering *Obergefell v. Hodges*,[9] the discussion of the broader application of *Bob Jones's* public policy doctrine – now to sexual orientation discrimination – has begun anew.[10]

In his feminist concurring opinion, Dean David Brennen, writing as Justice Brennen, examines *Bob Jones's* public policy doctrine in a new light, focusing on the intersection between race and gender. Brennen's opinion also demonstrates how the public policy doctrine of *Bob Jones* potentially applies to gender discrimination.

ORIGINAL OPINION

After *Brown v. Board of Education*[11] ended formal racial segregation in public schools, some segregationist white families formed racially discriminatory private schools.[12] For years after *Brown*, the IRS routinely recognized these schools' tax-exempt status with knowledge of their discriminatory practices.[13] In Revenue Ruling 71-447, the IRS finally announced that it would not recognize racially discriminatory private schools as tax-exempt, stating that "all charitable trusts, educational or otherwise, are subject to the requirement that the purpose of the trust may not be illegal or contrary to public policy."[14] Intense congressional debate and litigation followed.[15]

---

[7]   *See, e.g.*, Rev. Rul. 75-384, 1975-2 C.B. 204 (civil disobedience); I.R.S. Priv. Ltr. Rul. 2013-23-025 (Mar. 14, 2013) (support of polygamy).

[8]   United States v. Virginia, 518 U.S. 515 (1996); *see also* Faulkner v. Jones, 51 F.3d 440 (4th Cir. 1995) (single-sex admissions at The Citadel).

[9]   135 S. Ct. 2584 (2015); *see also* United States v. Windsor, 133 S. Ct. 2675 (2013) (striking down a portion of the federal Defense of Marriage Act).

[10] Laurie Goodstein & Adam Liptak, *Schools Fear Gay Marriage Ruling Could End Tax Exemptions*, N.Y. TIMES (June 24, 2015), http://www.nytimes.com/2015/06/25/us/schools-fear-impact-of-gay-marriage-ruling-on-tax-status.html?_r=0.

[11] 347 U.S. 483 (1954).

[12] *See* Swann v. Charlotte-Mecklenburg Bd. of Educ., 402 U.S. 1 (1971); Olatunde Johnson, *The Story of* Bob Jones University v. United States: *Race, Religion, and Congress' Extraordinary Acquiescence, in* STATUTORY INTERPRETATION STORIES 127–63 (William N. Eskridge Jr. et al. eds., 2011).

[13] Bob Jones Univ. v. United States, 461 U.S. 574, 577 (1983); Johnson, *supra* note 12, at 132.

[14] Rev. Rul. 71-447, 1971-2 C.B. 230 (citing RESTATEMENT (SECOND) OF TRUSTS § 377 cmt. c (AM. LAW. INST. 1959)).

[15] *See* Johnson, *supra* note 12, at 133–38.

Bob Jones University, a private religious school in South Carolina,[16] implemented various racially discriminatory policies, including a ban on interracial
dating or marriage.[17] The school justified its discriminatory policies on the
basis of religious beliefs, which the Supreme Court assumed were sincerely
held.[18] After various administrative proceedings, in 1975 the IRS revoked the
university's exemption retroactively.[19]

Neither § 501(c)(3) nor its regulations explicitly apply the public policy
limitation to the term "charitable." The Court found that Congress understood the term "charitable" in its common law sense,[20] which meant that the
public policy limitation was inherent.[21] Because the charitable tax exemption
confers a public benefit, an "institution's purpose must not be so at odds with
the common community conscience as to undermine any public benefit that
might otherwise be conferred."[22]

Having read the public policy limitation into § 501(c)(3), the Court determined that a public policy existed and was violated. The Court held that tax-
exempt status should be denied when there is *"no doubt* that the activity
involved is contrary to a *fundamental* public policy."[23] The Court's public
policy test sets two seemingly high bars: the public policy must be "fundamental"; and there must be "no doubt" that the policy is violated. Unfortunately,
the Court defines neither "fundamental" nor the quantum of certainty
required for there to be "no doubt."

Under any test,[24] the Court would have found that racial discrimination
in education violated a fundamental public policy: "[T]here can no longer
be any doubt that racial discrimination in education violates deeply and
widely accepted views of elementary justice."[25] The opinion recites a litany
of legislative, executive, and judicial actions over the thirty-year period following *Brown* to demonstrate that segregation in education violated federal
public policy. For judicial support, the Court cites an "unbroken line of
cases following" *Brown*.[26] Legislatively, the opinion highlights the passage of
the Civil Rights Act of 1964, the Voting Rights Act of 1965, and the Civil
Rights Act of 1968 as indicative of a federal public policy against racial

---

[16] *Bob Jones*, 461 U.S. at 579–83. The case included Goldsboro Christian Schools, a religious
K–12 private school with a racially discriminatory admissions policy, generally admitting only
white students. *Id.* at 583.
[17] *Id.* at 580–81.   [18] *Id.* at 602 n.28.   [19] *Id.* at 581–82.
[20] Congress held hearings but did not amend the statute. *Id.* at 599.   [21] *Id.* at 589.
[22] *Id.* at 592.   [23] *Id.* (emphasis added).
[24] Although hesitant, Justice Powell stated that "if any national policy is sufficiently
fundamental . . . it is the policy against racial discrimination in education." *Id.* at 607.
[25] *Id.* at 592.   [26] *Id.* at 593.

discrimination.[27] Finally, the Court describes various presidential actions – Republican and Democratic – to demonstrate the executive branch's stance against racial discrimination, including Truman's and Kennedy's executive orders barring discrimination and Eisenhower's deployment of the National Guard to enforce desegregation orders.[28]

The Court asserts that the public policy against racial discrimination already existed;[29] the Court merely discerned its existence from the government actions taken between *Brown* in 1954 and *Bob Jones* in 1983. Interestingly, the Court does not consider public opinion as an indicator of fundamental public policy.[30] Theoretically, elected officials should reflect public sentiment, thus mitigating the need for the Court to consider it.[31] On the other hand, the time lapse between *Brown* and *Bob Jones* begs the question: If there was no doubt that this was a fundamental public policy, why did it take thirty years to decide the obvious?

The controversy surrounding the government's role in litigating *Bob Jones* is as compelling as the case itself. The IRS first examined the university's exemption during the Nixon administration;[32] the Ford and Carter administrations defended the revocation.[33] Two days before the government's Supreme Court brief was due, the Reagan administration decided not to pursue the case.[34] Simultaneously, the Court of Appeals for the DC Circuit in *Wright v. Regan*[35] enjoined the IRS from recognizing the tax-exempt status of racially discriminatory schools. While *Wright* forced the Reagan administration to litigate *Bob Jones* further, the Supreme Court appointed an *amicus curiae* to defend the Fourth Circuit opinion upholding the denial of tax-exempt status on public policy grounds.[36]

Bob Jones was met with vocal disdain from some quarters. Bob Jones Jr. himself stated, "We're in a bad fix when eight evil old men and one vain and foolish woman can speak a verdict on American liberties."[37] Despite the

---

[27] *Id.* at 594.   [28] *Id.* at 594–95.   [29] *Id.* at 592–94.

[30] *Id.* at 598 (at the time of Rev. Rul. 71-447, "the position of ... the Federal Government ... was unmistakably clear").

[31] Justice Ginsburg has claimed that a problem with *Roe v. Wade* was that the Court was too far ahead of public opinion. Ruth Bader Ginsburg, *Speaking in a Judicial Voice*, 67 N.Y.U. L. Rev. 1185, 1200 (1992).

[32] Johnson, *supra* note 12, at 141.

[33] *Id.* at 141–42. The Supreme Court decided an Anti-Injunction Act issue before deciding the case on its merits. *See* Bob Jones Univ. v. Simon, 416 U.S. 725 (1974).

[34] Johnson, *supra* note 12, at 144.   [35] 656 F.2d 820 (D.C. Cir. 1981).

[36] Johnson, *supra* note 12, at 148.

[37] *Id.* at 127; *see also* James J. Fishman et al., Nonprofit Organizations 364 (5th ed. 2015).

Court's view that racial discrimination in education clearly violated existing public policy, the issue remained controversial.

Although *Bob Jones* holds that an organization cannot be tax-exempt if there is "no doubt" that it violates "fundamental" public policy, those terms remain undefined. The opinion only indicates that a fundamental public policy "violates deeply and widely accepted views of elementary justice."[38] The opinion never requires the government to take bipartisan action in order to make a public policy "fundamental." Because the policy prohibiting racial discrimination in education is "fundamental" under any measure, the Court did not need to articulate a more detailed test of general applicability. This void makes it impossible to determine whether any other public policy – such as a policy against gender or sexual orientation discrimination – also rises to the level of "fundamental."

In his feminist concurrence, Brennen either could have argued for a less onerous standard than "no doubt" of violation of a "fundamental public policy" or, alternatively, that gender discrimination already meets the Court's enumerated standard. He chose the latter.

Brennen notes that the university's policies against interracial relationships involve both racial and gender discrimination. The majority opinion is blind to the heightened impact of these policies on women of color – that is, to the intersection of race and gender discrimination. Brennen believes that the IRS could have revoked Bob Jones's exemption due to the violation of a fundamental public policy against gender discrimination as well.

To establish a fundamental public policy against gender discrimination, Brennen describes various judicial, legislative, and executive actions. Judicially, the feminist opinion cites cases prohibiting discrimination in medical school admissions[39] and in educational employment.[40] Legislatively, Brennen highlights Title IX,[41] which prohibits gender discrimination in educational activities. Finally, Brennen mentions various executive orders against gender

---

[38] Bob Jones Univ. v. United States, 461 U.S. 574, 592 (1983).

[39] Cannon v. Univ. of Chi., 441 U.S. 677 (1979); *see also* Kirstein v. Rector & Visitors of Univ. of Va., 309 F. Supp. 184 (E.D. Va. 1970) (male-only admissions at the University of Virginia unconstitutional).

[40] N. Haven Bd. of Educ. v. Bell, 456 U.S. 512 (1982).

[41] 20 U.S.C. § 1681 (Westlaw through Pub. L. No. 115-43); *see generally* Deborah L. Brake, *Title IX as Pragmatic Feminism*, 55 CLEV. ST. L. REV. 513 (2007).

discrimination and Nixon's proclamation of Women's Equality Day in 1973. As with the majority opinion, Brennen does not reference public opinion regarding gender equality at the time. Thus, the feminist opinion examines in parallel the government actions that established a policy against racial discrimination and those that establish a policy against gender discrimination.

Is Gender Equality a Fundamental Public Policy?

In *Bob Jones*, the Court purposefully identified a broad range of governmental actions against racial discrimination in education, and assumed that those actions automatically formed a "fundamental" policy. The history of the *Bob Jones* litigation demonstrates a lack of unanimity regarding the tax-exempt status of racially discriminatory schools. The litigation itself took over a decade, during which Congress hotly debated the issue. On the eve of oral argument, the Reagan administration balked. Given the congressional debates during this period (which the opinion specifically discussed[42]) and the Court's last-minute appointment of William Coleman to argue in defense of the Fourth Circuit's decision,[43] the Court knew that opinions on the issue were hardly monolithic. Therefore, the opinion promoted "deeply and widely held views of elementary justice"[44] that were not necessarily shared by all.

Other government actions taken during the pendency of the litigation highlight the ongoing discussion regarding gender equality. Although Congress passed the Equal Rights Amendment (ERA) in 1972,[45] the states did not ratify it by the June 30, 1982 deadline,[46] which expired before *Bob Jones* was argued before the Court.[47] In 1983, the House of Representatives rejected a second version of the amendment.[48]

During that time, some judicial decisions supported gender equality in education, while others did not. The Court first applied intermediate scrutiny to issues of gender discrimination in 1976.[49] On July 1, 1982 (one day after the ERA failed), the Court held in *Mississippi University for Women v. Hogan* that gender-based government action requires "exceedingly persuasive"

---

[42] *Bob Jones*, 461 U.S. at 599–603.   [43] Johnson, *supra* note 12, at 148.

[44] *Bob Jones*, 461 U.S. at 592.

[45] *See* Joan A. Lukey & Jeffrey A. Smagula, *Do We Still Need a Federal Equal Rights Amendment?*, Bos. B.J., Jan.–Feb. 2000, at 10.

[46] *Id.*   [47] Argument occurred on October 12, 1982.

[48] *See* Serena Mayeri, *A New E.R.A. or a New ERA? Amendment Advocacy and the Reconstitution of Feminism*, 103 Nw. U. L. Rev. 1223, 1287–88 (2009).

[49] Craig v. Boren, 429 U.S. 190, 197 (1976).

justification.[50] By contrast, a district court in 1970 approved the all-female admissions policy of Winthrop University, the alternative to the all-male military academy, The Citadel.[51] The Court described Winthrop as a "school for young ladies" that offered "courses . . . especially helpful to female students," including "needlework, cooking, [and] housekeeping."[52]

The *Bob Jones* litigation itself demonstrates executive branch hostility to gender equality. The Reagan administration feared that a public policy doctrine would allow the IRS to "make policy in areas in which public norms were less settled, such as attempting to revoke the tax-exempt status of women's colleges, requiring religious organizations to ordain women, or denying tax-exempt status to hospitals that perform abortions."[53] The rationale for abandoning *Bob Jones* was partially the fear that a public policy limitation might enable the IRS to deny exemptions due to gender discrimination.

In asserting a fundamental public policy against gender discrimination, Brennen's feminist concurrence may be ahead of where the debate actually stood at the time – and possibly even where it stands today. In that regard, the feminist concurrence may be no different than the majority opinion in *Bob Jones* with regard to racial discrimination. In each case, the opinion looks past public opinion and political posturing to find a truer notion of "elementary justice."[54]

Are Interracial Dating Prohibitions Gendered?

If a fundamental public policy against gender discrimination existed, the Court had to determine that there was "no doubt" that this policy had been violated. Bob Jones's policy against interracial relationships[55] is gender neutral on its face. Brennen's feminist opinion recognizes that differences in gender norms cause the policy to have a disproportionate impact on women. These racial and gender norms begin and are reinforced at the earliest ages through such things as Goldsboro Christian Schools' discriminatory elementary school admissions policy. Bob Jones's policy forced women to choose between the

---

[50] 458 U.S. 718, 724 (1982). In 1996, the Court held that the Virginia Military Institute's male-only admissions policy violated the Equal Protection Clause, citing *Hogan*. United States v. Virginia, 518 U.S. 515 (1996).

[51] Williams v. McNair, 316 F. Supp. 134 (D.S.C. 1970).

[52] *Id.* at 136; *see also* NANCY LEVIS ET AL., FEMINIST LEGAL THEORY: A PRIMER 94 (2d ed. 2016).

[53] Johnson, *supra* note 12, at 131 (citing Deputy Treasury Secretary R. T. McNamara).

[54] *See id.* at 162.

[55] Bans on interracial marriage were deemed unconstitutional in *Loving v. Virginia*, 388 U.S. 1 (1967).

economic opportunities of a college education and their intimate relationships. Faced with similar decisions, women culturally were (and are) more
likely to sacrifice their work lives to accommodate family. For example, a
2013 study by the Pew Research Center found "women experience family-
related career interruptions at a much higher rate than men do."[56] Choosing
family over opportunity disproportionately burdens women and "economically marginalize[s]" the skills required to enter the job market.[57]

Intersectionality

Brennen specifies the heightened burden placed on female students of color
and their relationships by Goldsboro's and Bob Jones's discriminatory policies.
His concurrence highlights specific harms caused when women experience
the intersection of discrimination due to gender and race simultaneously.
Intersectionality[58] highlights the fact the suffering inflicted on women of color
by racism and gender discrimination is compounded by the overlap between
the two. In addition, the interests of women of color as women can be put at
odds with their interests as minorities. Intersectionality challenges the Court to
recognize women as multifaceted individuals who do not experience discrimination identically or singularly.[59]

As Brennen notes, Goldsboro's discriminatory policies prevented early
relationships, intimate or otherwise, between members of different races from
even occurring. If such a relationship did develop, Bob Jones would expel
individuals who participated in, or simply encouraged, interracial relationships.[60] If a woman of color participated in an interracial relationship or
protested against the university's policy, she did so at her peril. Standing up
for her dignity, she risked certain expulsion and, choosing expulsion, she
economically marginalized herself and endangered her career more severely
than did a similarly situated man. Alternatively, she could silently suffer the

---

[56] Pew Research Ctr., On Pay Gap, Millennial Women Near Parity – For Now:
Despite Gains, Many See Roadblocks Ahead (2013).
[57] Joan Williams, Unbending Gender: Why Family and Work Conflict and What to
Do About It 65–66 (2000).
[58] *See generally* Kimberlé Crenshaw, *Demarginalizing the Intersection of Race and Sex: A Black
Feminist Critique of Antidiscrimination Doctrine, Feminist Theory and Antiracist Politics,*
1989 U. Chi. Legal F. 139; Angela P. Harris, *Race and Essentialism in Feminist Legal Theory,*
42 Stan. L. Rev. 581 (1990).
[59] *See generally* Geneva Brown, *The Wind Cries Mary – The Intersectionality of Race, Gender,
and Reentry: Challenges for African-American Women,* 24 St. John's J. Legal Comment.
625, 627 (2010).
[60] Bob Jones Univ. v. United States, 461 U.S. 574, 580–81 (1983).

university's racial discrimination to advance as a woman in an economic world stacked against her.

One commentator notes that choosing between work and home has a unique impact on some women of color: "Black women do not see participation in the labor force and being a wife and mother as mutually exclusive; rather, within Black culture, employment is an integral, normative, and traditional component of the roles of wife and mother."[61] Even the existence of a choice between career and family presupposes the ability to forgo a female income – an assumption that is simply not true for many women, especially women of color.[62]

The Road Not Taken

In lieu of demonstrating that gender discrimination complied with the *Bob Jones* standard, Brennen could have established a less stringent (or at least a less vague) standard for the public policy limitation.[63] Formulating such a test is fraught with difficulty. Requiring fewer governmental actions to support finding a fundamental public policy might make the test subject to the IRS's political whims, as feared by Justice Powell.[64] Alternatively, the IRS's use of a more lenient standard to deny exemption could impede the acceptance of otherwise recognized fundamental public policies in areas other than race.

Neither the original *Bob Jones* opinion nor the feminist concurrence specifically holds "that equal protection *requires* the denial of tax exemption."[65] Fundamentally, the original *Bob Jones* opinion and feminist concurrence concern statutory interpretation and agency power. Professor Judith Resnick notes that the original opinion "avoided the constitutional question of whether Congress could grant tax exemption to schools that discriminated on the basis of race."[66] One could provide that any discrimination that would violate the Equal Protection Clause under a strict scrutiny analysis creates a fundamental public policy for *Bob Jones* purposes.[67] This formulation may work for racial

---

[61] WILLIAMS, *supra* note 57, at 172 (citing Stephen D. Sugarman, *Reforming Welfare Through Social Security*, 26 U. MICH. J.L. REFORM 1 (1993)).

[62] *See, e.g.,* Dorothy E. Roberts, *The Future of Reproductive Rights for Poor Women and Women of Color*, 14 WOMEN'S RTS. L. REP. 305 (1992).

[63] *See* Johnson, *supra* note 12, at 159.

[64] *See* Charles O. Galvin & Neal Devins, *Tax Policy Analysis of* Bob Jones University v. U.S., 36 VAND. L. REV. 1353 (1983); *see also* Johnny Rex Buckles, *Reforming the Public Policy Doctrine*, 53 KAN. L. REV. 397 (2005).

[65] *See* Johnson, *supra* note 12, at 159; *see also* Judith Resnik, *Living Their Legal Commitments: Paideic Communities, Courts and Robert Cover*, 17 YALE J.L. & HUMAN. 17, 20–24 (2005).

[66] Resnik, *supra* note 65, at 40.

[67] *See generally* Samuel Brunson & David Herzig, *A Diachronic Approach to* Bob Jones University: *Religious Tax Exemptions After* Obergefell, 92 IND. L.J. 1175 (2017).

discrimination, but it would not work for gender discrimination: *Craig*, *Hogan*, and their progeny have not extended strict scrutiny to women.[68]

Brennen's concurrence does not go this route. Strict scrutiny analysis applies only to government action; private actors are not held to these standards. Brennen's approach evaluates private activities in light of the purpose of tax exemption. As his concurrence discusses, the charitable exemption supports the activities of the underlying charity, whether that support is in the form of incentives, endorsement, or real dollars through tax expenditures. Thus, Brennen asks whether the government should encourage discriminatory activity by private actors through the tax laws. If the government explicitly rejects an activity, it seems anomalous for the tax laws to circumvent that disapproval. In Brennen's words, "if the government should not do this, then those who are relieved from the obligation to support the government should likewise be barred."

Gender equality would satisfy such a test. Under an intermediate scrutiny analysis, the government cannot engage in invidious gender-based discrimination. Even if the government could constitutionally, it clearly should not. Congress explicitly rejected gender discrimination in education through Title IX, just as it had done for minority groups with the Civil Rights Act.[69] The tax laws should not circumvent this rejection of gender discrimination by supporting it indirectly through tax exemption.

The Road Forward: Sexual Orientation

At oral argument in *Obergefell v. Hodges*, Justice Alito questioned *Bob Jones*'s impact on the exemption of religious charities that oppose same-sex marriage.[70] Brennen's concurrence is unclear on whether prohibiting sexual orientation discrimination rises to the level of a fundamental public policy. There is no congressional equivalent of Title IX or the Civil Rights Act for the LGBTQ community; the most recent affirmative congressional statement is the now-defunct Defense of Marriage Act.[71] Using even heightened constitutional scrutiny as a proxy for a fundamental public policy might not protect the LGBTQ community, because it is unclear what level of

---

[68] *See* Nicholas A. Mirkay, *Is It "Charitable" to Discriminate?: The Necessary Transformation of Section 501(c)(3) into the Gold Standard for Charities*, 2007 W$_{IS}$. L. R$_{EV}$. 45, 68; *see also* *supra* text accompanying notes 49–50.

[69] David A. Brennen, *Tax Expenditures, Social Justice and Civil Rights: Expanding the Scope of Civil Rights Laws to Apply to Tax-Exempt Charities*, 2001 BYU L. R$_{EV}$. 167, 169.

[70] Brunson & Herzig, *supra* note 67, at 1183–84.

[71] Pub. L. No. 104-199, § 3, 110 Stat. 2419, 2419 (1996), *invalidated by* United States v. Windsor, 133 S. Ct. 2675 (2013).

scrutiny applies to sexual orientation classifications – either before or after *Obergefell*.[72]

Numerous families suffered from invidious discrimination in the thirty years between *Brown* and *Bob Jones*. The *Bob Jones* Court, fighting its "too activist" perception, pointed to earlier government action establishing a fundamental public policy, but provided no legal test for future use. Some argue that a similar caution should apply in extending *Bob Jones* to protect women or the LGBTQ community. In response to a similar argument in *Obergefell*, Justice Kennedy wrote:

> There may be an initial inclination in these cases to proceed with caution – to await further legislation, litigation and debate .... The dynamic of our constitutional system is that individuals need not await legislative action before asserting a fundamental right. ... An individual can invoke a right to constitutional protection when he or she is harmed, even if the broader public disagrees and even if the legislature refuses to act.[73]

BOB JONES UNIVERSITY v. UNITED STATES, 461 U.S. 574 (1983)

JUSTICE DAVID A. BRENNEN CONCURRING IN THE JUDGMENT

I join the Court's judgment; however, I do so for different reasons.

We granted certiorari to decide whether an organization may qualify as tax-exempt under Internal Revenue Code § 501(c)(3) if it operates a nonprofit private school that discriminates, on religious grounds, against individuals by denying them admission to the school based solely on whether they are involved in an interracial marriage or dating relationship.

I

A

Until 1970, the Internal Revenue Service did not consider the discriminatory nature of a private school's admissions policies when evaluating whether the school should be granted tax-exempt status under Code § 501(c)(3) and

---

[72] Obergefell v. Hodges, 135 S. Ct. 2584, 2604–08 (2015).   [73] *Id.* at 2605.

granted eligibility to receive charitable contributions that could be deducted by the individuals or corporations making those contributions. I.R.C. § 170.

After a 1970 injunction issued by the U.S. District Court for the District of Columbia that prohibited the IRS from granting tax-exempt status to private schools in Mississippi that discriminated on the basis of race, the IRS stated that it could "no longer legally justify allowing tax-exempt status [under § 501(c)(3)] to private schools which practice racial discrimination." *Green v. Kennedy*, 309 F. Supp. 1127 (D.D.C.), *app. dismissed sub nom. Cannon v. Green*, 398 U.S. 956 (1970); I.R.S. News Release (July 10, 1970), *reprinted in* Joint App. in No. 81-3, at A235. Additionally, the IRS announced that it could not "treat gifts to such schools as charitable deductions for income tax purposes [under § 170]." I.R.S. News Release, *supra*. Both parties to this case were officially notified by letter on November 30, 1970, of the official change in policy applicable to all private schools. *See* Letter from Internal Revenue Serv. to Bob Jones Univ., Def. Ex. 6, *reprinted in* Joint App. in No. 81-3, at A232.

On June 30, 1971, when ruling on the merits of the Mississippi challenge, the district court validated the IRS's amended construction of the Code, holding that racially discriminatory private schools were not entitled to exemption under § 501(c)(3), and those making donations to said discriminatory schools would not be eligible to receive charitable tax deductions. *Green v. Connally*, 330 F. Supp. 1150 (D.D.C.), *aff'd sub nom. Coit v. Green*, 404 U.S. 997 (1971) (per curiam). The court permanently enjoined the IRS from granting tax-exempt status to any school in Mississippi that lacked a publicly maintained policy of nondiscrimination.

The revised policy on discrimination was formalized in Revenue Ruling 71-447, 1971-2 C.B. 230:

> Both the courts and the Internal Revenue Service have long recognized that the statutory requirement of being "organized and operated exclusively for religious, charitable . . . or educational purposes" was intended to express the basic common law concept [of "charity"] . . . . All charitable trusts, educational or otherwise, are subject to the requirement that the purpose of the trust may not be illegal or contrary to public policy.

Citing the "national policy to discourage racial discrimination in education," the IRS ruled "a private school not having a racially nondiscriminatory policy as to students is not 'charitable' within the common law concepts reflected in sections 170 and 501(c)(3) of the Code." *Id.* at 231.

Petitioners, private schools with racially discriminatory admissions policies, challenge the application of these provisions to their institutions.

B

No. 81-3, Bob Jones University v. United States

Bob Jones University (University) is a nonprofit operating out of Greenville, South Carolina, whose purpose is "to conduct an institution of learning ... giving special emphasis to the Christian religion and the ethics revealed in the Holy Scriptures." Certificate of Incorporation, Bob Jones University, Inc., of Greenville, S.C., *reprinted in* App. in No. 81-3, at A118–19. The school educates nearly 5,000 students ranging from kindergarten to graduate school. Bob Jones University is devoted to teaching and spreading fundamentalist Christian religious beliefs. It operates as both a religious and educational organization, requiring its teachers to be zealous Christians and to teach according to the Bible. Further, prospective students are screened based on their religious beliefs, and their conduct, both inside and outside of the institution, is governed by University standards.

The University claims as one of its basic beliefs that the Bible forbids interracial dating and marriage. In furtherance of this belief, Negroes were unconditionally excluded until 1971. From 1971 to 1975, the University altered its policy to accept applications from Negroes, on the condition that they marry only within their race. In 1973, the University further amended its policy, allowing applications from unmarried Negroes if they had been members of the University staff for more than four years.

In response to *McCrary v. Runyon*, 515 F.2d 1082 (4th Cir. 1975), *aff'd*, 427 U.S. 160 (1976), which prohibited private schools from excluding students based on race, the University altered its policy yet again. Beginning in 1975, unmarried Negroes were entitled to enroll; however, University disciplinary policies barred interracial dating and marriage. The discriminatory rule read as follows:

There is to be no interracial dating

1. Students who are partners in an interracial marriage will be expelled.
2. Students who are members of or affiliated with any group or organization which holds as one of its goals or advocates interracial marriage will be expelled.
3. Students who date outside their own race will be expelled.
4. Students who espouse, promote, or encourage others to violate the University's dating rules and regulations will be expelled.

App. in No. 81-3, at A197. To further effectuate this policy, the University continues to deny admission to those who engage in interracial marriage, or those who even advocate interracial marriage or dating, effectively deciding with whom their students may and may not associate. *Id.* at A277.

In 1970, following the injunction issued in *Green v. Kennedy*, 309 F. Supp. 1127 (D.D.C. 1970), the University was formally notified by the IRS of the change in its policy, and the intention to challenge the tax-exempt status of private schools that enforced racially discriminatory admissions policies. Seeking assurance that they would remain tax-exempt, the University instituted an action in 1971 seeking to enjoin the IRS from revoking its tax-exempt status. The action culminated in *Bob Jones University v. Simon*, 416 U.S. 725 (1974), in which the Court held that the Anti-Injunction Act, I.R.C. § 7421(a), prohibited the University from obtaining judicial review by way of injunctive action before the assessment or collection of any tax. On April 16, 1975, the IRS notified the University of the proposed revocation of its tax-exempt status. On January 19, 1976, the University's tax-exempt status was officially retroactively revoked effective December 1, 1970, the day after the University was first officially notified of the change in IRS policy. In response, the University elected to file returns under the Federal Unemployment Tax Act for the period from December 1, 1970 to December 31, 1975, and paid a tax totaling $21.00 on one employee for the calendar year of 1975. Following the University's request for a refund of this tax being denied, the University instituted the present action, attempting to recover the $21.00 payment. In response, the Government counterclaimed for unpaid federal unemployment taxes for the taxable years 1971 through 1975, in the amount of $489,675.59, plus interest.

The U.S. District Court for the District of South Carolina held that revocation of the University's tax-exempt status was not within the delegated power of the IRS, was improper under IRS rulings and procedures, and violated the University's rights under the Religion Clauses of the First Amendment. *Bob Jones Univ. v. United States*, 468 F. Supp. 890, 907 (D.S.C. 1978). The court ordered the IRS to refund the $21.00 claimed by the University and rejected the IRS's counterclaim.

In reversing, the Court of Appeals for the Fourth Circuit cited *Green v. Connally*, 330 F. Supp. 1150 (D.D.C. 1971), with approval, concluding that § 501(c)(3) must be read against the background of charitable trust law. *Bob Jones Univ. v. United States*, 639 F.2d 147 (4th Cir. 1980). Under § 501(c)(3), an organization must be "charitable" in the common law sense and not be contrary to public policy in order to be eligible for an exemption. The Court of Appeals held that the University fell short of this requirement because its "racial policies violated the clearly defined public policy, rooted in our Constitution, condemning racial discrimination and, more specifically, the government policy against subsidizing racial discrimination in education, public or private." *Id.* at 151. The court held that the IRS acted within its statutory authority in revoking the University's tax-exempt status. Further, the court rejected the University's claim that depriving it of its tax exemption was in violation of the Free Exercise and Establishment Clauses of the First Amendment. The case was remanded to the district court with instructions to dismiss the University's claims for a refund and to reinstate the IRS's counterclaim.

C

No. 81-1, Goldsboro Christian Schools, Inc. v. United States

Goldsboro Christian Schools is a nonprofit corporation located in Goldsboro, North Carolina. The school is similar to Bob Jones University in that it requires Bible-related courses, and begins each class with prayer. One difference between the two schools is that Goldsboro, unlike Bob Jones University (which educates students from kindergarten to graduate school), only educates students from kindergarten through high school.

Since it was founded in 1963, Goldsboro Christian Schools has implemented a racially discriminatory admissions policy. Goldsboro asserts that these discriminatory policies are based on their genuine interpretation of the Bible, believing cultural or biological mixing of races is a violation of God's command. App. in No. 81-1, at 40–41. Although the school has traditionally accepted only Caucasian students, there have been instances where children from racially mixed families have been accepted, provided one of the parents is Caucasian.

Goldsboro never received from the IRS official status as a tax-exempt organization under § 501(c)(3). Upon being audited, the IRS officially determined that Goldsboro was not an organization described in § 501(c)(3). As a result, the IRS required Goldsboro to pay taxes under the Federal Insurance Contributions Act and the Federal Unemployment Tax Act.

Goldsboro paid the IRS $3,459.93 in taxes with respect to one employee for the years 1969 through 1972, and immediately filed suit seeking refund of the payment, alleging the IRS improperly denied Goldsboro § 501(c)(3) tax-exempt status. The IRS counterclaimed for $160,073.96 in unpaid Social Security and unemployment taxes for the years 1969 through 1972, including interest and penalties.

Although the District Court for the Eastern District of North Carolina assumed the racially discriminatory policy was based on a sincerely held religious belief, the court rejected Goldsboro's claim to tax-exempt status

under § 501(c)(3), finding that "private schools maintaining racially discriminatory admissions policies violate clearly declared federal policy and therefore
must be denied the federal tax benefits flowing from qualification under
Section 501(c)(3)." *Goldsboro Christian Sch., Inc. v. United States*, 436 F.
Supp. 1314, 1318 (E.D.N.C. 1977). Additionally, the court rejected the argument that the denial of tax-exempt status violated the Free Exercise and
Establishment Clauses of the First Amendment. Thus, the District Court
granted summary judgment in favor of the government. The Court of Appeals
for the Fourth Circuit affirmed, *Goldsboro Christian Sch., Inc. v. United States*,
644 F.2d 879 (4th Cir. 1981) (per curiam).

We granted certiorari in both cases, *Goldsboro Christian Sch. v. United
States*, 454 U.S. 892 (1981), and we affirm in each.

II

A

I agree with the majority's compelling reasons to consider racial nondiscrimination, specifically in the context of school, an "established public policy."

For proof that the judiciary has subscribed to the "established public policy"
against racial discrimination, the majority first cites to *Brown v. Board of Education*, 347 U.S. 483 (1954), which ended the practice of racial segregation
in schools. The majority then cites "an unbroken line of cases establish[ing]
beyond doubt this Court's view that racial discrimination in education violates
a most fundamental national public policy, as well as rights of individuals."
Runyon v. McCrary, 427 U.S. 160 (1976); *Norwood v. Harrison*, 413 U.S. 455
(1973); *Griffin v. Cty. Sch. Bd.*, 377 U.S. 218 (1964); *Cooper v. Aaron*, 358
U.S. 1 (1958).

To further buttress the "established public policy" against racial discrimination, the majority cites congressional action that supports its stance.
Congress, in Titles IV and VI of the Civil Rights Act of 1964, Pub. L. No.
88-352, 78 Stat. 241, 246, 252 (codified at 42 U.S.C. §§ 2000c et seq., 2000c-6,
2000-d et seq.), clearly expressed its agreement that racial discrimination
in education violates a fundamental public policy. Other sections of that
Act, and numerous enactments since then, attest to the public policy against
racial discrimination. *See, e.g.*, Voting Rights Act of 1965, Pub. L. No. 89-110,
79 Stat. 437 (codified at 42 U.S.C. § 1971 et seq.); Civil Rights Act of 1968, Pub.
L. No. 90-284, tit. VIII, 82 Stat. 73, 81 (codified at 42 U.S.C. § 3601 et seq.);
Emergency School Aid Act of 1972, Pub. L. No. 92-318, 86 Stat. 354 (repealed
effective Sept. 30, 1979; replaced by similar provisions in the Emergency

School Aid Act of 1978, Pub. L. No. 95-561, 92 Stat. 2252 (codified at 20 U.S.C. §§ 3191–3207 (1980 Supp.)).

Additionally, the majority cites to actions taken by the executive branch indicating the existence of an "established public policy" against racial discrimination. The majority brings to light Executive Order No. 9980, 3 C.F.R. 720 (1943–1948 Comp.), which banned discrimination in federal employment decisions, and Executive Order No. 9988, *id.* at 726, 729, which banned racial discrimination in classifications for the Selective Service. Various other executive orders are mentioned by the majority that belabor the point with which I, and most Americans, agree, namely that there is an "established public policy" against racial discrimination.

The majority fails, however, to recognize the gender discrimination that also implicitly takes place due to these schools' policies of dictating women's most intimate relationships and dealings. These policies affect whom women date and associate with, where they educate themselves, and where they work. While it may be the case that men are also subjected to these same prescriptions for personal behavior, the impact is especially pernicious on women of all colors who, similar to Negroes (male and female), have long been recognized in the law as subordinate citizens, and whose lives and bodies have long been controlled by men and the law. *See* U.S. Const. amend. XIX (women first given the right to vote as late as 1920); *Eisenstadt v. Baird*, 405 U.S. 438, 454–55 (1972) (finally ruling that treating similarly situated married and unmarried women differently violates the Constitution); *Cole v. Van Riper*, 44 Ill. 58, 64 (1867) ("It is simply impossible that a woman married should be able to control and enjoy her property as if she were sole, without leaving her at liberty, practically, to annul the marriage tie at pleasure; and the same is true of the property of the husband, so far as it is directly connected with the nurture and maintenance of his household."). To reach the conclusion that a gendered perspective should have also been analyzed when it comes to the discriminatory practices of Bob Jones University and Goldsboro Christian Schools, it must first be shown that there is an "established public policy" to protect women from the harm that results from gender discrimination.

This Court has recognized the importance of protecting women from discrimination, even in instances as specific as education. *See Cannon v. Univ. of Chi.*, 441 U.S. 677 (1979) (woman allowed to sue for gender discrimination after not being admitted to medical school). Further, this Court upheld the applicability of 20 U.S.C § 1681 – which prohibits discrimination on the basis of sex in education – to employment in the education setting. *N. Haven Bd. of Educ. v. Bell*, 456 U.S. 512 (1982). Clearly, this Court has recognized the prevailing notion that women should be offered protection from the harmful effects of gender discrimination in education and work settings. This Court recognizes and enforces the "established public policy" against gender discrimination.

Just as the Congress, due to the long history of harm to Negroes caused by legal discrimination, has been proactive in the protection of Negroes when passing laws, women of all colors have also been offered protection against discrimination – due in large part to a similar history of harm from legal discrimination. In the school context, there is an express prohibition of gender discrimination. 20 U.S.C. § 1681. That section states: "No person in the United States shall, on the basis of sex, be excluded from participation in, be denied the benefits of, or be subjected to discrimination under any education program or activity receiving Federal financial assistance." *Id.* In addition, gender discrimination was curtailed when the Nineteenth Amendment gave women the right to vote. U.S. Const. amend. XIX. Congress has certainly recognized a clearly "established public policy" against gender discrimination.

Finally, just as the executive branch has espoused an "established public policy" against race discrimination, it has done the same for gender discrimination. President Nixon furthered the "established public policy" against gender discrimination when he proclaimed August 26, 1973 (the fifty-third anniversary of the incorporation of the Nineteenth Amendment) as Women's Equality Day. Proclamation No. 4236, 3A C.F.R. 117 (1974). This tradition has since been continued by Presidents Ford, Carter, and Reagan, showing continued executive action toward an "established public policy" against gender discrimination. President Nixon's proclamation states: "In recent years, we have made other giant strides by attacking sex discrimination through our laws and by paving new avenues to equal economic opportunity for women. In virtually every sector of our society, women are making important contributions to the quality of American life." *Id.* Further, "there still exists elusive prejudices born of mores and customs that stand in the way of progress for women. We must do all that we can to overcome these barriers against what is fair and right." *Id.* Finally, the proclamation ends:

> I further urge all our people to use this occasion to reflect on the importance of achieving equal rights and opportunities for women and to dedicate themselves anew to that great goal. For the cause of equal rights and opportunities for women is inseparable from the cause of human dignity and justice for all.

Id. President Nixon's order not only helps establish that there is a "public policy" against gender discrimination but also offers evidence that such a policy has long existed and is "clearly established."

Further evidence of an "established public policy" against gender discrimination comes from Executive Order No. 11,478: "It has long been the policy of the United States Government to provide equal opportunity in Federal Employment on the basis of merit and fitness without discrimination because of race, color, religion, sex, or national origin." Exec. Order No. 11,478, 34 Fed. Reg. 12,985 (Aug. 12, 1969). Additional evidence of an "established public policy" against gender discrimination is buttressed by Executive Order No. 11,183, which banned gender discrimination in the selection process of White House Fellows. Exec. Order No. 11,183, 29 Fed. Reg. 13,633 (Oct. 3, 1964). Finally, Executive Order No. 10,980 further supplements the view that there is an "established public policy" against gender discrimination. Exec. Order No. 10,980, 26 Fed. Reg. 12,059 (Dec. 30, 1961). Executive Order No. 10,980 states that "women should be assured the opportunity to develop their capacities and fulfill their aspirations on a continuing basis irrespective of natural exigencies." *Id.* With these numerous examples, it is clear that the executive branch has subscribed to the "established public policy" against gender discrimination.

Just as the majority, relying on a history of racial subordination of Negroes, cites to evidence from the three branches of our government that there is an "established public policy" against race discrimination, likewise, based on a similar history of subordination of women, there is compelling evidence from actions taken by the three branches of the federal government of an "established public policy" against gender discrimination. In both instances, the government has taken action to curtail discrimination and to ensure that such ill treatment is no longer tolerated. If the majority is to allow the Treasury the power to deny tax-exempt status under § 501(c)(3) due to a violation of the "established public policy" against racial discrimination, then it should also do so due to a violation of the "established public policy" against gender discrimination.

B

Because there is an "established public policy" against gender discrimination, it is also important to consider how the admissions policies promulgated by these institutions implicitly discriminate against women and their choices about individuals with whom they may have intimate associations.

Bob Jones University's policy allows unmarried men and women to enroll, but prohibits interracial dating or marriage. The policy mandates that "students who are partners in an interracial marriage" will be expelled. The policy also states that students who "are members of or affiliated with any group or organization which holds as one of its goals or advocates interracial marriage," or who "date outside their own race," or who "espouse, promote, or encourage others to violate the University's dating" policy will be expelled. App. in No. 81-3, at A197. Finally, while Negro employees of the school can apply to become students, they must be unmarried and also wait until employed by the school for four years. As an example, if a young woman was enrolled at Bob Jones University and decided to date someone of a different race, or even support someone else who did, she would face expulsion if her secret were to be found out. In addition, a Negro woman employed by the University could be constrained in her relationship choices for a minimum of eight years if she were a new employee and chose a traditional four-year program. If a Negro woman lived out her life span as predicted by the Center for Disease Control, she would spend over 10 percent of life waiting to escape the grasp of the University's dating policy.

These rules designed to control students' behavior effectively tell women whom they can date, marry, associate with, or even support. If a young woman were awarded a scholarship to Bob Jones University, and happened to be in an intimate interracial relationship, she would face the ghastly decision to end the relationship or pursue higher education elsewhere. Again, this conundrum could last for a significant portion of the woman's entire life. Further, a female employee involved in an intimate interracial relationship would have to choose between quitting her job and seeking education elsewhere or concealing her relationship at the risk of expulsion and applying for admission to the University (which she would presumably receive a tuition discount for as an employee). In this instance, a woman may be in the position where her place of employment is the only place she can reasonably attend a university, yet the school maintains a policy that controls her most intimate associations.

Unlike Bob Jones University, which enrolls students from kindergarten through graduate school, Goldsboro Christian Schools enrolls only K-12 students. However, similar to Bob Jones University, Goldsboro Christian Schools also has a policy that limits whom young women may date or associate with. The Goldsboro Christian School prohibits what it calls "cultural or biological mixing of races" by refusing to accept mixed-race students. While the school traditionally accepts Caucasian students, it has accepted students from racially mixed families if one of the parents is Caucasian. Though the Goldsboro Christian Schools policy may appear less onerous than the Bob Jones University policy in terms of its impact on women, that appearance is illusory. Indeed, many long-term relationships that result in marriage start in high school. Thus, by significantly impairing young mixed-race male and female students' opportunity to attend the school, or only allowing certain mixed-race students to attend, Goldsboro Christian Schools is perpetuating the same type of harm as that caused by Bob Jones University.

These practices are in direct contradiction to the "established public policy" against gender discrimination, especially in light of the fact that the policy is rooted in the history of legal subordination of women. It makes no difference if one subscribes to the older feminist view that women should be treated the same as men to receive the same benefits as men, or to the modern feminist view that women fundamentally must be treated differently than men, because they are inherently different from men, in order to receive the same protections as men. Whichever theory one subscribes to, these admissions policies produce the same result: curtailment of a woman's freedom to associate with whomever she chooses. No matter the view, women are not being offered the same protections as men are under these admissions policies, especially when viewed in the historical context of pervasively discriminatory rules and regulations against women.

When making policy decisions, it is critical to analyze how any rule will affect different groups of people, either explicitly or implicitly. Although the admissions policies of these schools facially discriminate on the basis of race, they also impermissibly implicitly discriminate against women by determining with whom a woman can and cannot associate, or even support. Based on the reasoning of the majority in finding an "established public policy" against racial discrimination, there is also an "established public policy" against gender discrimination that further buttresses the denial of tax-exempt status under § 501(c)(3) and of the ability to accept deductible charitable contributions under § 170.

C

In addition to the race-biased and gendered nature of these policies that restrict the intimacy of women and men, one must not overlook the special harm these policies impart on Negro women due to the intersection of their status as women and as Negro. It is as if Negro women suffer two distinct types of harm as a result of the University's policies. On the one hand, as women, Negro women must continue to suffer the long history of subordination and powerlessness to control an important aspect of their personal lives by being restricted in their personal choices. *E.g., Loving v. Virginia*, 388 U.S. 1 (1967) (holding Virginia law preventing interracial marriages unconstitutional); *Hoyt v. Florida*, 368 U.S. 57, 61–62 (1961) ("Despite the enlightened emancipation of women from the restrictions and the protections of bygone years, and their entry into many parts of community formally considered to be reserved to men, woman is still regarded as the center of home and family life."). Men have not traditionally been victimized by society in this way. On top of this, being Negro, Negro women are also protected by the established public policy against race-based discrimination outlined by the majority. *E.g.*, Civil Rights Act of 1964, Pub. L. No. 88-352, tit. IV, VI, 78 Stat. 241, 246, 252 (codified at 42 U.S.C. §§ 2000c *et seq.*, 2000c-6, 2000-d *et seq.*); *Brown v. Bd. of Educ.*, 347 U.S. 483 (1954); Exec. Order No. 9980, 3 C.F.R. 720 (1943–1948 Comp.). In essence, Negro women suffer a two-pronged harm that is unique to their status as both female and Negro. Given the existence of established public policies against both types of harm, it is clear that the impact of both schools' policies on Negro women buttresses the conclusion that granting § 501(c)(3) tax-exempt status to either Bob Jones University or Goldsboro Christian Schools is inconsistent with appropriate government policy.

D

Importantly, this case is about *discrimination* and not merely unequal treatment. The law is replete with instances in which groups or individuals are appropriately treated differently from one another. *E.g.*, *Muller v. Oregon*, 208 U.S. 412 (1908) (ruling female-specific workplace protection legislation was constitutional); 29 U.S.C. § 212 (granting, among other things, specific protections under the Fair Labor Standards Act to children in the labor force); Older Americans Act of 1965, Pub. L. No. 89-73, 79 Stat. 218 (codified at 42 U.S.C. § 3001 *et seq.*) (providing specific protections to elderly individuals). The harm that the majority is addressing is the harm that stems from unwarranted distinctions that have resulted in clear harm to one group, often while simultaneously benefiting another group. In the case of racial distinctions, the majority's ruling is premised on the fact that society, through law, has long imposed burdens on Negroes that were not also imposed on Caucasians. U.S. Const. amend. XIII, § 1 (finally abolishing slavery in the United States after nearly 100 years); *id.* amend. XIV, § 1 (overruling *Dred Scott v. Stanford*, 60 U.S. 393 (1856), which denied Negro descendants of slaves U.S. citizenship); *id.* amend. XV, § 1 (granting Negroes the right to vote). These three amendments are proof that our Nation's most sacred document has recognized nearly a century of unequal treatment and undue hardships on Negroes, hardships not faced by their Caucasian counterparts. Even after these constitutional amendments, our Nation allowed young Negro children to face segregation in schools until *Brown v. Board of Education*, 347 U.S. 483 (1954), which abolished the "separate but equal" doctrine that led to inferior schooling for Negroes while Caucasian children were afforded better opportunities. In addition, it was apparent that discrimination and unequal treatment remained prevalent, as it was necessary to pass the Civil Rights Act of 1964 and the Voting Rights Act of 1965 to help curtail such treatment. That these laws were passed and decisions were made are proof in themselves that Negroes did not have the same legal protection as Caucasians in our legal system. Here, the government inappropriately long permitted private schools to exclude Negroes from admission. This concurring opinion asserts that a similar case can be made both for all women and for Negro women in particular.

Situations such as these where historical subordination exists are to be distinguished from structurally similar situations in which the group that is harmed has not been subjected to historical subordination. Thus, neither the majority's analysis with respect to racial discrimination nor this concurring analysis with respect to gender discrimination and the intersection of both race and gender discrimination necessarily applies equally to men or to Caucasians or to persons who are not Negro women. Stated differently, were this Court to face an issue of an all Negro school denying admission to Caucasians or a single-gender female school denying admission to men, this Court's analysis, and hence its ultimate ruling, might differ.

E

Finally, one must not lose sight of the benefit that is at stake. That is, both taxpayers in this case are seeking the right to earn income and not pay taxes on that income like all other citizens. The payment of income taxes is one of the most basic of civic responsibilities. It is a societal obligation that has existed for as long as societies themselves have existed. A grant of federal tax exemption, then, is a statement by society that it values greatly the contribution of the exempt party. *See Trinidad v. Sagrada Orden*, 262 U.S. 578, 581 (1924); *see also Walz v. Tax Comm'n*, 397 U.S. 664, 673 (1970). So much so, that the government is willing to forego collection of tax revenue.

The reason for this forbearance could be due to partial relief of the government obligation to provide the good or service that the exempt party is providing. *See* George G. Bogert et al., *The Law of Trusts and Trustees* § 361 (rev. 2d ed. 1977); *see also* H.R. Rep. No. 75-1860, at 19 (1938). It could also be due to certain economic imperfections that necessitate relief from this most basic of civic responsibilities. *Cf.* H.R. Rep. No. 75-1860, at 19 (1938). Whatever the reason, whenever some segment of society (e.g., tax-exempt entities) is relieved of the obligation to pay federal income tax, the obligation of others in society (e.g., taxpaying individuals) to pay income taxes necessarily increases. Thus, because the nonexempt citizens are all necessarily, in a very real way, "supporting" those entities that are exempt from income tax, it is critically important that the exempt party not engage in activities that society abhors. *See Norwood v. Harrison*, 413 U.S. 455, 469 (1973); *see also Walz*, 397 U.S. at 673. It is clear from the above analysis that society abhors the notion that the government should dictate women's most intimate relationships and dealings. If the government should not do this, then those who are relieved from the obligation to support the government likewise should be barred.

F

In conclusion, I support the ruling that these schools have violated "established public policy" by expressly discriminating against Negroes in their admissions policies. However, I do not believe the discrimination ends there. These policies also discriminate based on gender by dictating the race of the persons whom women may support or with whom they may associate. Further, the impact of the policy is especially burdensome on Negro women due to their status as both women and Negro.

8

Commentary on *Manufacturers Hanover Trust Co., as Executor of the Estate of Charlotte C. Wallace, v. United States*

MILDRED WIGFALL ROBINSON

INTRODUCTION

On November 5, 1923, when Charlotte C. Wallace was thirty-five years old, she created a trust in which she retained an income interest for life. She named her son Howard (then four years old) as the secondary life beneficiary, giving him an income interest for his life if he survived her and a general testamentary power of appointment over the trust remainder. Finally, under the terms of the trust, the remainder interest would be controlled by the terms of Charlotte's will if Howard predeceased her or survived her but failed to validly exercise the general power of appointment. Charlotte died on February 28, 1976. She was then eighty-eight years old. She was survived by Howard who was then fifty-seven years of age. Since Howard survived his mother, he succeeded to an income interest for life in the trust and acquired the right to dispose of the remainder interest as he wished to pursuant to the general power of appointment. Because he was still alive, however, he could not have exercised the general power of appointment. As a result, as a matter of property law (since title in fee simple absolute had not yet vested in any transferee), Charlotte retained a reversionary interest in the property.

For estate tax purposes, Code § 2037(a)(2) requires that the value of the decedent's reversionary interest be included in the decedent's estate if that value exceeds 5 percent of the value of the trust immediately before the decedent's death. As such, the issue in this case was whether the value of Charlotte's reversionary interest was greater than 5 percent of the trust's value at the time of her death. The reversionary interest would be included in Charlotte's estate only if its value exceeded 5 percent of the trust's value immediately before her death. As a consequence, calculations under actuarial tables would establish the interest's value for estate tax purposes – a value that would reflect the probability that the grantor of the trust would, at the age just prior to death, outlive the trust's successor beneficiary. Charlotte's executor used Unisex Table I to calculate the value of her reversionary interest and found that it was 4.9867 percent of the corpus value. As such, the executors did not include the value of the reversionary interest in the gross estate and paid no tax on the trust corpus. Treasury Regulations in effect at the time, however, required the executor to value the decedent's reversionary interest in accordance with gender-based mortality tables. Using the gender-based tables, the Internal Revenue Service determined that the value of Charlotte's reversion was 6.654 percent of the underlying corpus. The estate was assessed a deficiency that, in aggregate with interest and penalties, amounted to $458,662.98. The estate paid the deficiency and, after exhausting the administrative process, sued for a refund in the district court.

THE CASE

Manufacturers Hanover Trust Co., as executor of the decedent Charlotte C. Wallace's estate, brought an action for a tax refund in the U.S. District Court for the Southern District of New York. It challenged the IRS's use of gender-based mortality tables in calculating the present value of a reversionary interest. The executor alleged that the use of gender-based tables violated the Fifth Amendment's Equal Protection Clause, arguing that the challenged statutory scheme treated men and women differently and that the resulting gender classification was unjustified and constituted unlawful discrimination.

The IRS defended the use of gender-based tables, asserting that women on average had longer life expectancies than men. It argued that the use of gender-based tables did not violate equal protection but instead was an important tool in the quest to attain estate tax fairness and accuracy. In response to a motion for summary judgment, District Court Judge Charles Stewart ruled the use of the tables unconstitutional, finding that the practice did in fact distinguish between males and females and that the classification constituted impermissible discrimination. The IRS appealed. On appeal, Judge George Pratt held the use of gender-based tables to value reversionary interests distinguished between males and females, but found that the practice was substantially related to the important governmental objective of promoting fairness and equity in estate taxes by accurately valuing reversionary interests. As such, there was no equal protection violation. The district court decision was reversed. Judge Jon Newman dissented from the appellate court decision. He agreed with the finding of gender-based distinction but would have found the practice unconstitutionally discriminatory.

FEMINIST JUDGMENT

In a reimagined *Manufacturers Hanover Trust Co.* majority feminist judgment, Professor Mary Heen, writing for the U.S. Court of Appeals for the Second Circuit as Judge Heen, explains that in valuing the reversionary interest, the lives of both the decedent and the surviving income beneficiary must be considered. She establishes that the IRS's use of gender-based mortality tables operated to Charlotte's disadvantage as a female decedent survived by a male beneficiary because of presumptively greater female longevity inherent in gender-based tables. She explores the rigor of the assumptions underlying gender-based tables, noting that the tables do not correct for individual circumstances (economic status, health, or environmental conditions) and choices (deleterious behaviors) that could affect mortality, thus making individual risk assessment impossible. That leaves sex and age alone as the underlay for the mortality risk classification. Further, the assertion of greater longevity is questioned in light of the fact that approximately 80 percent of women do not, in fact, outlive their male counterparts. Because of the imprecise or impermissible underlying assumptions, and the heightened constitutional scrutiny given gender-based classifications, the tables' use in individual cases could not be justified, Heen says, without showing an overriding important governmental objective – here to attain estate tax fairness and accuracy. This imprecision, however, renders impossible the task of attaining tax fairness and accuracy. She rejects the IRS's assertion that the tables do not distinguish on the basis of gender in light of the demonstrably increased value of reversionary interests held by female decedents. This relatively greater value increased the likelihood of the reversionary interest's inclusion in the estate that, in turn, contributed to a greater tax burden, thus illustrating the discriminatory treatment embedded in what is presented as an objective actuarial determination. The female decedent here was unable to provide for her successors as generously as her similarly situated male counterparts would have. Thus, in Heen's analysis, the use of the gender-based mortality classification to determine tax liability constitutes overt discrimination based on gender, which would be impermissible unless the government could show that the practice was substantially related to and served an important government objective. The explanation proffered by the IRS – that the value of the reversionary interest was driven by probable greater longevity rather than sex – is rejected. Hence, Heen writes, gender was used as a proxy for longevity, and the use of an explicit gender-based classification is a practice previously held to be *per se* discriminatory. This case would be no exception.

She also notes that the practice of relying on such tables is relatively new (since 1970), was a departure from prior practice, and was shortly thereafter abandoned by the IRS as it returned to the use of unisex tables for future valuations of annuities, life estates, terms of years, remainders, and reversions.

COMMENTARY

Heen's opinion concludes that what purports to be the IRS's reliance on neutral standards (in that gender is appropriately considered given what appears to be greater female longevity) in resolving the issue of valuation in this instance is, in fact, a practice that utilizes an explicit gender-based classification that works to the disadvantage of female decedents. As such, she follows in the tradition of feminists like Clare Dalton by first describing the effect of reliance on the tables in this instance, then by exploring possible reasons for such reliance, and finally – having concluded that reliance upon the tables is inappropriate and unconstitutional – changing that reliance by prohibiting the use of the gender-based rules. The rules as reconstructed – moving from gender-based to unisex tables – appear to more fairly determine estate tax liability for all decedents irrespective of gender.

The decedent's estate would unquestionably have been subject to more liability based on her gender in spite of the fact that her death constituted absolute proof of her inability to live into the greater longevity that had been predicted for her under gender-based tables. She had, if you will, lost the "bet." Under these circumstances, reliance on unisex tables guarantees estate tax fairness and accuracy; the value of reversionary interests regardless of the owner's gender will be determined using the same mortality assumptions. In short, especially with regard to female decedents, the estate will not be held accountable for value that could not be enjoyed. This is a proposition that seems eminently reasonable. No doubt, if it were possible to ascertain the wishes of the now-deceased female transferor, it would be to transfer as much as possible to her successors in interest – an objective that would be inappropriately (and unconstitutionally) thwarted by the use of gender-based tables.

At first blush, the logic and conclusion in the feminist judgment seems unassailable, leading perhaps inexorably to reliance on unisex tables whenever question of valuation arises. The question, however, becomes subtler and more nuanced as the nature of the interest changes. Of necessity, valuing a reversion uses death as the critical point in time. On the other hand, life estates and interests for a term of years both involve attempts to determine value prospectively. A remainder interest may require either prospective or retrospective valuation dependent on whether it is created *inter vivos* or upon death. The difference in timing is critical.

Recall that Charlotte was thirty-five years of age in 1923 when she created her trust and that Howard was four years old. She was a mother planning for the financial well-being first for herself and then for her son. From an estate planning perspective, her plan appeared sound: provide income for herself throughout her life, then provide for Howard, taking care to control that wealth should he die childless and without having validly disposed of the property through his general power of appointment. Upon creation of the income interest, actuarial tables would absolutely predict relatively greater longevity for Charlotte on the basis of gender, and there would be no way of determining at that point whether she would be among the 80 percent of women who failed to outlive the male cohort or the 20 percent who would do so. In the latter case, reliance on unisex tables would impose upon her relatively greater liability because her retained interest would be undervalued. Indeed, Charlotte would understandably resist the imposition of gift tax liability upon value that was actuarially allocable to her retained interest. Valuation of a term of years created by a female would be similarly treated if retained by the transferor. In either case, the greater value of the retained interest under gender-based tables would reduce overall gift tax liability but not necessarily with discriminatory effect because of the prospective nature of the valuation. On the other hand, transfers to females could potentially be costlier to a transferor – male or female – using gender-based tables again because of the embedded presumption of greater female longevity. Again, on its face, in either case this appears unobjectionable; the value determined is presumptively the amount that would be required to support the interest created for the contemplated period.

Indeed, unless the underlying instrument imposed restrictions on aliena-tion, each of these interests could be sold at fair market value. Were this to occur, a purchaser of any of these interests would certainly take the life expec-tancy of the putative transferor into consideration as the parties bargained over price.

There would be, of course, no way to prospectively guarantee absolute alignment between imposition of liability and the quantum of the gift. This need not invalidate *a priori* reliance on gender-based tables, however. Liability is determined for both Subtitle A (income tax) and Subtitle B (gift tax) purposes annually on the basis of the law then extant. Similarly, estate tax liability is determined as of the date of death. There is no guarantee in any of these determinations that the underlying law will remain unchanged or that strategic choices will achieve the desired ends. Valuation of interests should not be accorded special treatment because of the possibility of either over- or undervaluation, so long as that process is undertaken in accordance with sound practices.

Note that all of the transactions examined so far are controlled by Subtitle B of the Code. Questions of valuation become no less difficult under Subtitle A of the Code and may, in fact, be of even more economic importance to women given the hugely increased presence of women in the civilian work force. The U.S. Department of Labor Women's Bureau reports that from 1948 to 2015, the number of women in the civilian labor force increased from approximately 17.3 million (28.4 percent) to 73.5 million (46.6 percent).[1] As of 2012, almost 50 percent of these women worked for employers that provided some type of retirement plan. Further, defined contribution plans providing an annuity option now constitute a substantial majority of such plans. The plan beneficiary may choose to elect either a one-time payout or periodic distributions over some predetermined period of time. With one-time payouts, the IRS would likely be unable to defend the use of gender-based tables to reach the value of the distribution for all of the reasons given by Heen in the rewritten opinion. After all, in the case of lump-sum retirement benefits (and analogous to determining the value of a reversion at death), the female beneficiary who opts for the lump sum is in precisely the same economic position as her male counterpart who has made the same choice. The calculus changes, however, if she opts to receive periodic payments for life.

An example makes the point. Assume that we have two employees – one male and one female. The male has a twenty-five-year life expectancy; the female has a thirty-year life expectancy. The employer provides to each an annuity with a present cash value of $100,000 payable for life. Assuming further that the $100,000 has not been tax sheltered, the rate of capital recovery must be determined as each payment is received in order to separate tax-free recovery of capital from taxable return on investment. Using unisex tables for this purpose, and holding life expectancy of twenty-five and thirty years constant for both recipients, each would have a (unisex) life expectancy of twenty-seven years and would annually receive $6,829. Pursuant to Code § 72(b)(1), the exclusion ratio for each would be 54.2 percent; $3,225 of each payment would be taxable income. For each annuitant, the total return would be approximately $184,000. Assuming (however unrealistically) that each annuitant lives only to the longevity predicted, the male will die two

[1] Women's Bureau, U.S. Dep't of Labor, *Civilian Labor Force by Sex, 1948–2015 Annual Averages*, https://www.dol.gov/wb/stats/Civilian_labor_force_sex_48_15_txt.htm (last visited Dec. 2, 2016).

years before the stream of payments ends; economic considerations would cease to matter. For the longer-lived female, however, the economic outlook after year twenty-seven could be quite dire. Assuming that the annuity is her only source of income, in the worst-case scenario, she would face possible destitution for the remaining three years of her life. On the other hand, using gender-specific actuarial tables generates different exclusion ratios, annual payments, and total incomes for the two employees. Specifically (and continuing to hold actuarial life expectancy constant), the male would be required to use an exclusion ratio of 56.4 percent, would receive annual payments of $7,095, and would recover the entire capital investment when his life ended in year twenty-five. His return would total approximately $177,000. Comparatively, the female would be required to use an exclusion ratio of 51.2 percent, and would receive annual payments of $6,505, but would not exhaust this income stream until the age of thirty. Her return over the life of the annuity would be approximately $195,000. In effect, she will have effectively traded a slower rate of capital recovery and less annual income for assured financial support over the course of her actuarial life and a higher return overall.

A gender-based actuarial determination thus has both pros and cons. It disadvantages a female in that her return would be actuarially lowered based on the assumption that she would be among the 20 percent or so of women who outlived their male counterpart – an outcome that certainly appears to be demonstrably impermissible discrimination. On the other hand, reliance on the gender-based determination could be more supportive of a woman's economic self-sufficiency over the course of her longer life. Gender-driven lower annual net receipts over a longer payout period is a troubling prospect made even more so given the realities of persistent male/female wage disparities and women's comparatively lesser economic readiness for the financial stresses of retirement. On balance, however, the risk may be preferable to the alternative: financial hardship driven by premature loss of the stream of income. As was the case with estate and gift tax questions of valuation, a unisex approach could prospectively undervalue a female's interest but now with financial risk exceeding attendant greater liability. In the income tax context, the statistically greater risk of financial hardship faced by women could be offset to some extent by factoring the real possibility of greater female longevity into the calculus. In short, the opinion as rewritten certainly achieves equality between male and female decedents whose estates are comprised in part of includable reversionary interests. Extending that same unisex treatment to all females who either give or receive life estates, interests for a term of years, or remainder interests that generate future tax consequences under either Subtitle A or Subtitle B goes too far, however. Taxpayers who hold interests that require prospective valuation will be both male and female, and economic consequences will differ for them accordingly. Greater female longevity is an actuarial reality. As such, the absolute rule that is the rewritten opinion's outcome (as well as present IRS practice) overcorrects in treating this aggregate body of taxpayers as an undifferentiated sexual monolith for which returns over time are presumptively equal.

To summarize, Heen is correct in asserting that it would be inappropriate to use race as a factor in determining value. Though often (albeit by no means always) observable, race remains impossible to capture definitively. Osagie Obasogie puts it this way: "While there may be genetic variations linked to a similar outward experience among various populations that can signal propensities in social and health outcomes, social categories of race do not capture these in any meaningful sense. Social categories of race and population differences are largely discordant and do not meaningfully map onto each other."[2] As such, as Heen so effectively points out, its impact on value will change as context changes. It also remains the case that race-based distinctions have generally been socially harmful overall and remain subject to strict judicial scrutiny. Biological sex shares some of these same characteristics. As Heen has argued so powerfully in this feminist judgment and in her scholarship more generally, differences in gender mortality can be explained, certainly in (large?) part and as mentioned earlier, by individual circumstances (economic status, health, or environmental conditions) and choices (deleterious behaviors) that could affect mortality. Further, while gender is not subject to strict scrutiny, it remains a suspect class. It is also the case that reinforcing gender-based distinctions has all too often proved harmful to women. That said, it remains true that, over time, a correlation between biological sex and increased longevity has persisted. Taking increased longevity into account to value economic interests prospectively would advantage women but without *unduly* disadvantaging men. Of equal importance, a gendered approach to valuation in the manner described would serve a legitimate governmental interest in responding constructively to the unique economic issues raised by women's relatively greater longevity. Moreover, this more nuanced approach need not be seen to be creating a Procrustean bed; if the longevity gap narrows or closes entirely, the periodic promulgation of new tables will reflect such changes. In the short term, it may well be preferable (during what may turn out to be only an interim period) to forgo the formality of uniform nongendered valuation rules for all purposes, opting instead for a gender-based

---

[2] OSAGIE K. OBASOGIE, BLINDED BY SIGHT: SEEING RACE THROUGH THE EYES OF THE BLIND 26 (2014).

approach to valuation processes. This should especially be the case where value is to be prospectively determined under either Subtitle A or Subtitle B and the female anticipates a series of payments for life. In the final analysis, in this set of transfers a gender-based approach could well be more supportive of women's financial well-being than reliance on facially neutral but economically insensitive unisex tables.

A final point: Heen is to be commended for her deep interest in the issues raised by this case in particular. She was a member of a team of lawyers from the American Civil Liberties Union Foundation filing a brief as *amici curiae* in the original case. The holding in that case was not the one for which she argued. With this rewritten opinion, she has now set that matter right.

MANUFACTURERS HANOVER TRUST CO., AS EXECUTOR OF THE ESTATE OF CHARLOTTE C. WALLACE v. UNITED STATES, 775 F.2D 459 (2D CIR. 1985)

MARY L. HEEN, CIRCUIT JUDGE, DELIVERED THE OPINION OF THE COURT

This case raises the issue of whether the use of gender-distinct mortality tables for federal estate tax valuation purposes denies female decedents equal protection of the law. The district court held below that the use of male and female mortality classifications for such valuation purposes does not have "the requisite direct and substantial relationship" to an important governmental objective, and therefore the classifications "constitute impermissible gender-based discrimination." *Mfrs. Hanover Tr. Co. v. United States*, 576 F. Supp. 837, 842, 844 (S.D.N.Y. 1983). Accordingly, the district court granted the estate's claim for a refund of estate taxes in the amount of $455,581.71, plus interest. We affirm the district court's judgment.

I

The facts of this case are not in dispute. Charlotte Wallace was in her mid-thirties with a four-year-old son when she established a trust in 1923. The trust agreement provided that the net income from the trust would be paid to her for her life, and at her death paid to her son, Howard Wallace. Under the agreement, she retained the right to direct in her will how the remainder of the trust would be paid, but only in the event that either (i) Howard did not survive her or (ii) Howard survived her but failed to exercise his testamentary general power of appointment under the trust agreement and had no children or descendants surviving him. Charlotte Wallace died in 1976 at the age of eighty-eight, and was survived by her son Howard Wallace, who was fifty-seven years old at the time of his mother's death. The parties agree that Charlotte Wallace's retained right under the trust agreement constitutes a reversionary interest; this raises a federal estate tax valuation issue for her estate.

Under Internal Revenue Code § 2037, if a reversionary interest in a trust exceeds 5 percent of the total value of the trust immediately before the decedent's death, the date of death value of the trust is included in the decedent's gross estate. I.R.C. § 2037(a)(2). In order to value a reversionary interest such as the retained interest at issue here, two lives are measured: the life of the decedent, Charlotte Wallace, and the life of the surviving income beneficiary, Howard Wallace.

Manufacturers Hanover Trust Company, the executor of the estate of Charlotte Wallace, valued the reversionary interest using life expectancies computed under a unisex or gender-merged mortality table. The computation resulted in a valuation percentage of 4.9867 percent for Charlotte Wallace's reversion. Because the retained interest did not exceed the 5 percent threshold provided by § 2037, the executor did not include the value of the trust in her gross estate, and accordingly, the estate paid total federal estate tax of $86,280.

The Internal Revenue Service, on the other hand, computed the present value of the reversionary interest using separate male and female mortality tables. Separate tables were specified at that time by Treasury Regulation § 20.2031-10(e) and (f). *See* Treas. Reg. §§ 20.2031-7(a), -10(d)–(f), 20.2037-1(c)(3).

The male and female mortality tables used by the Treasury Department in its regulations were based on United States Life Tables 1959–1961, published in 1964 by the U.S. Department of Health, Education, and Welfare (now the U.S. Department of Health and Human Services) (Table 2, "Life Table for Total Males" and Table 3, "Life Table for Total Females"). T.D. 7077, 1970-2 C.B. 183 (adopting these tables for decedents dying after December 31, 1970). If Charlotte Wallace had been male and Howard Wallace had been female, or alternatively, if Howard Wallace had been female (with all other facts remaining the same), the use of those gender-distinct tables would not have resulted in the payment of the additional estate tax, leaving a larger estate and a greater amount available for the beneficiaries. The gender-merged table utilized by the executor of Charlotte Wallace's estate to compute the value of her reversionary interest came from a different section of the same government publication on which the Treasury Department based its regulations (United States Life Tables 1959–1961, Table 1, "Life Table for Total Population").

The use of gender-distinct mortality tables by the IRS resulted in a valuation in excess of 5 percent (6.654 percent), and therefore the federal taxing authorities included the value of the trust in Charlotte Wallace's gross estate. Based on that calculation, the government assessed a tax deficiency in the amount of $455,581.71, plus interest, for a total of $458,662.98. The estate paid the assessed deficiencies in 1982 and commenced an action in the district court seeking a refund of the additional taxes paid, with interest.

The parties filed cross motions for summary judgment. On October 17, 1983, the district court granted Manufacturers Hanover's motion and denied the government's cross motion, concluding that the use of gender-based tables violated the equal protection component of the Fifth Amendment of the U.S. Constitution. *Mfrs. Hanover Tr. Co.*, 576 F. Supp. 837.

Shortly after the district court's decision, on October 31, 1983, the Treasury Department promulgated proposed regulations applicable to decedents dying after November 30, 1983, prescribing gender-merged tables to value reversions. Revision of Actuarial Tables and Interest Factors, 48 Fed. Reg. 50,087 (Oct. 31, 1983) (issuing proposed regulations eliminating the use of gender-based mortality tables prospectively but leaving gender-distinct tables applicable to estates of persons dying on or before and valuations effective on or before November 30, 1983). Those proposed regulations have now been finalized. Income, Estate, and Gift Taxes; Revision of Actuarial Tables and Interest Factors, 49 Fed. Reg. 19,973 (May 11, 1984) (finalizing rules to be codified at 26 C.F.R. pts. 1, 11, 20, 23). The revised regulations and gender-merged tables remain in effect today but do not apply to the case at hand.

II

The Due Process Clause of the Fifth Amendment imposes on the federal government requirements "comparable to those that the Equal Protection Clause of the Fourteenth Amendment imposes on the states." *Regan v. Taxation with Representation of Wash.*, 461 U.S. 540, 542 n.2 (1983); *Bolling v. Sharpe*, 347 U.S. 497 (1954). Governmental classifications that distinguish between males and females are "subject to scrutiny under the Equal Protection Clause," and to withstand constitutional scrutiny, such classifications "must serve important governmental objectives and must be substantially related to achievement of those objectives." *Craig v. Boren*, 429 U.S. 190, 197 (1976).

The party seeking to uphold the classification must show an "exceedingly persuasive justification." *Miss. Univ. for Women v. Hogan*, 458 U.S. 718, 724 (1982) (quoting *Kirchberg v. Feenstra*, 450 U.S. 455, 461 (1981)). The classification must also exhibit a direct and substantial relationship between the objective and the means employed. *Id.* at 724; *Wengler v. Druggists Mut. Ins. Co.*, 446 U.S. 142, 150 (1980). The requirement of a close relationship is to ensure that classifications do not rely on gender as a "proxy for other, more germane bases of classification." *Craig*, 429 U.S. at 198. The test must be applied free of role stereotypes or fixed notions concerning the innate characteristics of males and females. *Miss. Univ. for Women*, 458 U.S. at 723–77.

The government seeks to uphold its use of gender distinct mortality tables on two grounds: first, that the tables do not discriminate on the basis of gender; and second, even if they do, the discrimination is not unconstitutional. We conclude that both of the government's arguments fail for the reasons discussed below.

A

Despite the government's protestations to the contrary, the IRS applies a regulatory scheme that makes overt distinctions based on the gender of the individuals in question. In measuring the value of the reversionary interest in a trust, the government uses gender-based mortality classifications as a proxy for longevity. The use of gender-based classifications as a proxy for longevity has been repeatedly rebuffed by the U.S. Supreme Court and held to be gender-based employment discrimination unlawful under federal civil rights law. *See City of L.A., Dep't of Water & Power v. Manhart*, 435 U.S. 702 (1978); *Ariz. Governing Comm. for Tax Deferred Annuity & Deferred Comp. Plans v. Norris*, 463 U.S. 1073 (1983). We reach an analogous conclusion today under equal protection analysis with regard to the use of gender-distinct mortality classifications for tax valuation purposes.

Congress first adopted the 5 percent threshold of Code § 2037 in 1949. H.R. Rep. No. 81-1412, at 6–7 (1949). Although § 2037 taxes the privilege of transferring property by testamentary disposition or *inter vivos* substitute by taxing lifetime dispositions of property where the transferor can again possess or enjoy the property, the 5 percent threshold provides an exception to avoid taxation of transferred property in which the decedent holds merely a *de minimis* reversionary interest. Section 2037 does not prescribe how the 5 percent threshold should be determined, other than providing that the value of the reversionary interest "shall be determined (without regard to the decedent's death) by usual methods of valuation, including the use of mortality tables and actuarial principles, under regulations prescribed by the Secretary." I.R.C. § 2037(b).

For purposes of the estate tax, the value of the grantor's reversionary interest in a trust is calculated by determining the probability that a person of the decedent's age, just prior to death, would outlive the trust's beneficiary. Soon after the adoption of the 5 percent test, the Treasury Department promulgated regulations prescribing gender-merged mortality tables to be used to value reversionary interests for purposes of the test. Treas. Reg. § 20.2031-7; *see, e.g.*, Miscellaneous Amendments, 17 Fed. Reg. 5016, 5017 (June 4, 1952). In 1970, nearly twenty years later, the Treasury Department promulgated new regulations for decedents dying after 1970. Those regulations prescribed gender-distinct mortality tables to be used to value reversionary interests for purposes of the 5 percent test. T.D. 7077, 1970-2 C.B. 183. Because Charlotte Wallace died in 1976, the Treasury Department applied the gender-distinct tables applicable to decedents dying after 1970 in valuing her reversionary interest.

When gender-distinct tables are used in calculating an individual decedent's estate tax, the fact that the decedent is female will increase the value of the reversionary interest over what the value would be if the decedent were male, because, on average, women tend to live longer than men. Thus, the use of gender as a computational classifier results in the estates of women being taxed more frequently under the 5 percent test (leaving a smaller net estate for the beneficiaries of the estate) than the estates of men. Where all facts other than gender are identical, it is more likely that the estate of a female will exceed the 5 percent test than the estate of a male. When gender-based tables are used to compute the life expectancy of the beneficiary, the fact that the beneficiary is female will decrease the value of the reversionary interest from what it would be if the beneficiary were male. On the other hand, by using unisex or gender-merged tables, the gender of the persons whose lives are measured does not determine taxability.

It is apparent, therefore, that under the IRS practice of using gender-distinct mortality classifications, similarly situated male and female decedents are explicitly treated differently in a way that may affect the taxpayers' ultimate tax burdens. This constitutes overt discrimination based on gender. *See Wengler v. Druggists Mut. Ins. Co.*, 446 U.S. 142 (1980); *Moritz v. Comm'r*, 469 F.2d 466 (10th Cir. 1972), *cert. denied*, 412 U.S. 906 (1973); *see also Califano v. Goldfarb*, 430 U.S. 199, 208 (1977); *Weinberger v. Wiesenfeld*, 420 U.S. 636, 651–53 (1975). In *Moritz*, the court held unconstitutional under the equal protection component of the Fifth Amendment an income tax provision that denied a deduction for the dependent care expenses of a single, unmarried man but allowed a deduction for those of a single woman (or a married or widowed woman). In the court's view, the statutory scheme was not based on the relative burden of caretaking duties borne by taxpayers, but instead "made a special distinction based on sex alone, which cannot stand." *Moritz*, 469 F.2d at 470.

Nevertheless, the government argued in this case below that the regulations do not discriminate on the basis of gender because the tax burden turns on the "value of the transferor's reversionary interest, not his sex," and that this in turn depends "solely upon the probable longevity of the decedent and the transferee (discounted to present value), as derived by usual accounting measures." *Mfrs. Hanover Tr. Co. v. United States*, 576 F. Supp. 837, 840 (S.D.N.Y. 1983) (quoting from the Government's Memorandum of Law in Opposition at 25). Similar reasoning has been squarely rejected by the U.S. Supreme Court in *Manhart*, 435 U.S. at 712–13 (prohibiting an employer from requiring a higher pension contribution from female employees for benefits equal to those paid to men), and in *Norris*, 463 U.S. at 1083 (prohibiting lower periodic retirement plan benefits paid to female retirees based on equal contributions by men and women)

In holding the use of gender-based mortality tables to be *per se* discriminatory, the majority in *Norris* rejected Arizona's argument that the plan did not discriminate on the basis of sex because similarly situated men and women would obtain annuity policies at retirement with equal present actuarial values. Justice Marshall, writing for the Court, exposed the underlying fallacy of such an argument under Title VII of the Civil Rights Act of 1964, which prohibits employment discrimination on the basis of race, color, religion, sex, and national origin. Without the use of gender-based classifications in the first place, there would be no basis for postulating the actuarial equivalence or equal expected value of the annuity payouts. *Norris*, 463 U.S. at 1083. It is circular reasoning to use the expectancies generated by a predictor to justify using that predictor. *Id.*

That point can be illustrated by a simple example, as explained by Lea Brilmayer et al., *Sex Discrimination in Employer-Sponsored Insurance Plans: A Legal and Demographic Analysis*, 47 U. Chi. L. Rev. 505, 512–13 (1980):

> Consider the life expectancy of a newborn black male in South Carolina. Prediction of his life expectancy may or may not take into account his sex, race, and residence. If he is classified as a nonwhite male South Carolinian, his life expectancy is 58.33 years. If he is classified simply as a resident of the United States, his life expectancy is 70.75 years. The other possibilities range in between: he may be a nonwhite South Carolinian [62.64], or a male South Carolinian [63.85], a nonwhite male American [60.98], a male American [67.04], a nonwhite American [64.95], or a South Carolinian [67.96]. He has eight different life expectancies – and just on the basis of the three predictors introduced so far .... A newborn black female in South Carolina has a greater life expectancy only if one has already decided to use gender as a predictor; if gender is not used, the two infants have identical expectancies.

Thus, an equal expected value test is futile; it can be satisfied by either integrated or segregated tables .... [When employers classify on the basis of sex], they are treating every woman [as if she were] at the mean of the distribution for women, and every man as if he were at the mean of the distribution for men .... The important point is that no "true" expectancy can be generated by purely mathematical methods; considerations of social policy and administrative convenience are always called into play.

In *Manhart*, the Court viewed the use of gender-based mortality tables to be just as unacceptable under Title VII as it would be to utilize race-based tables. The majority rejected the argument that the actuarial distinctions used were based on "longevity" rather than gender and emphasized that the record contained no evidence that any factors other than sex (such as smoking or other behavioral or environmental factors) were taken into account in calculating the differential in employee contributions. Justice Stevens, writing for the Court, observed that "one cannot say that an actuarial distinction based entirely on sex is 'based on any factor other than sex.' Sex is entirely what it is based on." *Manhart*, 435 U.S. at 712–13.

The City of Los Angeles Department of Water in *Manhart* had required its female employees to make monthly payments to its pension fund which were nearly 15 percent higher than the monthly payments required of male employees, reducing the take-home pay of similarly situated women employees. The city justified its practice by claiming that gender-based mortality tables showed that women lived longer than men, and that women would therefore receive, on average, more in retirement benefits than men would receive over their lifetimes. The Supreme Court held that Title VII prohibited the use of gender-based actuarial classifications because they resulted in unlawful gender discrimination. The Court pointed out that many women "do not live as long as the average man and many men outlive the average woman," *id.* at 708, and that "individual risks, like individual performance, may not be predicted by resort to classifications proscribed by Title VII." *Id.* at 710. According to the Court, "even a true generalization about [a] class" cannot justify class-based treatment. *Id.* at 708; *Norris*, 463 U.S. at 1085 (quoting *Manhart*, 435 U.S. at 708).

The Supreme Court has applied similar concepts of "discrimination" under both Title VII and the Equal Protection Clause:

While there is no necessary inference that Congress, in choosing [the] language of [Section 703(a)(1) of Title VII], intended to incorporate into Title VII the concepts of discrimination which have evolved from court decisions construing the Equal Protection Clause of the Fourteenth

Amendment, the similarities between the congressional language and some of these decisions surely indicate that the latter are a useful starting point in interpreting the former. Particularly in the case of defining the term "discrimination" which Congress has nowhere in Title VII defined, those cases afford an existing body of law analyzing and discussing that term in a legal context not wholly dissimilar to the concerns which Congress manifested in enacting Title VII.

Gen. Elec. Co. v. Gilbert, 429 U.S. 125, 133 (1977). The use of gender as a class-based generalization for determining retirement benefits, unlawful under Title VII, has also been held to constitute a discriminatory gender-based classification under the Equal Protection Clause. As noted by the Indiana Supreme Court when it struck down the use of gender-based mortality tables that resulted in lower monthly annuity benefits to women under the state's teachers' retirement system, such discrimination constitutes an impermissible gender-based classification under the Fourteenth Amendment. *Reilly v. Robertson*, 360 N.E.2d 171 (Ind.), *cert. denied*, 434 U.S. 825 (1977).

Fairness to individual men and women requires that gender not be used as a proxy for longevity. As the U.S. Supreme Court has emphasized, the need for the requirement of a "direct, substantial relationship between objective and means" is "amply revealed by reference to the broad range of statutes already invalidated by this Court, statutes that relied upon the simplistic, outdated assumption that gender could be used as a 'proxy for other, more germane bases of classification,' to establish a link between objective and classification." *Miss. Univ. for Women v. Hogan*, 458 U.S. 718, 725–26 (1982) (quoting *Craig v. Boren*, 429 U.S. 190, 198 (1976)); *see, e.g., Kirchberg v. Feenstra*, 450 U.S. 455 (1981) (management of jointly owned property); *Wengler*, 446 U.S. 142 (spousal death benefits under workers' compensation laws); *Orr v. Orr*, 440 U.S. 268 (1979) (alimony); *Craig*, 429 U.S. 190 (sale of 3.2 percent beer); *Stanton v. Stanton*, 421 U.S. 7 (1975) (age of majority); *Weinberger*, 420 U.S. 636 (survivor's benefits under Social Security Act); *Frontiero v. Richardson*, 411 U.S. 677 (1973) (armed forces dependency benefits); *Reed v. Reed*, 404 U.S. 71 (1971) (administrators of estates).

In *Craig*, a vendor challenged the constitutionality of Oklahoma statutes prohibiting the sale of "non-intoxicating" 3.2 percent beer to males under the age of twenty-one and to females under the age of eighteen on the ground that the gender-based differential constituted invidious discrimination against males eighteen to twenty years of age. The state asserted the governmental objective of enhancing traffic safety, and relied on statistical surveys demonstrating that arrests of eighteen- to twenty-year-old males for drinking and driving greatly exceeded arrests of females in that age group, and that young males were overrepresented among those killed or injured in traffic accidents. On behalf of the Court's majority, Justice Brennan held that the differential had not been shown to be substantially related to achievement of traffic safety. The most relevant study showed that 2 percent of males and 0.18 percent of females in those age groups were arrested for driving while under the influence of alcohol. Although such a disparity was "not trivial in a statistical sense," the correlation was an "unduly tenuous 'fit'" to use gender as a statutory classification. *Craig*, 429 U.S. at 201–02. The Court concluded, after noting shortcomings of the statistical surveys, that gender was not an accurate proxy for drinking and driving, stating as follows:

> It is unrealistic to expect either members of the judiciary or state officials to be well versed in the rigors of experimental or statistical technique. But this merely illustrates that proving broad sociological propositions by statistics is a dubious business, and one that inevitably is in tension with the normative philosophy that underlies the Equal Protection Clause. Suffice it to say that the showing offered by the [state] does not satisfy us that sex represents a legitimate, accurate proxy for the regulation of drinking and driving.

Id. at 204. The Court then analogized gender-based statistical surveys to social science studies that have uncovered quantifiable differences in drinking tendencies dividing among both racial and ethnic lines. It observed that "the principles embodied in the Equal Protection Clause are not to be rendered inapplicable by statistically measured but loose-fitting generalities concerning the drinking tendencies of aggregate groups." *Id.* at 208–09 & n.22.

This case involves just the same sort of "statistically measured but loose-fitting generalities" concerning life expectancies of individuals based on aggregate tendencies of a group – defined by gender – to which they belong. The government here argues, and it is currently generally agreed, that women as a class have longer average life expectancies than men. Actuarial differences could unquestionably be identified in groups classified by race and national origin, as well as sex. For example, as noted by the Court in *Manhart*, the life expectancy of a white baby in 1973 was 72.2 years; a nonwhite baby could expect to live 65.9 years, a difference of 6.3 years. 435 U.S. at 709 n.15.

From a generalization about life expectancies, however, the government leaps to the conclusion that as a matter of biology men and women are not "similarly situated." The cases on which it relies, however, involve either absolute differences between men and women, *e.g.*, *Michael M. v. Superior Court of Sonoma Cty.*, 450 U.S. 464 (1981); *Geduldig v. Aiello*, 417 U.S. 484 (1974) (the capacity to become pregnant), or statutory schemes that, based on overriding considerations of national defense, have treated men and women differently with regard to military service, *Rostker v. Goldberg*, 453 U.S. 57 (1981) (excluding women from draft registration because they were, as a matter of law, not available for combat).

Here, the correlation between gender and longevity is based only on averages, not absolutes. No mortality table can predict the actual life expectancy of any individual, and some men do outlive women of the same age. In fact, most women do not live longer than most men of the same age. Based on the tables contained in Reg. § 20.2031-10, 80.6 percent of females aged sixty-five will have the same year of death as 80.6 percent of the males. The greater "life expectancy" of women compared to men therefore derives from the relatively small percentage of long-lived women and short-lived men in the entire group of men and women.

In sum, we conclude that the mortality classifications at issue are overtly gender-based, and consider next whether they withstand constitutional scrutiny as substantially related to an important governmental objective.

B

The government contends that the "important governmental objective" it seeks to promote by the use of gender-based mortality tables is actuarial accuracy in valuing reversionary interests of decedents' trusts. However, the government's assertion as to the alleged importance of the use of gender-based mortality tables is belied by two facts: (1) that their use in this context was a relatively new development (and departure from past practice), and (2) that the IRS itself recently revised its regulations to prospectively eliminate the use of gender-based tables.

As an initial observation, it should be noted that valuation under Code § 2037 differs significantly from most other purposes for which such tables have been used in the retirement and commercial insurance contexts. Typically, mortality tables are used to determine the amount of dollars paid to fund some kind of benefit, such as periodic retirement payments over a lifetime or a payment to a beneficiary upon the death of an insured. In that context, the life expectancies of those in a risk pool and assumptions about rates of return on investments determine the amount of dollars to be collected to fund the benefit for the group of retirees or the group of those insured. However, once the risk pool has been identified, adequate funding of the *overall* cost of such benefits can be ensured by the use of either gender-merged tables or by gender-distinct tables. Various degrees of cross subsidies of individual payouts may result, however, depending on actual mortality of individuals compared to average predicted life expectancies. Nevertheless, when insurance risks are grouped, the better risks always subsidize the poorer risks to some extent. As Justice Stevens pointed out in *Manhart*, nothing more than habit makes subsidies based on gender seem less fair in the pension context than subsidies by unmarried men of the benefits of married men, or subsidies by those who smoke, eat, or drink to excess of the benefits of the more temperate workers. *City of L.A., Dep't of Water & Power v. Manhart*, 435 U.S. 710 (1978); *see also* Brilmayer et al., *supra*, at 531–32; Barbara Bergmann & Mary Gray, *Equality in Retirement Benefits: The Need for Reform*, 8 Civ. Rts. Dig. 24, 25 (1975) (reporting an 84 percent overlap in the death ages of men and women and questioning the fairness of allocating to all women the greater retirement benefits costs of 8 percent of women who die later, and allocating to all men the lesser costs of 8 percent of men who die earlier rather than sharing such costs on a gender-neutral basis).

By contrast, the valuation under § 2037 does not concern a funding mechanism but instead only a theoretical construct, the present value of a decedent's reversionary interest in a trust the moment before death. The statute is not concerned with the actual fair market value of the interest. The present value just prior to death is calculated only for those persons who die, a circumstance that eliminates even a theoretical present value for their reversionary interest. The actual value will almost always be zero or very close to zero. What § 2037 does, according to the government, is to provide for the hypothetical valuation of the reversionary interest without regard to the decedent's death. *See* Rev. Rul. 80-80, 1980-1 C.B. 194; *see also* Rev. Rul. 66-307, 1966-2 C.B. 429.

When enacting the 5 percent threshold of § 2037 in 1949, Congress wanted the IRS to determine the theoretical value of a reversionary interest just prior to a decedent's death to avoid the tax inequity of including the value of an interest in a trust that was too slight to warrant the taxation of the entire trust corpus. 95 Cong. Rec. 14,411 (1949). The question raised by this case therefore is whether tax equity will be substantially advanced by the use of gender-based classifications in applying the 5 percent threshold. The government maintains that it is important to utilize the most accurate "averages" of life expectancy for the average man and woman to achieve tax equity in valuation. It argues that Congress has determined that a fair way of valuing reversionary interests is to use the average life expectancies of settlors and beneficiaries rather than individualized determinations, and that therefore it aimed to make the tax burden fair across groups of settlors and beneficiaries.

However, for nearly twenty years, until 1970, the Treasury Regulations for valuing § 2037 reversions required the use of unisex tables. Congress did not question the IRS's use of unisex tables at the time the predecessor to § 2037 was reenacted in the Internal Revenue Code of 1954. *See* H.R. Rep. No. 83-1337 (1954), *reprinted in* 1954 U.S.C.C.A.N. 4117, 4457, 4756, 5113.

Furthermore, notwithstanding the Treasury Department's use during 1971–1983 of gender-discriminatory tables for § 2037 purposes, the Treasury Department continued to use unisex tables for various purposes in other areas. *See, e.g.,* Treas. Reg. § 1.79-3(d)(2) (determining the cost of the portion of group term life insurance on the employee's life to be taken into account in computing the amount includable in the employee's gross income); Rev. Rul. 76-47, 1976-1 C.B. 109 (providing appropriate conversion factors for contributory defined benefit plans when normal retirement age is not age sixty-five and to determine the minimum accrued benefit derived from employee contributions and the actuarial adjustment required when the normal form of benefit is other than a single life annuity).

In addition, although race-based mortality tables were published in the source utilized by the Treasury Department for its 1970 gender-distinct mortality tables, United States Life Tables 1959–1961, in tables 4 through 9, the IRS did not attempt to apply mortality tables for the total white population, or for white females and white males when valuing the reversionary interest of Charlotte Wallace in this case, although arguably, according to the government's logic, those race-differentiated tables would have applied even more "accurate" averages. The government thus cannot now argue, much less bear its burden of proof, either that the use of gender-based tables is important for reasons of needed "accuracy" or that the use of unisex tables is unworkable.

As if to underscore this very point, the Treasury Department recently issued proposed regulations that eliminate the use of gender-distinct mortality tables to value annuities, life estates, terms for years, remainders, and reversions for purposes of federal income, estate, and gift taxation. *See* Revision of Actuarial Tables and Interest Factors, 48 Fed. Reg. 50,087–50,111 (Oct. 31, 1983) (applying unisex tables for estates of decedents dying after November 30, 1983). Thus, the government is at odds with itself in this case. The Justice Department here argues that the gender-based tables are important while the Treasury Department essentially concedes that they are not, and the Equal Employment Opportunity Commission, in a related context, takes the firm position that gender-distinct tables used to compute individual employee retirement contributions or benefits constitute impermissible sex discrimination. Brief for the United States and the Equal Employment Opportunity Commission as *Amici Curiae* Supporting Respondents at 7–10, 13–20, *Manhart*, 435 U.S. 702 (No. 76-1810) (arguing that Title VII bans such unequal treatment and explaining why unisex actuarial tables, which merge the life expectancies of men and women in a way similar to merged black and white life expectancies in tables used by the life insurance industry after the abandonment of traditional race-based actuarial tables, provide an available and practical alternative to gender-distinct tables); *see, e.g., E.E.O.C. v. Colby College*, 589 F.2d 1139 (1st Cir. 1978).

The significance of the dispute in this case has been substantially reduced for future decedents by the government's voluntary prospective abandonment of gender-distinct tables to value reversionary interests. Nevertheless, although the 5 percent threshold of § 2037 may itself have limited impact on the great majority of other economically less fortunate women than the decedent in this case, the decision of this court rests on principles of great significance to all women, with broad economic consequences. As emphasized by the court below, "[l]ike Title VII, the equal protection component of the Fifth Amendment is concerned with individual rights, which should not be determined on the basis of class composites." *Mfrs. Hanover Tr. Co. v. United States*, 576 F. Supp. 837, 843 (S.D.N.Y. 1983).

As various women's rights organizations argue in their brief in this case as *amici curiae*, the eradication of overt gender discrimination in the collection of federal taxes is essential if women workers are ever to achieve economic equality. They point out that older women workers are often doubly or triply disadvantaged by discrimination. When women workers who are covered by a retirement plan retire, they frequently receive benefits based on a history of discriminatorily depressed wages. Women thus accumulate lower dollar amounts in both public and private pensions; in addition, if gender-distinct mortality tables are utilized to compute benefits or to convert lump sums into lifetime annuities, they receive lesser periodic benefits at retirement than those received by similarly situated men. As a result, each female retiree is maintained at a lower economic level than her male counterpart for as long or short a time as she is alive to receive benefits, regardless of whether she is ultimately one of the few who outlives the average male participant or is one of the great majority of all women who do not outlive their male counterparts.

Even if women's retirement benefits were equal to those paid to similarly situated men, the Code and Treasury Regulations, which currently utilize gender-distinct life expectancy tables for the taxation of commercial lifetime annuity payments, place many individual women once again at a comparative disadvantage by requiring them to subsist on less after-tax income during their retirement years than similarly situated men. See I.R.C. § 72(b); Treas. Reg. § 1.72-9[1] (male and female life expectancy tables resulting in women retirees

---

[1] Citations are to the 1985 version of the Code and regulations. The regulations were changed prospectively after certain statutory adjustments were made in 1986. They now utilize unisex life expectancy tables, and the portion of any amount received as an annuity that is excluded from gross income under current § 72(b)(2) is limited to the unrecovered investment in the contract. – Eds.

being eligible to exclude a smaller portion of their investment in an annuity contract from their annual gross income than a similarly situated male retiree); *see also* Treas. Reg. § 1.101-7[2] (providing similar rules for taxation of annuitized payouts of life insurance proceeds). These factors have contributed to the placement of elderly women at the very bottom of the economic ladder in this country. Statistics published in the last decade show that women over age sixty-five had the lowest median income of any sex or age group, approximately one-half the median income for men in that age bracket.

In this case, the government has failed to sustain its burden of demonstrating that the Treasury Department's gender-based regulations are substantially related to an important governmental objective in determining the present value of reversionary interests. It is therefore our determination that the challenged classifications constitute unlawful gender discrimination under the equal protection component of the Fifth Amendment, and we unanimously affirm the district court's judgment below.

So ordered.

---

[2] *Id.*

9

Commentary on *Estate of Clack v. Commissioner*

GOLDBURN P. MAYNARD JR.

BACKGROUND

In *Estate of Clack v. Commissioner*, decided in February 1996, the U.S. Tax Court departed from its earlier interpretation of Code § 2056 and contingent qualified terminable interest property (QTIP) elections.[1] In effect, the *Clack* decision permitted a transfer to qualify for the estate tax marital deduction even in situations where an executor had the discretion to decide whether or not the surviving spouse would receive a lifetime interest in the transferred property. The case is important for severing the last link between the marital deduction and any coherent theories of marital property rights. The case is also part of a trend of judicial erosion of the estate tax base.[2]

Congress added the estate and gift tax marital deductions to the federal wealth transfer tax system in 1948.[3] This was in response to a three-decades-long reality: couples in common law states faced a more onerous tax burden than those in community property states. Attempts by taxpayers to equalize this treatment were often struck down on substantive grounds such as the assignment of income doctrine.[4] The Supreme Court of the United States permitted this disparate treatment for tax purposes, reasoning that there was a real distinction between the property rights of spouses in common law and community property jurisdictions: Legally, each spouse in a community property state had the right to one-half of income earned during the marriage and neither could legally control the disposition of the other half.[5]

---

[1] Estate of Clack v. Comm'r, 106 T.C. 131 (1996).
[2] *See, e.g.,* Goldburn P. Maynard Jr., *Perpetuating Inequality by Taxing Wealth*, 84 FORDHAM L. REV. 2429 (2016).
[3] Revenue Act of 1948, Pub. L. No. 80-471, § 351(b), 62 Stat. 110, 116.
[4] *See, e.g.,* Lucas v. Earl, 281 U.S. 111 (1930).   [5] *See* Poe v. Seaborn, 282 U.S. 101 (1930).

Property acquired by a spouse in a common law jurisdiction was completely and solely owned by that individual.[6]

The enactment of the estate and gift tax marital deductions in 1948 represents a legislative response to a practical reality: six common law states had adopted community property provisions between 1945 and 1947 in order to provide the kind of income splitting for tax purposes that was available in community property states. The oncoming wave of community property was troubling to 1940s American norms because it reduced marriage to an amoral (and unromantic) economic partnership. By giving women greater property rights, community property states were undermining traditional gender roles. Common law states were thought to uphold the more traditional American notion of marriage as a sacred compact rooted in the moral obligation of the husband to support and provide for his wife and offspring. Providing equal community property treatment between the states halted a potential redistribution of property rights between husbands and wives and helped prolong the economic dependence of women.[7]

To achieve a quasi–community property result, the Revenue Act of 1948 allowed for a deduction for marital transfers that was limited to one half of the non–community property. That is, a decedent in a non–community property state could devise up to half of his or her property to a surviving spouse and pay no estate tax on that devise. To be sure, this did not give spouses in common law jurisdictions the same property rights as spouses had in community property jurisdictions. The common law spouse did not necessarily have full ownership rights over the property, while the community property spouse could both manage and control the ultimate disposition of half of the couple's property. But Congress did require the common law spouse to control the ultimate disposition of the property to benefit from the legislative grace of the deduction.

Congress further liberalized the marital deduction in 1976, by expanding the deduction to the greater of $250,000 or one-half of the adjusted gross estate.[8] Because the exemption was so generous, this in effect made the deduction unlimited for modest estates. But the most sweeping changes to the marital deduction occurred in 1981.[9] The 1981 legislation removed the quantitative limits on the deduction. The purpose of this change was not to

[6] *See* Estate of Lee v. Comm'r, 11 T.C. 141, 144–45 (1948).
[7] Note, *The Marital Deduction in Federal Estate Tax: The Terminable Interest Rule*, 107 U. Pa. L. Rev. 1176 (1959).
[8] Tax Reform Act of 1976, Pub. L. No. 94-455, § 2002, 90 Stat. 1520, 1854.
[9] Economic Recovery Tax Act of 1981, Pub. L. No. 97-34, § 403, 95 Stat. 172, 301.

create parity between states, but rather to exempt from wealth transfer taxation any property that ultimately would become subject to taxation in the hands of the transferee spouse.[10] More significantly, the 1981 legislation fundamentally altered the marital deduction regime by further loosening the requirements that must be met in order for a transfer to qualify for the deduction. In addition to allowing the marital deduction for transfers in which the spouse did not have management rights, it extended the deduction to transfers over which the spouse had no right of disposition. This was the essence of the QTIP rule under Code § 2056(b)(7).

By the late 1980s, estate planners had devised an even more effective means of maximizing estate tax benefits: the contingent QTIP trust. The traditional understanding of the QTIP shared by the Internal Revenue Service had been that the decedent must specify the property that passed to the spouse, with the executor having the discretion to determine only which portion of the transferred property should be eligible for QTIP treatment.[11] In contrast, the contingent QTIP allowed the executor the discretion to determine both the amount of property passing to the spouse as well as its eligibility for QTIP treatment. Before *Clack*, the U.S. Tax Court had ruled that such discretion on the part of the executor had the ability to divest the surviving spouse of the lifetime income interest that was crucial to meeting the requirements for QTIP eligibility. However, between 1991 and 1995, the U.S. Courts of Appeals for the Fifth, Sixth, and Eighth Circuits reversed the Tax Court and permitted the marital deduction with respect to transfers to a contingent QTIP trust.[12] While bound by the decisions in those circuits, the Tax Court had more freedom to depart from the emerging appellate consensus in others. It is in this context that the Tax Court decided *Clack* in 1996.

ORIGINAL OPINION

The Tax Court's majority opinion written by Judge Wells, and joined by eight other judges on the court, held that transfers in which the executor had discretion to elect QTIP treatment, and possibly divest the surviving spouse of a property interest, qualified for the marital deduction pursuant to Code § 2056(b)(7). The *Clack* decision is a perfect illustration of the inherent unwieldiness of the Tax Court's nineteen-judge reviewed opinions. The

---

[10] H.R. Rep. No. 97-201, at 377 (1981).
[11] *See* I.R.S. Field Serv. Advisory, 1993 WL 1469427 (Jan. 1, 1993).
[12] Estate of Robertson v. Comm'r, 98 T.C. 678 (1992), *rev'd*, 15 F.3d 779 (8th Cir. 1994); Estate of Clayton v. Comm'r, 97 T.C. 327 (1991), *rev'd*, 976 F.2d 1486 (5th Cir. 1992); Estate of Spencer v. Comm'r, 64 T.C.M. (CCH) 937 (1992), *rev'd*, 43 F.3d 226 (6th Cir. 1995).

decision is striking also because the majority strangely refused to endorse a rationale for its interpretation of the statute. The full court review underscores both that the court departed from its previous line of reasoning as well as disagreements about the reasons for that decision.

The majority began by describing the cases in which the Tax Court previously disallowed the marital deduction for contingent QTIP trusts.[13] The court then explained the three reversals of its decisions by the appellate courts, emphasizing the divergence in the rationale of the circuits.[14] The court noted that there was a question as to the appropriate venue for the case. One interpretation would result in the court being bound by Eighth Circuit precedent, while the alternative would result in freedom from such concerns.[15]

The majority opinion then took a strange turn. Instead of delineating which of the competing appellate rationales it found persuasive, it simply acceded to the result by allowing the transfer to the contingent QTIP trust to qualify for the marital deduction.[16] The court also explained that its decision resolved any potential conflict between itself and the appellate courts, rendering the venue issue moot.[17] As such, the court endorsed the contingent QTIP trust as a plausible interpretation of the statute, without exploring the potential for widows being divested of the lifetime income interest. Rather than reconcile its current decision with its previous ones, the court just accepted the conclusion that a contingent QTIP trust should qualify for the marital deduction.

Six other judges on the court agreed with the result in four concurring opinions. These judges would have gone further than the majority by explicitly committing to a rationale for reversing its previous decisions. The remaining four judges produced three dissents defending the traditional interpretation barring marital deduction for contingent QTIP trusts as violating the marital deduction requirements. Judge Parker's dissent focused on the internal inconsistency and logical leaps required to fit the contingent QTIP within the statutory language and considered the venue issue.[18] Judge Halpern zeroed in on the lack of ambiguity in the statute, arguing that the court's previous decisions on the contingent QTIP had been reasonable interpretations.[19]

FEMINIST JUDGMENT

From a feminist perspective, *Clack* can be seen as a troubling step in the race to satisfy the estate tax avoidance prerogatives of wealthy men at the expense

---

[13] Estate of Clack v. Comm'r, 106 T.C. 131, 138–39 (1996).   [14] *Id.* at 140.   [15] *Id.* at 140–41.
[16] *Id.* at 141.   [17] *Id.*   [18] *Id.* at 152–53 (Parker, J., dissenting).
[19] *Id.* at 169–70 (Halpern, J., dissenting).

of property rights of women. This is all the more galling because the majority did not endorse any appellate court's reasoning. Professor Wendy Gerzog, writing a dissent as Judge Gerzog, reveals that beneath its neutral façade, the *Clack* decision was built on an edifice of gender stereotypes and stresses its disparate impact on women. She adopts a feminist methodology that uses practical reasoning and breaks with rhetorical conventions to expose the ways in which *Clack* uses a stilted reading of the statute and disregards accepted understandings of the Code to further winnow away the economic rights of women.

Feminists have long acknowledged the broader historical, cultural, economic, and social context of the family's role in the subordination of women.[20] With this wider lens, marriage can be viewed as a double-edged sword. It has hampered equality by promoting women's dependence and relying on a gendered division of labor that allocates uncompensated work to women.[21] But it has also provided a respite for women from a sexist marketplace by allowing them to gain access to the material benefits of a man's monetized labor.[22]

As the leading voice in critiquing the QTIP provisions, Gerzog's opinion springs from a complex but concrete perspective.[23] While she uses the term "surviving spouse" when referencing the statute or court opinions, Gerzog refers to the losers of the court's decision in *Clack* as "widows." This break with a contemporary rhetorical tendency to speak in gender-neutral terms of "surviving spouses" is meant to challenge the facial neutrality of the statute and the majority opinion. Cursory discussions of the "surviving spouse" by the court obscure the historical fact that men have typically earned more than women, and that women tend to outlive men. Consequently, the prototypical and stereotypical situation to which the QTIP trust is applicable is a propertied dead husband with a surviving (poorer) wife, with the husband possibly having children from a prior marriage. Gerzog, by her sustained focus on widows as the ones who bear the costs of these provisions, adds an explicitly gendered perspective that otherwise would be obscured.

---

[20] *See, e.g.*, Teresa Amott & Julie A. Matthaei, Race, Gender, and Work: A Multi-cultural Economic History of Women in the United States (rev. ed. 1996) (exploring the intersecting effects of race and gender on women of diverse backgrounds).

[21] *See* Reuben Gronau, *Home Production – A Forgotten Industry*, 62 Rev. Econ. & Stat. 408 (1980).

[22] Gary S. Becker, A Treatise on the Family 56 (enlarged ed. 1991).

[23] *See* Wendy C. Gerzog, *The Marital Deduction QTIP Provisions: Illogical and Degrading to Women*, 5 UCLA Women's L.J. 301 (1995) (illustrating how the QTIP provisions rely on gender-biased rationales and arguing for their repeal).

Gerzog's practical reasoning recalls that the QTIP trust is one manifestation of a longer struggle for the property rights of women during marriage.[24] State policies on property rights within and following marriage have long reflected a tension between the partnership and support theories of marriage. While the partnership theory views a marriage as a community in which both parties equally contribute to its wealth, the older support obligation theory justifies women's property rights by way of a man's moral obligation to take care of his wife and children.[25] Under this view, women need support but are not given control because of stereotypes about women's inability to manage property competently or the likelihood that they would be subject to the pressures of a controlling subsequent husband.

The power of Gerzog's opinion is that it exposes that the contingent QTIP has no underlying theoretical justification at all. The early twentieth-century tax advantage granted to community property husbands was based on the partnership theory and the complete property control their widows enjoyed over marital property. The 50 percent marital deduction undermined this theory by privileging transfers of less than fee simple ownership, but it at least maintained some part of the partnership theory by granting widows the right to determine the ultimate disposition of the property received. By granting the marital deduction for transfers to contingent QTIP trusts, the court no longer required the widow to have any control over the property. She is the mere vehicle for postponing taxation of transfers controlled entirely by the husband.

Gerzog provides context by showing how the QTIP abandoned the compromise between the two theories of marriage by explicitly jettisoning the partnership theory in favor of the support obligation theory. That is, as long as women were provided with money it was neither necessary for them to direct how the property was invested nor control ultimate disposition of the property. Gerzog underscores the paternalism of the QTIP provisions to highlight the impact of the blow to widows delivered by the court in *Clack*. The contingent QTIP trust allows the widow neither the control that the partnership theory embraced nor the guaranteed stream of income the support obligation theory contemplated. Instead, the widow is now placed in the precarious position of having her property rights determined by a third party, the executor.

---

[24] *See, e.g.,* VICTOR R. FUCHS, WOMEN'S QUEST FOR ECONOMIC EQUALITY (1988) (arguing that women's weaker economic position results primarily from conflicts between career and family).

[25] *See, e.g.,* Wissner v. Wissner, 338 U.S. 655, 660 (1950) (distinguishing between the moral support obligation and the business relationship between husband and wife under community property).

Gerzog's argument about the loss of material property rights by women is further supported by a careful analysis of the statute. By focusing on the discreteness of the statute's requirements and by making comparisons to other estate tax elections, Gerzog refutes the implication that the contingent QTIP trust is an acceptable interpretation of Code § 2056. Before *Clack*, the decedent's date of death served as the uncontroversial reference point for when a widow's rights were determined. After *Clack*, a widow had to wait until some later date for the executor to make a decision about her property rights. In effect, the court overturned conventional wisdom without a wise policy rationale to justify the change.

IMPLICATIONS

Because an overwhelming (if divided) majority of the Tax Court joined the *Clack* result, it is hard to argue that Gerzog's dissent alone could have stopped the inexorable weakening of the estate tax base that followed. Yet, this does not diminish the potential impact of Gerzog's opinion. It may well have been that Gerzog's dissent could have signaled the weakening of the estate tax base by highlighting the problem and shifting the narrative. Perhaps other courts would have been alerted to the radical step the *Clack* court took by disconnecting the marital deduction from theories of marital property. And maybe the IRS would not have abandoned its fight against the contingent QTIP trust that allows executors to divest widows of property interests.

The history of women's rights to marital property can be partly described by the efforts of husbands to undermine those rights. In the seventh century, widows had a dower right under English law.[26] This was a life estate in one-third of her late husband's property. The dower and its Germanic predecessor, the bride price, were both rooted in paternalistic stereotypes about women.[27] However, husbands were not willing to cede even this minimal property right for very long, historically speaking. Wanting to retain complete control of their property, by the eighteenth century, it became common for men in England to hold land in a trust that prevented their wives from acquiring dower rights.[28]

Similar gains by women to equal rights to marital property continually have been stymied and undermined.[29] The introduction of the joint return and

---

[26] *See* Ariela R. Dubler, *In the Shadow of Marriage: Single Women and the Legal Construction of the Family and the State*, 112 YALE L.J. 1641, 1660–64 (2003).

[27] *See, e.g.*, Mary Moers Wenig, *The Marital Property Law of Connecticut: Past Present and Future*, 1990 WIS. L. REV. 807, 812.

[28] Dower Act, 3 & 4 Will. 5, c. 105, § 4 (1833) (Eng.).

[29] *See, e.g.*, WILLIAM D. MACDONALD, FRAUD ON THE WIDOW'S SHARE (1960).

the marital deduction resulted in states reversing their decisions to adopt community property systems, which had given women more substantial rights to marital property. But this development was in tension with one of the goals of traditional tax reform: neutrality.[30] This view focuses on the efficiency of taxes, meaning that the best tax system is the invisible one. That is, choices between property systems should not be driven by tax benefits. This seems laudable, but in the name of the Code's aspirational neutrality, separate property husbands were given a tax benefit without the complementary relinquishment of control that community property husbands experienced. The reasoning that the Code should not affect a taxpayer's economic decisions obscures the fact that men disproportionately enjoy the ability to make choices and to benefit from the marketplace. Gerzog's opinion shows how the QTIP provisions similarly sacrifice widows' rights in favor of husbands' prerogatives to keep those wives from controlling property.

Gerzog's opinion also highlights just how anachronistic the QTIP provisions were and are. In contrast to the diminishing property rights of women under the estate and gift tax marital deductions, state marriage dissolution laws and elective share statutes generally moved toward a more explicit, if uneasy, embrace of a partnership theory of marriage.[31] The support obligation theory remains deeply entrenched in equitable division statutes, and more comprehensive elective share statutes purport to give effect to the central principles of the partnership theory.[32] For example, the 1990 Uniform Probate Code redesigned the elective share to grant widows a larger share of the augmented estate, thus moving the elective share closer to the community property system.[33] In contrast, the *Clack* court's allowance of the contingent QTIP allows the trustee discretion to determine the property rights of the widow, with no right vested in her.

Gerzog's opinion invites the reader to consider a nuanced understanding of discrimination. There is nothing in the QTIP provisions that refers to the gender of the spouse. Thanks to the work of feminists like Ruth Bader Ginsburg and Supreme Court cases like *Reed v. Reed*[34] and *Frontiero v. Richardson*,[35] this kind of facial discrimination is largely absent from U.S. law. Instead, what feminist scholars like Grace Blumberg underscored in the 1970s was that formal equality approaches were insufficient because

[30] *See* C. Eugene Steuerle, Contemporary U.S. Tax Policy 20–21 (2008).

[31] *See, e.g.*, Unif. Marital Property Act, 9A U.L.A. 19 (Supp. 1984).

[32] *See* Sheldon F. Kurtz, *The Augmented Estate Concept Under the Uniform Probate Code: In Search of an Equitable Elective Share*, 62 Iowa L. Rev. 981, 982–83 (1977).

[33] Unif. Probate Code § 2-202 cmt. (1990).   [34] 404 U.S. 71 (1971).

[35] 411 U.S. 677 (1973).

gender-neutral laws could have detrimental effects on women.[36] The work disincentive that Blumberg critiqued was not facially discriminatory, but resulted from the contemporary reality of women as secondary earners. The Code was neutral on its face but had a concrete effect in discouraging women from entering the job market.[37] Blumberg's article anticipated the work of Gerzog and other critical tax scholars, influenced by critical theory, feminist theory, and critical race theory, who are interested in exposing the role that legal structures play in creating and maintaining inequalities.[38]

Although Gerzog is correct in identifying the contingent QTIP trust as sexist, looking back, it is unlikely that a court would have struck down the QTIP provisions. Courts have been unwilling to strike down facially neutral statutes.[39] Scholars have shown that several sections of the Code have a distinctly disparate impact on historically disadvantaged groups, and yet these Code sections have not been struck down.[40] But such a pessimistic view undervalues the expressive force of dissents. It would have been a powerful statement to have a judge acknowledge structural inequality built into the system. Perhaps Gerzog's opinion could have set the stage for a series of dissents over time pointing out the structural sexism, racism, and heterosexism of the Code. This could in turn have influenced public opinion.

And herein lies another complicated aspect of Gerzog's opinion: the intersectional identities of the widows who are impacted by the QTIP provisions means that these women themselves participate in subordination of others.[41] To a lesser extent than their husbands, race and class provides social advantages to these widows that can be used to injure others. QTIP trusts are only used by the wealthy, and that wealth is (of course) a tremendous privilege, that wealth tends to be concentrated in one race, and so we are talking about a very narrow group of people who do not otherwise seem to be the subject of much critical inquiry. This is where Gerzog's opinion diverges from postmodern feminism's commitment to antiessentialism.[42]

---

[36] Grace Blumberg, *Sexism in the Code: A Comparative Study of Income Taxation of Working Wives and Mothers*, 22 Buff. L. Rev. 49 (1971).

[37] *Id.*

[38] *See, e.g.,* Symposium, *Critical Tax Theory: Still Not Taken Seriously*, 76 N.C. L. Rev. 1837 (1998).

[39] *See, e.g.,* Washington v. Davis, 426 U.S. 229 (1976); Griggs v. Duke Power Co., 401 U.S. 424 (1971).

[40] *See, e.g.,* Beverly I. Moran & William Whitford, *A Black Critique of the Internal Revenue Code*, 1996 Wis. L. Rev. 751.

[41] *See, e.g.,* Kimberlé Crenshaw, *Demarginalizing the Intersection of Race and Sex: A Black Feminist Critique of Antidiscrimination Doctrine, Feminist Theory, and Antiracist Politics*, 1989 U. Chi. Legal F. 139.

[42] *See, e.g.,* Martha Chamallas, Introduction to Feminist Legal Theory (3d ed. 2013).

Gerzog's practical legal reasoning is unapologetically interested in women's well-being, which more comfortably fits within the tradition of antisubordination feminists like Catharine MacKinnon.[43] Such an approach generally accepts status-based categories that postmodern feminists reject.[44] From this vantage point, Gerzog's opinion can be seen not as a universal statement on the rights of wealthy women to more privilege, but rather as highlighting one of the many ways in which male dominance is perpetuated. The opinion adds to the many data points from which theory is drawn rather than pretending to be universally representative.

ESTATE OF CLACK v. COMMISSIONER OF INTERNAL REVENUE, 106 T.C. 131 (1996)

JUDGE WENDY C. GERZOG, DISSENTING

The issue before the court is whether the decedent's contingent transfer of purported qualified terminable interest property (QTIP) to his surviving spouse, which was conditioned on the executor's making a QTIP election, constituted a qualifying income interest for life under Internal Revenue Code § 2056(b)(7)(B)(i)(II), thereby allowing an estate tax marital deduction for the value of the underlying assets in the QTIP trust.

The facts pertinent to the QTIP issue are as follows: The will of Willis Edward Clack provided that, if a QTIP election were made with respect to a marital trust created under his will, the trustee of that QTIP trust is required to pay net income to the decedent's widow at least quarterly. In addition, although not required by statute, the trustee had the power to invade the trust principal where necessary to maintain the decedent's widow in her accustomed standard of living. To the extent that the executor did not make a QTIP election, the assets would pass to the Family Trust, which was a discretionary trust that could benefit decedent's widow, children, and issue. By utilizing a QTIP trust, the disposition of which the widow could not control, the decedent ensured that his son, Richard, ultimately would own all of the decedent's business.

Apart from QTIP assets for which an election ultimately was made in an amount in excess of $4 million, the decedent's estate claimed a marital deduction of almost $200,000 for the aggregate nonprobate transfers to the

---

[43] See, e.g., Catharine A. MacKinnon, *From Practice to Theory, or What Is a White Woman Anyway*, 4 YALE J.L. & FEMINISM 13 (1991).

[44] See, e.g., Kimberlé W. Crenshaw, *Close Encounters of a Third Kind: On Teaching Dominance Feminism and Intersectionality*, 46 TULSA L. REV. 151 (2010).

decedent's widow of certain jointly held property, life insurance proceeds, and retirement property. Besides any benefit he might receive from the Family Trust, Richard received an interest in the business valued at a little less than $2.5 million, and decedent's other son, Robert, received a single payment annuity valued at approximately $26,000.

On audit, the government disallowed the portion of the claimed marital deduction attributable to the QTIP trust on the grounds that the executors could appoint the surviving spouse's interest to someone other than her during her lifetime, which would violate the qualifying income interest for life provisions of the QTIP statute. I.R.C. § 2056(b)(7)(B)(ii)(II). The majority found that the trust property qualifies as QTIP under § 2056(b)(7). 106 T.C. 131, 141.

Because I cannot join the majority's opinion for a variety of reasons, I write separately to express my views on the QTIP issue.

I

Before *Clack*, in three cases, the Tax Court had held for the government on essentially the same contingent QTIP issue and these cases were reversed by their respective appellate courts. *Estate of Spencer v. Comm'r*, 43 F.3d 226 (6th Cir. 1995), *rev'g* 64 T.C.M. (CCH) 937 (1992); *Estate of Robertson v. Comm'r*, 15 F.3d 779 (8th Cir. 1994), *rev'g* 98 T.C. 678 (1992); *Estate of Clayton v. Comm'r*, 976 F.2d 1486 (5th Cir. 1992), *rev'g* 97 T.C. 327 (1991).

In *Clayton*, the decedent created both a contingent income trust for which the estate claimed QTIP treatment and a trust in which his widow had no interest. The contingent income trust would give his widow a qualifying interest in the property, but only if the trustee made a QTIP election. If the trustee did not make that election, the property passed to the decedent's four children from his first marriage. *Clayton*, 976 F.2d at 1488. In *Robertson*, the decedent created one trust that qualified for the marital deduction under another Code section, and two other trusts which, if the executor elected, would give the decedent's third wife an otherwise-qualifying income interest in those trusts. However, if the executor did not so elect, she would lose her income interest and the property would transfer to a trust solely benefiting the decedent's sons from his second marriage. *Robertson*, 15 F.3d at 780. Finally, in *Spencer*, the decedent gave the executor almost complete discretion to determine the amount to be placed in Trust A, which, if funded, was designed to qualify for the QTIP marital deduction. 43 F.3d at 228. If the executor chose not to fund Trust A, the property would fund Trust B, a discretionary trust distributing income to the decedent's wife, his children, and grandchildren for their health, education, and/or support. *Id.* In both *Clayton* and *Spencer*, the trustee and/or executor was the decedent's widow. However, in *Robertson*, the executor was the decedent's son from his second marriage. *Robertson*, 15 F.3d at 780.

The Fifth Circuit in *Clayton* reviewed the history of the marital deduction and the QTIP provisions and found that the primary purpose of the statute was to ensure that property not taxed in the estate of the decedent spouse would be included in the surviving spouse's estate. 976 F.2d at 1490–91. The Eighth Circuit in *Robertson* adopted the Fifth Circuit's approach and rationale. 15 F.3d at 781.

However, omitted from the Fifth Circuit's opinion is an acknowledgment that the primary purpose of any form of the marital deduction is that there be a transfer from the decedent to the surviving spouse – that is, that the transfer must be a *marital* transfer. That requirement must be met for any transfer to qualify for this special benefit. However, the Fifth Circuit did not recognize the discreteness of each of the QTIP requirements and viewed its election requirement as ascendant. *Clayton*, 976 F.2d at 1498.

The Fifth Circuit rejected the position that the election, when used to allow a contingent interest to qualify for the marital deduction, was the equivalent of a power of appointment in favor of the trustee's children, and thus a disallowed QTIP interest. *Id.* at 1489. A power of appointment is defined as a power created by a person who owns or has the power to dispose of property, whereby the holder of the power can, within the restrictions of the instrument, designate the transferees of the property. Lewis M. Simes, *Future Interests* § 55 (2d ed. 1966).

Where the executor can give the property either to the surviving spouse or to other beneficiaries as prescribed in the decedent's will, the executor indeed has a special power of appointment. Moreover, where the executor can give the property either to the surviving spouse or to himself as a beneficiary permitted under the instrument, the executor indeed has a general power of appointment. In either instance, such a power to appoint the property to someone other than the surviving spouse is contrary to the QTIP provisions' prohibition against allowing anyone to hold a power to appoint the property during the surviving spouse's lifetime to anyone other than the surviving spouse. I.R.C. § 2056(b)(7)(B)(ii)(II).

The taxpayer urges this court to follow the Fifth and Eighth Circuits' conclusion that a power to elect or not elect QTIP is not a disqualifying power of appointment. The taxpayer cites the Fifth Circuit's statement that if the government's logic were followed, the executor's decision to make a partial QTIP election (i.e., not a full QTIP election) would thereby constitute a nonqualifying power of appointment. Br. for Pet'r 33. However, like the older power of appointment trust (PAT) marital deduction statute, the QTIP statute plainly states that a specific portion of property may constitute separate property for the purpose of QTIP treatment. I.R.C. § 2056(b)(7)(B)(iv). By contrast, a contingent income interest is not specifically allowed in the statute. In addition, the consequence of a partial QTIP election is that whether or not (or to what extent) the QTIP treatment is elected, the surviving spouse receives a qualifying income interest for life from her decedent husband, and the election serves to quantify the value of the property for which the decedent's estate qualifies for a marital deduction. With a contingent income interest, it is the executor who decides what interest the widow receives; it is the executor who decides whether or not the widow receives *any* property interest.

The majority would be extending the executor's powers to control the recipient of all of the interests in the property. That is, when an interest qualifies at decedent's date of death as a qualifying income interest for life under the QTIP statute, the life interest passes from the decedent to the surviving spouse. If the executor makes a timely partial QTIP election, he does not direct the ultimate beneficiary of that property, nor does he direct the ultimate beneficiary of any other property. He merely denotes the value of the property that will qualify for the marital deduction. By contrast, where the beneficiary's identity is determined by the executor, it is the executor, and not the decedent, who becomes the transferor. Thus, the power invested in the executor in a contingent income transfer violates the QTIP statute.

In *Spencer*, the Sixth Circuit rejected what it called the fiction of the relation-back position of the Fifth Circuit and held that the proper date for determining when property qualifies for QTIP status is the date on which the executor filed a QTIP election. 43 F.3d at 233. Since an election is the third element in the definition of QTIP property, the Sixth Circuit reasoned that no property could qualify until a proper election was made. *Id.* However, the election is a separate QTIP requirement, listed separately in the statute, and not referred to in any way as being part of any other QTIP requirement. The Sixth Circuit's explanation thus seems a conclusion not supported by logic.

Essentially, the majority accedes to the result of these three appellate decisions but does not specify which circuit's reasoning it is following. Rather, the majority states that adopting one or the other interpretation is unnecessary since the effect of the three circuit opinions is to allow the marital deduction for a contingent QTIP transfer. 106 T.C. at 141. Whether or not the majority wants to adopt the reasoning of another court, the majority needs to explain why and how our earlier reasoning on the issue of QTIP disqualification for trusts with contingent income interests is unsound.

I have joined with Judge Parker and Judge Halpern in their dissents because I agree that the majority is wrong both in terms of the statute itself and in the fact that the majority decision is inconsistent with most tax elections and determination dates in general.

In her dissenting opinion, Judge Parker maintains that while the QTIP election is a critical part of the definition of QTIP property, it is not an element of the definition of qualifying income interest for life, and that if Congress had intended the election to cure other defects in the QTIP property, Congress would have so stated. *Id.* at 162 (Parker, J., dissenting). She also convincingly states that the Fifth Circuit's relation-back approach is a legal fiction, which is imposed to ignore the executor's power over the property and is not, as the Fifth Circuit suggested, analogous to the legislatively created relation-back effect of qualified disclaimers. *Id.* at 153. Rather, it is a judicially created fiction without a congressional mandate.

I also find persuasive Judge Parker's treatment of the venue issue. The majority did not address venue. The venue issue is one of first impression. I note the strong policy arguments made by Judge Gerber, in concurring with the majority's judgment, that use of the decedent's date of death residence would limit forum shopping. 106 T.C. at 146 (Gerber, J., concurring). Yet Judge Parker relies on judicial precedents. Those favor the residence of the estate's executor or personal representative. In addition, she cites to a statute specific to U.S. Tax Court venue as controlling. *Id.* at 160, 167 (Parker, J., dissenting).

In his dissent, Judge Halpern rejected the majority's "three strikes and you're out" approach and stated that the Tax Court should decide the case on its own merit. *Id.* at 167. I wholeheartedly agree with that sentiment and responsibility. The majority ignores such cases as *Dickman v Commissioner*, 465 U.S. 330 (1984), in which the Supreme Court agreed with the Eleventh Circuit after many courts, over many years, had held to the contrary.

I also agree with Judge Halpern when he emphasized that the executor's power of appointment in the executor's ability to choose between the two trusts (the QTIP or the family trust) as the decedent's major beneficiary clearly violates the unambiguous directive of the statute that no one may appoint the decedent's qualifying income interest for life to anyone other than the widow during her lifetime. 106 T.C. at 170 (Halpern, J., dissenting).

Because there are other reasons for my dissent from the majority, I express them separately.

II

A

The marital deduction was enacted in 1948, and the underlying purpose was to give parity to married couples living in common law property states with those living in community property states; thus, the deduction was limited to one-half of the transferring spouse's property. In a community property state, only one-half of the couple's community property is taxed in the estate of the first spouse to die. The other half of their community property, to the extent unconsumed, is taxed in the surviving spouse's estate. Congress created the marital deduction to mirror this treatment. *See generally Ne. Pa. Nat'l Bank & Tr. Co. v. United States*, 387 U.S. 213 (1967); *Estate of Alexander v. Comm'r*, 82 T.C. 34, 38 (1984).

The marital deduction is restricted to transfers that pass from the decedent to his surviving spouse. The marital deduction is generally not available for transfers of nondeductible terminable interests, which are interests that will terminate (such as a life estate), if upon termination the property passes to someone other than the surviving spouse. There are reasons for excluding these interests. First, the property itself is not transferred from the decedent to the surviving spouse. Second, there is a potential for tax abuse, because the underlying property escapes taxation at its full fair market value in both spouses' estates. Joseph M. Dodge, *Redoing the Estate and Gift Taxes Along Easy-to-Value Lines*, 43 Tax L. Rev. 241, 345 (1988). Without the terminable interest rule, only the value of the remainder interest, which is minimal in comparison to the full fair market value of the underlying property, would be included in the estate of the first spouse to die. As the surviving spouse's life estate would be extinguished at her death, nothing would be included in that spouse's estate.

In 1981, Congress amended the marital deduction provisions in the following ways: (1) it eliminated the maximum restriction on the marital deduction from one-half of the decedent's estate and consequently made it an "unlimited marital deduction" and (2) it created a new type of transfer that would qualify for the marital deduction, a transfer from the decedent to his surviving spouse in a QTIP trust.

Before the 1981 QTIP legislation, in order to qualify for the marital deduction, the decedent had to give his widow either the property itself or somewhat equivalent control over the underlying property. The other exceptions to the terminable interest rule, I.R.C. §§ 2056(b)(5)–(6), require that the surviving spouse be given both an income interest and a power to appoint the property either to herself or to her estate. Before the QTIP legislation, a transfer of only the income interest, which when terminated would pass to a third party, would have failed to qualify for the marital deduction under the nondeductible terminable interest rule.

The QTIP statute requires that the decedent give the surviving spouse a "qualifying income interest for life" and that the executor make an election for the property to be classified as QTIP. The rationale for the QTIP provisions was the same as that of the unlimited marital deduction: (1) the property is "their" property (i.e., property of the marital unit) and (2) the trust property will ultimately be taxed in the surviving spouse's estate under Code § 2044 (or earlier subject to gift tax under Code § 2519 if the surviving spouse transfers her income interest during her lifetime). Staff of the Joint Comm. on Taxation, 97th Cong., *General Explanation of the Economic Recovery Tax Act of 1981*, at 233 (Comm. Print 1981) [hereinafter *1981 Joint Committee Explanation*].

B

The marital deduction QTIP provisions have three requirements: (1) that property pass from the decedent to his surviving spouse, (2) that the surviving spouse be entitled to a qualifying income interest for life, and (3) that the executor make a QTIP election. Each of these three requirements is discrete. The majority misinterprets the QTIP statute by elevating the significance of the QTIP election over the QTIP income requirement. That is, the majority emphasizes the significance of the QTIP election and, by allowing a contingent QTIP to qualify for the marital deduction, ignores the need to give the surviving spouse a vested property interest in order to make the deduction a *marital* deduction.

The majority interprets the third requirement, the executor's election, as the most important requirement of the three, and holds that it is integrally related to the first two requirements. Since elections are not usually interconnected with other requirements for other tax elections, it is unlikely Congress meant for this one to be so overriding, especially where such prominence is neither stated in the statute nor found in the statute's legislative history.

The purpose and importance of the election is to underscore that there will be future tax consequences to the executor's choice. *Estate of Higgins v. Comm'r*, 91 T.C. 61, 69–70 (1988), *aff'd*, 897 F.2d 856 (6th Cir. 1990). Once a QTIP election is made, it is irrevocable and it means that the property will be included in the surviving spouse's estate. While this latter consequence is one of the important policy reasons behind this section, it is not the only rationale for its enactment.

Congress created the QTIP provisions to allow decedents to control the ultimate beneficiary of their wealth while providing for the support and maintenance of their surviving spouses. *Estate of Spencer v. Comm'r*, 43 F.3d 226, 227 (6th Cir. 1995). The unlimited marital deduction, in addition, which was enacted at the same time as the QTIP provisions, reflected Congress's decision to treat a husband and wife as one unit who share *their* property for the purposes of transfer taxation, complementing its same decision in the income tax context. S. Rep. No. 97-144, at 127 (1981).

Estate tax elections are not generally intertwined with the substantive provisions of a statute. Tax elections are formalities, though not insignificant ones, because they bind the taxpayers to the elected tax treatment. In this case, the executor's QTIP election requires the decedent's widow to include the value of the trust in her gross estate at her death.

Code § 2032A, which reduces the estate tax value of a family farm in a decedent's estate, is another estate tax provision requiring an election. The statute was enacted to discourage the forced sale of family farms and other family businesses requiring great use of real estate that is included in the decedent's estate. Staff of the Joint Comm. on Taxation, 94th Cong., *General Explanation of the Tax Reform Act of 1976*, at 537 (Comm. Print 1976). Rather than being valued at its highest and best use (the normal rule for valuing estate assets), this property is, subject to certain limitations, valued by reference to its actual use. Like the QTIP election, the executor's election under § 2032A is irrevocable. The need to bind the taxpayer is clear in this Code section because if the taxpayer's family does not continue to use the real property for its qualifying use for at least ten years after decedent's death, the qualified heir (family member) must pay an additional tax.

The substantive requirements in this valuation reduction statute define "qualified real property" and "qualified heir" just as the QTIP provisions define a "qualifying income interest for life." Meeting the definitions of these special terms is a prerequisite for obtaining the estate tax benefits associated with these provisions. However, despite the affinity between these two estate tax provisions, no court has held that the substantive provisions defining "qualified real property" for special use valuation purposes should be determined on the date of the executor's election and not on decedent's date of death. This is so even though no property can literally comply with the definition of qualified real property until an election is made.

Likewise, the election under another estate tax provision, I.R.C. § 2032, to value all of decedent's property as of the alternate valuation date, like the QTIP election, is irrevocable and must be made within prescribed time limits. The election, like the QTIP election, serves an administrative function.

When the executor checks the box on the estate tax return, like in the case of a QTIP election, the executor notifies the Internal Revenue Service that the taxpayer is applying the valuation methods enunciated in that Code section and binds the taxpayer irrevocably to his election.

However, the alternate valuation date election (which reduces the value of the gross estate and estate tax liability) does not affect the substantive requirements for making an election. Those substantive requirements were enacted in 1984 to prevent the taxpayer from using the alternate valuation date to increase an asset's basis for income tax purposes where, for example, because of the availability of the marital deduction, inclusion of such property at an increased value would not increase the decedent's estate tax liability. H.R. Rep. No. 98-861, at 1243 (1984) (Conf. Rep.); H.R. Rep. No. 98-432, at 1521 (1984).

In the context of the alternate valuation date provision, it would be facetious to suggest that the election date is the pivotal date for determining whether the substantive parts of this provision are fulfilled. Yet, it also is illogical to suggest that the election date is the determination date for QTIP qualification under the substantive qualifying income interest requirement. The majority is putting the horse before the cart. Thus, I agree with the Commissioner that the taxpayer incorrectly tests the qualifications for the QTIP only *after* the election has been made. Reply Br. for Resp't 8. Such a methodology dilutes the other equally important requirements of the QTIP statute as well as the other stated purposes behind that legislation.

I also agree with the Commissioner when he explains that tax elections relate to tax treatment. Br. for Resp't 34. There is nothing in the legislative history of the QTIP provisions that suggests that the election requirement in this statute is any different from any other tax election or that the election is integral to the requirement that the surviving spouse be given a qualifying income interest for life. Clearly, if no election is made to take advantage of the benefits of the marital deduction, the government has no interest in examining the decedent's return to discover whether or not his estate could have qualified for QTIP marital deduction treatment. It is only when the estate elects to qualify for a special tax benefit that the return is reviewed to determine whether or not a transfer qualifies for that economic gain. At that point, each requirement of the QTIP is reviewed for qualification as of the time of the decedent's death.

As this court has often repeated, a deduction is a matter of legislative grace, and it is the taxpayer who must prove that he is entitled to a statutory benefit. *New Colonial Ice Co., Inc. v. Helvering*, 292 U.S. 435, 440 (1934). That burden is not met here. The taxpayer's arguments are contradicted by the statute, regulations, and legislative history.

C

Congress wanted a qualifying income interest under the QTIP rules to provide the surviving spouse with rights to income that are sufficient to satisfy the regulations applicable to power of appointment marital deduction trusts (PAT) at that time. H.R. Rep. No. 97-201, at 161 (1981); *1981 Joint Committee Explanation, supra,* at 235. The income interest under the power of appointment marital deduction regulations, which contain language virtually identical to the income provision for a QTIP, cannot be subject to a contingency and still qualify for the marital deduction.

Under the regulations, the surviving spouse's income interest must "give her substantially that degree of beneficial enjoyment of the trust property during her life which the principles of the law of trusts accord to a person who is unqualifiedly designated as the life beneficiary of a trust." Treas. Reg. § 20.2056(b)-5(f)(1). That specific regulation was cited in the legislative history of the QTIP provisions.

The QTIP regulations underline this parallel. When an otherwise qualifying income interest for life is contingent on the executor's election for QTIP treatment, that income interest fails to qualify for the QTIP marital deduction. Treas. Reg. § 20.2056(b)-7(d)(3), (h), ex. 6; *see* Br. for Resp't 28.

The taxpayer in this case has to some extent conceded the parallel between these two estate tax marital deduction provisions, but does not consider the PAT income rules in Code § 2056(b)(5) relevant to an analysis of § 2056(b)(7). Br. for Pet'r 37. Rather, the taxpayer erroneously focuses on the QTIP election under § 2056(b)(7)(B)(i)(III) and not on what is legislatively intended to be analogous (the required qualifying income interest for life under § 2056(b)(7)(B)(i)(II) that must be received by the surviving spouse).

D

Most estate tax determinations are made at the decedent's date of death. With respect to the marital deduction qualification date and, specifically, the test to determine whether the property transfer is a nondeductible terminable interest, the Supreme Court has held that decedent's date of death is the proper time to make that decision. *Jackson v. United States,* 376 U.S. 503 (1964). Yet, despite *Jackson,* the Sixth Circuit in *Estate of Spencer v. Commissioner,* 43 F.3d 226 (6th Cir. 1995), rejected the application of that holding as both distinguishable and not on point. The Sixth Circuit reasoned that *Jackson* dealt only with determinations of what constituted terminable interests rather than defining exceptions to that rule. The Fifth Circuit in *Clayton v. Commissioner*, 976 F.2d 1488 (5th Cir. 1992), did not cite or discuss *Jackson*; as this is the seminal Supreme Court case on the definition of a nondeductible terminable interest, the failure to cite or discuss *Jackson* is a serious omission. Br. for Resp't 33.

Jackson, a case from the 1960s, was decided at about the same time the prototype to the QTIP provisions was formulated, and was the accepted rule of law when the QTIP exception was framed. Indeed, *Jackson* is in line with the other estate tax cases that focus on the decedent's date of death as the determination date for inclusion of property.

Holding that the proper date to determine eligibility for the marital deduction under the QTIP provision is the date of the QTIP election, the Sixth Circuit maintained that "it would be contrary to the policy and meaning of the statute, as well as counterintuitive and against common sense, to apply the definition before the election can be satisfied." *Spencer*, 43 F.3d at 228. But it is more logical to infer from the statute that property should qualify under the substantive parts of the QTIP provisions before any election can be made. Moreover, such an inference would not be contrary to the policy of the QTIP provisions, which includes ensuring that the widow receives adequate lifetime support and thus requires that the trust satisfy the qualifying income for life requirements of the QTIP provisions from the moment of the decedent's death.

The taxpayer would have us distinguish *Jackson* on the basis that the facts in *Jackson* do not present a situation that involves a required statutory election. Reply Br. for Pet'r 8. But that viewpoint is one that assumes that Congress enacted the election requirement in the QTIP provisions as superseding all other QTIP requirements. There is absolutely nothing in the statute or legislative history of the QTIP provisions that supports the taxpayer's position.

The taxpayer, moreover, contends that the QTIP provisions require only that the widow be entitled to all the income from the property and states that the marital trust plainly fulfills that requirement, Br. for Pet'r 28–29; however, that argument mistakes the issue. The QTIP statute refers to the surviving spouse's legal right to the income at the decedent's death and not to any practical impediments that may delay income payments to her before the QTIP election is filed. With a contingent income interest, the surviving spouse has no entitlement to income at decedent's death. If there is no election, she has no right to any property interest. Where the income interest is, by contrast, a qualifying income interest for life, then even without a QTIP election, the surviving spouse has a right to that income interest.

E

Where the decedent provides for a contingent income interest, which is dependent on the executor's unfettered discretion, nothing has passed with certainty from the decedent to his widow. Rather, the interest passes from the executor, who decides to pass the income interest to the surviving spouse or to the alternative beneficiary the decedent has named. As such, the executor holds a special power of appointment. If, however, the executor is also the named alternative beneficiary, he holds a general power of appointment that for transfer tax purposes amounts to ownership. I.R.C. §§ 2514, 2041.

The Sixth Circuit analogized the executor's ability to deny the surviving spouse any property interest in the trust to a widow's ability to disclaim an interest in the estate. *Estate of Spencer v. Comm'r*, 43 F.3d 226, 234 (6th Cir. 1995). In *Spencer*, however, the appellate court was only able to draw this parallel because the widow in that case also fortuitously happened to be the decedent's chosen executor. This dual role will not always exist. Remember that the executor can be anyone that the decedent or the courts have appointed to that position. Indeed, it is just as likely that the executor is the decedent's adult child from an earlier marriage. That adult child may or may not have a good relationship with the decedent's widow.

Moreover, the QTIP provisions and the disclaimer statute reflect very real differences in the surviving spouse's property rights. With respect to a disclaimer, the property interest belongs to the widow. It is only if and when she chooses to disclaim the property she has been given by the decedent that she legally relinquishes her interest for transfer tax purposes. I.R.C. §§ 2518, 2044. By contrast, where the spouse's receipt of any income interest is dependent on the executor's discretion, the widow has nothing until the executor (potentially a third party) makes that decision. Thus, there is very little similarity between a contingent interest given to the surviving spouse, if the executor elects QTIP treatment, and her absolute right to disclaim property that she has received from the decedent.

Finally, the disclaimer statute provides *additional* benefits to the surviving spouse while a contingent QTIP interest only has the ability to destroy any benefit she might have received. Under the disclaimer requirements, the general rule is that if one disclaims, one may not subsequently hold another temporal interest in that property. *Id.* § 2518(b)(4)(B). Thus, if one receives a fee interest and disclaims a remainder interest, the disclaimer is not "qualified" if the person making the disclaimer retains an income interest in that same property – with one exception. The statute provides an exception for the surviving spouse who may disclaim an interest, but may then receive that disclaimed interest. *Id.* § 2518(b)(4)(A).

The Commissioner has argued that where there is a contingent property interest that relies on the executor's election, the property does not pass from the decedent. With a contingent income interest, the executor holds a power of appointment wherein he can choose between the surviving spouse as beneficiary or the decedent's named alternative beneficiaries. By contrast, where the widow receives a qualifying income interest for life and the executor merely elects QTIP treatment, she is the beneficiary unqualifiedly chosen by the decedent to hold a life interest in the property and the executor opts to select QTIP treatment for that transfer depending on which choice allows for a better tax result as directed by the decedent in his will or other governing instrument. Then, once the transfer qualifies for QTIP treatment, the underlying property itself, and not just the qualifying income interest for life, is deemed to pass from the decedent to the surviving spouse. The legislative history of the QTIP provisions supports this interpretation of the passing requirement. S. Rep. No. 97-592, at 20–21 (1982); H.R. Rep. No. 97-201, at 161.

With respect to a contingent income interest, the decedent has not given any vested interest to the surviving spouse, and therefore nothing has passed from the decedent to the surviving spouse with any certainty. Rather, it is the executor who creates the income interest in the surviving spouse because he has the unfettered option to pass the property to alternate beneficiaries and to pass no interest to the surviving spouse.

III

A

Since the enactment of the QTIP rules, QTIP trusts have become exceedingly popular estate planning devices. However, the QTIP provisions are sexist. They were rooted in a desire to aid wealthy men in second (or multiple) marriages who feared they would have to give their current wives much of their wealth in order to maximize the transfer tax benefits of the unlimited marital deduction when they really wanted to transfer their assets to children from their prior marriages. *See* Wendy C. Gerzog, *The Marital Deduction QTIP Provisions: Illogical and Degrading to Women,* 5 UCLA Women's L.J. 301 (1995). Although the language of the QTIP provisions is gender neutral, the application of the statute remains predominantly to reduce the property interests actually given to widows while allowing a much larger marital deduction to their deceased husbands.

Significantly, the majority's holding will only aggravate the statute's sexism and will become the new typical form of the marital deduction. In so doing, the majority attenuates the fiction that these transfers reflect marital unity. Because women are most often the surviving spouse, the majority's ruling will encourage additional inequality between men and women in a marriage.

The source of the QTIP's qualifying income interest for life provision is the current beneficial enjoyment test that was proposed by the American Law Institute (ALI) Federal Estate and Gift Tax Project in the late 1960s. ALI Proposal number seventeen reads: "The terminable interest rule in relation to marital deduction transfers should be abolished and a current-beneficial-enjoyment test adopted, under either a dual tax system or a unified tax." *Federal Estate and Gift Taxation: Recommendations Adopted by the American Law Institute and Reporters' Studies* 358–59 (1969). The current beneficial enjoyment test provides that any transfer that gives the widow a limited, present enjoyment of the property would qualify for a marital deduction not equal to a partial temporal interest in the property but equal to the full value of the underlying property itself. *Id.* at 355. In 1969, the Treasury Department also touted this proposal. Harry L. Gutman, *Reforming Federal Wealth Transfer Taxes After ERTA,* 69 Va. L. Rev. 1183, 1256 (1983).

The following facts support the argument for the QTIP's sexism. First, although the language of the 1981 statute is gender neutral, *all* of the ALI examples posited the decedent as a man and his surviving spouse as a woman. Second, in support of this proposal, the Treasury Department presented statistics on the number of years widows survived their husbands, but never offered any statistical information on how many years widowers survived their wives. Third, the legislative history of the QTIP provisions, together with the statistical realities that women are generally the surviving spouse, are also evidence of this prototype. Finally, with a QTIP, the marital deduction is allowed even though the decedent/husband directs the ultimate disposition of the property after the surviving spouse/widow's death, even though his widow receives only an income interest in the property, and it is the executor designated by the decedent (who need not be the widow) who makes the QTIP election.

The legislative history is replete with statements of a particular intent for the QTIP provisions to give a tax benefit to remarried men with children from earlier marriages. 127 Cong. Rec. 17,288, 17,289 (1981); *Major Estate and Gift Tax Issues, Part 1 of 2: Hearing Before the Subcomm. on Estate and Gift*

Taxation of the S. Comm. on Fin., 97th Cong. 151, 158–59 (1981); *Major Estate and Gift Tax Issues, Part 2 of 2: Hearing Before the Subcomm. on Estate and Gift Taxation of the S. Comm. on Fin.*, 97th Cong. 150–54, 156, 178–79, 184, 207 (1981) [hereinafter *1981 Senate Hearing Part 2*] (various testimony). Yet, there is no justifiable policy goal in giving a special tax break to remarried men with children from an earlier marriage when the decedent retains deathbed control of the underlying property that he transfers to a nonspouse.

Consider, for example, the three contingent income cases cited in this dissenting opinion, as well as the instant case. In all four cases, the decedents were men making transfers to their wives and children. Half of these cases (*Clayton* and *Robertson*) involved multiple marriages and children from prior marriages. *Clack* and *Spencer* did not have that marital history.

The QTIP provisions are inequitable to women as they allow a marital deduction for transfers to third parties that are only ostensibly made to the widow. The widow does not need to accede to the QTIP election and she neither selects nor joins in the selection of the ultimate beneficiary of the property. Therefore, although purportedly enacted to show that husbands and wives share decisions about their property, the actual QTIP requirements do not reflect that rationale.

B

The Fifth Circuit in *Clayton* wondered whether this court and the IRS believed that the QTIP was some sort of congressional paternalism aimed at protecting the continued support of the surviving spouse. *Estate of Clayton v. Comm'r*, 976 F.2d 1486, 1498 (5th Cir. 1992). This paternalistic view of women replicates certain aspects of the common law of coverture. *Thompson v. Thompson*, 218 U.S. 611, 614–15 (1910) ("At the common law the husband and wife were regarded as one. The legal existence of the wife during coverture was merged in that of the husband, and, generally speaking, the wife was incapable of making contracts, of acquiring property or disposing of the same without her husband's consent."). While much of that doctrine has been eroded by state and federal law, vestiges of coverture do indeed imbue the QTIP provisions. The legislative history of the QTIP provisions indicates that this statute was rooted in paternalist thinking.

At the 1981 Senate hearings, representatives from the American Bar Association's Tax Section spoke in support of adding the QTIP form of the marital deduction so that a decedent could leave property in trust for his spouse, providing income to her for life but with no power to dispose of the remainder, and still have that property qualify for the marital deduction. *1981 Senate*

Hearing Part 2, supra, at 179 (joint statement of Harvie Branscomb Jr. and John S. Nolan, Chairman and Chairman-elect, Section of Taxation, American Bar Association). Likewise, a representative from the Estate and Gift Tax Committee of the American College of Probate Counsel (College) suggested that their clients ordinarily wished to give their spouses a life estate, but wanted to control the ultimate disposition of the property, particularly with the contemporary reality of divorce and multiple marriages. *Id.* at 154 (testimony of John A. Wallace, American College of Probate Counsel).

The 1981 Committee Reports and the Joint Committee Explanation, however, emphasized that to be a qualifying income interest for life, the income interest must *not* be an interest for a term of years or a life estate that could terminate on the surviving spouse's remarriage or on another specified condition. H.R. Rep. No. 97-201, at 161 (1981); *1981 Joint Committee Explanation, supra*, at 235–36. Thus, when it enacted the QTIP provisions, Congress specifically wanted the surviving spouse to receive a robust income interest for life. The majority's reading of the statute allows, and indeed encourages, her spousal income interest to be destroyed.

If Congress had been chiefly concerned with ensuring that the property be taxed in the surviving spouse's estate or at the time of an earlier transfer, Congress could have simply clarified that if such a contingency occurred, it would be considered an earlier transfer by the surviving spouse and subject to taxation. Although the ALI had suggested that tax treatment in its 1960s prototype of the QTIP (i.e., that the surviving spouse be taxed on the transfer prior to her death if she is given a current interest until she remarries or for some stated period of time), John H. Alexander, *Federal Estate and Gift Taxation: The Major Issues Presented in the American Law Institute Project*, 22 Tax L. Rev. 635, 662 (1967), Congress rejected that proposal in 1981 and it is not in the QTIP statute as enacted.

The College recommended that, to avoid undue complexity, the marital deduction election be limited to benefit solely the surviving spouse. It urged Congress not to adopt the 1969 Treasury Department study suggestion that would have allowed a marital deduction whereby the transfers could benefit multiple beneficiaries besides the widow during her lifetime; rather, the College recommended that the QTIP rule not allow others to receive current rights in the property during the widow's lifetime.

Since the QTIP statute does not allow anyone other than the surviving spouse to be a beneficiary of the QTIP trust during her lifetime, it is unlikely that Congress wanted the QTIP provisions to be interpreted in a way that would indirectly produce the same effect. By making the surviving spouse's income interest contingent on the executor's election, others could receive a current benefit during the surviving spouse's lifetime and it is that *possibility* that should disqualify the trust from QTIP treatment. Br. for Resp't 29–30.

IV

By summarily concluding that the QTIP election was of primary importance in the statute, the majority implicitly, and the concurring opinion of Judge Beghe explicitly, minimizes the financial benefits of deferral. *See* 106 T.C. at 139–40, 150. Yet, what is all too clear with the popularity of this deduction, and particularly with the QTIP version of the marital deduction, is that it is a sought-after and integral part of typical estate planning for wealthy married couples. This deduction allows optimization of such tax benefits as lower combined rates, two exemptions, and the opportunity for the surviving spouse to continue to minimize taxes through lifetime annual tax-free gifts.

From the creation of the marital deduction in 1948, the financial benefits of the marital deduction were clear. In a community property state, married taxpayers by law split their estates so that they could benefit from lower, combined estate tax rates. As the taxpayer has acknowledged, the rationale for the marital deduction was to alleviate the financial burden of high progressive tax rates that adhered to married couples in common law property states. Br. for Pet'r 18–19. That is, when the wealthier spouse dies first, he is able to defer the tax on one-half of his estate, which would have been taxed at much higher tax rates if he had been subject to taxes on all of his estate at his earlier death. With the marital deduction, the couple's total wealth could be divided in two so that the couple was able to have both halves of the total wealth run through the lower tax brackets of two individuals. That transfer tax legislation thus replicated the benefits of the joint income tax return option offered to married couples that Congress enacted at that same time.

The current estate tax rates begin at 37 percent and rise to a maximum rate of 55 percent. Under the majority opinion, like in most wealthy decedents' estates, with the marital deduction the taxpayer owes no tax; without the marital deduction and without the ability to equalize the two estates and have two separate runs at the lower estate tax rates, the taxpayer would be subject to the transfer tax at his death and much more of his estate would be taxed at the highest rate of 55 percent. Moreover, by saving approximately $500,000 in estate taxes at his death, the estate would not need to liquidate its major asset, the decedent's business interests, to pay estate taxes.

Most significantly, finally, are the benefits of using both the widow's and the decedent's own unified credits in making transfers to third parties. The unified credit is currently equal to an exemption of $600,000 of property transfers.

Therefore, where a decedent owns $1.2 million in assets and where his widow owns none of her own property, the QTIP allows a decedent to transfer $1.2 million tax-free to third parties, or twice as much as would be exempt to him as an individual.

Deferral allows continued growth undiminished by estate tax payments at the decedent's death. While it is true that when the surviving spouse dies, the property is included in her estate, in the intervening years between the two spouses' deaths, the estate tax laws may change and the couple's total tax bite would benefit from any reduction in total taxes caused by such a postponement. Married couples would also benefit from any lower rate applicable to the surviving spouse's estate tax inclusion of the decedent spouse's assets if the widow has a lower rate because she has consumed much of her own estate for her needs.

Throughout the history of the estate tax, the amount of decedent's property that is exempt from the tax has increased, and that rise has outpaced inflation. In 1981, under the 1976 Tax Reform Act phase-in, the unified credit applied to an exemption equivalent of $175,626. By 1986, under the 1981 legislation, that exemption equivalent grew to $600,000. Staff of S. Comm. on Fin., 97th Cong., *Summary of the Economic Recovery Tax Act of 1981*, at 17 (Comm. Print 1981). In addition, under the 1981 legislation, the gift tax annual exclusion (i.e., the amount of gifts a donor may make annually to an unlimited number of donees free of transfer tax) rose from $3,000 to $10,000 per donee per year. *Id.* By using the larger annual exclusion, the surviving spouse may also reduce the value of her estate and, thereby, her estate tax rate.

Because most widows outlive their husbands, that reality may result in a lower overall value being subject to estate taxes. That may be particularly true in a multiple marriage situation when the QTIP is often applied to a much younger widow, allowing for a greater number of years to pass before the government is entitled to collect estate taxes on the decedent's wealth transfers that qualify for the marital deduction. Citing the legislative history of the QTIP, the taxpayer describes the quandary between a decedent's surrendering control to his spouse by employing a PAT (or by making an outright property transfer to his widow) or forgoing the economic benefits of the estate tax marital deduction by transferring his property directly to his children. Br. for Pet'r 20–21.

Thus, while the majority has stated that there is no loophole involved in the QTIP statute, that is not accurate. The marital deduction provides real financial incentives to a decedent whose transfer qualifies for that benefit. Otherwise, the taxpayer would not be litigating this issue.

V

A

The majority of this court adds insult to injury to the "women-deserve-only-income" position of the QTIP provisions by creating a situation where a woman does not deserve even a vested right in the income from the property that qualifies for the marital deduction. Under the majority's holding, the widow's receipt of support after her husband's death depends on the decision of the executor (often a child from a previous marriage) that she merits even that limited property interest. That means that there is even less of a marital transfer required to qualify for the *marital* deduction.

The majority today interprets the QTIP provisions as not requiring that the decedent transfer the vested income interest that the statute plainly provides. The majority opinion is contrary to the real congressional (albeit paternalistic) intent to provide support for the decedent's widow.

Although a widow may renounce all her interests under the will, including the QTIP life interest, and elect to take her statutory share under state law, that option generally only governs a portion of a decedent's probate assets (usually one-third to one-half). Moreover, that option is often illusory in the case of wealthy decedents who obtain good estate planning advice and who thereby own most or all of their assets in nonprobate form.

The QTIP provisions were enacted in order to create a limited interest in the widow while allowing her husband to control the ultimate disposition of the underlying property. With the majority opinion sanctifying a contingent QTIP income interest as qualifying for the marital deduction, where the decedent has not named his widow as executor, that widow must now hope that a third party will elect QTIP treatment so that she will at least receive the income from the trust. Her powerlessness may be contrasted with the QTIP benefits received by third parties not in the marital unit. If the QTIP election is made, those nonmarital beneficiaries will likely benefit from the widow's additional estate tax exemption and lower rates. By its ruling today, the majority is adding insult to injury.

B

As a result of the majority opinion, executors who are enabled to choose the identity of the beneficiary of the income interest in the property may face conflict of interest issues, particularly where they are also beneficiaries under the decedent's will. Where it is very likely that the executor is a child from one of the decedent's prior marriages in the multiple marriage situation Congress envisioned when it enacted the QTIP provisions, the likelihood of litigation over the executor's exercise of his power is increased.

Robertson illustrates this likely outcome. On November 2, 1983, when the will was probated, the decedent's son from his second marriage was named executor. On April 11, 1984, the widow filed a petition for removal of the executor. That suit was settled on August 1, 1984, naming that son together with the widow as coexecutors. On October 13, 1989, and subsequently on January 11, 1991, on its own motion, the Probate Court replaced these coexecutors, successively, with a third party. *Estate of Robertson v. Comm'r*, 98 T.C. 678, 679 (1992).

VI

The majority has conceded the issue of the availability of the marital deduction for trusts with contingent income interests. If the surviving spouse is lucky, the executor will make the QTIP election and she will receive income from the trust. The QTIP provisions are already degrading to women in that they allow a marital deduction for the full value of the underlying assets transferred to the QTIP trust while the widow only receives the income from those assets. The majority ignores the legislative history of the QTIP provisions; this history encourages a decedent to provide unequivocal support for his widow during her lifetime. Winnowing away at the widow's interest so that she gets to hold merely a contingent income interest, the majority endorses an interpretation of marriage that further undermines any sharing theory of that relationship. The law is left with the view that marriage as a status is sufficient to qualify for the lucrative deferral benefits of the estate tax marital deduction. The majority opinion will cause a further loss of dignity and property to women. It will dilute even further the marital aspect of the "marital" deduction.

I would hold for the Commissioner in this case.

10

Commentary on *Cheshire v. Commissioner*

MICHELLE LYON DRUMBL

BACKGROUND

Married U.S. taxpayers have the ability to file joint income tax returns, an option that is not available in many other countries. The vast majority of married taxpayers choose the joint filing option. It is convenient. For many couples, joint filing also offers economic benefits in the form of a "marriage bonus." This refers to the situation where the joint income tax liability of the married couple will be *less* than it would have been if the taxpayers had been unmarried and had filed individual returns. The marriage bonus typically is experienced by single-earner couples. In contrast, a "marriage penalty" typically is experienced by couples with two high earners. For these couples, their joint liability will be *higher* than it would have been if they had been unmarried and had filed individual returns. However, the marriage penalty can also hit couples with two relatively low-earners. They may find that their collective income exceeds the cap for earned income tax credit eligibility, for example, even though one or both of them would have been eligible for the earned income tax credit if they had been unmarried.

Despite this framework, most couples prefer "married filing jointly" status over "married filing separately." Those who file separately are ineligible for a number of tax benefits (including the earned income tax credit) that are available to joint filers. Thus, in most circumstances, it is in a married couple's collective financial interest to file jointly rather than separately, even factoring in the possibility of a marriage penalty.[1] This explains, at least in part, why nearly 95 percent of married couples elect to file a joint return.[2]

---

[1] Due to particularities in the Code, some married couples do fare better filing separately. There are also nontax financial reasons to consider filing separately. *See* Victoria J. Haneman, *The Collision of Student Loan Debt and Joint Marital Taxation*, 35 VA. TAX REV. 223, 227 (2016) (discussing income-based repayment of student loans).

[2] INTERNAL REVENUE SERV., PUB. NO. 1304, INDIVIDUAL INCOME TAX RETURNS 2014, at 95 tbl.1.6 (2016).

With the "privilege" of joint filing comes the obligation (or "price") of joint and several liability. This joint liability survives a subsequent divorce or death, regardless of which spouse created the liability or which spouse agrees to pay it in a divorce settlement. A taxpayer can seek relief from the joint liability under the so-called innocent spouse provisions of the Internal Revenue Code. Decades of case law provide factual examples illustrating how harsh joint liability can become following a divorce. *Cheshire v. Commissioner*[3] is an example of a less financially sophisticated spouse finding herself in unexpected tax trouble because she trusted her marital partner.

Kathryn Cheshire was an elementary school teacher. Her husband of twenty-two years, David Cheshire, retired from Southwestern Bell Telephone Co. at the end of 1991. In March 1993, Mr. Cheshire prepared a joint income tax return for the 1992 tax year. Mrs. Cheshire signed it and assumed he would file the return timely, as he had done in the past. Not long after, Mr. Cheshire served time in jail for a DWI conviction, the couple legally separated, and they divorced seventeen months later. In August 1994, Mrs. Cheshire received a letter from the Internal Revenue Service indicating that the 1992 return had not been filed. She found the signed original in a desk drawer, and Mr. Cheshire's certified public accountant advised her to file it and remit payment for the $23.86 balance shown due as soon as possible. Unfortunately for Mrs. Cheshire, her troubles with the IRS were only beginning.

The IRS determined that the Cheshires understated their 1992 income and disallowed certain Schedule C expenses. It additionally imposed a penalty for filing a late return and an accuracy-related penalty based on the amount of the deficiency.

Most of the problems on the return stemmed from retirement distributions Mr. Cheshire had received in 1992, which totaled $229,924. Of this amount, Mr. Cheshire rolled over $42,183 into a qualified account. He deposited most of the balance into a joint bank account. Mrs. Cheshire knew about these distributions. She also knew that much of the money was used to pay for household and family expenses, including a family truck, a car for their daughter, and the payoff of the mortgage on the family residence. Mrs. Cheshire had asked Mr. Cheshire about the tax consequences of the retirement distributions before she signed the 1992 joint return. Mr. Cheshire lied: He told her that he had consulted his accountant and had been advised that the proceeds used to pay off the mortgage on their home ($99,425) would reduce the amount of their taxable income. Mrs. Cheshire trusted Mr. Cheshire on this point, believing that he had consulted the

---

[3]　115 T.C. 183 (2000).

accountant and that retirement distributions used to pay off a mortgage would have such a tax-favored status. She signed the return, which reported that Mr. Cheshire had received a $199,771 retirement distribution, of which $56,150 was taxable income.

Mrs. Cheshire filed a petition in Tax Court for relief under the Code's innocent spouse provisions, which had been recently expanded. She argued that she did not know of the substantial understatement when she signed the return, and that it would be inequitable under the circumstances to hold her liable for the understatement.

The IRS conceded that Mrs. Cheshire was entitled to partial relief, including relief from certain other savings distributions, the disallowed Schedule C deductions, and the penalty for failure to file a return in a timely manner. But it denied her relief with respect to the understated taxable amount of the retirement distribution and the interest earned in the joint account to which it was deposited, as well as the accuracy-related penalty.

A majority of the U.S. Tax Court, consisting of twelve judges, held that Mrs. Cheshire was not entitled to innocent spouse relief under Code § 6015(b) or (c) because she had actual knowledge of the retirement distributions and the interest earned on the joint account. It further determined that the IRS did not abuse its discretion in denying equitable relief under § 6015(f) with respect to the retirement distribution proceeds and interest income.[4] However, the Tax Court found the denial of relief to be an abuse of discretion with respect to the accuracy-related penalty.

Mrs. Cheshire appealed her case to the U.S. Court of Appeals for the Fifth Circuit. She argued that she had no knowledge that the portion of the retirement distribution used to pay off the mortgage would be taxable, having believed her husband's word on this tax treatment. The Fifth Circuit affirmed the Tax Court's decision, stating that "ignorance of the law cannot establish an innocent spouse defense to tax liability."[5] Mrs. Cheshire then appealed to the Supreme Court of the United States, which denied her petition for writ of certiorari.

ORIGINAL OPINION

Cheshire v. Commissioner was one of the first cases in which the U.S. Tax Court was called upon to interpret the newly liberalized innocent spouse

---

[4] At the time the court decided the case, the standard of review for § 6015(f) relief was abuse of discretion. Following 2006 amendments to § 6015(e)(1), the Tax Court determined that Congress intended a de novo standard of review in § 6015(f) cases. Porter v. Comm'r, 132 T.C. 203, 206–10 (2009).

[5] Cheshire v. Comm'r, 282 F.3d 326, 335 (5th Cir. 2002) (citing Park v. Comm'r, 25 F.3d 1289, 1293–94 (5th Cir. 1994), and Sanders v. United States, 509 F.2d 162, 169 & n.14 (5th Cir. 1975)).

provisions that were enacted in 1998. The predecessor statute for innocent spouse relief, Code § 6013(e), was narrowly drawn. As initially passed in 1971, a spouse could seek relief if the joint return omitted an item of income that was attributable to the other spouse, but only if the omission was in excess of 25 percent of the amount of gross income stated in the return. In 1984, § 6013(e) was amended to allow relief if there was a "substantial understatement" attributable either to a grossly erroneous item with respect either to omitted income or to a claim of deduction, credit, or basis "in an amount for which there is no basis in fact or law."

In 1998, Congress further expanded the situations in which a spouse could seek relief. It repealed § 6013(e) and enacted § 6015, which provided three alternative and distinct forms of relief under § 6015(b), (c), and (f). The accompanying House Report described Congress's concern "that the innocent spouse provisions of present law are inadequate" and stated its intention that the proposed changes would "generally make[] innocent spouse status easier to obtain."[6] Section 6015(b) closely tracks the traditional innocent spouse relief of § 6013(e) but slightly loosens the eligibility requirements by dropping the 25 percent standard. Section 6015(c) provides a new form of relief by allowing a spouse meeting certain requirements to elect to allocate the deficiency such that his or her liability is attributable only to items allocable to the taxpayer seeking innocent spouse relief. Among other requirements, § 6015(c) is not available in cases in which the requesting spouse has actual knowledge of "any item giving rise to a deficiency (or portion thereof)," and the burden is on the IRS to determine actual knowledge existed at the time the return was signed. For those spouses who cannot qualify under § 6015(b) or (c), § 6015(f) allows the possibility of equitable relief, which had not been available to taxpayers prior to the 1998 law.

The Tax Court's decision in *Cheshire* turned on the meaning of the words "knowledge of the understatement," which form part of the requirement of § 6015(b)(1)(C), and the phrase "actual knowledge . . . of any item giving rise to a deficiency" in § 6015(c)(3)(C). Former § 6013(e)(1)(C) had a similar requirement ("no knowledge of the understatement"), and in that context the Tax Court (and Fifth Circuit, among others) interpreted "knowledge" to mean that the requesting spouse had "actual knowledge of the underlying transaction that produced the omitted income."[7] In other words, ignorance of

---

6   H.R. Rep. No. 105-364, pt. 1, at 61 (1997) ("The Committee believes it is inappropriate to limit innocent spouse relief only to the most egregious cases where the understatement is large and the tax position taken is grossly erroneous.").

7   *Cheshire*, 115 T.C. at 193 (citing Reser v. Comm'r, 112 F.3d 1258, 1265 (5th Cir. 1997), *aff'g in part, rev'g in part* 70 T.C.M. (CCH) 1472 (1995), and Bokum v. Comm'r, 94 T.C. 126, 148 (1990), *aff'd*, 992 F.2d 1132 (11th Cir. 1993)).

the law was not grounds for innocent spouse relief under § 6013, if the spouse knew of the transactions or items giving rise to the income.

Mrs. Cheshire conceded that she had actual knowledge of the retirement distribution and the interest earned on the joint account. She did not, however, have actual knowledge that her husband was incorrect in taking the position that distribution proceeds used to pay off the mortgage were not taxable. She argued that § 6015's legislative history supported a different meaning of knowledge than had been applied under § 6013: that a taxpayer is entitled to relief unless the requesting spouse has "actual knowledge *that an item on a return is incorrect.*" Her interpretation of the statute is consistent with the idea that Congress intended § 6015 to provide broader relief than § 6013(e). Mrs. Cheshire's interpretation is also consistent with the legislative history showing that Congress was concerned taxpayers would abuse the innocent spouse rules by signing returns they knew to be false and then requesting relief from liability.

The majority Tax Court opinion rejected Mrs. Cheshire's interpretation: "Were we to accept the knowledge standard petitioner advocates ... then potentially any spouse who is not a certified public accountant or tax attorney would be allowed to escape paying income tax. We do not believe Congress intended such a result."[8] In his dissenting opinion, which three other judges joined, Judge Colvin found that "the majority's construction of section 6015(c)(3)(C) squarely conflicts with the legislative history of section 6015(c)."[9]

When Mrs. Cheshire appealed her case to the Fifth Circuit Court of Appeals, a group of tax attorneys filed an *amici curiae* brief explaining in detail how the legislative history of § 6015(c) demonstrates Congress intended the knowledge requirement to mean knowledge that the item in question would give rise to a deficiency. But the Fifth Circuit found the legislative history ambiguous, and found that Mrs. Cheshire's proposed interpretation "runs afoul of the general rule that ignorance of the law is not a defense to a tax deficiency."[10] In reviewing the Tax Court's denial of equitable relief under § 6015(f), the Fifth Circuit emphasized the fact that Mrs. Cheshire received the unencumbered marital house and the family car in the divorce. Because the home mortgage and car were both paid off from the retirement distribution proceeds, the appellate court found it was reasonable for the IRS to conclude that Mrs. Cheshire "received significant benefit from the tax understatement."[11]

Cheshire is significant because it is one of the first decisions under the newly enacted § 6015, and it set the Tax Court on a pathway of interpreting § 6015(c) narrowly in future cases. It has not been overruled.

---

[8] *Id.* at 197. [9] *Id.* at 202. [10] *Cheshire*, 282 F.3d at 336. [11] *Id.* at 338.

FEMINIST JUDGMENT

Professor Danshera Cords, writing as Judge Cords, rewrites the opinion of the Tax Court in *Cheshire* and reaches the opposite conclusion that the original opinion does. Cords decides that Mrs. Cheshire is entitled to relief under § 6015(c) with respect to the amounts that Mr. Cheshire led her to believe were nontaxable because they were placed in qualified assets. Unlike the Tax Court's original decision, Cords's reimagined majority reads the legislative history to support Mrs. Cheshire's interpretation of § 6015(c). Cords finds that Mrs. Cheshire acted in good faith and believed her husband when he said the portion of the distribution used to pay off the mortgage was not taxable. Cords grants relief with respect to this portion of the understatement, finding the IRS did not meet its burden of proof by showing Mrs. Cheshire had actual knowledge that this portion of the proceeds would in fact be taxable. Cords finds that Mrs. Cheshire did not receive a tax benefit, within the meaning of § 6015(d)(3)(B), from Mr. Cheshire's erroneous deduction for the mortgage payoff. Like the original decision, Cords does not grant relief with respect to amounts deducted from the retirement proceeds other than the portion used to pay off the mortgage.

As the original decision did, Cords also finds that the IRS abused its discretion in not granting relief from the § 6662(a) accuracy-related penalty.

The most significant aspect of Cords's feminist judgment is how her interpretation of § 6015(c) differs from the original opinion. Cords's interpretation of "knowledge" is broader than that adopted by the Tax Court. Had her feminist judgment been the actual decision in the case, Cords would have set a different precedent for the court's interpretation of that subsection's "knowledge" element going forward. Her feminist judgment would have allowed for the court in future cases to weigh the wife's role and determine whether her good faith inquiries were sufficient, without requiring her to act adversarially as an auditor.

Cords's opinion provides context for her broader interpretation of § 6015(c). It offers a brief historical examination of joint liability, citations to scholars who had, prior to the decision, written about how joint filing and joint liability reinforce traditional gender roles, and a discussion of testimony from innocent spouses who participated in the congressional hearings preceding the enactment of the current statutory framework.

As Cords's feminist judgment notes, the option to file a joint return preceded the concept of joint and several liability. While married taxpayers could file joint returns as early as 1918, Congress did not mandate joint and several liability on these returns until 1938. In the intervening twenty years, the issue was litigated repeatedly. Cords references the *Cole* case, in which the Ninth Circuit reversed the Board of Tax Appeals in holding that joint and several liability did not attach to a joint return.[12] In its brief in the *Cole* case, the IRS referred to joint filing as "an unusual privilege" because electing it reduced a couple's overall tax liability.[13] The legislative history accompanying the Revenue Act of 1938, which mandated joint liability, seized upon the IRS's use of the word "privilege":

> Section 51(b) of the bill expressly provides that the spouses, who exercise the privilege of filing a joint return, are jointly and severally liable for the tax computed upon their aggregate income. It is necessary, for administrative reasons, that any doubt as to the existence of such liability should be set at rest, if the privilege of filing such joint returns is continued.[14]

In the rewritten opinion, Cords cites to the work of Richard Beck and Amy Christian, both of whom have explored the historic justifications of joint liability, and both of whom argue for the elimination of joint and several liability. Far from being an "unusual privilege," joint filing actually presents a certain amount of risk and dilemma, especially for married low-income taxpayers who must file jointly to claim the earned income tax credit.[15] Cords describes traditional gender roles within marriage and acknowledges the potential hardship that can result from joint liability. She also expresses skepticism that eliminating joint filing would be a "satisfying solution." In her role as a Tax Court judge, however, Cords accepts that Congress has chosen to retain joint filing and to provide innocent spouse relief as the appropriate resolution for potential hardship resulting from joint liability. Cords knows that it is not appropriate for a Tax Court judge to simply ignore, or attempt to rewrite, the Code.

Indeed, back in 1967, when the Code provided no possibility of innocent spouse relief, Tax Court Judge Hoyt expressed sympathy for one wife's joint filing hardship while acknowledging the court's inherent limits in providing a remedy:

> Although we have much sympathy for petitioner's unhappy situation and are appalled at the harshness of this result in the instant case, the inflexible

---

[12] Cole v. Comm'r, 81 F.2d 485 (9th Cir. 1935).   [13] *Id.* at 489.

[14] H.R. REP. No. 75-1860, at 29–30 (1938).

[15] There is a strong argument that Congress should eliminate the "married" filing statuses, in part because the innocent spouse relief process is flawed and also because of demographic trends. *See* Michelle Lyon Drumbl, *Decoupling Taxes and Marriage: Beyond Innocence and Income Splitting*, 4 COLUM. J. TAX L. 94, 125 (2012).

statute leaves no room for amelioration. It would seem that only remedial legislation can soften the impact of the rule of strict individual liability for income taxes on the many married women who are unknowingly subjected to its provisions by filing joint returns.[16]

As this quote illustrates, innocent spouse relief originally was imagined and presented as a gendered issue. In 1971, when the first provision for innocent spouse relief was enacted, it was described as relief for unsuspecting house-wives whose breadwinning husbands engaged in tax fraud or illegal activity without their knowledge. Members of Congress expressed concern about "the grave injustice" resulting from joint and several liability in a situation in which a husband embezzles funds unbeknownst to his wife, fails to report the proceeds, and later deserts his wife.[17]

To be sure, both § 6013(d)(3) (mandating joint and several liability) and § 6015 (offering a path to relief from it) are gender neutral. Both spouses, regardless of gender, are jointly and severally liable, and either gender can be eligible for innocent spouse relief. But joint and several liability is an excellent example of a facially gender-neutral legal concept that in practice disadvan-tages women. IRS statistics suggest there is truth behind the stereotype that a wife is more likely to be the lower earner and more likely to request innocent spouse relief.[18] Empirical data support the conclusion that "[n]ot only do women bring more [innocent spouse] cases [in Tax Court], courts appear to be more sympathetic to wives than to husbands."[19]

Cords notes that it would be unreasonable to place one spouse in the role of an auditor of the other. Indeed, this would introduce an adversarial role into the marital dynamic, which Cords finds inappropriate. Cords's rewritten opinion seems to comport with Catharine MacKinnon's writings on domin-ance and subordination. In her 1984 essay, "Difference and Dominance: On Sex Discrimination," MacKinnon writes: "Gender is also a question of power, specifically of male supremacy and female subordination. The question of equality, from the standpoint of what it is going to take to get it, is at root a question of hierarchy."[20]

---

[16] Scudder v. Comm'r, 48 T.C. 36, 41 (1967); *see also* S. Rep. No. 91-1537, at 2 (1970).

[17] *See* S. Rep. No. 91-1537, at 2.

[18] "Nearly 90% of the claims filed for relief from Joint and Several Liability are filed by women with earned income that is approximately 25% of the total income on a joint return." Nat'l Taxpayer Advocate, FY 2001 Annual Report to Congress 128 (2001).

[19] Stephanie Hunter McMahon, *An Empirical Study of Innocent Spouse Relief: Do Courts Implement Congress's Legislative Intent?*, 12 Fla. Tax Rev. 629, 662 (2012).

[20] Catharine A. MacKinnon, *Difference and Dominance: On Sex Discrimination*, *in* Feminism Unmodified: Discourses on Life and Law 32, 40 (1987).

Still, it is important to remember that not all innocent spouses are women, and perhaps even more important to recognize that themes of dominance can transcend traditional gender roles. Among different-sex married couples in 2013, women out-earned their husbands in 38 percent of households.[21] This figure is up from the time that *Cheshire* was decided in 2000, when just under 30 percent of wives earned more than their husbands.[22] Though at first blush, innocent spouse relief appears to be a gender issue, it could be equally framed in modern U.S. society as a class issue. Any spouse, regardless of gender, who in relative terms is less well educated, less financially sophisticated, or earns less than his or her partner is potentially vulnerable under the Code's joint filing and joint liability structure. In any marriage, whether between different-sex partners or same-sex partners, where there is a power and income imbalance, joint filing is inherently problematic because the spouse with greater income and knowledge is likely to exercise control over the decision of whether to file jointly. While the married household may benefit as a collective unit, the other spouse is left on the hook for the entire joint liability even if he or she would have owed no tax at all if filing separately.

Income disparity between spouses creates a power hierarchy. When there is an income disparity between spouses, the Code's incentives to file jointly rather than separately interject (or exacerbate) an uncomfortable power dynamic in the marriage. Imagine a marriage in which one spouse earns nearly $300,000 and the other spouse earns just a few thousand dollars in a part-time job. The lower-earning spouse (regardless of gender) may suspect or even know that the breadwinner does not intend to report his or her entire income, or plans to intentionally inflate deductions. Fearing or knowing this, the lower-earning spouse decides to prepare a separate income tax return. Upon discovering this decision, the breadwinner becomes enraged. Why? Because the lower-earning spouse's decision to file separately will "cost" the couple the benefit of income splitting. Filing a separate return will result in an individual tax liability more than $20,000 higher as compared to what the liability on a joint return would be.[23] With the separate return, the lower-earning spouse is protected from the IRS, but not from the fury of the breadwinner.

---

[21] BUREAU OF LABOR STATISTICS, U.S. DEP'T OF LABOR, WOMEN IN THE LABOR FORCE: A DATABOOK 87 tbl.26 (2015) (including households in which the husband may have no earnings at all).

[22] *Id.*

[23] For a case with similar facts (though somewhat different income figures), see Bozick v. Comm'r, 99 T.C.M. (CCH) 1242 (2010).

Innocent spouse requests often involve victims of domestic abuse (physical, emotional, and/or verbal) and/or controlling behavior that includes one spouse restricting the other's access to financial information or accounts. Since *Cheshire* was decided, the IRS has issued guidance setting forth the factors it will use to determine when equitable relief is appropriate. The most recent guidance is set forth in Revenue Procedure 2013-34, which supersedes Revenue Procedure 2003-61. Among other things, the 2013 revenue procedure gives greater deference to the presence of abuse as a factor and acknowledges that abuse can negate other factors (including, specifically, knowledge).[24] IRS Form 8857, used to request innocent spouse relief, devotes an entire page to gathering information about any domestic violence or spousal abuse that may have occurred. The form names examples of specific types of abuse or control and allows the requesting spouse to check the boxes that apply. One box asks whether the requestor's spouse made "most or all the decisions for you, including financial decisions." The IRS thus shows sensitivity to domestic violence and spousal abuse, and recognizes the many forms it can take beyond physical abuse. The form for relief also seems to recognize the potential for power imbalance in marriage, and the damaging effects of that. At the same time, Congress has not gone far enough. After extensive hearings on this subject in 1998, it did not take any steps to eliminate joint liability. Instead, Congress chose to liberalize innocent spouse relief. As a result, income tax liability continues to be an arena in which power imbalances between spouses may have negative consequences for the less powerful or less wealthy spouse. Though a spouse can request relief, doing so can be an expensive process, as well as a long and emotionally grueling one that may require revealing the most intimate of life's details to a federal agency tasked with enforcing revenue laws.

Had Cords's decision been the one that the Tax Court issued in 2000, it would have set an important precedent for interpreting the newly liberalized innocent spouse statute. It would have acknowledged that there can exist a corrosive power imbalance in a marriage between those who are financially savvy and those who are not. Importantly, it would have sent a signal to married couples that if one spouse chooses to lie or misrepresent the tax consequences to the other spouse, the former will bear the risk that the joint liability will later be severed.

From a feminist perspective, abolishing joint liability ultimately may be the preferred step toward advancing spousal equality because it would abolish a

---

[24] *See* Rev. Proc. 2013-34, §§ 3.08, 4.02(3)(a), 2013-43 I.R.B. 397, *modifying and superseding* Rev. Proc. 2003-61, 2003-2 C.B. 296.

system that reinforces hierarchy of power between spouses. But any first step toward disempowering a financially controlling spouse would have been a more positive one than the steps taken in the actual decision by the Tax Court in *Cheshire*.

CHESHIRE v. COMMISSIONER OF INTERNAL REVENUE, 115 T.C. 183 (2000)

OPINION BY JUDGE DANSHERA CORDS

David and Kathryn Cheshire, husband and wife, filed a joint federal income tax return for 1992. The Internal Revenue Service determined a deficiency consisting of a $66,069 understatement of tax, an addition to tax of $16,518 under Internal Revenue Code § 6651(a)(1), and an accuracy-related penalty of $13,214 under § 6662(a). The taxpayer, Kathryn Cheshire, has contested this determination and claims that she is entitled to innocent spouse relief pursuant to § 6015(b), (c), and/or (f).

After concessions by the IRS, two issues remain for decision. The first issue is whether the taxpayer is entitled to innocent spouse relief pursuant to § 6015(b), (c), and/or (f) with respect to the omitted portions of the retirement distributions Mr. Cheshire received from Southwestern Bell Telephone Co. and the omitted interest income from a joint bank account. The second issue is whether the taxpayer is entitled to relief from the § 6662(a) accuracy-related penalty.

All Rule references are to the Tax Court Rules of Practice and Procedure. All dollar amounts are rounded.

I

Some of the facts have been stipulated and are so found. The stipulation of facts and the attached exhibits are incorporated herein by reference.

The taxpayer resided in Cedar Creek, Texas, at the time she filed her petition. She resided in the family home that she and Mr. Cheshire had purchased in 1985.

A

The taxpayer and David Cheshire were married on June 20, 1970. At approximately the same time, the taxpayer received a Bachelor of Science degree in secondary education.

She began work in 1970 as an elementary school teacher, work that she continued until 1973 when she left the workforce to raise the couple's two children. She stayed home with the children from 1974 through 1984. In 1984, the taxpayer returned to teaching.

The Cheshires purchased the family home in Cedar Creek, Texas, in 1985. They incurred a $99,000 mortgage on the home.

Mr. Cheshire acted as the financial head of the Cheshire household. He prepared their jointly filed federal income tax returns. Although the taxpayer asked questions regarding their financial and tax matters, she relied on Mr. Cheshire to investigate, seek advice and counsel, and accurately report their income and liabilities on their income tax returns.

B

Effective January 1, 1992, Mr. Cheshire retired from Southwestern Bell Telephone Co. (Southwestern Bell). At the time of his retirement he received a total lump sum distribution from his retirement accounts of $229,924: Nations Bank of Texas, Trustee, for "SBNCNPP EMP LUMP SUM" ($199,771); Southwestern Bell LESOP for salaried employees ($5,919); Southwestern Bell savings plan for salaried employees ($23,263); Southwestern Bell ESOP ($971). From this total lump sum distribution, $42,183 was rolled over into a qualified account.

Mr. Cheshire deposited $184,377 into account No. 9633-09 at Austin Telco Federal Credit Union on January 31, 1992. The taxpayer knew that Mr. Cheshire had deposited this portion of the retirement lump sum distribution into this account. In addition, $29,786 was deposited into this account between January 29 and February 4, 1992. The record does not establish the source of these deposits. The account earned a total of $1,168 in interest during 1992.

Mr. Cheshire, as financial head of the household, controlled the funds in this account. Mr. Cheshire conducted eight transactions, exclusive of the rollover, that exhausted the retirement distribution. He:

(1) financed his new sole proprietorship, Academic Resources Management Systems (ARMS);

(2) and (3) opened two brokerage accounts at Edward D. Jones & Co., using $40,000 and $5,301, respectively;

(4) paid off the mortgage on the family residence for $99,425;

(5) purchased a 1992 Ford Explorer for $20,189;

(6) purchased a car for one of the couple's children;

(7) opened a college bank account for their daughter with $10,000; and

(8) opened a second account at the Austin Telco Federal Credit Union (account no. 25239-87) into which he transferred the remaining proceeds of the retirement distributions, from which he wrote a check for $6,300 payable to "A.R.M.S.", which presumably went to his sole proprietorship.

C

In March 1993, as he was preparing to begin a jail sentence for a conviction for driving while intoxicated following his second DWI arrest, Mr. Cheshire prepared the couples' joint 1992 federal income tax return. The taxpayer inquired about the tax consequences of the retirement distribution before signing the return. Mr. Cheshire assured her that the $99,425 that the couple used to pay off the mortgage was not taxable according to the certified public accountant he had consulted, J. D. Mican. The taxpayer had no reason to inquire further.

In addition to believing that Mr. Cheshire had consulted with Mr. Mican regarding the tax consequences of paying off the mortgage on the family residence, the taxpayer also believed that Mr. Cheshire timely filed the tax return. In August 1994, the IRS notified the taxpayer that it had not received the Cheshires' 1992 federal income tax return.

While searching for a copy of the missing return, the taxpayer discovered the original unfiled return and a check for the amount of tax shown as due, $23.86. The taxpayer consulted Mr. Mican and followed his advice to immediately submit the return and payment to the IRS. At the time, Mr. Cheshire was in jail on the DWI conviction relating to his March 1993 arrest.

Then, in October 1994, the IRS notified the taxpayer that the $8,502 of estimated tax payments shown on the 1992 tax return had not been made. On advice of Mr. Mican, and despite Mr. Cheshire's assurances that he had made the payments, the taxpayer borrowed the money needed to make the $8,502 estimated tax payment.

In its Notice of Determination, the IRS determined that the Cheshires (1) had understated the amount of taxable income resulting from retirement distributions by $131,591, interest income by $717, dividend income by $132, capital gains by $1,889, and self-employment tax by $353; (2) had overclaimed $14,843 in Schedule C expenses related to Mr. Cheshire's business, ARMS; and (3) were liable for an addition to tax pursuant to Code § 6651(a)(1) for late filing and for a § 6662(a) accuracy-related penalty.

Prior to trial, the IRS conceded that the taxpayer was entitled to innocent spouse relief with respect to the Schedule C expenses, self-employment taxes,

certain capital gains, dividend income, interest income, portions of the retirement income, and the § 6651(a)(1) addition to tax.

D

At some point during their marriage, Mr. Cheshire developed a problem with
alcohol. As a result of his alcohol abuse, Mr. Cheshire was arrested multiple
times for driving while intoxicated and served a jail sentence for a conviction
for DWI. Following his release from jail in June 1993, Mr. Cheshire was
involved in a hit-and-run, alcohol-related motor vehicle accident. In August
1993, the couple permanently separated.

The couple divorced on December 5, 1994. Pursuant to the divorce decree,
Mr. Cheshire transferred to the taxpayer Mr. Cheshire's interest in the family
residence and the 1992 Ford Explorer. At the time of divorce, neither property
was encumbered.

II

A

Married individuals who file a joint return are jointly and severally liable
for their federal income tax liability. I.R.C. § 6013(d)(3). In other words,
once a joint return is filed, each spouse is responsible for all tax due, whether
reported or not.

Courts and commentators have long struggled over the justification for
imposing joint and several liability. Indeed, the U.S. income tax regime is
unusual in its choice to impose joint and several liability on spouses for tax
liabilities. *See* Richard C.E. Beck, *The Innocent Spouse Problem: Joint and
Several Liability for Income Taxes Should Be Repealed,* 43 Vand. L. Rev. 317,
382–89 (1990); Amy C. Christian, *Joint and Several Liability and the Joint
Return,* 66 U. Cin. L. Rev. 535, 542 (1998). Historically, the administrative
difficulty of apportioning the liability resulting from the joint return has
justified joint and several liability, perhaps based on the rationale that once
a couple is married, they become a single economic unit. Beck, *supra,*
at 342–46.

Before Congress specifically addressed whether liability was individual and
related to the source of the income or joint and several, the IRS took the
position that joint returns required joint and several liability. I.T. 1575, II-1
C.B. 144 (1923). That ruling held that "a single joint return is one return
of a taxable unit and not two returns of two units on one sheet of paper."

Id. Initially, the courts were ambivalent about this position. Although the Board of Tax Appeals initially agreed, the Ninth Circuit Court of Appeals reversed. *Cole v. Comm'r,* 29 B.T.A. 602 (1933), *rev'd,* 81 F.2d 485, 490 (9th Cir. 1935). Following the Ninth Circuit's decision in *Cole,* other courts agreed that joint and several liability did not attach to spouses filing joint tax returns. *Crowe v. Comm'r,* 86 F.2d 796 (7th Cir. 1936); *Seder v. Comm'r,* 38 B.T.A. 874 (1938); *Hyman v. Comm'r,* 36 B.T.A. 202, 208 (1937); *Flaherty v. Comm'r,* 35 B.T.A. 1131 (1937); *Darling v. Comm'r,* 34 B.T.A. 1062 (1936); *see also* Christian, *supra,* at 542. In 1938, Congress resolved the issue, enacting a provision establishing joint and several liability. Revenue Act of 1938, Pub. L. No. 554, ch. 289, § 51(b), 52 Stat. 447, 476.

Although women have entered the workforce in ever-increasing numbers, the division of household chores has remained gendered. *See generally* Anne L. Alstott, *Tax Policy and Feminism: Competing Goals and Institutional Choices,* 96 Colum. L. Rev. 2001, 2002–03 (1996) (citing Gillian K. Hadfield, *Households at Work: Beyond Labor Market Policies to Remedy the Gender Gap,* 82 Geo. L.J. 89, 89 (1993)). Despite women's increasing presence in the paid workforce, they also generally remain the principal family caregivers. As a result, when children are born or family members become ill, the responsibility of caring for them often falls almost exclusively on the women in the family. These responsibilities, coupled with the lower wages paid to women and the time out of the workforce often required for bearing and raising children, make women more vulnerable to being viewed as the secondary earner. This is exacerbated by the tax rate structures, which effectively tax the woman's wages as though they are at the couple's highest marginal tax rate. A woman's earnings may thus be viewed as even less economically valuable and more easily dispensed with when there is a need for caregiving.

However, it is not unusual within a marriage for a couple to divide responsibilities. The tax law, including joint marital filing, contributes to the maintenance of traditional household roles within marital relationships. Alstott, *supra,* at 2011. Wives often bear the lion's share of the burden for dependent care. *Id.* at 2011–12. As a result, husbands often continue to possess more knowledge of the couple's finances, including the true state of the tax liabilities, and do not disclose all of that information to their wives. Reasons for the retention of more traditional gender roles vary, but include control, belief about one's spouse's ability or need to understand, and a general sense that this is simply the way that things are done. *See, e.g.,* Marjorie E. Kornhauser, *Money, Marriage & Taxation,* 16 N.Y.L. Sch. J. Hum. Rts. 140, 145–46 (1999). Hardship can result in cases involving unequal sharing of financial information within the marital unit, because of joint and several liability especially when a couple divorces, or the more knowledgeable spouse abandons the marriage or dies (stereotypically the husband, although this is not always the case), leaving the less knowledgeable spouse to pay a liability of which she was unaware.

Many feminists and other advocates have argued that the appropriate resolution to the potential hardship is the elimination of joint filing. Beck, *supra*. This is not a satisfying solution under the current Code because many tax incentives are unavailable to married persons who do not file a joint tax return. *See, e.g.,* I.R.C. §§ 32(d) (allowing the use of the earned income tax credit for married taxpayers only if a joint return is filed), 221(e) (requiring married couples to file a joint return to claim the deduction for interest on student loans); Jerome Borison, *Innocent Spouse Relief: A Call for Legislative and Judicial Liberalization,* 40 Tax Law. 819, 831–32 (1987). Although Congress could easily solve the problem of ineligibility for married taxpayers who file separate returns, it has not chosen to do so.

Congress has instead chosen to impose a *de facto* penalty on married taxpayers eligible for any of these limited benefits. As a limited concession to the possibility that joint and several liability may not be appropriate in all instances, Congress instead allows limited relief to spouses who can demonstrate that they did not know and had no reason to know of the understatement of income or that it would be inequitable to hold the complaining spouse liable for the joint tax liability. *See* I.R.C. § 6015 (formerly I.R.C. § 6013(e)). Unfortunately, as we see in this case, neither addressing the liability as though separate returns were filed nor attempting to address the liability on purely equitable grounds would satisfy all that the feminists and scholars might like to see from the tax law, but the law often lags behind changes in social behavior.

B

Prior to enactment of Code § 6013(e) in 1971, relief from joint and several liability was nearly impossible. A spouse, usually the wife, seeking any relief for a tax liability had to establish that the conditions under which she had signed the return amounted to fraud or duress. In these cases, the courts held that because of the duress, no joint return was filed for purposes of § 6013. *Brown v. Comm'r,* 51 T.C. 116, 121 (1968). The courts held that if duress were present, a return was not filed voluntarily and, therefore, would not be treated as a joint return to which joint and several liability could attach. *Id.* at 119 (citing *Furnish v. Comm'r,* 262 F.2d 727, 733 (9th Cir. 1958), and *Stanley v. Comm'r,* 45 T.C. 555, 560–62 (1966)). Establishing that a tax return was signed under duress required that the spouse alleging duress demonstrate that "the pressure applied did in fact so far affect the individual concerned as to deprive him of contractual volition" as determined under state law. *Id.* (quoting 17 C.J.S., *Contracts* § 175). Proving duress was extraordinarily difficult.

To mitigate the potential hardship of establishing that one's volition had been overcome, in 1971, Congress enacted former § 6013(e), the earliest version of "innocent spouse" relief. Section 6013(e) permitted relief to a spouse who could prove that (1) a joint tax return was filed; (2) the return contained a substantial understatement of tax attributable to the other spouse's grossly erroneous items; (3) at the time the spouse seeking relief signed the return, he or she did not know or have reason to know of the substantial understatement; and (4) under the circumstances, it would be inequitable to hold the spouse seeking relief liable for the substantial understatement. Act of Jan. 12, 1971, Pub. L. No. 91-679, § 1, 84 Stat. 2063; *see* Deficit Reduction Act of 1984, Pub. L. No. 98-369, § 424, 98 Stat. 494, 801–03 (amending § 6013(e) to provide relief in erroneous deduction cases); S. Rep. No. 91-1537, at 2 (1970).

The new § 6013(e) "innocent spouse" provision had the potential to make it easier to obtain relief in many appropriate cases without eliminating the possibility of a spouse defending against the liability on the grounds of duress. However, it presented "innocent spouses" with several challenges. First, its language regarding whether the spouse "had reason to know" of the substantial understatement was broadly interpreted. H.R. Rep. No. 105-599, at 249 (1998) (Conf. Rep.). Second, no relief was available in cases where the understatement was not "substantial" or there was not a "gross omission," as defined therein. *Id.* Third, because these terms were defined relative to the tax liability, they had nothing to do with the financial means of the party seeking relief. *Id.* Finally, a spouse was considered to have "had reason to know" of a substantial understatement if a "reasonable person in the [spouse's] position could have been expected to know of the substantial understatements at the time of signing the returns." *See Sanders v. United States*, 509 F.2d 162, 166–67 (5th Cir. 1975). In *Sanders*, the court rejected the IRS's proposed more restrictive standard that would have required the taxpayer to prove that he or she had no opportunity to determine that there had been an omission of income. *Id.*

Scholars and advocates argued that the thresholds set in § 6013(e) were too high. First, relief was only available when there was a gross omission of income. Second, there must have been a substantial understatement of tax. Third, the spouse seeking protection must have satisfied the requirement that she or he lacked knowledge or reason to know of the omission.

Fourth, application of joint and several liability must have been shown to be inequitable. Not only did § 6013(e) create numerous hurdles, but some of them were more difficult to overcome than others. Although the joint and several liability statute and § 6013(e) were gender neutral on their face, innocent spouse relief has been far more frequently used by women to seek protection from collection of their husbands' tax liabilities. *See, e.g.,* Christian, *supra*, at 536–37. Because the gross omission and substantial understatement of tax requirements were absolute requirements and unrelated to the income of the spouse against which collection was being sought, a claim might not even be available, despite the hardship. Given the gender gap in wages, the unavailability of any avenue for relief could be devastating.

In an effort to remove some of the perceived hurdles, in 1998 Congress repealed § 6013(e) and replaced it with § 6015. Internal Revenue Service Restructuring and Reform Act of 1998, Pub. L. No. 105-206, § 3201(a), (e)(1), 112 Stat. 685, 734. Because § 6015 is relatively new, we have had limited opportunity to hear cases requesting relief under this section.

C

Section 6015 provides three alternative paths to relief for joint and several liability. First, § 6015(b) allows complete relief to innocent spouses who are able to demonstrate that they meet very stringent requirements, similar to those in § 6013(e). Second, § 6015(c) allows apportionment of liability away from an innocent spouse in certain circumstances. Third, § 6015(f) allows equitable relief when it is warranted and relief is otherwise unavailable pursuant to § 6015(b) or (c).

Section 6015(b) provides the greatest possible relief to a requesting spouse, but also contains the most rigorous requirements. A requesting spouse who satisfies the requirements of § 6015(b) is entitled to complete relief from joint and several liability. Because the relief is generous, the requirements are stringent:

SEC. 6015(b) Procedures for relief from liability applicable to all joint filers.

(1) In general. Under procedures prescribed by the Secretary, if—
    (A) a joint return has been made for a taxable year;
    (B) on such return there is an understatement of tax attributable to erroneous items of one individual filing the joint return;
    (C) the other individual filing the joint return establishes that in signing the return he or she did not know, and had no reason to know, that there was such understatement;

(D) taking into account all the facts and circumstances, it is inequitable to hold the other individual liable for the deficiency in tax for such taxable year attributable to such understatement; and

(E) the other individual elects (in such form as the Secretary may prescribe) the benefits of this subsection not later than the date which is 2 years after the date the Secretary has begun collection activities with respect to the individual making the election,

then the other individual shall be relieved of liability for tax (including interest, penalties, and other amounts) for such taxable year to the extent such liability is attributable to such understatement.

. . .

(3) Understatement. For purposes of this subsection, the term "understatement" has the meaning given to such term by section 6662(d)(2)(A).

Although these requirements are very similar to those found in § 6013(e), Congress provided greater leniency, removing the requirements that there be a substantial understatement of tax, a gross omission of income, and a conclusion that failure to grant relief would be inequitable. As discussed in Part II.D of this opinion, *infra*, these changes are significant. These changes were intended to, and often do, result in very different consequences for spouses seeking relief pursuant to § 6015(b) when no such relief would have been available under § 6013(e).

In addition, the drafters of § 6015 provided a second, more flexible path to relief for requesting spouses who had filed joint returns and were divorced or separated from, or no longer living with, the spouse with whom they had filed the return. These spouses could be eligible for relief if they did not have actual knowledge of, and had not received a tax benefit from, the understatement or omission. This more flexible, second path to relief is located in § 6015(c).

SEC. 6015(c) Procedures to limit liability for taxpayers no longer married or taxpayers legally separated or not living together. —

(1) In general. Except as provided in this subsection, if an individual who has made a joint return for any taxable year elects the application of this subsection, the individual's liability for any deficiency which is assessed with respect to the return shall not exceed the portion of such deficiency properly allocable to the individual under subsection (d).

(2) Burden of proof. Except as provided in subparagraph (A)(ii) or (C) of paragraph (3), each individual who elects the application of this subsection shall have the burden of proof with respect to establishing the portion of any deficiency allocable to such individual.

(3) Election.
  (A) Individuals eligible to make election.
    (i) In general. An individual shall only be eligible to elect the application of this subsection if—
      (I) at the time such election is filed, such individual is no longer married to, or is legally separated from, the individual with whom such individual filed the joint return to which the election relates; or
      (II) such individual was not a member of the same household as the individual with whom such joint return was filed at any time during the 12-month period ending on the date such election is filed.
    (ii) Certain taxpayers ineligible to elect. If the Secretary demonstrates that assets were transferred between individuals filing a joint return as part of a fraudulent scheme by such individuals, an election under this subsection by either individual shall be invalid (and section 6013(d)(3) shall apply to the joint return).
  (B) Time for election. An election under this subsection for any taxable year may be made at any time after a deficiency for such year is asserted but not later than 2 years after the date on which the Secretary has begun collection activities with respect to the individual making the election.

Finally, not all cases can be resolved equitably pursuant to § 6015(b) or (c):

  (C) Election not valid with respect to certain deficiencies. If the Secretary demonstrates that an individual making an election under this subsection had actual knowledge, at the time such individual signed the return, of any item giving rise to a deficiency (or portion thereof) which is not allocable to such individual under subsection (d), such election shall not apply to such deficiency (or portion). This subparagraph shall not apply where the individual with actual knowledge establishes that such individual signed the return under duress.

Section 6015(d) provides for an allocation of any deficiency based on the innocent spouse's share of the joint income:

SEC. 6015(d) Allocation of deficiency. For purposes of subsection (c)—

(1) In general. The portion of any deficiency on a joint return allocated to an individual shall be the amount which bears the same ratio to such deficiency as the net amount of items taken into account in computing the deficiency and allocable to the individual under paragraph (3) bears to the net amount of all items taken into account in computing the deficiency.

(2) Separate treatment of certain items. If a deficiency (or portion thereof) is attributable to—
  (A) the disallowance of a credit; or
  (B) any tax (other than tax imposed by section 1 or 55) required to be included with the joint return; and such item is allocated to one individual under paragraph (3), such deficiency (or portion) shall be allocated to such individual. Any such item shall not be taken into account under paragraph (1).
(3) Allocation of items giving rise to the deficiency. For purposes of this subsection—
  (A) In general. Except as provided in paragraphs (4) and (5), any item giving rise to a deficiency on a joint return shall be allocated to individuals filing the return in the same manner as it would have been allocated if the individuals had filed separate returns for the taxable year.
  (B) Exception where other spouse benefits. Under rules prescribed by the Secretary, an item otherwise allocable to an individual under subparagraph (A) shall be allocated to the other individual filing the joint return to the extent the item gave rise to a tax benefit on the joint return to the other individual.
  (C) Exception for fraud. The Secretary may provide for an allocation of any item in a manner not prescribed by subparagraph (A) if the Secretary establishes that such allocation is appropriate due to fraud of one or both individuals.

Section 6015(d) would require that we allocate the items giving rise to the deficiency "in the same manner as it would have been allocated if the individuals had filed separate returns for the taxable year."

Recognizing that there might be cases where looking at equitable principles would be the best approach, Congress permitted the Secretary that option pursuant to § 6015(f):

SEC. 6015(f). Equitable Relief. Under procedures prescribed by the Secretary, if—

(1) taking into account all the facts and circumstances, it is inequitable to hold the individual liable for any unpaid tax or any deficiency (or any portion of either); and
(2) relief is not available to such individual under subsection (b) or (c), the Secretary may relieve such individual of such liability.

Section 6015 applies to any liability for tax arising on or before July 22, 1998 that remains unpaid as of such date as well as to any liability for tax arising after that date. H.R. Rep. No. 105-599, at 251 (1998) (Conf. Rep.).

Because language in §§ 6013(e) and 6015(b) is very similar, it was somewhat unrealistic to expect that § 6015(b) would be interpreted entirely without reference to § 6013(e). However, the complete repeal of § 6013(e) indicates that Congress intended that there be significant change. The IRS has argued in this and other cases before this court that the similarity in language between §§ 6013(e) and 6015(b) should produce the same results. Indeed, we have even concluded that "[d]espite difference between the former provision and the new one, cases interpreting old section 6013(e) remain instructive as to our analysis of whether a taxpayer 'knew or had reason to know' of an understatement pursuant to new section 6015(b)," in cases arising under § 6015(b) after July 22, 1998. *Butler v. Comm'r*, 114 T.C. 276, 283 (2000).

Unfortunately, the newly enacted provisions contain a number of ambiguous terms. As we discuss below, these terms are made even more ambiguous by the differing contexts in which they are used within § 6015. Although the legislative history clearly indicates that Congress had in mind a fundamental reform of the innocent spouse relief provisions, the language in § 6015(b) is similar to that of former § 6013(e). Nonetheless, § 6015 should be read as a part of the larger statute. In the absence of new regulations and in the face of Congress's repeal of § 6013(e), we must determine how the term "items," which is used repeatedly in § 6015, is to be interpreted.

As explained below, the context and legislative history indicate that Congress intended to give a broad reading to the term "items" as used in §§ 6015(c) and 6015(d). However, given the close textual and substantive similarities between §§ 6013(e) and 6015(b), we believe that Congress intended the phrase "erroneous items" in § 6015(b)(1)(B) to be given its historic judicial and regulatory interpretation.

D

The taxpayer and the IRS have argued vigorously on brief regarding whether the similarities in language between § 6015(b) and (c) are intended to yield the same result as would have been obtained under § 6013(e) relating to whether the taxpayer knew or had reason to know of the omitted items of income. However, there are substantial differences between the text in § 6015(b) and (c). Moreover, a requesting party may receive relief under only one provision, although a request for relief may be made in the alternative. We therefore proceed with our analysis examining § 6015(b) first, as it provides the most stringent requirements.

Although the legislative history clearly indicates that Congress had in mind a fundamental reform of the innocent spouse relief provisions, the language in

§ 6015(b) is similar to that of former § 6013(e). Nonetheless, § 6015 should be read as a part of the larger statute. On this point, unlike others in the IRS Restructuring and Reform Act of 1998, the legislative history is silent, so we look to the hearings for indications of the legislators' intent. The Senate conducted a public hearing on February 11, 1998 devoted to issues surrounding former § 6013(e) and the relief it provided to an innocent spouse. S. Rep. No. 105-174, at 7 (1998). The senators conducting the hearings repeatedly expressed concern that the existing provisions did not afford wives adequate protection from their husbands' financial misdeeds and from the IRS's failure to pursue the husbands. *IRS Restructuring: Hearings on H.R. 2676 Before the S. Comm. on Fin.*, 105th Cong. 141–84 (1998) [hereinafter *IRS February 11 Hearing*].

The Senate Report, the House Conference Report, and the statements of the members of the Senate Finance Committee during the testimony evince a clear motivation to make relief easier for taxpayers to obtain. The witnesses were four taxpayers who were directly affected by the requirements of the prior statute who were simply trying to make things work for their families, tried to do the right thing, but did not understand their tax obligations and liabilities. During the hearings, the Senate Finance Committee heard the testimony of four divorced women who were being pursued by the IRS for collection of large tax liabilities resulting from their husbands' activities. *See id.* at 144–64.

One of the witnesses testified that at the time of her testimony in 1998 she was unable to retire because of a liability incurred by her ex-husband in the course of his business in 1968, 1969, and 1970. *Id.* at 153 (testimony of Josephine Berman of South Orange, N.J.). She alleged that she was pursued and harassed by IRS agents and cajoled into signing waivers of the statute of limitations on collections for a tax debt resulting from a disallowed deduction resulting from a subchapter S corporation. *Id.* She testified that, "I was never involved in any of my husband's business activities, nor was I ever included in any business or tax decisions. As was typical for those times, I was the homemaker and he was the breadwinner." *Id.* at 154. Later, after the couple divorced, she lost the home in which she raised the children and her meager retirement savings to pay the taxes resulting from the disallowed tax liability. *Id.*

The legislative language removed was that which most clearly created those roadblocks. *See* S. Rep. No. 105-174, at 55 ("The Committee is concerned that the innocent spouse provisions of present law are inadequate . . . . The Committee intends that this election be available to limit the liability of spouses for tax attributable to items of which they had no knowledge."). It is unfortunate that neither the statute nor the legislative history clearly defines the overlapping terms, but we think the intent to expand the availability of relief is clear. During the hearings, Senator Roth noted that

> [o]ne of the major issues that we have uncovered, one that concerns me greatly, relates to the treatment of innocent spouses who are caught in the cross-hairs of an IRS examination or collection effort who are often left to foot the bill alone once their marriages have come to an end.

See IRS February 11 Hearing, supra, at 161.

The enactment of § 6015 was intended to cure some of these inequities. Indeed, the legislative history indicates that Congress intentionally repealed § 6013(e), replacing it with § 6015 to create a new, more attainable standard. Congress was making a statement that it wanted to afford greater rights, more flexibility, and an easier path to innocent spouse relief than was available under § 6013(e).

We are bound to follow Congress's intent. Although we cannot know what all 535 members of Congress intended, in the absence of other indications, the plain language of the statute makes clear that they intended a significant change from the status quo. Joint and several liability has always imposed a risk, particularly in couples who do not equitably share control over and participation in the financial dealings of the couple.

When couples are in different economic positions, the wife or former wife is more frequently the spouse who lacks earning power, because women's wages tend to be more marginal. Child-rearing and caretaking responsibilities often leave a former wife in possession of the family home, making her the easier target for collection actions, because she is easier to locate, even though she may not have the resources to pay a past tax liability. *See IRS February 11 Hearing, supra,* at 161. Joint filing and joint and several liability all reinforce traditional gender roles under which the male spouse is the primary bread-winner and, therefore, in control of the family finances. *See generally* Alstott, *supra* (citing Alicia H. Munnell, *The Couple versus the Individual under the Federal Personal Income Tax,* in *The Economics of Taxation* 247, 263–65 (Henry J. Aaron & Michael J. Boskin eds., 1980), and Grace Blumberg, *Sexism in the Code: A Comparative Study of Income Taxation of Working Wives and Mothers,* 21 Buff. L. Rev. 49, 52–54 (1971)). Ninety percent of litigated inno-cent spouse requests are made by women. *See* Stephen A. Zorn, *Innocent Spouse, Reasonable Women, and Divorce: The Gap between Reality and the Internal Revenue Code,* 3 Mich. J. Gender & L. 421, 424–25 (1996). The Cheshires maintained a very traditional family structure. Mrs. Cheshire took care of the family, Mr. Cheshire took care of finances and taxes. Mrs. Cheshire was not actively engaged in the financial affairs of the family.

Although she was a college graduate, her education trained her to teach at the elementary and secondary levels. She left the business affairs of the family to her husband.

The taxpayer was not willfully blind to the potential for tax. The taxpayer had asked Mr. Cheshire about the tax consequences of the retirement distribution. First, he lied to the taxpayer about having gotten information from their accountant, Mr. Mican, about the tax consequences. Second, Mr. Cheshire misled her regarding the use of some of the proceeds of the retirement distributions. Even as he was preparing to go to jail in March 1993, he was completing the 1992 tax return. Mr. Cheshire was an alcoholic, with at least two alcohol-related criminal driving convictions at the time of their separation. She inquired about the tax consequences of the retirement distribution.

The taxpayer's request for relief pursuant to § 6015(b) is denied. Section 6015(b) requires the requesting spouse to demonstrate that he or she "did not know and had no reason to know" about the "understatement of tax attributable to the erroneous item." That burden is placed upon the taxpayer. As we held in *Butler*, the standards established under § 6013(e) and contained in § 6015(b) are interpreted in the same manner. For purposes of § 6015, the legislative history is not clear enough for us to conclude that Congress intended us to write on an entirely new slate. However, as we discuss next, § 6015(c) demonstrates substantially broader changes and an intent to provide a fresh start to an innocent spouse.

Section 6015(c) presents several slightly different questions of interpretation. This section was intended to make obtaining relief easier, but also provides some systemic safeguards that protect against fraud and abuse. *See* S. Rep. No. 105-174, at 55. Instead of requiring that the requesting spouse demonstrate that he or she "did not know and had no reason to know" of the "understatement of tax attributable to erroneous items of one individual" as required in § 6015(b)(1), the Secretary must demonstrate that the requesting spouse "had actual knowledge ... of any item giving rise to a deficiency (or portion thereof)" pursuant to § 6015(c)(3)(C). In distinguishing between the terms "erroneous item" and "item," the burden of proof and knowledge standards are significant. These differences require that we revisit our analysis.

Section 6015(c) was intended to provide an eligible electing spouse the ability to seek relief only for that portion of the liability that is allocable to the other spouse. I.R.C. § 6015(c)(1). Section 6015(c)(3) requires that the couple be divorced, legally separated, or not living together. If relief is granted, the liability is not forgiven, but it is allocated only to the spouse to whom it is attributable. Moreover, the legislative history indicates that the taxpayer's situation is the kind of situation that Congress intended to resolve with this new provision. Specifically, the Senate Finance Committee indicated that the reason for adding § 6015(c) was that:

> The Committee generally believes that an electing spouse's liability should be satisfied by the payment of the tax attributable to that spouse's income and that an election to limit a spouse's liability to that amount is appropriate.

> The Committee intends that this election be available to limit the liability of spouses for tax attributable to items of which they had no knowledge. The Committee is concerned that taxpayers not be allowed to abuse these rules by knowingly signing false returns, or transferring assets for the purpose of avoiding the payment of tax by the use of this election.

S. Rep. No. 105-174, at 55–56.

We begin by observing that the IRS bears the burden of proof and must demonstrate that the taxpayer had actual knowledge of the item that gave rise to the deficiency. I.R.C. § 6015(c)(3)(C).

Earlier this year, in another case calling for consideration of the meaning of "item" as used in § 6015, we concluded that a husband who knew that his wife had an income-producing Schedule C business could qualify as an innocent spouse under § 6015(c) if the Commissioner failed to show that the putative innocent spouse had knowledge of the item giving rise to the deficiency when he signed the return. *Charlton v. Comm'r*, 114 T.C. 333 (2000). In *Charlton*, we concluded that a husband who knew of his wife's Schedule C business, but had not reconciled the return to the bank statements lacked "actual knowledge" for purposes of § 6015(c). Proving that the husband had knowledge of the business and access to the bank statements did not satisfy the IRS's burden to demonstrate actual knowledge of the "items" of income produced by the business. The IRS must demonstrate that the claimant spouse has made use of that access.

Here, the IRS has not demonstrated that the taxpayer had actual knowledge regarding the taxable amount of the lump-sum distribution. Had the Cheshires filed separately, the distribution would have been taxable to Mr. Cheshire. The taxpayer questioned Mr. Cheshire about the use of the proceeds. He informed her, untruthfully, that he had consulted a CPA, that the returns were accurately prepared, and that payments were timely made.

This is exactly the type of case about which Congress was concerned when enacting § 6015(c)(3). Innocent spouse cases where a putative innocent spouse requests relief pursuant to § 6015(c)(3) present an entirely different context from cases where a taxpayer has a mistaken belief about the law and to allow the taxpayer to rely on that belief would result in a loss to the Treasury.

Here there is no loss to the Treasury. Mr. Cheshire, who misused the funds, who failed to get the accountant's advice as he had claimed, and who benefited from their use will be required to pay the tax and penalty in full if the taxpayer receives innocent spouse relief; this is the substantively correct result, as the tax liability was Mr. Cheshire's.

There is little more that the taxpayer could have done short of auditing the tax returns to avoid joint and several liability. To do so would have upset the family harmony and, therefore, would not have been a reasonable action to expect of her. *See generally* Alstott, *supra*. As a result, the IRS has failed to satisfy its burden of proof.

To the extent that the taxpayer was led to believe that the proceeds of the retirement distributions had been placed in qualified assets, the taxpayer is entitled to be treated as though she had filed a separate return pursuant to the election in § 6015(c). The taxpayer is relieved of the tax liability for the retirement distribution. Tax liability for the retirement distribution is allocated to Mr. Cheshire pursuant to § 6015(c)(1) because the distribution would have been taxable to him had the Cheshires filed separate returns.

Although some of the funds from the distribution were used to pay for liabilities and expenses of the family while the Cheshires remained married, the taxpayer did not receive a tax benefit in the manner that the term is used in § 6015(d)(3)(B). The reason for this is that the taxpayer did not receive a tax benefit from the erroneous deduction for the mortgage payoff taken on the original return. That deduction reduced only the amount of the retirement distribution on which tax was paid. As such, the only party to benefit was Mr. Cheshire, insofar as it offset income attributable to him. Therefore, all of the benefit, in the sense used in § 6015(d)(3)(B), accrued to Mr. Cheshire and is properly allocable to the income and tax liability that belong to him. The taxpayer is not being enriched by escaping repayment of a prior tax benefit that § 6015(d)(3)(B) seeks to recapture from the putative innocent spouse.

We conclude that the taxpayer is entitled to relief pursuant to § 6015(c) for the tax attributable to the improper deduction claimed for the mortgage payoff. No such relief is available for any other amount deducted.

After concessions and application of § 6015(c), an understatement of tax remains resulting from the IRS's denial of relief from the § 6662(a) accuracy-related penalty. We must decide whether it was an abuse of discretion for the IRS to deny relief for this penalty under the circumstances.

Section 6015(f) permits the Secretary to exercise discretion and grant relief if "taking into account all the facts and circumstances, it is inequitable to hold the individual liable for any unpaid tax or any deficiency (or any portion of either)" and § 6015(b) or (c) are not available grounds for relief.

Unfortunately, not only is the language of this additional subsection ambiguous on its face but Congress also left us with no legislative history in either the House Report or the Conference Report as guidance. This subsection was added in conference.

We must decide whether it is an abuse of discretion on the part of the IRS to have denied the taxpayer relief on equitable innocent spouse grounds. *Butler v. Comm'r*, 114 T.C. 276 (2000); *Fernandez v. Comm'r*, 114 T.C. 324 (2000); *Charlton*, 114 T.C. 333. We review the IRS's denial of equitable innocent spouse relief pursuant to § 6015(f) under an abuse of discretion standard. *Butler*, 114 T.C. at 291. Whether the IRS's denial of equitable innocent spouse relief was an abuse of discretion is a question of fact. *See Hospital Corp. of Am. v. Comm'r*, 81 T.C. 520, 594 (1983).

We hold that this was an abuse of the IRS's discretion. Pursuant to § 6664(c)(1), § 6662(a) does not apply to "any portion of an underpayment if it is shown that there was a reasonable cause for such portion and that the taxpayer acted in good faith with respect to such portion."

Having had the opportunity to view the credibility of the witnesses at trial, we find the testimony of the taxpayer to be credible. The taxpayer in good faith believed that the tax returns were correct at the time they were submitted. She made reasonable inquiries of her husband regarding the tax consequences of the proceeds of the retirement distribution. Mr. Cheshire assured the taxpayer that he had consulted with a certified public accountant and was properly reporting the income, that the estimated tax payments had been made timely and that the return was filed timely. Short of auditing their accounts and preparing the returns herself, an unreasonable expectation to impose on a wife in this particular case, there is nothing further that the taxpayer could have done to satisfy her obligation to ensure that her taxes were prepared accurately.

Appropriate orders will be issued.

11

Commentary on *Magdalin v. Commissioner*

KATHERINE PRATT

BACKGROUND

The legal issue in *Magdalin v. Commissioner*[1] was whether the federal income tax allows a medically fertile gay man to take a medical expense deduction for the costs he incurred for *in vitro* fertilization (IVF), egg donation, and gestational surrogacy in order to have children biologically related to him. More broadly, the case raises significant concerns – including feminist concerns – about assisted reproductive technology and access to parenting and family formation for same-sex couples. Parenting children is a defining, essential part of flourishing and identity for most, but not all, people.[2] Legally recognized parent-child relationships can be formed through (1) (hetero)sexual reproduction; (2) alternative reproduction (i.e., assisted reproductive technology [ART], including artificial insemination, IVF, egg donation, and surrogacy); or (3) adoption or foster care. Adoption and foster care typically are not the preferred path to parenting for couples and individuals who cannot become parents through sexual reproduction.[3] Infertile different-sex couples, same-sex couples, and individuals thus increasingly use ARTs to become parents,[4] and

---

[1] 96 T.C.M. (CCH) 491 (2008), *aff'd*, 2010-1 U.S. Tax Cas. (CCH) ¶ 50,150 (1st Cir. 2009).

[2] Katherine Pratt, *Inconceivable? Deducting the Costs of Fertility Treatment*, 89 CORNELL L. REV. 101 (2004).

[3] Most would-be parents want a genetic connection to their children. Also, adoption and fostering are cumbersome, uncertain paths to parenting. Competition for healthy children, with no special needs, is fierce among would-be adoptive parents, and agencies often prefer to place children with married different-sex couples.

[4] Barriers to ART access may be formal (e.g., some state laws deny access to unmarried couples and individuals) or informal (e.g., some providers deny ART access to married or unmarried gay and lesbian couples and individuals). *See* Judith F. Daar, *Accessing Reproductive Technologies: Invisible Barriers, Indelible Harms*, 23 BERKELEY J. GENDER L. & JUST. 18, 43–48 (2008). Also, some states allow surrogacy only if the intended parents can prove "medical"

family law has developed new "intentional" and "functional" parentage tests to legally recognize the parent-child relationship of "intended" parents who nurture children conceived and born with ARTs.[5]

Infertile women and different-sex couples, gay couples, and single gay men incur significant costs for ARTs. In addition, fertile lesbian couples must incur the costs of IVF if, as is common, they want one partner to gestate the child and the other to provide the egg that is fertilized. On average, gay would-be parents incur the highest ART costs to conceive and bear children because they require IVF, egg donation, and gestational surrogacy, while other would-be parents often incur only some of these costs.[6] Although the costs of ARTs generally are not reimbursed by health insurance, a tax deduction for such costs can reduce the net out-of-pocket costs of the ARTs. Federal law allows an income tax deduction for taxpayers' expenses for "medical care," as that term is defined in Code § 213(d)(1)(A).[7] The specific question in *Magdalin v. Commissioner* was whether the taxpayer's IVF, egg donation, surrogacy, and related costs of using ART were tax deductible as "medical care."

The term "medical care" is defined in § 213(d)(1)(A) to include amounts paid "for the diagnosis, cure, mitigation, treatment, or prevention of disease, *or* for the purpose of affecting any structure or function of the body."[8] The Internal Revenue Service consistently has interpreted the term "disease" broadly, to encompass mental or physical illnesses, conditions, injuries, impairments, and disorders.[9]

The term "medical care" does not include expenses incurred for the "general well-being" of the taxpayer[10] or "cosmetic surgery or similar procedures."[11] Many § 213 cases involve taxpayers trying to deduct as a medical

---

infertility. *See* Fla. Stat. Ann. § 742.15 (West 2016); 750 Ill. Comp. Stat. Ann. 47/20 (West 2016).

5   *See* Douglas NeJaime, *Marriage Equality and the New Parenthood*, 129 Harv. L. Rev. 1185, 1187 (2016) (observing that early family parentage tests were based on biological/genetic connection and marital status, but courts developed newer "intentional" and "functional" parentage tests in the context of ARTs).

6   Although fertile women whose spouses or partners are women or infertile men can use low-cost, nonmedical ARTs to conceive children, such women who are not in a married different-sex couple may choose to use medical insemination, because it creates stronger parental rights in some states. Medical insemination is much less costly than IVF, egg donation, and surrogacy.

7   I.R.C. § 213(a) (Westlaw through Pub. L. No. 115-43) (allowing a deduction for unreimbursed "medical care" expenses in excess of 10 percent of adjusted gross income).

8   *Id.* § 213(d)(1)(A) (emphasis added); Treas. Reg. § 1.213-1(e) (as amended in 1979).

9   *See, e.g.*, Treas. Reg. § 1.213-1(e)(1)(v)(a).   10   *See id.* § 1.213-1(e)(1)(ii).

11   I.R.C. § 213(d)(9).

expense the cost of a recreational item, such as a vacation or a swimming pool, which is usually purchased for nonmedical, personal-consumption reasons.[12] In these cases, courts distinguish between nondeductible personal-consumption expenses and deductible medical expenses by looking for a "direct or proximate relation" between the expense and the ostensible medical problem.[13] Another group of § 213 cases involves fees paid to nonmedical providers, such as lawyers, for items that are not recreational but are generally characterized as nondeductible personal expenses.[14] The IRS and courts classify these types of fees as medical expenses only if the services provided by the person are necessary (using a "but for" test) to treat the taxpayer's medical condition.[15]

In contrast, some § 213 cases involve expenses for procedures or treatments that are *inherently medical* in nature,[16] including fees for doctors' services, diagnostic tests, surgery, prescription drugs, and hospital expenses.[17] It is much more difficult for the IRS to argue that this type of care is not "medical care." The assumption is that most medical treatment originates out of the taxpayer's medical need, not out of pure personal-consumption motives,[18] despite the fact that certain medical expenses may include an element of personal consumption.[19] The fact that a medical procedure is "elective" does not take the procedure out of the definition of "medical care"; what matters is whether

[12] *See, e.g.,* Evanoff v. Comm'r, 44 T.C.M. (CCH) 1394 (1982) (denying a medical expense deduction for the cost of a home pool used for therapy where there was a community pool nearby).

[13] *See, e.g.,* Havey v. Comm'r, 12 T.C. 409, 412 (1949).

[14] *See, e.g.,* Jacobs v. Comm'r, 62 T.C. 813 (1974) (denying a medical expense deduction for the cost of divorce, even though the divorce was recommended by a psychiatrist as a first step toward treating mental illness).

[15] *See, e.g.,* Gerstacker v. Comm'r, 49 T.C. 522 (1968) (taxpayer could deduct legal fees incurred to establish a guardianship for his spouse because guardianship was necessary to commit her to a mental institution for medical treatment).

[16] *See* Huff v. Comm'r, 69 T.C.M. (CCH) 2551 (1995) (distinguishing between "inherently medical" treatments and nonmedical treatments (e.g., massage) intended to improve general well-being).

[17] Care that is inherently medical includes: "hospital services, nursing services, . . . medical, laboratory, surgical, dental and other diagnostic and healing services, X-rays, medicine and drugs . . . , artificial teeth or limbs, and ambulance hire." Treas. Reg. § 1.213-1(e)(1)(ii) (as amended in 1979).

[18] *See* William D. Andrews, *Personal Deductions in an Ideal Income Tax,* 86 Harv. L. Rev. 309, 314 (1972).

[19] *See* Mark G. Kelman, *Personal Deductions Revisited: Why They Fit Poorly in an "Ideal" Income Tax and Why They Fit Worse in a Far from Ideal World,* 31 Stan. L. Rev. 831, 866–68 (1979); *see also id.* at 864–65 (noting the income elasticity and price elasticity of medical care).

the procedure is for the diagnosis, cure, mitigation, treatment, or prevention of "disease" (broadly construed), or for the purpose of affecting functioning.[20]

In administrative pronouncements issued decades ago, the IRS ruled that taxpayers can deduct the costs of obstetrical care, prescription contraceptives, tubal ligations, vasectomies, and legal abortions, notwithstanding the absence of "disease."[21] In more recent decades, the IRS stated in Publication 502 (nonbinding advice provided by the IRS to lay taxpayers) that taxpayers can deduct the costs of "fertility enhancements" (e.g., IVF or surgery to reverse prior voluntary sterilization) to "overcome your inability to have children."[22] Also, in a single tax controversy, the IRS allowed a medically infertile taxpayer to deduct the cost of egg donation, although that IRS decision pertains only to the taxpayer involved in that controversy.[23] Conversely, the IRS asserted in a U.S. Tax Court case that taxpayers cannot take a medical expense deduction for surrogacy costs; however, no decision or opinion was reported in the case, which the IRS settled in favor of the taxpayer.[24] *Magdalin* is the first judicial opinion to directly address the question of whether IVF, egg donation, and surrogacy costs are deductible under § 213 as "medical care."

ORIGINAL OPINION

In December 2008, U.S. Tax Court Judge Wherry held that William Magdalin could not deduct the IVF, egg donor, and surrogacy costs that he incurred to conceive and bear two biological children.[25] Judge Wherry concluded that Magdalin's ART expenses were not expenses for "medical care" because (1) the taxpayer "had no medical condition or defect, such as, for example,

---

[20] *See* Katherine Pratt, *Deducting the Costs of Fertility Treatment: Implications of* Magdalin v. Commissioner *for Opposite-Sex Couples, Gay and Lesbian Same-Sex Couples, and Single Women and Men*, 2009 WIS. L. REV. 1283.

[21] Treas. Reg. § 1.213-1(e); Rev. Rul. 73-200, 1973-1 C.B. 140 (cost of birth-control pills is "medical care"); Rev. Rul. 73-201, 1973-1 C.B. 140 (cost of a legal abortion or vasectomy is "medical care"); Rev. Rul. 73-603, 1973-2 C.B. 76 (cost of tubal ligation procedure is "medical care").

[22] I.R.S. Pub. No. 502, Medical and Dental Expenses (2016).

[23] I.R.S. Priv. Ltr. Rul. 2003-18-017 (Jan. 9, 2003).

[24] Sedgwick v. Comm'r, No. 10133-94 (T.C. filed June 14, 1994); *see also* I.R.S. Information Letter 2002-0291 (2002) (concluding that surrogacy expenses are not deductible medical expenses).

[25] The decision was an unofficial "memorandum" decision, which indicates that the Chief Judge of the Tax Court thought that Judge Wherry was not making new law in the case. Memorandum decisions are not treated as binding precedent in the Tax Court. *See, e.g.,* Nico v. Comm'r, 67 T.C. 647, 654 (1977). The rewritten feminist opinion of Jennifer Bird-Pollan, writing as Judge Bird-Pollan, is a "reviewed" decision (in which all Tax Court judges participate), which indicates that the Chief Judge viewed the case as significant and establishing new law.

infertility, that required treatment or mitigation through IVF procedures";
and (2) the medical procedures "did not affect a structure or function of
his body."[26] The court added that, because the taxpayer did not suffer from
infertility:

> We therefore need not answer lurking questions as to whether (and, if so, to
> what extent) expenditures for IVF procedures and associated costs (e.g., a
> taxpayer's legal fees and fees paid to, or on behalf of, a surrogate or gestational
> carrier) would be deductible in the presence of an underlying condition . . . .
> We leave such questions for another day.[27]

Judge Wherry seemed to agree with the IRS argument that deductibility under
§ 213 requires that the taxpayer satisfy the "disease" prong of § 213's definition
of "medical care,"[28] citing as support the § 213 regulations, which provide that
medical expense deductions "will be confined strictly to expenses incurred
primarily for the prevention or alleviation of a physical or mental defect or
illness."[29] He also cited § 213 cases,[30] including *Havey v. Commissioner*[31] and
Jacobs v. Commissioner,[32] that require a showing of a "but for" (or direct and
proximate) relationship between the expense and a disease or medical condition. In the cited cases, however, the issue was whether the taxpayer could
deduct expenses that were not inherently medical (vacation travel in *Havey*
and divorce expenses in *Jacobs*). In *Magdalin*, the taxpayer deducted *inherently medical* expenses (i.e., ovarian stimulation, egg extraction, and IVF
expenses), plus ancillary expenses (e.g., egg donation and surrogacy contract
expenses), without which his children could not have been conceived, ges-
tated, and born.[33]

There is no discussion in the *Magdalin* opinion of the administrative
pronouncements regarding the deductibility of reproductive care, and no
recognition of the role of the "structure or function" prong of § 213's definition
of "medical care" in the context of determining the deductibility of the costs of
reproductive care. Judge Wherry also rejected the taxpayer's constitutional
claims "that it was his civil right to reproduce, that he should have the freedom
to choose the method of reproduction, and that it is sex discrimination to

---

[26] Magdalin v. Comm'r, 96 T.C.M. (CCH) 491, 493 (2008), *aff'd* 2010-1 U.S. Tax Cas. (CCH)
¶ 50,150 (1st Cir. 2009).

[27] *Id.*

[28] *Id.* at 492; Opening Brief for Respondent at 16–19, *Magdalin*, 96 T.C.M. (CCH) 491
(No. 7880-07) (arguing that a medical expense is deductible only if it satisfies the "disease"
prong of the § 213(d)(1)(A) definition, even if it satisfies the "structure or function" prong of
that definition).

[29] *Magdalin*, 96 T.C.M. (CCH) at 492 (quoting Treas. Reg. § 1.213-1(e)(1)(ii)).   [30] *Id.*

[31] 12 T.C. 409 (1949).   [32] 62 T.C. 813 (1974).   [33] *Magdalin*, 96 T.C.M. (CCH) at 491–92.

allow women but not men to choose how they will reproduce."[34] He concluded that, on the facts of the case, there were no constitutional issues to resolve.[35]

Under the original opinion, the tax deductibility under § 213 of the costs of various types of fertility treatment thus turns on: (1) whether the taxpayer has been diagnosed with "medical" infertility; (2) the taxpayer's sex, marital status, and sexual orientation; and (3) what the IRS and judges implicitly consider to be "natural" or "normal" reproduction.[36] As Anthony Infanti has observed, the case also illustrates how the tax law constitutes "the body" "of" "the taxpayer, his spouse, or a dependent," by aggregating the bodies of married taxpayers who reproduce, but not aggregating the bodies of an intended parent, egg donor, and surrogate.[37]

Two subsequent medical expense deduction cases have cited *Magdalin* approvingly. In a recent tax refund case in federal district court, Judge Lazzara denied a medical expense deduction for IVF, egg donation, and surrogacy expenses incurred by a gay man in an unsuccessful attempt to have children.[38] Also, in a 2013 memorandum decision, Tax Court Judge Morrison denied a § 213 deduction for expenses a male taxpayer incurred for his fiancé's IVF treatment, noting that the taxpayer and his fiancé were not married and the taxpayer failed to prove that he suffered from medical infertility.[39]

FEMINIST JUDGMENT

The feminist opinion of Jennifer Bird-Pollan, writing as Judge Bird-Pollan, holds that the costs of ARTs, including IVF, egg donation, and surrogacy, are for "medical care" and thus are deductible under § 213, notwithstanding that (1) the taxpayer did not suffer from medical infertility and (2) the medical procedures did not affect the structure of the single male taxpayer's "body." Bird-Pollan's rationale is that reproduction is a type of human "functioning" and "medical care" as defined by § 213, and thus includes costs incurred for a medical substitute for sexual reproduction. In her view, a taxpayer need not prove that he or she suffered from a "disease" or that the medical treatment

---

[34] *Id.* at 493; Opening Brief of Petitioner at 7–9, *Magdalin*, 96 T.C.M. (CCH) 491 (No. 7880-07).

[35] *Magdalin*, 96 T.C.M. (CCH) at 493. [36] Pratt, *supra* note 20, at 1334–37, 1345.

[37] Anthony C. Infanti, *Dismembering Families, in* CHALLENGING GENDER INEQUALITY IN TAX POLICY MAKING: COMPARATIVE PERSPECTIVES 159 (Kim Brooks et al. eds., 2011).

[38] Morrissey v. United States, 226 F. Supp. 3d 1338 (M.D. Fla. 2016). The taxpayer appealed the court's decision.

[39] Longino v. Comm'r, 105 T.C.M. (CCH) 1491 (2013), *aff'd* 2015-1 U.S. Tax Cas. (CCH) ¶ 50,104 (11th Cir. 2014).

affected the structure of the taxpayer's own "body," much less that the treatment was medically necessary. Reproduction is a "function" of a taxpayer's body; all reproductive care thus is "medical care."[40] In addition, she implicitly rejects the notion that conceiving and bearing biological children is similar to cosmetic surgery and therefore excluded from the definition of "medical care."

The narrow implications of the feminist opinion relate specifically to the interpretation of the income tax term "medical care" and the deductibility of ART costs. Bird-Pollan holds, in a case of first impression, that medical costs of ARTs, including IVF, egg donation, and surrogacy costs, are deductible as medical care under § 213. Had this been the actual decision, it would have been a very significant legal development for would-be parents who plan to use ARTs. Her decision responds to Anthony Infanti's critique of the original *Magdalin* opinion – that the tax law aggregates the bodies of married taxpayers who reproduce, but "dismembers" the bodies of an intended parent, egg donor, and surrogate. Bird-Pollan's decision raises new boundary questions, however, about whether there are limits on the amount of ART expenses that may be deducted as medical care. For example, if an intended parent pays a premium for the eggs of a particularly intelligent or talented donor, is the cost of the egg donation deductible in whole or only in part?

In theory, Bird-Pollan's decision in *Magdalin* furthers the reproductive autonomy of persons who cannot bear and raise children through (hetero) sexual reproduction. The § 213 subsidy for ARTs is an upside-down subsidy, however (notwithstanding the adjusted gross income floor for the deduction). The § 213 deduction reduces taxes only for taxpayers who pay for costly ARTs and itemize deductions; lower-income taxpayers typically do not itemize deductions.[41] In addition, the tax savings from the deduction are greatest for taxpayers who are in the highest tax brackets. The deduction is not valuable

---

[40] Although Bird-Pollan's holding in the rewritten *Magdalin* opinion probably is limited to *legal* reproductive medical care, this limitation generally would not be an issue for intended parents; even if they reside in a state that prohibits surrogacy, they can arrange for surrogacy in a state that allows it. This limitation might apply to reproductive procedures that are universally prohibited, however, such as human cloning.

[41] Internal Revenue Serv., Dep't of Treasury, Statistics of Income – 2014 Individual Income Tax Returns, at 46 tbl.1.2 (2016) (taxpayers who itemize deductions include around 25 percent of lower- and middle-income taxpayers and 80 percent of high-income taxpayers with more than $100,000 of income). Taxpayers who have a flexible spending account can exclude from income up to $2,600 of reimbursements for medical care in 2017. Rev. Proc. 2016-55, § 3.16, 2016-45 I.R.B. 707. Similarly, distributions from Health Savings Accounts to pay qualifying medical expenses are excluded from income. I.R.C. § 223(d)(2)(A), (f) (Westlaw through Pub. L. No. 115-43).

for low-income taxpayers who want to conceive and bear children through ARTs but cannot afford it or have no positive tax liability.

Thinking beyond the technical tax issue addressed in *Magdalin v. Commissioner*, the case raises significant concerns – including feminist concerns – about assisted reproductive technology and access to parenting for gay and lesbian couples and individuals. Consider first the implications for access to parenting and family formation. Gay and lesbian couples and individuals cannot conceive and bear children through sexual reproduction, and adoption and fostering are inadequate substitutes for those who want to parent healthy children from birth and have a genetic connection to their children. That leaves ART as the single best route to parenting and family formation for gay and lesbian couples and individuals. Family law has developed "intentional" and "functional" parentage tests, which support parental rights of intended gay and lesbian parents who use ARTs.[42]

Notwithstanding recent positive legal developments for same-sex couples who want to parent, conservatives continue to oppose ARTs and legal recognition of same-sex marriage and nontraditional families. Conservative writers oppose compensated egg donation and surrogacy on religious grounds or based on the view that ARTs are not "natural" procreation. These writers often also take the view that gay and lesbian couples and individuals should not be allowed to parent, because they cannot "procreate" unassisted and lead deviant lifestyles that are harmful to children.[43] Such arguments, which harken back to discredited "natural law" arguments made in support of antimiscegenation statutes, are contrary to evidence that "many same-sex couples provide loving and nurturing homes to their children, whether biological or adopted."[44] Religious and natural-law opposition to gay and lesbian parenting continues nonetheless and is reflected in state statutes that bar ART access to intended parents who cannot prove medical infertility and in ART providers' refusals to give gay and lesbian intended parents access to ARTs.

Is the promotion of access to parenting and family formation a "feminist" concern? Feminist writers hold diverse views on parenting and, more specifically, on mothering. For decades, feminists aligned with the antisubordination strain of feminism questioned whether the cultural expectation of full-time mothering traps women in subordinated stereotypes that limit their

---

[42] NeJaime, *supra* note 5, at 1187.

[43] *See* Courtney Megan Cahill, *Obergefell and the "New" Reproduction*, 100 Minn. L. Rev. Headnotes 1, 6 (2016) (noting that the Supreme Court in *Obergefell* rejected "hoary stereotypes about sexual minorities as sterile pedophiliacs prone to unfamiliar, and unfamilial, behavior").

[44] Obergefell v. Hodges, 135 S. Ct. 2584, 2600 (2015).

life choices and opportunities. These writers' influential views gradually changed the cultural zeitgeist and made it more socially acceptable for women to delay motherhood or decide to be childless. This, in turn, produced economic gains for women, as they increased their paid participation in labor markets. More recently, third-wave feminists have embraced motherhood anew – sometimes in rhapsodic terms that seemingly depict parenting, specifically "mothering," as essential for a happy and fulfilling life.[45] This recent endorsement of mothering stands in stark opposition to earlier feminist writing that attributed the subordination of women to the prevalent mandatory-mothering societal norm. However, the third-wave pro-parenting stance simply might be an expression of the *nearly* universal desire – of women *and men* alike – to parent and nurture children.

The proliferation of gay parenting adds a new frame on parenting and mothering that can break down traditional gender stereotypes. Feminists observe that both women and men can – and do – "mother" children, contrary to historically gendered views of nurturing and mothering children. In addition, feminists champion the rights of disadvantaged groups, including gay and lesbian couples and individuals. Feminists thus should support increased access to parenting and family formation for gay and lesbian couples and individuals.

Bird-Pollan's *Magdalin* decision shows how the 2015 same-sex marriage decision in *Obergefell v. Hodges*[46] might increase reproductive freedom for gay and lesbian would-be parents. Following *Obergefell*, Courtney Cahill argued that the decision has far-reaching implications for the regulation of ARTs, rendering legal distinctions between sexual procreation and alternative reproduction "constitutionally suspect."[47] Bird-Pollan's *Magdalin* opinion would have anticipated Cahill's views about how a subsequent decision like *Obergefell* could alter the legal conceptualization of alternative reproduction. In addition, Bird-Pollan's approach is consistent with Cahill's more recent argument to reject "reproductive binarism" (legal distinctions between sexual reproduction and alternative reproduction) in favor of a unitary legal approach to reproduction, with a focus on procreative intent instead of procreative mechanics.[48]

A perhaps unintended consequence of Bird-Pollan's decision, had it been the original opinion, is that it likely would have increased the number of

---

[45] Bridget J. Crawford, *Third-Wave Feminism, Motherhood and the Future of Feminist Legal Theory, in* GENDER, SEXUALITIES AND LAW 227 (Jackie Jones et al. eds., 2011).

[46] *Obergefell*, 135 S. Ct. at 2600.   [47] Cahill, *supra* note 43.

[48] *See generally* Courtney Megan Cahill, *Reproduction Reconceived*, 101 MINN. L. REV. 617 (2016).

women who serve as egg donors and surrogates. Feminist opinions on compensated egg donation and surrogacy are conflicted. Some feminist writers approve of compensated surrogacy and egg donation on the grounds that allowing surrogates and egg donors to enter into enforceable agreements furthers their autonomy and freedom to do what they want with their own bodies. Others counter that surrogacy contracts impair surrogates' autonomy, because such contracts sometimes require that surrogates relinquish control over their bodies during pregnancy.[49]

In addition, some feminist writers and critical race theorists oppose compensated egg donation and surrogacy on the grounds that such practices potentially exploit and oppress women, especially low-income women and women of color.[50] For example, some feminist writers argue that the increasing prevalence of ARTs and increasing reproductive medical tourism to the global south create a dystopia in which poor women of color are relegated to the status of paid breeders or reproductive slaves.[51] Some writers question whether such subordination could ever be truly voluntary, in light of the fact that the compensation paid to an Indian surrogate is a multiple of the wages the surrogate otherwise could earn. Gay and lesbian intended parents probably are much less likely to engage in medical tourism than married different-sex intended parents, however, because gay and lesbian intended parents would be concerned that other countries might discriminate against them and deny them parental rights and access to their child. They are more likely to contract with surrogates in American states that permit surrogacy and are less hostile to gay and lesbian families.

A related, but distinct feminist concern is that allowing compensated egg donation and surrogacy commodifies women's reproductive organs and gametes and treats them like reproductive spare parts. Feminists expressing this concern sometimes liken compensated egg donation and surrogacy to compensated organ donation, which is prohibited in the United States, primarily on anticommodification grounds.

Some feminist writers also oppose the societal and legal oppression of gay and lesbian couples and individuals. Consistent with this approach, existing

---

[49] For example, some surrogacy contracts purport to allow the intended parents to decide whether a surrogate will undergo amniocentesis, have an abortion if the fetus has genetic abnormalities, or have a C-section delivery.

[50] *See, e.g.,* Lisa C. Ikemoto, *The In/Fertile, the Too Fertile, and the Dysfertile,* 47 HASTINGS L.J. 1007, 1028 (1996).

[51] Writers note, for example, that agreements for Indian gestational surrogates often require surrogates to live in a segregated compound, apart from their families, to enable the agents of the intended parents to exercise control over the diet and lifestyle of surrogates during pregnancy.

rules and norms that deny gay and lesbian couples and individuals access to parenting and family formation are a feminist concern. In addition, gay men have even less access to parenting than do lesbian women; the disproportionate exclusion of gay men from parenting raises particular concerns about stereotyping and bias against gay men. Feminists who recognize the critical importance of parenting and family formation for the flourishing of most *women and men* – regardless of sexual orientation – will celebrate Bird-Pollan's feminist judgment.

MAGDALIN v. COMMISSIONER OF INTERNAL REVENUE, 96 T.C.M. (CCH) 491 (2008)

OPINION BY JUDGE JENNIFER E. BIRD-POLLAN

This case involves a petition for reconsideration of deficiencies for the taxpayer's 2004 and 2005 tax years. In the notice of deficiency, the Internal Revenue Service disallowed medical expense and charitable contribution deductions in both tax years. The IRS also increased the amount of taxable dividends included in the taxpayer's income for 2005. The taxpayer has not challenged the recalculation of taxable dividends or charitable contributions, so the focus of this opinion is on the IRS's denial of the taxpayer's medical expense deductions in 2004 and 2005.

I

The taxpayer, William Magdalin, is a medical doctor with a license to practice in Massachusetts. He is unmarried and the father of four children, two of whom were conceived via the use of an egg donor, *in vitro* fertilization (IVF), and a surrogate gestational carrier, the expenses of which are the subject of this dispute. Although the IRS does not mention this in its brief, the taxpayer is a gay man, who was previously married to a woman. Reply Br. for Pet'r 7–8. The taxpayer's first two children were conceived and born during his marriage without the help of assisted reproductive technology. Suppl. Stipulation of Facts 1.

In July 2004, having decided to attempt to have biological children on his own, the taxpayer signed an Anonymous Egg Donor Agreement. Under the terms of the agreement, an anonymous egg donor would donate eggs, which would then be fertilized with the taxpayer's sperm. Upon successful fertilization, the embryo would be transferred to a gestational carrier using the IVF method. The taxpayer also entered into a Gestational Carrier Agreement with the woman who would carry the fertilized egg to term and give birth to the taxpayer's biological child. The process was ultimately successful, and the gestational carrier gave birth to the taxpayer's child on September 17, 2005.

In November 2005, the taxpayer entered into a second Gestational Carrier Agreement with another woman, and that second carrier was impregnated with an embryo created from the taxpayer's sperm and the egg of a donor (not the gestational carrier), again using the IVF process. The second carrier gave birth to the taxpayer's child on August 12, 2006.

In order to complete the procedures described above, the taxpayer incurred a variety of expenses. In 2004, the taxpayer paid $3,500 for his own legal fees relating the Anonymous Egg Donor Agreement, $500 for the egg donor's legal fees relating to the Anonymous Egg Donor Agreement, $10,750 for the egg donor's other fees and expenses, $8,000 for the gestational carrier's fees and expenses, $25,400 for the IVF clinic's fees, and $2,815 for prescription medications for the first gestational carrier. In total, the taxpayer paid $50,965 in expenses in 2004 relating to his efforts to reproduce.

In 2005, the taxpayer paid $750 for his own legal fees under the Anonymous Egg Donor Agreement, $17,000 for the first gestational carrier's additional fees and expenses, $14,270 for his own legal fees relating to the second Gestational Carrier Agreement, $1,000 for the second gestational carrier's legal fees relating to the Gestational Carrier Agreement, $2,615.10 for the IVF clinic's fees, $300 to the Lawrence General Hospital for costs related to the delivery of his first child, $1,181.25 for legal fees relating to the issuance of his first child's birth certificate, and $838 for prescription drugs for the two carriers. In total, the taxpayer paid $37,954.35 in expenses in 2005 relating to his efforts to reproduce.

No evidence was presented by either party that any of the taxpayer's expenses were compensated for by insurance or otherwise. The IRS does not challenge the accuracy of any of these claimed expenses.

The taxpayer claimed all of the above expenses as medical expense deductions. After applying the 7.5 percent floor, the taxpayer claimed $34,050 in medical expenses on his 2004 Schedule A as part of his itemized deductions, and for 2005, he claimed $28,230 in medical expenses on Schedule A. On March 22, 2007, the taxpayer received a notice of deficiency from the IRS for both tax years, indicating that the IRS was disallowing all medical expenses related to the births of his two children. On April 3, 2007, the taxpayer filed a timely petition with this court.

II

Congress has enacted a sweeping definition of "gross income," Internal Revenue Code § 61(a), that taxes all income from whatever source derived absent a specific statutory exclusion to the contrary. *Comm'r v. Glenshaw Glass Co.*, 348 U.S. 426, 429–30 (1955) ("But Congress applied no limitations as to the source of taxable receipts, nor restrictive labels as to their nature. And the Court has given a liberal construction to this broad phraseology in recognition of the intention of Congress to tax all gains except those specifically exempted."). By contrast, deductions are unavailable to taxpayers unless specifically authorized by a statutory provision, and even then those deductions are read narrowly as a matter of statutory interpretation. *New Colonial Ice Co. v. Helvering*, 292 U.S. 435, 440 (1934) ("Whether and to what extent deductions shall be allowed depends upon legislative grace; and only as there is clear provision therefor can any particular deduction be allowed.").

The justification for Congress's allowance of a deduction for an expense differs depending on the type of expense in question; however, with regard to certain expenses, the justification is that allowing the deduction results in a more accurate measurement of that taxpayer's ability to pay. This justification has been offered with respect to the deduction available to taxpayers under Code § 213 for medical expenses. William D. Andrews, *Personal Deductions in an Ideal Income Tax*, 86 Harv. L. Rev. 309, 314 (1972). Because taxpayers with significant medical expenses have less income remaining after paying those expenses, Congress has accepted the view that it is an appropriate adjustment to a taxpayer's gross income to allow a deduction for extraordinary medical expenses paid by that taxpayer. While any payment of a medical expense would reduce a taxpayer's ability to pay, Congress limits the deduction to cases where the expenses exceed a floor, determined as a percentage of the taxpayer's adjusted gross income. The Joint Committee on Taxation articulated this view in its report on the 1982 tax bill: "The primary rationale for allowing an itemized deduction for medical expenses is that 'extraordinary' medical costs – those in excess of a floor designed to exclude predictable, recurring expenses – reflect an economic hardship, beyond the individual's control, which reduces the ability to pay Federal income tax." Staff of Joint Comm. on Taxation, 97th Cong., *General Explanation of the Revenue Provisions of the Tax Equity and Fiscal Responsibility Act of 1982*, at 24 (Comm. Print 1982). However, Congress worried that allowing a deduction both incentivized taxpayers' overconsumption of healthcare, and that, because the floor had been too low, the deduction was insufficiently tied to the concept of ability to pay.

Under Code § 213(a), a taxpayer may deduct unreimbursed expenses paid during a taxable year for "medical care" rendered to the taxpayer, the taxpayer's spouse, or the taxpayer's dependents. Medical care is defined in the statute as "amounts paid for the diagnosis, cure, mitigation, treatment, or prevention of disease, or for the purpose of affecting any structure or function of the body." I.R.C. § 213(a). This two-pronged test makes clear that Congress intends to allow a medical expense deduction in instances where the expense at issue is either connected with a disease or with affecting a structure or function of the body of the recipient of the medical care. The IRS has made clear that the structure/function prong of § 213 covers instances where the person's body lacks some structure or function or the person needs outside assistance to compensate for the structure or functioning of the body. E.g., Rev. Rul. 73-189, 1973-1 C.B. 139 (costs incurred by kidney transplant recipient as well as prospective kidney donors deductible as medical care); Rev. Rul. 57-461, 1957-2 C.B. 116 (blind person's costs related to seeing-eye dog deductible as medical care).

Congress's allowance of a deduction for medical expenses represents a deviation from the general rule in Code § 262 that personal expenses are nondeductible. As mentioned above, Professor William Andrews has argued that medical expenses are unlike "regular" personal expenses, in that they are generally involuntary and affect a taxpayer's ability to pay. Andrews, *supra*, at 314. In 1990, Congress amended § 213 regarding cosmetic surgery in a way that seems to confirm Professor Andrews's interpretation of the rule. Under that amendment, by preventing the deduction of costs paid for cosmetic surgery "unless the surgery or procedure is necessary to ameliorate a deformity arising from, or directly related to, a congenital abnormality, a personal injury resulting from an accident or trauma, or disfiguring disease," I.R.C. § 213(d)(9)(A), Congress attempts to confirm that voluntary, "purely" cosmetic surgery expenses (as distinguished from involuntary surgery expenses that serve a therapeutic purpose because they relate to correcting the effects of a disease, congenital abnormality, or personal injury) are not the kind of medical expenses contemplated as deductible under the statute. Yet, thinking of the statute as permitting a deduction only in instances where the medical care in question is involuntary or related purely to treating a disease, injury, or defect captures neither the spirit nor the letter of the law.

Many expenses that fall squarely within the realm of "voluntary" costs are nonetheless incurred in order to receive medical care, as that term is conceptualized in the statute. Even staying within the realm of reproduction, the IRS has readily conceded that the cost of abortions, birth control pills, vasectomies, and tubal ligations – all methods used to prevent or terminate pregnancy and all "elective" procedures – are deductible as medical care under § 213. I.R.S. Pub. No. 502, Medical and Dental Expenses (2004). This case is difficult because it addresses an issue that is treated as medical in our society, but is, in most instances, elective: conceiving, gestating, and giving birth to one's own children, whether or not alternative reproductive technologies are involved.

III

This court has not yet considered the issue raised in this case. The IRS has previously challenged the deductibility of costs in a similar case, but in that instance the parties settled before seeking a judgment from this court. *Sedgwick v. Comm'r*, No. 10133-94 (T.C. filed June 7, 1994). As a result, the deductibility of the egg donation, surrogacy, and related costs that the taxpayer incurred for the purpose of bearing his own biological children is a matter of first impression. In order to allow the taxpayer to deduct the costs at issue in this case, we must distinguish those costs as medical, rather than merely personal. Nothing in the Code or the Treasury Regulations explicitly identifies whether or not these costs are medical. Because the IRS has not yet addressed the issue of the deductibility of such costs in this particular context, it makes sense for this court to review how the IRS has historically treated other costs associated with pregnancy and reproduction for purposes of § 213.

While no statute or Treasury Regulation clarifies exactly how the taxpayer's costs should be treated, Treasury Regulation § 1.213-1(e)(1)(ii) (emphasis added) does state that "amounts paid for operations or treatments affecting any portion of the body, *including obstetrical expenses* . . . are deemed to be for the purpose of affecting any structure or function of the body" and are therefore deductible. In accordance with this Treasury Regulation, the IRS has consistently permitted a medical expense deduction for amounts paid by taxpayers in the normal course of pregnancy and childbirth, including pre-pregnancy check-ups for those planning a pregnancy. In this way, the IRS has regularly treated medical care for pregnancy and childbirth as "medical" rather than "personal" for purposes of analyzing expenses under §§ 213 and 262. Further, this treatment prescribed under the Treasury Regulations contemplates pregnancy and childbirth accomplished by traditional means, and not requiring additional intervention.

Accordingly, even "normal" pregnancy and childbirth that do not require extraordinary medical intervention can create expenses that are "medical" for purposes of § 213, because those expenses affect a function of the body – namely reproduction – and thus satisfy one of the two independent tests for deductibility under § 213. Indeed, when this Treasury Regulation was promulgated in 1960, the wide array of assisted reproductive technologies available today was nearly unthinkable. As a result, the Treasury Regulation, unsurprisingly, does not explicitly address the expenses raised in this case. This court is not bound by the past actions of the IRS, but looking to indications of IRS policy does help inform the court as we evaluate how to proceed in this case. In application of the statute in the past, the IRS has held that costs paid in the ever-expanding world of reproductive technologies are deductible medical expenses so long as they are paid to "overcome an inability to have children." I.R.S. Pub. No. 502, *supra*, at 7.

Part of what makes the analysis in this case so difficult is the unusual nature of pregnancy, childbirth, and parenting in the human experience. *See* Katherine Pratt, *Inconceivable? Deducting the Costs of Fertility Treatment*, 89 Cornell L. Rev. 101 (2004). Reproduction is necessarily an act that an individual cannot undertake alone. Whether a person chooses to engage in the traditional method of reproduction or to seek medical intervention, more than one person *must* be involved. Further, for many people, pregnancy and childbirth are the only times in their lives that they regularly visit a doctor or spend time in a hospital. Viewed from that perspective, pregnancy and childbirth seem inherently medical (rather than purely personal), bringing them under the purview of § 213. At the same time, there is reason to think of the decision to have children as inherently personal – one of the most personal decisions an individual can make. When considered this way, there are legitimate arguments to be made that no costs associated with pregnancy and childbirth for any taxpayer should be deductible. Allowing no deduction for any of the costs associated with pregnancy and childbirth to be deductible medical expenses, however, will disproportionately disadvantage women, since most of these costs are incurred in connection with the treatment of women's bodies. As a result, as theoretically consistent as it might be, this court is not advocating for eliminating pregnancy and childbirth from the category of costs considered medical expenses for purposes of § 213.

While it might be most appropriate for all of pregnancy and childbirth to be outside of the realm of § 213 altogether, this is not the view that the Treasury Department took in its decades-old Treasury Regulations or that the IRS has taken in its enforcement of the tax laws. The IRS has published a series of revenue rulings providing taxpayers with guidance on how various costs related to reproduction or the avoidance of reproduction will be treated for purposes of the medical expense deduction under § 213. Furthermore, the IRS annually updates and issues its Publication 502, *Medical and Dental Expenses*, *supra*, instructing taxpayers as to which of their costs will be treated as deductible medical expenses by the IRS. Neither those revenue rulings nor the IRS publication bind this court's decision. Nor are previously published revenue rulings or publications produced for the benefit of taxpayers binding on the actions of the IRS going forward; however, because taxpayers rely on information provided by the IRS in these fora, they provide a fruitful addition to our examination of the issue.

Several revenue rulings issued in 1973 introduced the IRS's view of the deductibility of a variety of costs associated with childbirth or the prevention of childbirth. Rev. Rul. 73-603, 1973-2 C.B. 76 (holding that a woman may deduct the costs of a medical procedure undertaken to make her sterile, whether or not the procedure is medically necessary); Rev. Rul. 73-201, 1973-1 C.B. 140 (holding that both vasectomies and elective abortions are "medical care" for purposes of § 213); Rev. Rul. 73-200, 1973-1 C.B. 140 (holding that the costs of birth control are costs incurred for "medical care" for purposes of § 213). The IRS's positions in these revenue rulings are collected and clarified in Publication 502, *supra*, which identifies expenses that the IRS accepts as medical expenses eligible for deduction by taxpayers. Included in that publication's list are birth control pills, vasectomies, sterilization, and legal abortions. Each of these costs is incurred by taxpayers in connection with childbearing or the avoidance of childbearing. The IRS's identification of these costs as eligible to be deducted as medical expenses indicates its conclusion that these costs associated with childbearing or the avoidance of childbearing are by their very nature medical expenses. And because none of these expenses is associated with a disease, the first prong of the definition of "medical care" in § 213, these expenses must be deductible under the second prong of that definition because they affect a structure or function of the body. In these cases, the most obvious explanation is that the costs affect reproduction, which is a function of the body, either by enhancing or inhibiting the reproductive function of the body.

Professor Andrews's distinction, that voluntary costs are nonmedical and should be considered personal expenses while medical costs are generally involuntary and should be deductible because they affect ability to pay, seems to break down in the face of the revenue rulings and Publication 502. Taking birth control pills, undergoing a sterilization procedure, or having a legal abortion are all voluntary choices made by a taxpayer. And yet the IRS has conceded that all of these costs are deductible medical expenses. It seems that, from the IRS's perspective, the voluntary/involuntary distinction is inappropriate, at least in the arena of conception, pregnancy, and childbirth (or their avoidance).

Since the IRS's published interpretation of § 213 has included costs related to conception, pregnancy, and childbirth, the next question is whether the costs associated with the conception, pregnancy, and childbirth of the taxpayer's two children are meaningfully different from the costs the IRS has historically permitted to be deducted as medical expenses. The IRS's argument is that neither prong of the § 213 definition applies to the costs incurred by the taxpayer, because he did not suffer from any "disease" and the costs incurred by the taxpayer did not affect the structure or function of his own body. Therefore, the IRS concludes that the costs are not for "medical care" as defined in § 213.

In defending this position, the IRS writes that it "does not believe that procreation is a covered function of petitioner's male body within the meaning of § 213(d)(1)." Resp't's Opening Br. 11. The IRS goes on to claim that "[p]etitioner was able to procreate naturally so petitioner's expenses were not medically indicated." *Id.* The IRS's argument here assumes that the taxpayer should have made affirmative choices that would have led to his procreating in a way that would have avoided the necessity of the expenses at issue, namely by having heterosexual intercourse with a woman in order to impregnate her. But it is also evident to this court that, without involving at least one other person, it is objectively false that taxpayer would have been able to procreate. Indeed, this is true for all individuals who wish to procreate. Every individual body, male or female, is structurally and functionally incapable of reproduction on its own. Some taxpayers overcome this lack by finding a different-sex person with whom to procreate. This option is, in most cases, a less expensive path. As we have seen repeatedly in other contexts, however, when a taxpayer is faced with a variety of options for receiving medical care to address a disease or to affect a structure or function of the body, there is no statutory or regulatory requirement that the taxpayer find the least expensive care in order to take a deduction. *See* Rev. Rul. 75-317, 1975-2 C.B. 57 (situation 2) (confirming the ability to choose in obtaining deductible nursing services between a licensed professional and an unlicensed spouse or friend). In this case, the taxpayer's body – like every other human body – could not reproduce without some kind of intervention. The IRS suggests one method of intervention (i.e., sex with a woman), but the taxpayer chose to seek medical intervention in the form of surrogacy and IVF to address this functional lack.

The IRS has addressed similar issues in different contexts in the past. In Rev. Rul. 68-452, 1968-2 C.B. 111, the IRS permitted a medical expense deduction to a taxpayer in need of a kidney donation for amounts paid by him for the kidney donor's expenses. The IRS seeks to distinguish this revenue ruling by claiming that the kidney recipient incurred the expense because of a problem in the functioning of the kidney recipient's body, but that the taxpayer here suffers from no such problem with the functioning of his own body and therefore should be denied the deduction. However, since the taxpayer's body could not have performed the function of procreation without some external support, this court rejects the distinction that the IRS attempts to draw. Both the kidney recipient and the taxpayer in the instant case had bodies that needed outside assistance in order to fully carry out a function of their bodies. Both the kidney recipient and the taxpayer in this case incurred expenses related to a third party (i.e., the kidney donor and the egg donor/gestational surrogate, respectively), which served to assist their bodies in completing the desired function.

Similarly, in Rev. Rul. 64-173, 1964-1 C.B. 121, the taxpayer was permitted to deduct costs related to paying a third party to accompany the taxpayer's blind child during the school day. As in the instant case, the taxpayer in Rev. Rul. 64-173 elected to involve a third party in order to address a functional problem of the body of the taxpayer's dependent child. Whether or not the taxpayer in Rev. Rul. 64-173 could have addressed the functional problem through other means was not at issue there, as it is not at issue here. The taxpayer's blind child's body failed to perform one of its functions, and the expenses incurred to address that issue gave rise to a medical expense deduction for the taxpayer. The taxpayer in Rev. Rul. 64-173 could have sought alternative means to address the child's inability to see, but the IRS did not respond to the taxpayer's claimed medical expense deduction with that suggestion. The disparate response by the IRS to a taxpayer with a blind child and a male taxpayer needing medical assistance to reproduce indicates again that the IRS is acting in this case as though reproduction and its attendant costs are not quite medical. But this treatment is inconsistent with the way the IRS has treated costs associated with conception, pregnancy, and childbirth in the past.

As a practical matter, allowing deductions associated with conception, pregnancy, and childbirth, as the IRS has in the past, but disallowing the deduction claimed by the taxpayer in this case creates disparate treatment on the basis of facts about the taxpayer that should be nondeterminative in this context. Indeed, the IRS makes explicit reference to the "male body" of the taxpayer, as an element of its decision to deny the deduction. Resp't's Opening Br. 11. This fact, combined with the fact that the taxpayer here is a gay man, which fact is at the heart of the expenses he incurred to reproduce, raise specters of discrimination on the part of the government. Interpreting the statute in a way that ignores these nondeterminative facts avoids the risk that the government might engage in discrimination. The most expensive assisted reproductive technology (ART) procedures are those associated with IVF. IVF is often used by aspiring different-sex parents with a structural or functional problem that makes it impossible for the woman to carry a pregnancy to term. However, there is also a large category of people who, by the very nature of their identity, will also require IVF in order to facilitate reproduction. The IRS argues that the taxpayer in this case has no structural or functional disorder that prevents his having a child. The unstated implication is that the "correct" way for the taxpayer to have a child would be to engage in heterosexual sexual intercourse, impregnating a woman, who would then be the mother of his child. By definition, using the criteria proposed by the IRS, gay men (whether coupled or uncoupled) or single heterosexual men who incur costs associated with becoming biological parents will never be allowed to deduct those costs as medical expenses. Further, lesbian couples who choose, as is common to do, to use the biological egg of one parent to impregnate the other parent, will have the costs associated with those procedures denied as medical deductions as well. These very expensive procedures, which are a necessary step for most gay and lesbian couples and many single people to reproduce, are costs every bit as necessary for reproduction in those contexts as the costs for heterosexual couples that have been considered and approved by the IRS for deduction as medical expenses in the past. Distinguishing these costs, and denying the deduction in the case of the taxpayer and others in his situation smacks of discrimination, and finds no justification in the existing law. Interpreting the statute in a way that treats all taxpayers equally avoids the risk of discrimination based on characteristics that should be irrelevant to this determination, such as sexual orientation or gender identity.

IV

In applying the statutory distinction between medical and personal expenses, the IRS has had to make fine distinctions when taxpayers have attempted to deduct costs that seemed more personal than medical. While the IRS has sought to make principled distinctions, sometimes the distinctions have been drawn on a more arbitrary basis. In instances where the taxpayer has pushed back, this court has gotten involved in analyzing the nature of those distinctions. In a case from 1949, the taxpayer sought to deduct as medical expenses the costs associated with trips to resorts in Arizona and Atlantic City, New Jersey – trips that had been recommended by a medical doctor in response to the taxpayer's wife's heart condition. Despite the taxpayer's claim that the trips were taken for medical purposes, this court found that the trips were too personal in nature to justify a medical expense deduction. *Havey v. Comm'r*, 12 T.C. 409 (1949). By contrast, where a taxpayer fully justified to the satisfaction of the IRS examiner the medical necessity of his trip to Florida for treatment of his postoperative throat and lung condition, the IRS conceded, on those particular facts, the deductibility of the medical expense. Rev. Rul. 55-261, 1955-1 C.B. 307. In the same revenue ruling, the IRS held that the cost of a special mattress and plywood boards for the relief of an arthritic condition was deductible, as were the costs associated with an air conditioning unit, when the taxpayer could substantiate the medical need for the air conditioning; however, maternity clothing, wigs, and toothpaste, which involve "amounts expended for the preservation of general health or for the alleviation of physical or mental discomfort which is unrelated to some particular disease or defect," were held nondeductible. Requiring taxpayers to extract a principle from these individual rulings, which the IRS and this court repeatedly claim are extremely fact dependent, asks the taxpayer to do more than many experts trained in this area are able to do.

If one sought to identify a principle based on these decisions, it might be that permitting taxpayers to deduct certain costs as medical expenses, however necessary to ongoing well-being they might be, could open the floodgates to a deluge of taxpayer expenses deducted under a claim of medical necessity, despite providing significant personal benefit. This court can understand why the IRS is opposed to reading the statute in that way. However, in the instant case, where the taxpayer's male body lacks the necessary functionality to allow the taxpayer to procreate unaided, the costs deducted by the taxpayer for the conception, gestation, and birth of his two children were unavoidable medical expenses. Allowing the taxpayer to deduct these costs will not open the door for taxpayers to deduct hot tubs or beach vacations. Becoming a parent is a deeply personal event, but the personal/medical distinction breaks down when it comes to reproduction. Because the IRS has not elected to treat all expenses related to pregnancy and childbearing as nonmedical nondeductible expenses, this court believes that the proper approach is to treat all such expenses as medical, rather than requiring an investigation into taxpayers' reproductive choices. The taxpayer's "choice" to have children via ART is no different from the choices made by the many other taxpayers whose bodily functions allow them to have children in the more traditional, and usually less expensive, way. The IRS has allowed medical expense deductions for those taxpayers when they incur costs as a result of their reproductive choices, and this court believes the taxpayer is entitled to the same treatment.

We note as well that our approach in this case will allow taxpayers to deduct more of the costs associated with pregnancy and childbirth in the future. Because our interpretation of § 213 treats an inability to procreate as a structural or functional lack for purposes of the deduction, any single person, of any gender, who decides to reproduce will be authorized to treat as medical expenses the costs associated with that procreation. In addition, any same-sex or different-sex couples who incur such costs associated with reproduction will be authorized to deduct those costs as medical expenses. While this might well dramatically widen the universe of taxpayers seeking to take a deduction for these types of expenses, this court believes such a result is required by the statute. Further, this court does not expect that permitting a deduction in the case before us here will result in a significant increase in the number of taxpayers seeking deductions. Because of the 7.5 percent floor imposed by § 213, most minimal costs associated with reproduction will remain nondeductible. Only significant expenses, such as those incurred in connection with IVF and surrogacy, will rise to the level of deductibility. Regardless of whether or not the IRS fears that the number of claims for medical expense deductions related to reproduction will increase as a result of this ruling, deductibility is required in this case, as Congress has not amended the statute to eliminate any medical expense deduction for reproduction. Because expenses incurred by some taxpayers (namely those in heterosexual relationships) in order to procreate are deductible, this court believes that an outcome disallowing a deduction for similar expenses when the costs are incurred by a single taxpayer or a same-sex couple smacks of discrimination. In this case, the taxpayer's male body lacked the functional ability to reproduce. Section 213 allows a deduction for medical expenses incurred in order to affect a structure or function of the taxpayer's body. Therefore, the taxpayer is entitled to a deduction for the expenses he incurred for the surrogacy and IVF necessary to allow him to procreate.

While issuance of a birth certificate is not a part of the functioning of a body, the legal fees associated with the issuance of the birth certificate were a necessary cost associated with the medical expenses considered thus far. This court has regularly held that legal fees can be deductible medical expenses when there is a direct or proximate relationship between the legal fee and the provision of medical care. *Lenn v. Comm'r*, 75 T.C.M. (CCH) 1892 (1998). The IRS itself has acknowledged that legal fees relating to a donor contract are deductible medical expenses. I.R.S. Priv. Ltr. Rul. 2003-18-017 (Jan. 9, 2003). In this case, the end goal of allowing the taxpayer to become the legal parent of his child required incurring legal expenses associated with the issuance of a birth certificate that appropriately reflected the child's parentage. Just as the legal fees associated with the surrogacy contracts in this case were medical care for purposes of the § 213 deduction, the fees associated with the issuance of the birth certificate were part of the "medical care" for these purposes. Without the fees associated with the issuance of the birth certificate, the taxpayer would not have been legally recognized as the father of his own child. Therefore, such fees should be considered "medical care" for purposes of § 213 and the expenses should be deductible as medical expenses.

The court has considered all of the IRS's contentions, arguments, requests, and statements. To the extent not discussed here, we conclude that they are meritless, moot, or irrelevant.

To reflect the foregoing, with respect to the medical expense deductions claimed for the egg donation, IVF, and the gestational surrogacy for the taxpayer's two children, as well as the expenses incurred in connection with the production and filing of a birth certificate for one of the taxpayer's children,

Decision will be entered for the taxpayer.

Reviewed by the court.

12

Commentary on *O'Donnabhain v. Commissioner*

NANCY J. KNAUER

BACKGROUND

In 2001, at the age of fifty-seven, Rhiannon O'Donnabhain incurred $25,000 in medical expenses for gender confirmation surgery and related transition care.[1] The extraordinary expenses she incurred in 2001 were the culmination of many years of personal struggle. Although O'Donnabhain had been assigned the male gender at birth and given a traditional male name, she began secretly identifying as female as early as elementary school. O'Donnabhain served in the Coast Guard, worked as a construction engineer, married, and raised three children. After her marriage dissolved in 1996, O'Donnabhain entered therapy and received the diagnosis of Gender Identity Disorder (GID) in 1997. For the next four years, O'Donnabhain engaged in a process of gender transition that included counseling, hormone therapy, and surgical procedures. She had to pay all the expenses associated with her gender care out of pocket because, at the time, it was very rare for such expenses to be covered by insurance. Following her surgery, "O'Donnabhain finally ha[d] a sense of comfort with her body. Feelings of conflict and pain . . . disappeared as she . . . succeeded in integrating her physical, mental, and emotional selves."[2]

Since 1942, taxpayers such as O'Donnabhain who incur significant medical expenses not covered by insurance have been allowed to deduct their expenses

---

[1] The summarized facts are based on O'Donnabhain's petition to the Tax Court, statements made by her attorneys, and the findings of the Tax Court. O'Donnabhain v. Comm'r, 134 T.C. 34 (2010); Petition, *O'Donnabhain*, 134 T.C. 34 (No. 6402-06), *available at* https://www .glad.org/wp-content/uploads/2010/02/odonnabhain-tax-court-petition.pdf; Gay & Lesbian Advocates & Defs., Win in O'Donnabhain Tax Court Case: GID Qualifies as Medical Care (Jan. 2012), *available at* https://www.glad.org/wp-content/uploads/2017/01/odonnabhain-win.pdf.

[2] Petition, *supra* note 1, at 7.

under Code § 213.[3] The medical expense deduction has been described as a "wherewithal" deduction because it recognizes that extraordinary or unusually large medical expenses can impair a taxpayer's ability to pay in a particular taxable year. Currently, expenses for medical care are deductible as an itemized deduction to the extent such expenses exceed 10 percent of a taxpayer's adjusted gross income, but the floor was 7.5 percent for the year in question.[4] The deductibility of these expenses for federal income tax purposes can produce a tax savings that acts as a subsidy to help offset the cost of the care. The amount of the savings depends on a taxpayer's particular tax situation and marginal tax rate. Nontaxpayers obviously receive no benefit from the deduction. Although only a relatively small number of taxpayers will incur expenses related to gender transition medical care, the extraordinary nature of the expenses, their high cost, and the likelihood that they would not be covered by insurance would seem to make them prime candidates for the deduction.

O'Donnabhain claimed a deduction for her transition-related medical expenses on her 2001 federal income tax return and received a refund check for more than $5,000, which was due in large part to her medical expense deduction. Shortly after receiving her refund, she was notified that her income tax return was being audited. The audit examiner eventually disallowed her medical expense deduction on the ground that the procedures she underwent were "cosmetic" in nature. In 1990, Congress had amended § 213 to exclude expenses for "cosmetic surgery or other similar procedures."[5] The exclusion was designed to reach procedures that are purely aesthetic, unlike gender confirmation surgery and other forms of transition-related medical care that are not only medically necessary, but can literally be a matter of life and death for transgender individuals. The Code defines "cosmetic surgery" for purposes of the medical expense deduction as "any procedure which is directed at improving the patient's appearance and does not meaningfully promote the proper function of the body or prevent or treat illness or disease."[6]

O'Donnabhain requested reconsideration of the disallowance of the deduction by the regional Internal Revenue Service Appeals Office. Although the Appeals Officer initially seemed inclined to allow the deduction, the regional office requested and received advice from the Chief Counsel's Office of the IRS in Washington, DC, which affirmed the denial of the deduction and

[3] I.R.C. § 213 (Westlaw through Pub. L. No. 115-43).
[4] *Id.* § 213(a). For several tax years following the change, the applicable floor remained 7.5 percent for taxpayers aged sixty-five and older. *Id.* § 213(f).
[5] *Id.* § 213(d)(9).   [6] *Id.* § 213(d)(9)(B).

represented the final decision by the IRS. The advice came in the form of a Chief Counsel's Advice Memorandum (CCA), dated October 14, 2005.[7] The CCA based its denial of O'Donnabhain's medical expense deduction on the bare assertion that "whether gender reassignment surgery is a treatment for an illness or a disease is controversial."[8] The only authority cited in the CCA to support the conclusion that medical treatment for gender identity disorder is "controversial" was an online article from a religious blog called *First Things*.[9] The CCA concluded that "[o]nly an unequivocal expression of Congressional intent that expenses of this type qualify under section 213 would justify the allowance of the deduction in this case."[10]

On January 6, 2006, the IRS issued a notice of deficiency that disallowed the deduction for medical expenses on the grounds that the expenses related to O'Donnabhain's gender confirmation surgery were not medical care within the meaning of § 213 and constituted "cosmetic surgery" under § 213(d)(9).[11] These conclusions were directly at odds with the great weight of medical opinion, which the IRS had chosen to ignore. Medical experts and LGBT advocacy organizations roundly criticized the IRS for its position, noting that GID was an established medical disorder listed in Section 302.85 of the *Diagnostic and Statistical Manual of Mental Disorders–IV*.[12] As Dr. Marshall Forstein, an associate professor of psychiatry at Harvard Medical School, remarked, "It's absolutely clear that transgender identity is a condition discussed in diagnostic manuals. It seems the IRS is now in the business of practicing medicine without a license."[13]

ORIGINAL OPINION

On March 31, 2006, O'Donnabhain petitioned the Tax Court for redetermination of the deficiency. It was by all accounts a case of first impression. O'Donnabhain was represented by the Gay & Lesbian Advocates & Defenders, an LGBT advocacy organization based in Boston. O'Donnabhain's argument was straightforward. She argued that she was entitled to the medical expense deduction because her transition care was "medically necessary and directed toward the cure, mitigation and treatment of [her] diagnosed gender

---

[7] I.R.S. Chief Couns. Adv. Mem. 2006-03-025 (Oct. 14, 2005).   [8] *Id.*   [9] *Id.*   [10] *Id.*

[11] Petition, *supra* note 1, at 2.

[12] Am. Psychiatric Ass'n, Diagnostic and Statistical Manual of Mental Disorders–IV, at 537–38 (4th ed. 1994).

[13] Anthony Faiola, *Woman Suing IRS over Sex-Change Tax Claims*, Wash. Post, Oct. 7, 2007, at A3.

identity disorder ('GID')."[14] The IRS's argument was more complex and multileveled, as set forth in a brief that was 209 pages long and followed by a 72-page response brief.[15] The IRS argued that GID was not a disease within the meaning of the statute and that the procedures O'Donnabhain had attempted to deduct did not "treat" GID because there was no evidence of their efficacy. To the contrary, the IRS contended that the procedures in question were "cosmetic surgery" because they were not medically necessary. Finally, the IRS argued that O'Donnabhain did not have GID because she had been incorrectly diagnosed. The primary source of authority for these assertions was a medical expert who testified that "GID is a mental disorder . . . but not a disease or an illness."[16]

Nearly four years later, on February 10, 2010, a fractured Tax Court ruled in favor of allowing a deduction for some, but not all, of the claimed medical expenses related to O'Donnabhain's transition care. Writing for an eight-judge majority, Judge Gale allowed the deduction for O'Donnabhain's hormone therapy and gender confirmation surgery because the procedures treated disease within the meaning of § 213, but disallowed a deduction for breast augmentation surgery on the ground that it constituted cosmetic surgery.[17] The majority made detailed and specific findings that GID was a "disease" within the meaning of the statute and that hormone therapy and gender confirmation surgery were not cosmetic because they were for the treatment of a disease. The holding with respect to the breast augmentation surgery was specific to the facts presented and did not represent a broader finding that the cost of breast augmentation would be disallowed as a medical expense deduction in all cases. In O'Donnabhain's case, the majority placed great weight on a notation in O'Donnabhain's medical records that her breasts had already developed in response to hormone therapy and "had a very nice shape."[18] Over a year later, the IRS acquiesced to the decision and issued a notice on November 21, 2011, that it would follow the majority opinion in *O'Donnabhain* in all future cases and would no longer follow the CCA.[19] At that point, almost ten years had elapsed since O'Donnabhain had first claimed the deduction on her 2001 federal income tax return.

In addition to the majority opinion, three judges filed concurring opinions, and five judges dissented in part and concurred in part, meaning that they would have disallowed all of O'Donnabhain's medical expenses. Judge

---

[14] Petition, *supra* note 1, at 2.
[15] O'Donnabhain v. Comm'r, 134 T.C. 34, 96 n.1 (2010) (Halpern, J., concurring).
[16] *Id.* at 46 (majority opinion).   [17] *Id.* at 77.   [18] *Id.* at 72.
[19] I.R.S. Actions Relating to Decisions of the Tax Court, 2011-47 I.R.B.

Holmes's concurrence was notable for the way he bristled at the "crash course on transsexualism that this case has forced on us."[20] He also faulted the majority opinion, saying that it "drafts our Court into culture wars in which tax lawyers have heretofore claimed noncombatant status."[21] The dissenting opinions objected to what they perceived to be the majority's judicial activism, but Judge Gustafson's twenty-one-page dissent that was joined by four other judges stands apart for the clear disdain with which he described O'Donnabhain and GID more generally. Gustafson maintained that transition care is medically unethical because such treatment "has given up on the mental disease, has capitulated to the mental disease, has arguably even changed sides and joined forces with the mental disease."[22] In his view, individuals with GID should be treated to cure the disease, but not given access to gender confirmation procedures. Consistent with this belief, Gustafson only begrudgingly referred to O'Donnabhain with female pronouns for events that occurred after her gender confirmation surgery in 2001.[23]

The original decision of the Tax Court is considered a victory by many LGBT advocates.[24] O'Donnabhain was allowed to deduct the majority of the expenses related to her transition care. The disallowance of the costs of the breast augmentation surgery was specific to O'Donnabhain's circumstances and did not represent a blanket disallowance. For many transgender taxpayers, the availability of the deduction would reduce the after-tax cost of expensive procedures that could otherwise be out of reach financially. The ruling did not, however, directly help transgender taxpayers who could not use the deduction because they owed no federal income tax or lacked the means to pay the high out-of-pocket expenses associated with gender confirmation surgery. Nevertheless, it constituted federal recognition that GID is a legitimate medical condition and gender confirmation surgery is medically necessary to treat GID. These findings had positive ramifications far beyond the tax laws, as advocates argued for expanded insurance coverage in government programs and in the private sector. When O'Donnabhain filed her 2001 taxes, health insurance plans routinely had blanket exclusions for transition-related medical care. By 2016, sixteen states prohibited these exclusions, and 40 percent of all Fortune 500 companies provided transgender-inclusive medical benefits.[25]

---

[20] *O'Donnabhain*, 134 T.C. at 86 (Holmes, J., concurring).   [21] *Id.* at 85.
[22] *Id.* at 122 (Gustafson, J., dissenting).   [23] *Id.* at 109 n.2.
[24] Gay & Lesbian Advocates & Defs., *supra* note 1.
[25] Human Rights Campaign, Corporate Equality Index 2016: Rating American Workplaces on Lesbian, Gay, Bisexual, and Transgender Equality 7, *available at* http://hrc-assets.s3-website-us-east-1.amazonaws.com//files/assets/resources/CEI-2016-FullReport.pdf.

That same year, the Department of Health and Human Services issued broad regulations under Section 1557 of the Affordable Care Act that prohibit discrimination based on gender identity and could result in nationwide coverage for transition-related medical care.[26]

The victory in *O'Donnabain v. Commissioner*, however, was not without cost.[27] In order to qualify for the deduction, transgender taxpayers have to prove that they have a "disease" and that the expenses claimed are for the treatment of a "mental defect or illness."[28] The original opinion thus added one more item to the long list of transition-related milestones that are only available to transgender individuals who are first diagnosed with a "disease," "disorder," or "defect," including access to hormone therapy, gender confirmation surgery, and corrected gender markers on legal documents.[29] On a personal level, O'Donnabhain had spent nearly ten years embroiled in a legal dispute that questioned who she was at the most fundamental and intimate level. At each juncture along the way – audit, appeals, Chief Counsel's Office, and the Tax Court – O'Donnabhain had been forced to explain herself, her life experience, and why it mattered. Despite her compelling personal story of resilience, the Tax Court chose to see O'Donnabhain through the lens of disease and mental defect, repeatedly noting that her disorder was "severe."[30] The American Psychiatric Association eventually recognized the risk of stigmatization attached to a GID diagnosis and reclassified GID as Gender Dysphoria in the latest addition of the *Diagnostic and Statistical Manual of Mental Disorders, Fifth Edition (DSM–5)* published in 2013.[31] The new classification focuses on the distress caused by the condition and "removes the connotation that the patient is 'disordered.'"[32]

---

[26] *HHS Issues Regulations Banning Trans Health Care Discrimination*, NAT'L CTR. FOR TRANSGENDER EQUAL. (May 16, 2016), http://www.transequality.org/blog/hhs-issues-regulations-banning-trans-health-care-discrimination. The 2016 election of Donald Trump as President has placed the longevity of the 1557 Regulations in doubt. If Congress repeals the Affordable Care Act, then the regulations under the Act would no longer have any effect.

[27] Anthony C. Infanti, *LGBT Taxpayers: A Collision of "Others,"* 13 GEO. J. GENDER & L. 1 (2012) (analyzing *O'Donnabhain* and the "violence wrought by the carving out of the intersection of tax with sexual and gender identity").

[28] *See* Dean Spade, *Resisting Medicine, Re/Modeling Gender*, 18 BERKELEY WOMEN'S L.J. 15, 18 (2003) (discussing the "oppressive relationship between medicine and gender transgressive people").

[29] *See* Dean Spade, *Documenting Gender*, 59 HASTINGS L.J. 731 (2008) (discussing barriers to obtaining legal documents that conform to gender identity).

[30] O'Donnabhain v. Comm'r, 134 T.C. 34, 79 (2010).

[31] AM. PSYCHIATRIC ASS'N, DIAGNOSTIC AND STATISTICAL MANUAL OF MENTAL DISORDERS–V § 302.6 (5th ed. 2013).

[32] Am. Psychiatric Ass'n, *Gender Dysphoria* (2013), *available at* http://www.dsm5.org/documents/gender%20dysphoria%20fact%20sheet.pdf.

FEMINIST JUDGMENT

The rewritten feminist opinion stands in sharp contrast to the original majority opinion. Professor David Cruz, writing as Judge Cruz for the U.S. Tax Court, focuses first and foremost on the taxpayer rather than her "disorder." By centering on the taxpayer and affirming her lived experience, Cruz approaches the question of deductibility from a decidedly different vantage point. Although Cruz reaches the same result as the original opinion with respect to the deductibility of gender confirmation surgery, he rules that the breast reconstruction surgery should also be deductible because both procedures were medically necessary. Instead of forcing O'Donnabhain's claim through the portal of disease and disorder, Cruz identifies an alternative interpretation of the Treasury Regulations that had so thoroughly pathologized and medicalized O'Donnabhain. When Cruz does address GID as a disease, he is conscious of the risk of stigmatization that surrounds the problematic relationship between identity and diagnosis. The result is an affirming and nuanced decision that "emphatically" rejects any suggestion that the procedures could be considered "cosmetic surgery" within the meaning of the statute.

From the opening sentences of the rewritten opinion, it is clear that Cruz places O'Donnabhain securely in the foreground. He begins his opinion: "Rhiannon O'Donnabhain is a taxpayer. She is also a transgender woman." Cruz meets the taxpayer on her own terms and with respect for her identity. To the contrary, the original opinion repeatedly contests O'Donnabhain's identity and describes the taxpayer in very different terms: "Rhiannon G. O'Donnabhain (petitioner) was born a genetic male with unambiguous male genitalia."[33] The first time the original opinion refers to O'Donnabhain with a female pronoun, there is a footnote awkwardly attached midsentence to the word "she."[34] The footnote explains that the use of female pronouns to refer to O'Donnabhain reflects "petitioner's preference."[35] By way of contrast, Cruz addresses the same issue as follows: "[W]e refer to Rhiannon O'Donnabhain by her chosen name and with pronouns that correspond with her gender identity, and do not relegate this explanation to a footnote, as a way of accepting and respecting her and her identity." The opinion then continually refers to O'Donnabhain by her name rather than the more generic "taxpayer" or "petitioner" that is commonly used in Tax Court opinions.

From this strong taxpayer-centric position, Cruz turns to the plain language of the statute to evaluate O'Donnabhain's claim. He focuses on the

[33] *O'Donnabhain*, 134 T.C. at 35.   [34] *Id.* at 35 n.3.   [35] *Id.*

disjunctive definition of "medical care" in § 213(d)(1)(A) that provides that expenses qualify as medical care if they are paid for (1) the diagnosis, cure, mitigation, treatment, or prevention of disease; or (2) for the purpose of affecting any structure or function of the body.[36] The original opinion had accepted the IRS's argument that both prongs of the definition were modified by Treasury Regulations that required all "[d]eductions for expenditures for medical care allowable under section 213 [to] be confined strictly to expenses incurred primarily for the prevention or alleviation of a physical or mental defect or illness."[37] To Cruz, this argument simply makes no sense given traditional rules of statutory construction and the past positions of the IRS that procedures such as vasectomies and abortions qualify as medical expenses notwithstanding the fact that they that do not treat a disease, but rather relate to a structure or function of the body. He concludes that O'Donnabhain's expenses are deductible because they were "for the purpose of affecting any structure or function of the body."[38] Cruz is arguably more able to see the objective shortcomings in the IRS's argument because he does not share its view of O'Donnabhain as defined primarily by her alleged disease, disorder, or defect.

After making the case for a strong disjunctive reading of the definition of medical care, Cruz addresses the risk that that the IRS might appeal to the U.S. Court of Appeals for the First Circuit and engages the merits of the IRS's argument for disallowance head on, namely that GID is not a disease within the meaning of the statute and transition-related medical care is not treatment for a disease as required by the statute. This pragmatic turn, however, is done deliberatively and with full recognition of the risk of stigmatization. Cruz acknowledges: "[W]e run the grave risk of contributing to a stigmatizing discourse wherein transgender individuals, including O'Donnabhain, must classify themselves as 'defective,' 'ill,' or 'diseased,' in the statutory and regulatory terminology, to obtain a deduction for expenses that are patently medical in nature." With this nuanced approach and primary concern for the dignity and agency of the taxpayer, Cruz easily concludes that transition care constitutes medical care for purposes of § 213.

As a final matter, Cruz considers the argument that O'Donnabhain's transition care constitutes "cosmetic surgery" and finds "most emphatically" that it is medically necessary and therefore not "merely cosmetic." Cruz reaches this decision by taking judicial notice of the pressures and violence that transgender individuals face on a daily basis as they attempt to navigate

---

[36] I.R.C. § 213(d)(1)(A) (Westlaw through Pub. L. No. 115-43).
[37] Treas. Reg. § 1.213-1(e)(1)(ii) (as amended in 1979).   [38] I.R.C. § 213(d)(1)(A).

the gender binary and "bring their bodies into alignment with their gender identity." The distance between the original opinion and the rewritten opinion demonstrates how much work remains to be done to secure dignity and equality under the law for transgender taxpayers. But the rewritten opinion also provides an important template for judicial empathy and cultural competency – a template that can help ensure that future transgender legal victories are won in a larger and more nuanced frame.

O'DONNABHAIN v. COMMISSIONER OF INTERNAL REVENUE, 134 T.C. 34 (2010)

OPINION BY JUDGE DAVID B. CRUZ

Rhiannon O'Donnabhain is a taxpayer. She is also a transgender woman. The tax laws of this country afford taxpayers, transgender or not, deductions for the costs of medical care. The Commissioner of Internal Revenue denied O'Donnabhain's claimed deductions for certain medical expenses associated with her gender confirmation. This was error, and we now reverse.

I

Many of the facts have been stipulated, and the stipulated facts and attached exhibits are incorporated in this opinion by this reference. The parties have stipulated that this case is appealable to the U.S. Court of Appeals for the First Circuit. In addition, we refer to Rhiannon O'Donnabhain by her chosen name and with pronouns that correspond with her gender identity, and do not relegate this explanation to a footnote, as a way of accepting and respecting her and her identity. Respect for her also counsels that we not dwell on details of her anatomy and medical procedures beyond what is necessary for us to resolve this dispute about what costs, if any, for procedures undertaken to change her embodiment and way of living in the world to match her gender identity – "transition care" – she may claim as a medical expense deduction.

When she was born in 1943, O'Donnabhain's genitalia appeared male, and she was given a conventionally male name and identified as male on her birth certificate. During her childhood she realized that she was not comfortable with her gender of rearing (her assigned gender), and sometime around ten years of age she began wearing conventionally female clothing in secret. She continued to do this throughout her adolescence, a time when her discomfort with her assigned gender intensified. She continued secretly dressing consistently with her gender identity throughout her adulthood, even as she married a woman and brought three children into the world with her. O'Donnabhain separated from her spouse in 1992, and in 1996 they were divorced.

In 1996, Rhiannon O'Donnabhain began seeing Licensed Independent Clinical Social Worker Diane Ellaborn for assistance in dealing with her discomfort living as a man and her desire to live as the woman she understood herself to be. Ellaborn diagnosed O'Donnabhain as having gender identity disorder (GID) and transsexualism. Ellaborn referred her to endocrinologist Stuart Chipkin for hormone therapy to feminize her appearance. Starting in September 1997, she took hormones under the supervision of four physicians, including two who served as her primary care physicians. She also underwent electrolysis from September 1997 through 2005. Starting in March 2000, O'Donnabhain's gender presentation was female on a full-time basis; that month she underwent surgeries to feminize the appearance of her face and to reduce her Adam's apple. After meeting with two physicians and securing their approval, in October 2001 she underwent what is sometimes termed sex reassignment surgery, but what we will refer to as gender confirmation surgery, including genital reconstruction surgery and breast surgery with implants. She received further genital gender confirmation surgery in May 2002 and underwent still further genital and facial surgeries in 2005.

In her federal income tax return for 2001, O'Donnabhain claimed itemized deductions for medical expenses she paid that year for endocrine therapy and for gender confirmation surgeries including genital/gonadal, facial, and breast. The Commissioner denied those claimed deductions in a notice of deficiency. O'Donnabhain timely appealed that denial.

II

Few would accuse the Internal Revenue Code of simplicity. *See, e.g.,* James W. Colliton, *Standards, Rules, and the Decline of Courts in the Law of Taxation,* 99 Dick. L. Rev. 265, 265 (1995) ("The tax law is the most complex body of statutory law that exists in our legal system."). Although its primary aim is to raise revenue by taxing income, it effectuates, and often makes trades-offs among, numerous public policies. One common way it does this is by allowing deductions from a taxpayer's income that reduce the amount of tax owed. As a general matter, the Code specifies that, "[e]xcept as otherwise expressly provided ... no deduction shall be allowed for personal, living, or family expenses." I.R.C. § 262(a).

That general principle, however, does not by itself resolve this case, for Congress, representing the interests of the American people, has since 1942 expressly provided for tax deductions for medical expenses, which, although personal, can be deductible. *See* Revenue Act of 1942, ch. 619, § 127(a), 56 Stat. 798, 825. Currently, Code § 213(a) provides that "[t]here shall be allowed as a deduction the expenses paid during the taxable year, not compensated for by insurance or otherwise, for medical care of the taxpayer, his spouse, or a dependent . . . to the extent that such expenses exceed 7.5 percent of adjusted gross income." Section 213(d)(1)(A) defines "medical care" as "amounts paid . . . for the diagnosis, cure, mitigation, treatment, or prevention of disease, or for the purpose of affecting any structure or function of the body."[39]

This general definition is subject to an exclusion for cosmetic surgery, which itself is subject to three alternative saving conditions. As a general matter § 213(d)(9)(A) excludes from the definition of "medical care" "cosmetic surgery or other similar procedures," and § 213(d)(9)(B) defines "cosmetic surgery" (for purposes of this exclusion) as "any procedure which is directed at improving the patient's appearance and does not meaningfully promote the proper function of the body or prevent or treat illness or disease." Even if something is cosmetic surgery or a similar procedure, however, § 213(d)(9)(A) does not exclude it from medical care if "the surgery or procedure is necessary to ameliorate a deformity arising from, or directly related to, a congenital abnormality, a personal injury resulting from an accident or trauma, or disfiguring disease."

So, as a matter of statutory language and elementary logic, Rhiannon O'Donnabhain's medical expenses are deductible if (1) either (A) they are "for the diagnosis, cure, mitigation, treatment, or prevention of disease" or (B) they are "for the purpose of affecting any structure or function of the body";[40] and (2) (A) either they are not "directed at improving the patient's appearance" or they do "meaningfully promote the proper function of the body or prevent or treat illness or disease" or (B) they are "necessary to ameliorate a deformity arising from, or directly related to, a congenital abnormality, a personal injury resulting from an accident or trauma, or disfiguring disease." Condition (1) brings a procedure within the general definition of "medical care." One of its subconditions must be satisfied for deductibility. In addition, either a procedure must not be cosmetic surgery, or if it is, it must satisfy one of the saving conditions in § 213(d)(9)(A). Condition (2)(A) is the negation of the definition of "cosmetic surgery," and condition (2)(B) restates the saving conditions.

---

[39] One might think this a better definition of "medical care expenses" than "medical care" simpliciter, but we will let the inartful statutory drafting pass.

[40] Although *Jacobs v. Commissioner*, 62 T.C. 813, 818 (1974), required "the present existence or imminent probability of a disease, defect, or illness" for a medical care deduction, its analysis was limited to the first prong of § 213(d)(1)(A).

III

To be deductible, expenses claimed as medical expenses must be "for the primary purpose of, and directly related to ... medical care." *Haines v. Comm'r*, 71 T.C. 644, 647 (1979). Whether an expense is for the primary purpose of, or directly related to, medical care is a question of fact. *See, e.g., id.* at 647. Under the second prong of § 213(d)(1)(A), a taxpayer's expenditures prima facie count as medical care if they are "for the purpose of affecting any structure or function of the body." As explained below, transition care procedures generally, and Rhiannon O'Donnabhain's transition care in particular, easily satisfy that condition. Accordingly, unless they also amount to cosmetic surgery or similar procedures and do not satisfy any of the saving conditions, which will be addressed in Part VI of this opinion, O'Donnabhain is entitled to deduct these amounts.

The expenses at issue in this case, for which O'Donnabhain claimed deductions on her 2001 tax return that the Commissioner later disallowed following audit, include the following: $382 for endocrine therapy, comprising both prescription hormones and the unreimbursed cost of office visits with Dr. Susana Ebner, one of her physicians; $300 to Ms. Ellaborn for psychotherapy; $260 to Dr. Alex Coleman, a licensed psychotherapist with a doctoral degree in clinical psychology, who examined her and provided a second recommendation for her gender confirmation surgery, as required by the generally accepted standard of care applicable to her genital reconstructive surgery; $19,195 to Dr. Toby Meltzer for surgical procedures, including $14,495 for vaginoplasty and other procedures and $4,500 for breast augmentation, and $200 towards a portion of petitioner's postsurgical stay at Dr. Meltzer's facility; $1,544 in travel and lodging costs away from home first for presurgical consultation with Dr. Meltzer and later for her surgery; and $60 for medical equipment (dilators) necessary as follow-up to her vaginoplasty. The total expenses for which the Commissioner disallowed O'Donnabhain a deduction thus totaled $21,741. Yet each of these expenses was for the purpose of affecting a structure or function of the body.

For a transgender woman such as Rhiannon O'Donnabhain, hormonal treatment with estrogens can result in (*inter alia*) breast growth, some redistribution of body fat in a way that makes her body appear more conventionally feminine, softening of her skin, reduction in body hair, slowing or stopping loss of cranial hair, and reduced size of testicles. Each of these is a change in the structure of the body. While there can be other effects, such as decreased upper body strength and reduction in the firmness of erections, the preceding structural effects are generally what are desired in order to help the transgender woman more readily be accepted as a woman and to help reduce any distress occasioned by the discrepancy between the transgender woman's gender identity (female) and the way she and/or others may perceive her body (typically male). According to the World Professional Association for Transgender Health (WPATH), the goal of treatment here is helping bring about "lasting personal comfort with the gendered self in order to maximize overall psychological well-being and self-fulfillment." World Prof'l Ass'n for Transgender Health, *Standards of Care for Gender Identity Disorders* 1 (6th ed. 2001). The purpose of endocrine therapy is thus to affect structures of the body.

The same is true of the surgical aspects of transition care: Gender confirming surgeries in general and O'Donnabhain's in particular also are "for the purpose of affecting ... structure[s] or function[s] of the body." Her surgeon explained that the operation "creates an intact, functioning, sensate clitoris that is capable of having an orgasm and a vaginal vault that is adequate for intercourse." Trial Tr. 658–59. Similarly, the breast surgery he performed on O'Donnabhain was "about creating a female chest" as distinguished from a chest that appears male even with the breast growth she experienced from the hormones she took. *Id.* at 623–25. Clearly these procedures affected the structure and function of her body, intentionally so.

The therapy, consultation, travel, lodging, and medical equipment claimed for 2001 all contributed to the success of O'Donnabhain's surgery. Her 2001 therapy with Ellaborn, whom she had been seeing for years, was an integral part of her transition care. The genital surgical recommendation Ellaborn provided after assessing her in 2001 was one of two required recommendations, and O'Donnabhain's examination by Dr. Coleman was necessary for him to be able to provide the second recommendation. The travel and lodging for which O'Donnabhain claimed deductions were in the service of enabling her surgery, both the presurgical consultation with her surgeon in Oregon and the actual trip there for the surgery. All of these expenses were thus "for the purpose of affecting ... structure[s] or function[s] of the body" or, in the case of the travel and lodging, "primarily for and essential to" such "medical care." I.R.C. § 213(d)(1)(B). Finally, the dilators for which O'Donnabhain claimed a deduction also were "for the purpose of affecting ... structure[s] or function[s] of the body." They were used postsurgery to ensure that her vaginal canal remained open and capable of receiving a phallus.

Because all of the medical expenses for which she claimed a deduction for 2001 were "for the purpose of affecting ... structure[s] or function[s] of the body," they satisfy the second prong of § 213(d)(1)(A). Since that section is framed disjunctively (i.e., "A or B"), meeting that one condition is sufficient to bring her claims properly within § 213(d)(1)(A). The statutory text appears unambiguous that meeting either condition makes an expense "medical care," so relying on the statutory text alone, we would conclude that O'Donnabhain's deducted expenses were all for medical care and turn then to the question whether they were nevertheless excluded by § 213(d)(9)(A)'s disallowance of a deduction for cosmetic surgery.

A complication arises, however, due not to the text of the statute, but to the Treasury Department's implementing regulations. Treas. Reg. § 1.213-1. This regulation addresses a range of issues related to "Medical, Dental, etc." expenses. *Id.* In a section on definitions, the regulation first essentially restates the statutory definition:

> The term *medical care* includes the diagnosis, cure, mitigation, treatment, or prevention of disease. Expenses paid for "medical care" shall include those paid for the purpose of affecting any structure or function of the body or for transportation primarily for and essential to medical care.

Id. § 1.213-1(e)(1)(i). The next subsection provides, *inter alia*, that

> [d]eductions for expenditures for medical care allowable under section 213 will be confined strictly to expenses incurred primarily for the prevention or alleviation of a physical or mental defect or illness . . . . However, an expenditure which is merely beneficial to the general health of an individual, such as an expenditure for a vacation, is not an expenditure for medical care.

Id. § 1.213-1(e)(1)(ii). The Commissioner relies on this regulation to argue that "[t]o be deductible as medical expenses, [O'Donnabhain's gender confirmation surgeries] and hormone therapy must be for the treatment of a disease or illness." Opening Br. for Resp't 153–54.

Treasury Regulation § 1.213-1(e)(1)(ii) is curious. The generality of its language might suggest that it applies to both prongs in the statutory definition of deductible "medical care." Yet recall what those two prongs of that statutory definition are. The first category of deductible medical expenses embraces "amounts paid . . . for the diagnosis, cure, mitigation, treatment, or prevention of disease." I.R.C. § 213(d)(1)(A). The second category extends to expenditures "for the purpose of affecting any structure or function of the body." *Id.* If Reg. § 1.213-1(e)(1)(ii)'s "confined strictly" proviso applied to both prongs of the statutory definition of medical expenses, then a taxpayer could deduct expenses that were "for the purpose of affecting any structure or function of the body" only if they were also incurred "primarily for the prevention or alleviation of a physical or mental defect or illness." But if they are for preventing or alleviating physical or mental defects or illnesses, they would seem also to be for "diagnosis, cure, mitigation, treatment, or prevention of disease." The only application the second prong of the statutory definition of "medical care" could have then would be where a mental or physical defect or illness and its effects do not count as disease. The Commissioner has treated "defect[s] or illness[es]" and "disease" interchangeably, *see, e.g.*, Opening Br. for Resp't 153–54 (not distinguishing among "defects," "diseases," or "illnesses" in addressing the statutory and regulatory provisions addressed here), and the regulations have treated "disease" as used in the statute as synonymous with "a physical or mental defect or illness" ever since the first version of the regulations promulgated in 1943. *See* T.D. 5234, 1943 C.B. 119, 130. Applying the regulation's "confined strictly" proviso to the "structure or function" prong of the statutory medical care definition would nigh render that prong completely superfluous given the first, "disease" prong of that definition.

Congress deliberately chose to frame the definition of "medical care" in the disjunctive – expenses are deductible if they *either* address disease *or* affect bodily structure or function. Absent clear indication, we should not read a Treasury Regulation in a way that effectively reads one of those prongs out of the statute, for Code § 7805 only gives the IRS the authority to interpret the statute, not to rewrite it. This is particularly true where doing so could threaten to overturn the IRS's settled opinion that procedures such as abortion, Rev. Rul. 73-201, 1973-1 C.B. 140, and vasectomies, *id.*, qualify as "medical care" because they affect a structure or function of the body even though they do not diagnose, cure, mitigate, treat, or prevent a "disease."

The structure of Reg. § 1.213-1(e)(1)(ii) does not dictate that the "confined strictly" proviso should apply to both prongs of the "medical care" definition. It contains a potpourri of provisions relating to the Code's treatment of medical expenses. It first relies on the second prong of the statutory definition of "medical care" – "for the purpose of affecting any structure or function of the body" – to deem certain expenses categorically to be for "medical care." It then superimposes a legal restriction on deductible medical expenses: Regardless of whether they meet either or both prongs of the statutory definition, the regulation bars deductibility of unlawful operations or treatments. *Id.* Next comes the "confined strictly" proviso. *Id.* Following that, the regulation offers a string of various costs that do count as payments for medical services, including hospital services and drugs as specified elsewhere in the regulation. It closes with the exclusion for things merely beneficial to general health. If anything, by *not* invoking the "confined strictly" language in the first sentence, treating certain expenses as deductible based on the second prong of the statutory medical care language without reference to "defect or illness,"

Reg. § 1.213-1(e)(1)(ii) supports reading the proviso as applicable only to the first (disease-based) prong of the statutory definition of medical care.

Moreover, the Commissioner's current interpretation of Reg. § 1.213-1(e)(1)(ii) conflicts with the position the IRS took in the 1970s, when it ruled that face lifts and electrolysis were deductible medical care because they satisfied the "function or structure" prong of § 213(d)(1)(A). See Rev. Rul. 82-111, 1982-1 C.B. 48 (electrolysis); Rev. Rul. 76-332, 1976-2 C.B. 81 (facelifts). Those rulings did not require that those procedures be for "the prevention or alleviation of a physical or mental defect or illness," as would have been required to satisfy the regulation's "confined strictly" proviso had it been applicable to § 213(d)(1)(A)'s "function or structure" prong. The Commissioner has not attempted to justify its new interpretation of the regulation, and his unreasoned assertion of its new scope does not overcome our preceding analysis.

Accordingly, we now hold that the "confined strictly" proviso of Reg. § 1.213-1(e)(1)(ii) applies only to that part of § 213(d)(1)(A) that defines "medical care" expenses as extending to "amounts paid ... for the diagnosis, cure, mitigation, treatment, or prevention of disease." By adopting this more limited construction of the regulatory proviso, we avoid the need to determine whether we must, as we have in the past, see, e.g., Ga. Fed. Bank, F.S.B. v. Comm'r, 98 T.C. 105 (1992), hold a regulation invalid as inconsistent with Congress's statutory intent. Moreover, the Commissioner has not argued here that any doctrine of judicial deference compels our acceptance of his view of the proviso, which his brief merely assumes rather than argues applies to both prongs of the medical care definition.

Accordingly, provided it does not amount to cosmetic surgery, a question which we address below, O'Donnabhain's transition care is deductible if it is "for the purpose of affecting any structure or function of the body" (the second, or "structure or function," prong of § 213(d)(1)(A)). As we have shown, it is readily apparent that her transition care expenses were for the purpose of affecting a structure or function of her body, and they consequently count as presumptively deductible expenses for "medical care."

IV

Although we have concluded that O'Donnabain's transition care expenses satisfy the second, "structure or function" prong of the statutory definition of medical care and that the "confined strictly" proviso of Reg. § 1.213-1(e)(1)(ii) does not apply to that prong, in the interest of judicial economy we will next address the first, "disease" prong of the statutory definition. For reasons not wholly clear to us, the Commissioner has opposed this taxpayer's claimed medical expense deductions with something bordering on ferocity: The Commissioner's opening brief before this court was 218 pages long (in contrast to O'Donnabhain's 87 pages). It seems plausible that he may wish to appeal his loss before us to the U.S. Court of Appeals for the First Circuit, as the parties have stipulated he may, and because of that prospect, we deem it prudent to provide the Court of Appeals with our considered judgment about how other parts of the statutory and regulatory framework for medical care deductions apply to O'Donnabhain's claims.

We do so, however, advisedly and not without hesitation. For once we turn from the relatively simple analysis of whether Rhiannon O'Donnabhain's transition care was for the purpose of affecting a "structure or function of the body," and attempt to analyze whether her care involved "the diagnosis, cure, mitigation, treatment, or prevention of disease," I.R.C. § 213(d)(1)(A), or was "incurred primarily for the prevention or alleviation of a physical or mental defect or illness," Treas. Reg. § 1.213-1(e)(1)(ii), we run the grave risk of contributing to a stigmatizing discourse wherein transgender individuals, including O'Donnabhain, must classify themselves as "defective," "ill," or "diseased," in the statutory and regulatory terminology, to obtain a deduction for expenses that are patently medical in nature.

And we do so as persons not identified as transgender. Our life experiences are in key respects different from those of transgender persons. Our points of reference – different from (though in light of the Fourteenth Amendment clearly not superior to) those of transgender individuals regardless of whatever commonalities we do share with them, our fellow taxpayers, our fellow persons – and our obligation to do justice under law make it imperative that we seek truly to listen to one such as Rhiannon O'Donnabhain. And those different social locations can contribute to the risk of not apprehending her, not appreciating her, not treating her with the equal dignity, concern, and respect to which she is entitled from our common society and the law that serves us all. That the author of this opinion is a gay man and identifies as a member of various LGBT communities is no guarantee against misrecognition or mistake; it could even lead to overconfidence about this court's level of understanding.

The circumstance that our conclusion that a transgender person is mentally ill would depend, as it does here, on judgments by the medical profession affords meager reassurance about the perilousness of our task. As the Commissioner has recognized, the medical profession long conceived of lesbian, gay, and bisexual persons as mentally ill, and it has ratified a horrifying range of "cure" efforts. Opening Br. for Resp't 163–64 (analogizing gender identity disorder to homosexuality, which had been classified as a mental disorder by the U.S. psychiatric profession); *see* David B. Cruz, *Controlling Desires: Sexual Orientation Conversion and the Limits of Knowledge and Law,* 72 S. Cal. L. Rev. 1297, 1303–13 (1999) (canvassing "grisly" history of "cure" efforts). The medical profession's treatment of women has also been far from exemplary, as the Supreme Court has noted. *See United States v. Virginia,* 518 U.S. 515, 537 n.9 (1996) (quoting a Harvard medical professor and others who "maintained that the physiological effects of hard study and academic competition with boys would interfere with the development of girls' reproductive organs"). The medical profession's deeds were often no better than those views when it came to women; ovariotomies, for example, were for decades "a popular method ... for [treating] alleged psychological disorders from which women were thought to suffer, including 'nymphomania', and especially for nervous and psychological problems such as hysteria and 'ovarian insanity.'" Julie M. Spanbauer, *Breast Implants as Beauty Ritual: Women's Sceptre and Prison,* 9 Yale J.L. & Feminism 157, 176 (1997) (quoting Diana Scully, *Men Who Control Women's Health* 49 (Teachers College Press 1994) (1980)). Even without taking into account the full range of the history of medicine's maltreatment of persons with disabilities, these gendered examples counsel caution in characterizing the mental health of persons such as O'Donnabhain who seek to bring their bodies into greater alignment with their gender identity.

Analogizing to the depathologization of sexual orientation, where the American Psychiatric Association (APA) concluded in 1973 that to be lesbian, gay, or bisexual was not (without more) to be mentally ill, the Commissioner argues that being transgender, or more specifically, being diagnosed with gender identity disorder (GID) within the meaning of the *Diagnostic and Statistical Manual of Mental Disorders, 4th Edition, Text Revision* published by the APA (DSM-IV-TR), does not count as having an illness or disease within the meaning of § 213. In his view, it is not some pathology within transgender persons that makes them mentally ill; rather, GID should be seen as a social phenomenon, a "conflict[] that [is] primarily between the individual and society." Opening Br. for Resp't 171.

Were we the final word on the meaning of the statute and regulation, we might be inclined to agree. For as we have explicated above, transition care for transgender persons such as O'Donnabhain is deductible medical care under the "structure or function" prong of the statutory definition regardless of whether or not the condition it treats is deemed a defect, illness, or disease. Because private insurance providers commonly deny coverage for transition-related care, and because a 1989 National Coverage Determination held what it termed "transsexual surgery" (or "sex reassignment surgery" or "intersex surgery") to be excluded from Medicare coverage, *see* NCD 140.3, Transsexual Surgery, the § 213 medical expense deduction operates as a kind of backup insurance in this case for transgender persons, making the substantial costs of gender confirmation surgeries more affordable. Were we assured that transgender persons would be entitled to deduct from their income the often high expenses that transition care can necessitate, we would be more moved by the concern not to stigmatize them with an "illness" label. While we certainly agree that people with illnesses, physical or mental, ought not be viewed as "less than" others, we cannot deny that many in U.S. society do not agree. "To be diagnosed with [GID] is to be found in some way, to be ill, sick, wrong, out of order, abnormal, and to suffer a certain stigmatization as a consequence of the diagnosis being given at all." Judith Butler, *Undoing Gender* 76 (2004). Avoiding the illness label, at least in this context, may help transgender persons to avoid some of that unwarranted stigmatization.

But we are not necessarily the last word here. The Commissioner wants to deny not only that Rhiannon O'Donnabhain has any defect or illness or disease but also that her transition care is deductible medical care. He could appeal our judgment and challenge our legal interpretation, first to the First Circuit Court of Appeals and then to the U.S. Supreme Court if need be. The sums at issue are significant, particularly for O'Donnabhain, who has also had to contend with other health problems and lack of a job and dependency on savings for her daily subsistence as of 2006. It is no surprise, then, that she and her counsel, some of whom regularly represent LGBT persons, have chosen to embrace her GID diagnosis and to argue that with it, she is entitled to deduct the expenses of her transition care under the "disease" prong of the statutory definition of medical care. As Professor Butler has argued, "we ought not to underestimate the benefits that the diagnosis has brought, especially to trans people of limited economic means." *Id.* at 77.

While our job is to interpret and apply the laws Congress has enacted, it is also to do justice under those laws. The Supreme Court has admonished that "[t]axation is an intensely practical matter, and laws in respect of it should be construed and applied with a view of avoiding, so far as possible, unjust and oppressive consequences." *Farmers' Loan & Trust Co. v. Minnesota*, 280 U.S. 204, 212 (1930). In the interest of doing justice to the real, individual human person before us, Rhiannon O'Donnabhain, and so that if an appeal follows the reviewing court or courts will have the benefit of our expertise with the nation's tax laws, we turn now to whether her transition care costs should be understood as deductible expenses paid "for the diagnosis, cure, mitigation, treatment, or prevention of disease" under § 213(d)(1)(A) and subject to the regulatory proviso that "[d]eductions for expenditures for medical care allowable under section 213 will be confined strictly to expenses incurred primarily for the prevention or alleviation of a physical or mental defect or illness." Treas. Reg. § 1.213-1(e)(1)(ii).

V

Under § 213(d)(1)(A), if an expenditure is "for the diagnosis, cure, mitigation, treatment, or prevention of disease," it is for "medical care" and *prima facie* deductible under the statute. Under the regulatory proviso, "[d]eductions for expenditures for medical care allowable under section 213 will be confined strictly to expenses incurred primarily for the prevention or alleviation of a physical or mental defect or illness." Treas. Reg. § 1.213-1(e)(1)(ii).

A

Rhiannon O'Donnabhain argues that she is entitled to deduct her expenditures for the procedures at issue because they were treatments for GID, a condition that she contends is a "disease" for purposes of § 213. It is clearly settled by more than half a century of case law that "disease" for purposes of § 213 includes mental disorders. *See Fay v. Comm'r*, 76 T.C. 408 (1981) ("learning disability, accompanied by emotional stress"); *Jacobs v. Comm'r*, 62 T.C. 813, 818 (1974) (severe depression); *Fischer v. Comm'r*, 50 T.C. 164, 170, 173 (1968) (deep-rooted, severe neurotic blocks); *Starrett v. Comm'r*, 41 T.C. 877, 878, 881 (1964) (anxiety reaction); *Hendrick v. Comm'r*, 35 T.C. 1223, 1236–37 (1961) (emotional insecurity); *Sims v. Comm'r*, 39 T.C.M. (CCH) 700 (1979) ("some sort of learning disability, accompanied by emotional or psychiatric problems"). These cases found mental conditions to be "diseases" where there was evidence that mental health professionals regarded the condition as creating a significant impairment to normal functioning and warranting treatment.

The Commissioner maintains that O'Donnabhain's expenditures did not treat any "disease" because in his view GID is not a disease within the meaning of the statute. Central to his argument is his contention that "disease" as used in § 213 has the meaning advocated by his expert, Dr. Park Dietz,[41] namely "a condition [arising] as a result of a pathological process [occurring] within the individual and [reflecting] abnormal structure or

---

[41] Dietz is a licensed physician board certified in psychiatry and, at the time of trial, a clinical professor of psychiatry and behavioral sciences at the UCLA School of Medicine, but he claimed no expertise in treating patients presenting with GID symptoms.

function of the body at the gross, microscopic, molecular, biochemical, or neuro-chemical levels." Opening Br. for Resp't 113. Because they do not view GID as having been shown to be caused by anything within the body, Dietz and the Commissioner contend that GID is a mental disorder but not a disease or illness. We disagree with the Commissioner's hairsplitting, agree with O'Donnabhain, and conclude that GID is a mental illness or disease within the meaning of § 213 and Reg. § 1.213-1.

For purposes of § 213, our case law establishes that a condition can qualify as a "disease" or "illness" without regard to any demonstrated organic or physiological origin or cause. See *Fay*, 76 T.C. 408; *Jacobs*, 62 T.C. 813; *Fischer*, 50 T.C. 164; *Starrett*, 41 T.C. 877; *Hendrick*, 35 T.C. 1223; *Sims*, 39 T.C.M. (CCH) 700. The Commissioner cites no authority in support of his preferred, narrow definition, and we have found none. The absence of any consideration of etiology in the case law is consistent with the legislative history and the regulations. Both treat "disease" as synonymous with "a physical or mental defect," which suggests Congress intended a more colloquial sense of the term "disease" than the narrower interpretation the Commissioner advocates. When medical science recognizes a condition as an illness, disorder, or disease without insisting on a particular etiology, as it does with GID, it would not be "practical," *Farmers' Loan & Trust Co.*, 280 U.S. at 212, to embrace that narrow view, for most mental disorders listed in the DSM-IV-TR do not have demonstrated organic causes. Nor would it be just for us to deny taxpayers the relief of a medical expense deduction by adopting a narrow definition of "disease" based on various philosophical sources, Trial Tr. 804–07, not evident in the text or legislative history of the statute. Superimposing that definition would deny countless taxpayers financial amelioration of the costs of meaningful care that medicine routinely provides. In sum, we reject the Commissioner's interpretation of "disease" because it is incompatible with the stated intent of the regulations and legislative history to cover "mental defects" generally and is contradicted by a consistent line of cases finding "disease" in the case of mental disorders without regard to any demonstrated etiology.

We have found mental conditions to be "diseases" where there was evidence that mental health professionals regarded the condition as creating a significant impairment to normal functioning and warranting treatment, see *Fay*, 76 T.C. 408; *Jacobs*, 62 T.C. 813; *Fischer*, 50 T.C. 164; *Hendrick*, 35 T.C. 1223, or where the condition was listed in a medical reference text, see *Starrett*, 41 T.C. 877. Both factors involve deference by a court to the judgment of medical professionals. GID is listed as a mental disorder in the DSM-IV-TR, which both sides' experts agree is the primary diagnostic tool of U.S. psychiatry. GID and transsexualism are also listed in numerous medical reference texts, with descriptions of their characteristics that are similar to those in the DSM-IV-TR. Although there is not unanimity within psychiatry about the validity of the GID diagnosis, the evidence shows that the prevailing view in the profession regards GID as a mental disorder or disease; this is especially true of those mental health professionals who actually treat transgender persons.

GID meets the statutory definition of a defect, illness, or disease not merely because of its characterization by the medical community but also because it can be a serious, psychologically debilitating condition. Absent treatment, GID in transgender women like Rhiannon O'Donnabhain is sometimes associated with suicide attempts and attempts to remove one's penis and/or testicles. Even if "the pain and suffering experienced by GID patients is primarily inflicted by an intolerant society" as the Commissioner has argued, the pain and suffering are indisputably real and flow from the discrepancy between the gender a person was assigned at birth and the person's gender identity. For those transgender persons who seek medical assistance to transform their bodies to better reflect their gender identity, it is that conflict between the individual's body and gender identity that marks "a behavioral, psychological, or biological dysfunction in the individual," hence a mental illness; it does not constitute what the DSM distinguishes from mental illnesses as a mere "conflict[s] that [is] primarily between the individual and society." DSM-IV-TR, *supra*, at xxi–xxii. O'Donnabhain's expert Dr. George Brown is a licensed physician, board certified in adult psychiatry by the American Board of Psychiatry and Neurology and a member of the American Psychiatric Association since 1983. At the time of trial, he was a professor and associate chair of the Department of Psychiatry at East Tennessee State University and chief of psychiatry at James H. Quillen Veterans Affairs Medical Center in Johnson City, Tennessee. He has been an active member of WPATH since 1987, including serving on its board of directors, participated in the development of the *Standards of Care*, and has extensive experience treating transgender patients. Dr. Brown testified that the incongruity between anatomical sex and gender can make "looking in the mirror itself a painful experience" for transgender persons, and people with GID "suffer a lot of distress as a result of the incongruity between how they see themselves inside and what their body looks like on the outside." Trial Tr. 282.

Moreover, every U.S. Court of Appeals that has ruled on the question has concluded that GID poses a serious medical need for purposes of the Eighth Amendment, which has been interpreted to require that prisoners receive adequate medical care. *Estelle v. Gamble*, 429 U.S. 97, 103 (1976). Seven of the Courts of Appeals have concluded that severe GID or transsexualism constitutes a "serious medical need" for purposes of the Eighth Amendment. *See De'lonta v. Angelone*, 330 F.3d 630, 634 (4th Cir. 2003); *Allard v. Gomez*, 9 F. App'x 793, 794 (9th Cir. 2001); *Cuoco v. Moritsugu*, 222 F.3d 99 (2d Cir. 2000); *Brown v. Zavaras*, 63 F.3d 967, 970 (10th Cir. 1995); *Phillips v. Mich. Dep't of Corr.*, 932 F.2d 969 (6th Cir. 1991); *White v. Farrier*, 849 F.2d 322 (8th Cir. 1988); *Meriwether v. Faulkner*, 821 F.2d 408, 411–13 (7th Cir. 1987); *see also Maggert v. Hanks*, 131 F.3d 670, 671 (7th Cir. 1997) (describing gender dysphoria as a "profound psychiatric disorder"). No Court of Appeals has held otherwise.

Keeping in mind the caveats we raised in Section III.B, *supra*, and in view of GID's widely recognized status in diagnostic and psychiatric reference texts as a legitimate diagnosis, the seriousness of the condition as described in learned treatises in evidence and as acknowledged by both O'Donnabhain's and the Commissioner's experts in this case, the severity of petitioner's impairment as found by the mental health professionals who examined her, and the consensus in the U.S. Courts of Appeals that GID constitutes a serious medical need for purposes of the Eighth Amendment, we conclude and hold that GID is a "disease" for purposes of § 213 and a "mental defect" and "illness" for purposes of Reg. § 1.213-1(e)(1)(ii).

Regardless of whether GID counts as a "disease," the Commissioner has also argued that Rhiannon O'Donnabhain was properly denied a medical expense deduction for her transition care because she did not have GID. We reject this claim. Diane Ellaborn was licensed under state law to make a diagnosis of GID. Ellaborn's testimony concerning her diagnosis was persuasive. She considered and ruled out comorbid conditions, including depression and transvestic fetishism, and she believed her initial diagnosis was confirmed by O'Donnabhain's experience with the steps in her course of treatment. A second licensed professional concurred, as did O'Donnabhain's expert, a recognized authority in the field. The Commissioner's expert who opined to the contrary did not even interview O'Donnabhain, whereas all three witnesses who supported petitioner's GID diagnosis did interview her. This court has generally deferred in § 213 disputes to the judgment of the medical professionals who treated the patient. *See, e.g., Fay*, 76 T.C. at 414; *Jacobs*, 62 T.C. at 818; *Fischer*, 50 T.C. at 173–74. Based on the evidence at trial, we conclude that O'Donnabhain was properly diagnosed with GID.

B

To qualify as medical care under the "disease" prong of § 213, Rhiannon O'Donnabhain's therapy, consultation, travel, lodging, surgery, and medical equipment claimed for 2001 must have been "for the diagnosis, cure, mitigation, treatment, or prevention of" her GID. I.R.C. § 213(d)(1)(A). To satisfy the "confined strictly" proviso of the regulation, those procedures must have been "confined strictly to expenses incurred primarily for the prevention or alleviation of" her GID. Treas. Reg. § 1.213-1(e)(1)(ii).

We interpret "treatment" to have its ordinary meaning. *Crane v. Comm'r*, 331 U.S. 1, 6 (1947); *Old Colony R.R. Co. v. Comm'r*, 284 U.S. 552, 560 (1932). "Treat" is defined in standard dictionaries as, for example: "to deal with (a disease, patient, etc.) in order to relieve or cure," *Webster's New Universal Unabridged Dictionary* 2015 (2003); "to care for or deal with medically or surgically," *Merriam Webster's Collegiate Dictionary* 1333 (11th ed. 2008); "to seek cure or relief of," *Webster's Third New International Dictionary* 2435 (2002). A treatment should bear a "direct or proximate therapeutic relation to the ... condition" sufficient "to justify a reasonable belief the [treatment] would be efficacious." *Havey v. Comm'r*, 12 T.C. 409, 412 (1949). No particular degree of effectiveness need be shown. Our precedent and rulings allow deductibility of treatments lacking rigorous scientific review such as naturopathic cancer treatments, *Dickie v. Comm'r*, 77 T.C.M. (CCH) 1916 (1999); Navajo sings as cancer treatment, *Tso v. Comm'r*, 40 T.C.M. (CCH) 1277 (1980); and services of Christian Science practitioners, Rev. Rul. 55-261, 1955-1 C.B. 307. The key question under § 213(d)(1) is whether the treatment is therapeutic to the individual involved. *See Fischer v. Comm'r*, 50 T.C. 164, 174 (1968). This is essentially a test looking to the good-faith, subjective motivation of the taxpayer. There is no doubt that O'Donnabhain meets it with regard to all her transition care at issue here.

1

As WPATH has made clear, not every transgender person needs psychotherapy as a prerequisite for endocrine therapy or sex confirmation surgeries. *Standards of Care, supra*, at 11. However, "psychotherapy can be very helpful in bringing about the discovery and maturational processes that enable self-comfort." *Id*. All medical care is individualized, so the variable propriety of this therapeutic modality does not mean that psychotherapy does not "treat" a transgender person's GID. Moreover, the *Standards of Care* generally prescribe one letter from a mental health professional to a physician for the patient to receive endocrine therapy or breast surgery, and two such letters for genital surgery. *Id*. at 7–8.

Rhiannon O'Donnabhain underwent psychotherapy with Diane Ellaborn to seek relief for her gender conflict starting in August 1996. O'Donnabhain saw her for individual therapy in 1996, for group therapy from 1997 to 2000, and for additional individual sessions preparatory for surgery in 2001, the taxable year at issue in this case. Trial Tr. 55, 65, 112. Ellaborn's licensure as a Licensed Independent Clinical Social Worker in Massachusetts for more than two decades prior to 2001 allows her to diagnose and treat psychiatric illnesses, such as GID, with which she has extensive experience. Since 1990 she has assessed over 1,000 patients for gender issues and has treated 400–500 clients with severe GID. We do not intimate that a professional history anywhere near this extensive is necessary for psychotherapy with a mental health professional to count as treatment, but Ellaborn's experience underscores the seriousness of the care she provided O'Donnabhain.

We have long recognized that psychotherapy "treats" mental illness. In *Starrett v. Commissioner*, 41 T.C. 877 (1964), we considered a claimed deduction for psychoanalysis. It was undisputed that Starrett was suffering from anxiety reaction, a psychoneurosis that amounted to a "disease" within the meaning of § 213. We thought it "clear" that

> he certainly had the intention ... to be thereby relieved of the physical and emotional suffering attendant upon the specific disease from which he had suffered throughout his adult life. ... [T]he amounts paid ... are clearly "amounts paid for the diagnosis, cure, mitigation, treatment," and "prevention" of a specific "disease."

Id. at 881.

So too, the amounts Rhiannon O'Donnabhain paid to Ellaborn and to Dr. Coleman for therapy were amounts paid "for the diagnosis, cure mitigation, [and] treatment," I.R.C. § 213(d)(1)(A), of GID, which we concluded above is a disease within the meaning of the statute. We believe this clear, and the Commissioner nowhere argues otherwise in his 218-page posttrial brief. (Indeed, in questioning whether O'Donnabhain has GID, as opposed to "transvestic fetishism," the Commissioner's brief relies on an article advocating psychotherapy as the proper treatment. Opening Br. for Resp't 27–28.)

It follows that O'Donnabhain's psychotherapy in 2001 was "medical care," and her expenses for it are deductible.

2

Similarly, we conclude that, where prescribed, hormone or endocrine therapy and gender confirming surgeries in general, and Rhiannon O'Donnabhain's in particular, "treat" GID within the meaning of § 213. This is true both of genital surgery and of breast surgery.

Standard psychiatric texts recommend hormone therapy as medical treatment for GID or transsexualism. Endocrine therapy involves giving patients hormones, which are drugs or biologicals that require a prescription of a physician for their use by an individual. In the case of a transgender woman such as Rhiannon O'Donnabhain, "[e]strogens (female hormones) will stimulate breast development, widening of the hips, loss of facial hair and a slight increase in voice pitch." Ex. 48-P (L. Fleming Fallon, *Sex Reassignment Surgery*, in *Gale Encyclopedia of Surgery* (Anthony J. Senagore ed., database updated Nov. 2006)). For a transgender man, "[a]ndrogens (male hormones) will stimulate the development of facial and chest hair and cause the voice to deepen." *Id.*

The *Standards of Care* generally call for treating a person with GID according to an individualized plan involving one or more of three major components. These components, referred to as a "triadic" treatment sequence, are: hormones consistent with the patient's gender identity (estrogens for transgender women such as Rhiannon O'Donnabhain, androgens for transgender men); a "real-life" experience, that is, living full-time as a member of the gender corresponding to one's gender identity (rather than the gender one was assigned at birth) as a prerequisite to surgery; and surgery to change sex characteristics, which may involve genital surgery and/or breast surgery. *Standards of Care, supra,* at 3. O'Donnabhain followed the typical order for triadic therapy – first hormones, then the real-life experience, then surgery – but the order can vary, and "not all persons with gender identity disorders need or want all three elements of triadic therapy." *Id.*

It is true these standards officially represent only the membership – numbering about 350 – of the WPATH, formerly known as the Harry Benjamin International Gender Dysphoria Association, an association of medical, surgical, and mental health professionals specializing in the understanding and treatment of GID. However, most psychiatrists and mental health professionals who treat GID are members of WPATH. As a consequence, WPATH has more expertise with GID than any other professional organization; it has been promulgating versions of its *Standards of Care* since 1979. And while medicine has alternative or competing standards of care for some conditions, the WPATH *Standards of Care* are the only existing standards for the medical treatment of GID. The *Standards of Care* and triadic therapy are the accepted medical treatment for individuals with GID. The only significant disagreement with the *Standards* within the psychiatric profession comes from a minority who believe genital reconstruction surgeries to be unethical. In contrast, at least six standard psychiatric texts, including publications of the American Psychiatric Association, describe the *Standards of Care,* and the use of hormone therapy and gender confirmation surgery, as the accepted and appropriate treatment for GID.

In U.S. society where there is widespread belief in gender dimorphism and in the importance of genitalia to one's gender, Rhiannon O'Donnabhain exercised her autonomy to deal with what medical science has identified as her gender identity disorder. She enlisted the aid of competent medical health professionals to pursue a well-recognized course of treatment to deal with her GID and to enable her to lead a happier, *healthier* life. The evidence showed that her treatments, including her surgical ones whose costs she claims here as medical expenses, alleviated her suffering. This certainly counts as "treatment." This conclusion is not foreclosed here by the fact that the documentation of the insufficiency of the breasts she developed from hormones alone before surgery was not what the *Standards of Care* prescribe; after all, the *Standards of Care* are only guidelines. The evidence at trial, including the unrebutted testimony of O'Donnabhain's surgeon Dr. Meltzer, showed that the breast augmentation surgery was not simply a matter of a woman (here, a transgender woman) preferring to have larger breasts for appearance's sake. Rhiannon O'Donnabhain's breast surgery, like her genital surgery, was for the purpose of treating her GID and transsexualism.

In sum, psychotherapy, prescribed endocrine or hormone therapy, and genital and breast surgery all "treat" GID, and therefore count as medical care within the meaning of § 213. Accordingly, Rhiannon O'Donnabhain may deduct all her claimed costs for those, as well as for such incidental costs as for travel and lodging for surgery and surgical consultations and postsurgical medical supplies, all of which she has adequately substantiated, provided they do not run afoul of the statutory exclusion for "cosmetic surgery."

VI

As noted in Part II, as a general matter § 213 excludes from the definition of "medical care" "cosmetic surgery or other similar procedures," I.R.C. § 213(d)(9)(A), but transition care will not fall within the scope of that exclusion if it is not "directed at improving the patient's appearance," or if it "meaningfully promote[s] the proper function of the body or prevent[s] or treat[s] illness or disease." *Id.* § 213(d)(9)(B). Neither endocrine therapy nor genital or breast surgery that is part of a transgender person's transition care is cosmetic surgery or a "similar procedure." (Because we conclude that transition care does not amount to cosmetic surgery, we have no need to consider whether it meets the saving conditions specified in § 213(d)(9)(A).)

The Commissioner has argued that the hormonal and surgical procedures O'Donnabhain underwent were "cosmetic surgery or other similar procedures" not "necessary to ameliorate a deformity arising from, or directly related to, a congenital abnormality," that they were "directed at improving the patient's appearance and [do] not meaningfully promote the proper function of the body or prevent or treat illness or disease." We think this obtuse.

At a statutory level, procedures that "treat illness or disease" do not count as cosmetic surgery. So, under our alternative holding that transition care, such as O'Donnabhain's, "treats" GID, a significant mental illness and hence disease, such care is not cosmetic surgery or a similar procedure. Nor under our first holding, that transition care, such as O'Donnabhain's, is medical care because it is "for the purpose of affecting any structure or function of the body," is transition care cosmetic surgery or a similar procedure. It is not "directed at" improving the patient's appearance, for that is not the purpose or end of transition care; it is merely the means, or more properly part of the means, of advancing patients' health by affecting the structures and functions of their bodies.

At a deeper level, although at times the Commissioner's posttrial brief reads like modern feminist theory, invoking the World Health Organization's view that gender is a social construction, its reduction of transition care to satisfaction of mere aesthetic preferences (admittedly in a sexist society) trivializes transgender persons' pursuit of mental and physical well-being in a fashion more reminiscent of the earlier, biological essentialism of certain self-professed feminists like Janice Raymond, who viewed transgender women not as women but as delusional men duped by a patriarchal medical establishment. *See generally* Janice Raymond, *The Transsexual Empire: The Making of the She-Male* (1979). We see nothing in the Code that compels such a benighted view of transgender persons.

Now, as we noted, the Commissioner contends that Congress intended to limit deductibility of procedures directed at improving appearance to those that are "medically necessary," as evidenced by certain references to "medically necessary" procedures in the legislative history of the enactment of the cosmetic surgery exclusion of § 213(d)(9), notwithstanding the statute's failure to use either the phrase "medically necessary" or "medical necessity." We find it unnecessary to resolve whether the statute contains such a restriction, for we conclude that prescribed transition care generally, and O'Donnabhain's in particular, is medically necessary.

As noted above, the evidence at trial showed that numerous medical textbooks characterize GID as a mental illness and accept the triadic treatment approach of the WPATH *Standards of Care*; that most mental health professionals with extensive experience treating transgender persons belong to WPATH, which views transition care as medically necessary for those patients for whom it is indicated; and that the therapists and doctors who treated

Rhiannon O'Donnabhain judged her transition care medically necessary *for her* to treat her severe GID. Moreover, although not dispositive, our conclusion is supported by the fact that several courts have also concluded in a variety of contexts that gender confirmation surgery for severe GID or transsexualism is medically necessary. *See Meriwether v. Faulkner*, 821 F.2d 408, 412 (7th Cir. 1987); *Pinneke v. Preisser*, 623 F.2d 546, 548 (8th Cir. 1980); *Sommers v. Iowa Civil Rights Comm'n*, 337 N.W.2d 470, 473 (Iowa 1983); *Doe v. Minn. Dep't of Pub. Welfare*, 257 N.W.2d 816, 819 (Minn. 1977); *Davidson v. Aetna Life & Cas. Ins. Co.*, 420 N.Y.S.2d 450, 453 (Sup. Ct. 1979).

We reach our conclusion with attention to whether our reasoning reinforces problematic, essentialist views of what one must be to be a woman or to be a man. The concern is that some transgender persons' pursuit of various procedures as medically necessary to their living as a member of their gender might be read to imply that the resultant bodily features are constitutive of persons of that gender. For example, though not at issue in this case, Rhiannon O'Donnabhain had a tracheal shave in 2000 to reduce her Adam's apple, thus reducing the likelihood of her gender being called into question. Most of the largest insurance companies in the United States deem tracheal shaves not medically necessary. Does our deeming this procedure medically necessary imply that to be a woman is to have a (relatively) small Adam's apple, or at a minimum that normative women have small Adam's apples?

The concern is ameliorated by the fact that courts often treat the medical necessity of a transition procedure or what a person's legal sex is as not necessarily invariant across contexts. For example, such questions arise in Eighth Amendment inmate care cases, *e.g., Allard v. Gomez*, 9 F. App'x 793 (9th Cir. 2001), and Medicaid and Medicare cases, *e.g., J.D. v. Lackner*, 145 Cal. Rptr. 570, 573 (Ct. App. 1978), and the answers to the questions in those contexts need not *a priori* be the same as in the tax context. Even in rejecting claims that a transgender person should be legally treated as a member of their gender (rather than of their natally assigned gender), courts have treated the person's legal sex as potentially varying across contexts.

In one of the unfortunately pathbreaking decisions denying recognition of a transgender woman's lived sex, Judge Ormrod in *Corbett v. Corbett* treated transgender woman April Ashley's sex for purposes of English marriage law as distinct from her sex in other legal contexts. [1970] 2 All E.R. 33, 47 (Eng.). Although the Ministry of National Insurance treated Ms. Ashley as a woman, Judge Ormrod approached Ashley's sex determination as a question to be answered "[f]or the limited purposes of this case." *Id.* at 48. "The question then becomes what is meant by the word 'woman' in the context of a marriage, for I am not concerned to determine the 'legal sex' of the respondent at large." *Id.* Similarly, *In re Estate of Gardiner* involved a dispute over intestate inheritance by a putative widow, transgender woman J'Noel Gardiner. 42 P.3d 120 (Kan. 2002). In ruling against her and the validity of her marriage, the Supreme Court of Kansas concluded that "J'Noel remains a transsexual, and a male *for purposes of marriage under*" the Kansas marriage statute. *Id.* at 137 (emphasis added). *Cf. In re Marriage of Simmons*, 825 N.E.2d 303, 312 (Ill. App. Ct. 2005) (holding against transgender man Sterling Simmons in a marital dissolution and custody case because he was "not a man *within the meaning of the [Illinois Parentage Act]*, and . . . therefore, the statute does not apply" (emphasis added)).

Moreover, like the variability of sex across legal contexts, the individualization of the course of medical treatment pursuant to the WPATH *Standards of Care* helps avoid implications of necessity. The *Standards* are clinical *guidelines* "intended to provide flexible directions for the treatment of persons with gender identity disorders." *Standards of Care, supra,* at 1. For example, the *Standards of Care's* default position is that breast augmentation surgery "*may* be performed" as transition surgery for a transgender woman patient "if the physician prescribing hormones and the surgeon have documented that breast enlargement after undergoing hormone treatment for 18 months is not sufficient for comfort in the social gender role." *Id.* at 20 (emphasis added). "Individual professionals and organized programs may modify them. Clinical departures from these guidelines may come about *because of a patient's unique* anatomic, social, or psychological *situation*. . . ." *Id.* at 2 (emphasis added).

As a consequence, different individuals may be women or men in different ways. A statement that for one person a particular physical feature, such as a nonprominent Adam's apple as achieved via tracheal shave, is necessary, is thus not a statement about what all women are like.

This court recognizes that sex generalizations could come into decisions about transition care insofar as a key part of why an anatomical feature is necessary – either for transgender persons' acceptance of their own bodies or for others to accept them – is because of norms/expectations/beliefs about how women are or how men are, at least as underpinnings of norms/expectations/ beliefs about whether a particular person will be perceived as a man or as a woman. Certainly, women as a group have great physical variation, as do men as a group. We should not, however, jump to the conclusion that attempting to come close to an actual or ideal physical norm for a gender is not "necessary" for any trans person. While nontransgender women may be mistaken for men and nontransgender men mistaken for women, the consequences of doubt about one's sex or misgendering seem likely on average worse for transgender persons whose genitals, breasts, or identity documents' gender markers may not match expectations. Due regard for the well-being of transgender persons counsels more tolerance for conclusions regarding the necessity of their attempts to bring their bodies into alignment with their gender identity and/or to forestall doubt in others, or challenges or violence from others, through means such as tracheal shaves or breast augmentation or double mastectomies.

The evidence amply shows that psychotherapy, endocrine or hormone therapy, and gender confirmation surgeries are medical care for transgender persons. They are both for the purpose of affecting the structure and/or function of the body and for the purpose of treating gender identity disorders. They most emphatically are not merely cosmetic procedures, and the Commissioner's contention that they are was not substantially justified. Thus, Rhiannon O'Donnabhain's expenditures for these procedures were for "medical care" as defined in § 213(d)(1)(A), for which a deduction is allowed under § 213(a).

To reflect the foregoing and concessions by the parties, we reverse the disallowance of the deductions contested in this appeal and award Rhiannon O'Donnabhain reasonable litigation costs.

Reviewed by the court.

13

Commentary on *United States v. Windsor*

ALLISON ANNA TAIT

BACKGROUND

The story of the relationship between Edie Windsor and Thea Spyer is about tax, but it is also a love story. The two women met in 1965, at a time when lesbians were worried more about discrimination and violence than about marriage rights and tax deductions. Windsor was a technology manager at IBM at the time and Spyer was a psychologist with a private practice. They were introduced to each other one evening at Portofino, an Italian restaurant in Greenwich Village that was a safe haven for lesbians. After two years of constant companionship, despite the fact that same-sex marriage was not legal anywhere in the United States at the time, Spyer asked Windsor to marry her and gave her a circular diamond pin to commemorate the promise. The couple stayed together until Spyer's death, more than forty years later, and led a charmed life, in many respects. The two women lived and worked in Manhattan, where they had a strong circle of friends and high-paying jobs. Vacations were spent at a cottage they owned in the Hamptons as well as traveling the world.

When New York City gave same-sex couples the right to register as same-sex partners in 1993, Spyer and Windsor registered. But it was not until 2007, forty years after Spyer's marriage proposal, that the couple married in Canada. The marriage was prompted by concerns about Spyer's health, since she had been diagnosed with multiple sclerosis years earlier and it was progressively becoming more serious. New York recognized their marriage as valid upon their return from Canada because the marriage was valid in the jurisdiction in which it was performed. The federal government, however, did not.

Accordingly, when Spyer died in 2009, Windsor was required to pay $363,053 in federal estate taxes because the federal government did not recognize their marriage. Section 3 of the Defense of Marriage Act (DOMA), which had been enacted by Congress and signed into law by then-President Bill Clinton in 1996, defined "marriage" for all federal purposes as being only a union between one man and one woman.[1] This federal ban on recognizing Windsor and Spyer's marriage for federal tax purposes barred Windsor from benefiting from the estate tax marital deduction upon Spyer's death. Had Spyer and Windsor's marriage been federally recognized, there would have been no estate tax bill because one "spouse" can transfer unlimited assets to a surviving spouse on death without any tax liability.[2] Consequently, Windsor claimed that Section 3 of DOMA violated the constitutional guarantee of equal protection and applied to the Internal Revenue Service for a refund of the taxes paid. The IRS, bound by DOMA, denied the refund, and Windsor appealed the decision.[3]

ORIGINAL OPINION

When the case reached the Supreme Court of the United States, on appeal from a decision by the Second Circuit in Windsor's favor, the majority of the Court agreed with Edie Windsor. The Second Circuit, ruling on the case, concluded that DOMA violated Windsor's equal protection rights and subjected the law to heightened scrutiny.[4] The U.S. Supreme Court, with Justice Anthony Kennedy writing for the majority, affirmed the lower court's opinion and held that Section 3 of DOMA violated Windsor's equal protection as well as due process rights.[5]

Before addressing the merits of Windsor's equal protection claim, Justice Kennedy began his analysis by addressing two threshold questions concerning Article III of the U.S. Constitution and prudential standing.[6] These questions emerged as a result of the unusual "decision of the Executive not to defend the constitutionality of section three of DOMA in court while continuing to deny refunds and to assess deficiencies."[7] Kennedy concluded, however, that the payment of money to Windsor from the Treasury constituted a "real and immediate" economic injury that gave the United States Article III standing to bring the case.[8] The United States also had jurisprudential standing, the Court concluded, because of the intervention of the Bipartisan Legal Advisory

---

[1] Defense of Marriage Act, Pub. L. No. 104-199, § 3, 110 Stat. 2419, 2419 (1996).
[2] I.R.C. § 2056 (Westlaw through Pub. L. No. 115-43).
[3] United States v. Windsor, 133 S. Ct. 2675, 2683 (2013).
[4] Windsor v. United States, 699 F.3d 169 (2d Cir. 2012).   [5] *Windsor*, 133 S. Ct. at 2693.
[6] *Id.* at 2685.   [7] *Id.*   [8] *Id.*

Group (BLAG) formed by the House of Representatives and that group's "sharp adversarial presentation of the issues."[9]

After dispatching the standing questions, Kennedy addressed the merits of the case.[10] Kennedy reasoned that DOMA violated basic due process rights because states such as New York, possessed of the historical authority to regulate domestic relations, had utilized this decision-making power to enable and support same-sex marriage. These states had thereby chosen to enhance "the recognition, dignity, and protection of the class in their own community."[11] The federal government had, on the other hand, treated this same class quite differently, singling out same-sex couples in order "to impose restrictions and disabilities."[12] In so doing, Kennedy concluded, the federal government had violated the liberty interests and due process rights of same-sex couples.

Kennedy also concluded that Section 3 of DOMA was unconstitutional because it violated the constitutional guarantee of equal protection under the law. Kennedy stated that DOMA's "principal effect" was to "identify a subset of state-sanctioned marriages and make them unequal."[13] DOMA created a two-tiered system of marriage in which some marriages were better than others. Same-sex spouses living in states that sanctioned their marriages were subject to the insecurity of being married in the eyes of the state but not the federal government.[14] This dual system of categorization had the capacity, Kennedy stated, to cause harm not only to the dignity of these same-sex couples but also to their financial health and to the psychological well-being of their children. Justice Kennedy did not discuss levels of scrutiny in this equal protection analysis, which is the usual framework for such an analysis, or specifically apply anything other than the lowest level of review (i.e., rational basis review).

Chief Justice Roberts and Justices Alito and Scalia all filed separate dissents, and Justice Thomas joined parts of both Alito's and Scalia's dissents. The dissents, in the main, focused on questions of jurisdiction, federalism, and scrutiny in equal protection analysis. Scalia's dissent, the most vociferous of the three dissents, took issue with the majority opinion for glossing over significant standing questions in a "jaw-dropping ... assertion of judicial supremacy."[15] Scalia also heavily criticized Kennedy's merits analysis as "rootless and shifting,"[16] calling the majority's reasoning an indeterminate

---

[9] *Id.* at 2688.   [10] *Id.* at 2693.   [11] *Id.* at 2692.   [12] *Id.* at 2693.   [13] *Id.* at 2694.

[14] *Id.* ("This places same-sex couples in an unstable position of being in a second-tier marriage.").

[15] *Id.* at 2698 (Scalia, J., dissenting); *see id.* at 2700 ("We have never before agreed to speak – to 'say what the law is' – where there is no controversy before us.").

[16] *Id.* at 2705.

mix of due process and equal protection as well as an incomplete equal protection analysis, failing as it did to specify any particular level of scrutiny. "Some might conclude," Scalia stated, "that this loaf could have used a while longer in the oven. But that would be wrong; it is already overcooked. The most expert care in preparation cannot redeem a bad recipe."[17]

FEMINIST JUDGMENT

In an opinion that speaks, in many ways, directly to the Scalia critique, Professor Ruthann Robson, writing as Justice Robson, crystallizes the equal protection argument and brings clarity to the question of what precise legal protections should be afforded to claims grounded in sexual orientation discrimination. In so doing, Robson adds clarity to the doctrinal analysis and substance to the discussion of gender.

Robson begins, however, by bringing the story of the two women into focus. Robson deliberately incorporates personal narrative into the statement of facts in order to highlight the lived experience of Windsor and Spyer and to connect with a particular feminist modality. Using information from Windsor's brief, Robson uncovers a small sample of the hardships, large and small, that the women experienced because of their sexual orientation, both in the workplace and in the larger social context. Bringing in the details of the lived realities of and obstacles experienced by Windsor and Spyer, Robson underscores for the reader that "narratives have the capacity to reveal truths about the social world that are [otherwise] flattened or silenced."[18] For example, Robson mentions Spyer's expulsion from college when a campus security guard saw her kissing a woman and Windsor's fear of losing her job when the FBI interviewed her for a security clearance. Robson also tells the story of Windsor's diamond pin, revealing that Spyer gave Windsor the pin instead of a ring in order to avoid "unwelcome questions" from friends and colleagues. Robson highlights the anxieties and injuries of hidden sexuality, as well as the charms and joys of their life together. In this way, Robson connects the law story to the love story, strategically deploying personal narrative in order to "mak[e] abstract claims more tangible"[19] and provide a "wealth of particularized detail that will not permit [the feminist] experience to be ignored."[20]

---

[17] *Id.* at 2707.
[18] Patricia Ewick & Susan Sibley, *Subversive Stories and Hegemonic Tales: Toward a Sociology of Narrative*, 29 LAW & SOC'Y REV. 197, 199 (1995).
[19] Kathryn Abrams, *Hearing the Call of Stories*, 79 CALIF. L. REV. 971, 975 (1991).
[20] *Id.* at 1051.

Like Kennedy, Robson begins by addressing the question of Article III and prudential standing – and agreeing with Justice Kennedy's approach. But Robson moves quickly to the heart of the opinion: equal protection. In the third section of her opinion, Robson embraces Windsor's equal protection claim, concluding that DOMA is unconstitutional on equal protection grounds alone. Before engaging in her equal protection analysis, Robson acknowledges that due process is a potential source of protection for same-sex marriage rights. Robson, however, states her preference for the equal protection rationale, reasoning that the equal protection rights guaranteed by the Fifth and Fourteenth Amendments provide a "more explicit safeguard of prohibited unfairness than due process of law."

Kennedy himself did not provide any in-depth analysis of Windsor's due process rights. Kennedy mentioned the words "due process" only three times in the whole opinion. And as Scalia scathingly observed, "The majority never utters the dread words 'substantive due process,' perhaps sensing the disrepute into which that doctrine has fallen, but that is what those statements mean."[21] Nevertheless, even Kennedy's brief mention of due process rights coupled with language about dignity and social worth have been perceived as fitting quite "comfortably within the Court's existing right-to-marry jurisprudence."[22]

Robson's rejection of the due process framework as the dispositive analytic is, therefore, responsive to critics who find Kennedy's approach to due process reasoning unsatisfying in its brevity. More importantly to the feminist agenda, Robson's approach is also responsive to critics who have been concerned with the use of due process to further – and unnecessarily – entrench the import-ance of marriage in the legal imagination. Due process, these critics have argued, "reifies marriage as a key element in the social front of family, further marginalizing nonmarital families."[23] In Robson's opinion, she chooses equal protection over due process in order not only to remedy discrimination but also to curtail the sociolegal glorification of marriage.

Isolating and expanding the equal protection rationale, then, Robson con-cludes that equal protection is theoretically preferable and that sexual orienta-tion classifications merit intermediate scrutiny within the tiered framework of equal protection analysis, such as gender and sex classifications. Kennedy's opinion "did not invoke any of the traditional doctrinal structures of equal protection analysis, such as suspect classification analysis, fundamental rights

---

[21] *Windsor*, 133 S. Ct. at 2706.

[22] Douglas NeJaime, Windsor's *Right to Marry*, 123 YALE L.J. ONLINE 219, 229 (2013).

[23] Clare Huntington, Obergefell's *Conservatism: Reifying Familial Fronts*, 84 FORDHAM L. REV. 23, 23, (2015).

analysis, or the associated mechanism of heightened scrutiny."[24] Consequently, Robson's application of intermediate scrutiny answers the long-asked question about what level of scrutiny sexual orientation cases merit and brings legal precision to Kennedy's rhetorical flourishes.

Clarifying the relevant level of scrutiny allows Robson to follow a well-lighted path cleared by Justice Ginsburg in her mapping of intermediate scrutiny analysis in the context of gender in *United States v. Virginia*.[25] Robson therefore proceeds directly to an analysis of whether the federal government's justifications for DOMA are "exceedingly persuasive" and whether the challenged classification serves important governmental objectives.[26] She concludes that the interests articulated by BLAG do not meet the test. For example, protecting state sovereignty and democratic self-governance are, she observes, legitimate governmental interests. Nevertheless, as she points out, DOMA actually infringes on such sovereignty rather than facilitating it. Similarly, Robson notes that preserving government resources is a legitimate concern, but that the enforcement of DOMA actually requires *increased* expenditures for "managing the conflicts caused by federal nonrecognition of same-sex marriage." The justifications must be "genuine, not hypothesized or invented *post hoc* in response to litigation."[27] Reliance on the states' justifications here, Robson concludes, fails to meet that test.

Among the various state justifications, Robson singles out one particular set – "defending and nurturing the institution of traditional, heterosexual marriage" and "defending traditional notions of morality" – for extended treatment. Speaking directly to the question of sexual orientation, sex, and gender, Robson concludes that these particular justifications cannot prevail because they rely on "overbroad generalizations" about men and women that derive from and also replicate heteronormativity. Robson likewise reasons that the nurturing of traditional marriage is an inappropriate government interest because such an interest is grounded in outdated and harmful notions about both female sexuality and the role it plays in relation to male desire. According to Robson, this unacceptable mix of marriage and morality harms both men and women in multiple ways.

The proffered state interest of defending traditional marriage harms straight women – even if they are not directly implicated in Windsor's struggle – by consigning them to the confines of masculine authority. This justification assumes, as Robson points out, a female sexuality that is in service of and

[24] Susannah W. Pollvogt, *Marriage Equality,* United States v. Windsor, *and the Crisis in Equal Protection Jurisprudence,* 42 HOFSTRA L. REV. 1045, 1045–46 (2014).
[25] 518 U.S. 515 (1996).   [26] *Id.* at 533.   [27] *Id.*

captive to male desire. In other words, traditional marriage undermines the feminist agenda of actualizing female autonomy. In addition, state interest in traditional marriage harms not only women in general but lesbians in particular. If traditional marriage relegates straight women to heteronormative sites of domesticity, it exiles lesbian women to uncharted spheres where they are subject to eternal nonrecognition. Lesbian women, in this context, are neither subjects nor objects of desire; against this backdrop of "tradition," they are neither cultural nor sexual citizens.

Robson's opinion and use of equal protection doctrine bars traditional marriage from acting as the measuring stick for legitimate, state-sanctioned relationships. In so doing, Robson opens the door for increased fluidity – of gender, sexuality, and identity – within marriage. Rejecting both the due process reification of marriage as well as the state-based defense of marriage, Robson clears space for the expression of "different talents, capacities, or preferences of males and females regarding parental stability and gendered roles." Rejecting gendered stereotypes about marriage participants, Robson's reasoning enables individuals to exist and flourish outside of the predetermined roles of "husband" and "wife." In this way, Robson gestures at the possibility of a legal marital status that destabilizes both gender roles and conventional household economies, imagining men as homemakers and women as primary earners. What is more, this disruptive vision of marriage allows for another, even more transgressive version of marriage, one in which neither gender nor sex plays a role, a relationship that has no basis in either sexual preference or gender constraint.

One strong indicator of this break with heteronormativity is evident in Robson's treatment – or rather, elision – of children. Kennedy, in the majority opinion, insisted strongly on the harms wrought by DOMA on the children of same-sex couples, stating that the law "humiliate[d] tens of thousands of children now being raised by same-sex couples."[28] Kennedy mentioned children close to a half-dozen times in his opinion, and ensuing opinions examining the constitutionality of state-level same-sex marriage bans maintained this focus on the dignitary harm to children, assuming that same-sex couples aspired to homonormativity, in the sense of replicating and adopting the same domestic patterns as conventional different-sex couples.[29] The mention

---

[28] United States v. Windsor, 133 S. Ct. 2675, 2694 (2013).

[29] *See* Anthony C. Infanti, *The House of* Windsor: *Accentuating the Heteronormativity in the Tax Incentives for Procreation*, 89 WASH. L. REV. 1185, 1187 (2014) ("A key component of all of these decisions has been the effect of prohibitions against same-sex marriage on the family and, particularly, on the children of same-sex couples.")

of children in the original *Windsor* decision is particularly notable – or jarring – given the fact that Windsor and Spyer had no children and children played no part in either their love story or their tax story. Robson, declining to equate intimacy in marriage with procreative desires and childrearing, mentions children only once. When she does invoke children, it is in the context of the state's invalid defense of traditional marriage. Defending traditional marriage, Robson remarks, can prove harmful in the context of children by "elevating a biological component to parenting that denigrates every adoptive or nonbiological parent, whether male or female." Gender does not make marriage, nor does biology alone make a parent.

Robson's use of equal protection and clarification of the level of scrutiny have, therefore, significant consequences. Her equal protection reasoning provides solid grounds for eradicating gender stereotypes as well as sexual orientation discrimination. Likewise, her equal protection reasoning disables the reification of marriage as an institution and the attachment of privilege to marriage itself. In these respects, her opinion offers real feminist traction in a way that Kennedy's opinion did not. Furthermore, Robson's use of intermediate scrutiny provides a platform and the tools for claimants in subsequent discrimination cases based on sexual orientation, helping gays and lesbians combat discrimination in domains other than marital. Setting the standard for lower courts at intermediate scrutiny and binding them to such precedential authority would help future gay and lesbian claimants who challenged laws targeting them based on sexual orientation. As one scholar remarked after Kennedy's failure to identify a heightened (or any) standard of scrutiny in *Obergefell*, "This heightened level of scrutiny would in turn give gays and lesbians a measure of repose, affording them the same certainty that racial minorities and women have that laws targeting them are unlikely to be upheld by courts today."[30] In the workplace, aware of a heightened scrutiny level, government employers might have increased reason to monitor and deter discriminatory behavior. Intermediate scrutiny could, then, have the potential to mitigate the intensity of hostile work environments for LGBTQ employees.

In her closing section, because federalism was a lens of analysis in Kennedy's opinion, Robson ends by referencing the theme of federal authority over marriage law and policy. She writes that the striking down of DOMA's marital definition as unconstitutional will certainly restore an important historical right to the states and increase equality. Nevertheless, Robson points out that federal tax law will continue to privilege and promote marriage even after

---

[30] Peter Nicholas, *Obergefell's Squandered Potential*, 6 Calif. L. Rev. Circuit 137, 138 (2015); *see Obergefell v. Hodges*, 135 S. Ct. 2584 (2015).

DOMA has been stricken from the books. Social policy inheres in choices made about the tax system, Robson states, and while marriage equality might be realized, we have yet to make visible the position of and harm to those individuals who live outside or on the margins of marriage. An example Robson uses is the present treatment of married couples as taxpayers and the use of the joint return. The adoption of the joint tax return as a method for remedying unequal tax treatment of married couples in common law and community property states has embedded "the fiction of marital unity" into the tax laws, furthering outdated coverture values and rewarding the specialization of household labor.

In making this point, Robson gestures at future work that might be taken up in order to address marital supremacy in the tax context. This work involves recognizing the relationships that *Windsor* leaves behind and the interests that tax reform obscures – namely couples who are unmarried and thus lack the legal status to benefit from rules such as the marital deduction, and couples who, even though married, lack the wealth to benefit from marital tax rules. Citing to important and cogent tax scholarship that takes a feminist stance in addressing these issues, Robson observes that, even in a post-*Windsor* world, the current tax system privileges the already privileged, that is to say high-wealth, hetero- and homonormative couples in more traditional marriages.

One obvious but unstated characteristic of Windsor and Spyer's relationship was that it took place against a backdrop of not only discrimination but also privilege. Their story unfolded in well-appointed Manhattan apartments and cottages in the Hamptons. They both had good incomes and their life together was one of financial comfort. This wealth was confirmed by the facts of the case. That Windsor paid $363,053 in federal estate taxes upon Spyer's death meant Spyer's estate was subject to estate tax and therefore in excess of $3.5 million at the time of her death in 2009. Windsor was, ultimately, able to benefit from the marital deduction and avoid transfer tax. Nevertheless, as feminist tax scholars have highlighted, the tax system was written to protect and benefit high-wealth heterosexual spouses, usually husbands, in marriages defined by income or wealth asymmetry between the spouses.[31]

For example, various forms of wealth transfer, such as the Qualified Terminable Interest Property trust, authorize a high-wealth spouse to limit the control of the other spouse over his money and property after his death and allow him to decide unilaterally who will receive that money and property after his wife's death, recreating the life estate and reenacting a fiction of

---

[31] *See, e.g.,* Wendy Gerzog, *The Marital Deduction QTIP Provisions: Illogical and Degrading to Women,* 5 UCLA WOMEN'S L.J. 301 (1995).

marital unity. These tax laws "reflect a 'deeply patriarchal outlook' that a male decedent must ensure that his widow will not squander the estate or disinherit the decedent's children."[32] These tax rules are unlikely to benefit most lesbian couples because they do not possess the wealth for the rules to matter. Moreover, working and living at the intersection of gender and sexual orientation discrimination, lesbian couples are less likely to amass wealth than their straight and male counterparts. And finally, even if lesbian couples do inherit or acquire wealth, the tax rules are not necessarily designed to benefit these couples because they are more likely inclined to choose less gendered and patriarchal forms of wealth holding. What Windsor won was an equal protection victory. What she obtained, however, was equal access to a tax system built to help married men control wealth.

In closing her opinion, Robson highlights these failings of the current tax system, acknowledging that "heteronormativity has been one of the core building blocks of our federal tax system."[33] Nevertheless, as Robson writes, "tax laws, like all other laws, should have as their mandate progress toward equality." The work of equal protection, Robson suggests, is not over. *Windsor* was a bright moment in the legal struggle against discrimination. *Windsor* did not, however, make the tax laws more equitable or less marriage-centric. *Windsor* left to the future larger fights about the gender and class biases inscribed in the tax laws.

UNITED STATES v. WINDSOR, 133 S. CT. 2675 (2013)

JUSTICE RUTHANN ROBSON DELIVERED THE OPINION OF THE COURT

We have before us a constitutional challenge to Section 3 of the Defense of Marriage Act (DOMA), Pub. L. No. 104-199, 110 Stat. 2419 (1996), passed by Congress and signed by President William J. Clinton. Section 3 of DOMA amended the Dictionary Act, 1 U.S.C. § 7, to limit the definition of "marriage" to only a "legal union between one man and one woman as husband and wife" and likewise to limit the definition of "spouse" to only "a person of the opposite sex who is a husband or wife." In short, Section 3 of DOMA prohibits

---

[32] Lily Kahng, *The Not-So-Merry Wives of* Windsor: *The Taxation of Women in Same-Sex Marriages*, 101 CORNELL L. REV. 325, 353 (2016).

[33] Infanti, *supra* note 29, at 1187.

the federal government from recognizing same-sex marriages as marriages even if state laws recognize those marriages.

Thus, DOMA prohibited the Internal Revenue Service from according the same tax treatment under the federal estate tax laws to Edith Windsor, the married same-sex partner of decedent Thea Spyer, as would have been accorded were they a different-sex married couple. Under federal law, estates over a certain amount ($3.5 million for decedents dying in 2009) are subject to estate tax. However, Internal Revenue Code § 2056 allows for a marital deduction, which generally operates as a total exemption from tax on certain transfers made to a spouse. But because DOMA precluded the applicability of § 2056 to Spyer's estate, Windsor paid $363,053 in estate taxes. Windsor sought a refund, which the IRS denied, citing DOMA. Windsor sought relief in federal court, challenging the constitutionality of Section 3 of DOMA as violating the guarantee of equal protection of the law, as applicable to the federal government through the Fifth Amendment to the U.S. Constitution.

While Windsor's suit – as well as numerous other challenges to Section 3 of DOMA – was pending, the federal government came to agree with the merits of her constitutional claim. Attorney General Eric Holder announced that the Department of Justice (DOJ) would no longer defend DOMA's constitutionality because the Attorney General and the President believe that a heightened standard of scrutiny should apply to classifications based on sexual orientation and that Section 3 of DOMA is unconstitutional under that standard. Letter from Eric H. Holder Jr., Attorney Gen., to John A. Boehner, Speaker, U.S. House of Representatives 5 (Feb. 23, 2011), https://www.justice.gov/opa/pr/letter-attorney-general-congress-litigation-involving-defense-marriage-act. Prompted by the Executive Branch's decision not to defend the constitutionality of DOMA, the Bipartisan Legal Advisory Group of the U.S. House of Representatives (BLAG) successfully moved to intervene to defend the constitutionality of the statute. After considering the merits, U.S. District Judge Barbara Jones entered summary judgment in favor of Windsor, *Windsor v. United States*, 833 F. Supp. 2d 394 (S.D.N.Y. 2012), on the equal protection claim. Importantly, however, as the letter from the Attorney General stated, Section 3 of DOMA would "continue to be enforced by the Executive Branch." It is uncontroverted that Windsor has not received the refund of taxes paid by Spyer's estate. Nevertheless, the somewhat uncommon configuration of this case raises the preliminary issue of whether there is a sufficient "case or controversy" under Article III of the Constitution to empower this Court to consider the merits.

We hold that there is an Article III case or controversy and that Section 3 of DOMA is an unconstitutional violation of equal protection as applicable to the United States through the Fifth Amendment's Due Process Clause, independent of any federalism or Tenth Amendment concerns. We consider these issues in turn after a brief discussion of the background facts.

I

We adapt our statement of the facts from the Brief on the Merits of Respondent Edith Windsor, given that they are uncontroverted. We include this background to provide a contextualized narrative of the real people involved in this challenge to Section 3 of DOMA. *See* Kathryn Abrams, *Hearing the Call of Stories*, 79 Calif. L. Rev. 971 (1991). This case is about estate taxes paid to the federal government in the amount of over three hundred thousand dollars, although it is also about much more.

As Windsor's brief relates, in the early 1960s, at a time when lesbians and gay men risked losing their families, friends, and livelihoods if their sexual orientation became known, respondent Edith Windsor and her late spouse Thea Spyer fell in love and embarked upon a relationship that would last until Dr. Spyer's death forty-four years later.

The depth, commitment, and longevity of their relationship and eventual marriage are all the more remarkable given the times they lived through. Dr. Spyer was expelled from college when a campus security guard observed her kissing another woman. Ms. Windsor entered into a brief, and unsuccessful, marriage to a man in the early 1950s because she did not believe that it was possible for her to live openly as a lesbian. Shortly after her first marriage ended, Ms. Windsor moved to New York City, where she received a graduate degree in mathematics. She eventually became a highly successful computer programmer at IBM, achieving the highest technical rank at the company, a notable achievement for a woman at the time. Sadly, discriminatory federal laws threatened her ability to pursue her career. Ms. Windsor supported herself during graduate school by working as a programmer on the UNIVAC computer for the Atomic Energy Commission. But an executive order prohibited companies that had contracts with the government from employing gay men or lesbians. *See* Exec. Order No. 10,450, 18 Fed. Reg. 2489 (1953). Thus, when the FBI requested an interview in connection with her security clearance, Ms. Windsor rightly feared that she would lose her job if she were asked about her sexual orientation, although the FBI never raised the subject. Similarly, by hiring Ms. Windsor (who never disclosed her sexual orientation), IBM later unknowingly ran afoul of that same executive order.

Threats of disclosure and harassment also forced lesbians like Ms. Windsor and Dr. Spyer to lead important parts of their lives in secrecy. Ms. Windsor and Dr. Spyer met at one of the few restaurants in New York City where lesbians were welcomed in 1963. Four years later, they moved in together and became engaged, although there was then no prospect of their being able to marry legally. To avoid unwelcome questions about the identity of Ms. Windsor's "fiancé" from coworkers, Dr. Spyer proposed with a diamond brooch, instead of a diamond ring.

Their life together was full of all the joys and sorrows that any couple faces. In addition to paying their taxes, they worked, traveled, spent time with friends, and participated in their communities. Ms. Windsor spent her career at IBM. Dr. Spyer, who earned a doctorate in clinical psychology, maintained an active private practice.

In 1977, Dr. Spyer was diagnosed with progressive multiple sclerosis, a disease of the central nervous system that causes irreversible neurological damage and often, as in Dr. Spyer's case, paralysis. Ms. Windsor supported Dr. Spyer as her disability worsened, requiring first a cane, then crutches, then a manual wheelchair, and then a motorized wheelchair that Dr. Spyer could operate with her one usable finger. Their life together became the subject of an award-winning documentary film, *Edie and Thea: A Very Long Engagement* (2009).

Eventually, Dr. Spyer's health had so deteriorated that it became clear she would not live long enough to hold their wedding ceremony in New York, as the couple had long hoped. Therefore, joined by a physician and several close friends, Dr. Spyer, then seventy-five, and Ms. Windsor, then seventy-seven, flew to Toronto, Canada, where they were wed on May 22, 2007. They spent their last two years together as a married couple. Dr. Spyer died of a heart condition on February 5, 2009. Grief-stricken, Ms. Windsor suffered a severe heart attack and received a diagnosis of stress cardiomyopathy, or "broken heart syndrome."

Dr. Spyer left her entire estate to Ms. Windsor, who was appointed executor. Because DOMA prohibited recognition of their marriage, the estate was required to pay more than $363,000 in federal estate taxes.

II

No matter how sympathetic a situation might be, the judiciary is constrained by the Constitution as to the wrongs federal courts might remedy. The purpose of the "case or controversy" provision, U.S. Const. art. III, § 2, cl. 1, is to "limit the business of federal courts to questions presented in an adversary context and in a form historically viewed as capable of resolution through the judicial process." *Flast v. Cohen*, 392 U.S. 83, 95 (1968). Accordingly, there is no Article III case or controversy when the parties desire "precisely the same result." *Moore v. Charlotte-Mecklenburg Bd. of Educ.*, 402 U.S. 47, 48 (1971) (per curiam); *see GTE Sylvania, Inc. v. Consumers Union of U.S., Inc.*, 445 U.S. 375, 382–83 (1980). It is essential that all parties at all stages of the litigation have standing to invoke the federal judicial power. To hold otherwise would be to allow an advisory opinion, a practice we have long prohibited. *See Hayburn's Case*, 2 U.S. 408 (2 Dall. 409) (1792).

As a threshold matter, we conclude that this case comes within Article III's extension of judicial power to "cases or controversies," despite the unusual developments in this litigation.

When she filed her complaint, Windsor easily satisfied the well-established requirements for standing, which we reiterated just last term. *See Clapper v. Amnesty Int'l USA*, 133 S. Ct. 1138, 1147 (2013) (to establish Article III standing, an injury must be "concrete, particularized, and actual or imminent; fairly traceable to the challenged action; and redressable by a favorable ruling"). Generally, the term "taxpayer standing" describes situations in which an individual who has paid taxes argues she has a "continuing, legally cognizable interest in ensuring that those funds are not *used* by the Government in a way that violates the Constitution." *Ariz. Christian Sch. Tuition Org. v. Winn*, 563 U.S. 125, 134 (2011); *Hein v. Freedom from Religion Found., Inc.*, 551 U.S. 587, 599 (2007) (plurality opinion). Here, however, Windsor has a classic cognizable economic injury of the type most easily recognized in that she alleged that the government owed her a specific amount of money. Moreover, it is uncontroverted that the district court had power to render its ruling, even after the United States essentially agreed with the merits of Windsor's constitutional challenge. After the district court's judgment, the United States did not remit the refund, consistent with its position that the Executive Branch would continue to "enforce" DOMA. Instead, both DOJ and BLAG filed notices of appeal to the Second Circuit and the Solicitor General of the United States filed a petition for writ of certiorari with this Court. In our grant of certiorari, we specifically directed the parties to brief the issues of whether "the Executive Branch's agreement with the court below that DOMA is unconstitutional deprives this Court of jurisdiction to decide this case; and whether the Bipartisan Legal Advisory Group of the United States House of Representatives has Article III standing in this case," *United States v. Windsor*, 133 S. Ct. 786 (2012). Thereafter, this Court appointed Professor Vicki C. Jackson to brief and argue as *amicus curiae*, in support of the positions that the Executive Branch's agreement with the court below that DOMA is unconstitutional deprives this Court of jurisdiction to decide this case and that BLAG lacks Article III standing in this case. *United States v. Windsor*, 133 S. Ct. 814 (2012).

We find that the United States retains standing before this Court so that there is a sufficient case or controversy under Article III. The United States is subject to a court judgment to refund a specific amount to the taxpayer, Edith Windsor, which the United States has not done but has instead pursued further judicial review in resistance to the taxpayer's claim. That the United States, through the DOJ and the President, may agree with the merits of Windsor's claim is not determinative. As in *INS v. Chadha*, 462 U.S. 919 (1983), in which the executive had determined that the federal statute was unconstitutional but the U.S. Immigration and Naturalization Service was enforcing the decision of the House of Representatives under the statute, there is a live case or controversy here. In *Chadha*, depending upon the outcome of the case, Chadha would or would not be deported by the INS; here, depending upon the outcome of the case, Windsor will or will not be issued a substantial tax refund, paid by the U.S. Treasury.

Our consideration of prudential standing, an issue distinct from Article III standing, does not warrant a contrary result. We recognize that just because this Court has power under Article III to hear this case does not mean that this Court should exercise its discretionary review when there is not sufficient adversarial argument. The adversarial nature of this litigation, however, is well demonstrated by the appearance of BLAG as well as by the numerous *amicus* briefs supporting BLAG's position. Although it is not determinative, and may not even be relevant, we also note that BLAG is financed by taxpayer funds, into the millions of dollars, as it vigorously presses its arguments that DOMA is constitutional.

It is to the merits of those constitutional arguments that we now turn.

III

While it was not until the Fourteenth Amendment that our nation's dedication to the principle of equality was introduced into our Constitution, its application not only to state governments but also to the federal government is clear. As we have found, while the "equal protection of the laws" phrase in the Fourteenth Amendment is a "more explicit safeguard of prohibited unfairness than due process of law," the Fifth Amendment's Due Process Clause includes equal protection because it is "unthinkable that the same Constitution would impose a lesser duty on the Federal Government" than on state governments. *Bolling v. Sharpe*, 347 U.S. 497, 499–500 (1954); *accord Weinberger v. Wiesenfeld*, 420 U.S. 636 (1975) (equal protection component of Fifth Amendment applied to gender-based Social Security Act provision on benefits); *U.S. Dep't of Agric. v. Moreno*, 413 U.S. 528 (1973) (equal protection component of Fifth Amendment applied to Food Stamp Act that rendered ineligible any household containing an individual unrelated to any other member of the household); *Frontiero v. Richardson*, 411 U.S. 677 (1973) (equal protection component of Fifth Amendment applied to enforcement of gender-based federal statutes governing benefits for members of the uniformed services). Section 3 of DOMA must be measured against our equal protection doctrine and our nation's continuing commitment to equality.

Section 3 of DOMA makes a classification based upon sexual orientation and upon gender, limiting marriage for purposes of federal law to a legal union between "one man and one woman." We need not consider whether the legally operative classification should be sexual orientation or gender. We hold that equal protection challenges on the basis of sexual orientation classifications deserve intermediate scrutiny, similar to the gender and sex classifications that sexual orientation classifications resemble and upon which they rely. We eschew a separate analysis of sexual orientation classifications using the factors developed from *United States v. Carolene Products Co.*, 304 U.S. 144, 153 n.4 (1938), and articulated in *City of Cleburne v. Cleburne Living Center*, 473 U.S. 432 (1985). We specifically reject an inquiry into factors such as "political powerlessness" and "history of past discrimination" in light of our cases such as *Adarand Constructors, Inc. v. Pena*, 515 U.S. 200, 224 (1995), in which we have valued the principle of "consistency," holding that the "stand- ard of review under the Equal Protection Clause is not dependent" on whether the class is being "burdened or benefited by a particular classifica- tion." Moreover, while the "tiers of scrutiny" have been subject to criticism, they nevertheless are valuable shorthand for the degree of judicial inquiry that various classifications merit. Like sex and gender, classifications based on sexuality require an important government interest and the means chosen to accomplish that government interest must be substantially related to that interest. Section 3 of DOMA fails both of these requirements.

The government interests supporting the passage of DOMA are explicitly detailed in a forty-five-page House of Representatives Report, H.R. Rep. No. 104-664 (1996). This report enumerates four specific government interests: the government's interest in defending and nurturing the institution of traditional, heterosexual marriage; the government's interest in defending traditional notions of morality; the government's interest in protecting state sovereignty and democratic self-governance; and the government's interest in preserving scarce government resources. Additionally, BLAG now asserts additional gov- ernment interests that it argues should be considered as supporting Section 3 of DOMA: preserving each sovereign's ability to define marriage for itself at a time when states are beginning to experiment with the traditional definition;

ensuring national uniformity in eligibility for federal benefits and programs based on marital status; preserving past legislative judgments, conserving financial resources, and avoiding uncertain and unpredictable effects on the federal fisc; proceeding with caution when faced with the unknown consequences of an unprecedented redefinition of marriage, a foundational social institution, by a minority of states; and retaining the traditional definition of marriage for the same reasons states might retain that definition, including providing a stable structure to raise unintended and unplanned offspring, encouraging the rearing of children by their biological parents, and promoting child-rearing by both a mother and a father. Br. on the Merits for Resp't the Bipartisan Legal Advisory Group of the United States House of Representatives (BLAG) 30–49.

Most of these articulated interests do not rise to the level of important. As we stated when considering whether the exclusion of women from a public university violated equal protection, to qualify as "important," the "justification must be genuine, not hypothesized or invented *post hoc* in response to litigation. And it must not rely on overbroad generalizations about the different talents, capacities, or preferences of males and females." *United States v. Virginia*, 518 U.S. 515, 533 (1996).

The asserted interests in the House Report relating to "defending and nurturing the institution of traditional, heterosexual marriage" and "defending traditional notions of morality" unacceptably rely on the overbroad generalizations about males and females that are inherent in heteronormativity. These asserted interests both assume and seek to mandate a female sexuality, for example, that is directed exclusively at males. It exiles women who are not entirely male-directed sexually from both marriage and morality. Even if we were to agree with BLAG that Section 3 of DOMA merits mere rational basis review, it is well established that the "bare congressional desire to harm a politically unpopular group" cannot justify disparate treatment of that group under equal protection principles, *see Moreno*, 413 U.S. at 534–35, and that invocations of "morality" are not legitimate interests, *see Lawrence v. Texas*, 539 U.S. 558, 578 (2003) ("The Texas statute furthers no legitimate state interest which can justify its intrusion into the personal and private life of the individual."); *id.* at 583 (O'Connor, J., concurring) ("Moral disapproval of a group cannot be a legitimate governmental interest under the Equal Protection Clause because legal classifications must not be 'drawn for the purpose of disadvantaging the group burdened by the law.'" (quoting *Romer v. Evans*, 517 U.S. 620, 633 (1996)).

The interests asserted by BLAG are largely invented *post hoc* in response to the litigation challenging the constitutionality of Section 3 of DOMA; they are not genuine interests, but are hypothesized after the fact. Additionally, the interests asserted for maintaining the traditional definition of marriage for the same reasons as states might do so rely on overbroad generalizations about the different talents, capacities, or preferences of males and females regarding parental stability and their gendered roles, as well as elevating a biological component to parenting that denigrates every adoptive or nonbiological parent, whether male or female.

Considering the two interests contained in the House Report that might rise to the level of important – namely, the government's interest in protecting state sovereignty and democratic self-governance and the government's interest in preserving scarce government resources – the means chosen by Section 3 of DOMA prohibit the federal government from recognizing same-sex marriages even if a state does so. This prohibition is not substantially related to protecting state sovereignty or protecting scarce resources. In fact, the prohibition undercuts both of these articulated interests. Section 3 of DOMA dishonors state sovereignty rather than protecting it because it deviates from the long-standing practice of the federal government, including the IRS, of generally accepting state determinations of marital status. *See Boyter v. Comm'r*, 668 F.2d 1382, 1385 (4th Cir. 1981) ("We agree with the government's argument that under the Internal Revenue Code a federal court is bound by state law rather than federal law when attempting to construe marital status."). Additionally, DOMA essentially makes the federal government a party to one state's infringement of another state's sovereignty in tax situations involving married same-sex partners who have economic interests such as property, employment, or tort actions in a state that does not honor the same-sex marriage that they entered into in another sovereign state.

Section 3 of DOMA unnecessarily requires scarce resources to be spent when it requires the federal government to depart from its usual practice and to treat the property and other rights of married couples differently for federal tax purposes from how they are treated under state law. For example, scarce federal resources have been spent deciding whether or not to have the federal tax treatment of California registered domestic partners follow their treatment under state community property laws, providing guidance to affected taxpayers, and ultimately in monitoring affected taxpayers' reporting of their incomes for federal tax purposes because confusion and error are the inevitable by-product of a decision to adopt dissonant federal and state treatment of the same events or transactions. *Compare* I.R.S. Chief Couns. Mem. 2010-21-050 (May 5, 2010), *and* I.R.S. Priv. Ltr. Rul. 2010-21-048 (May 5, 2010), *with* I.R.S. Gen. Couns. Mem. 2006-08-038 (Feb. 24, 2006), available at http://www.irs.gov/pub/irs-wd/0608038.pdf. Additionally, DOMA actually causes states to expend their scarce resources managing the conflicts caused by the federal nonrecognition of same-sex marriage: when the federal and state tax returns do not "look the same," this will typically mean state tax officials must inspect the tax returns more carefully to resolve the differences and may trigger unnecessary audits of those returns, inconveniencing the affected taxpayers. *See* Carlton Smith & Edward Stein, *Dealing with DOMA: Federal Non-Recognition Complicates State Income Taxation of Same-Sex Relationships,* 24 Colum. J. Gender & L. 29, 33 (2012). This interest in conserving scarce resources also misapprehends the reality of marriage recognition in federal tax and other regulations. In Windsor's particular situation, the federal government will forfeit tax revenue by reason of the estate tax marital deduction, I.R.C. § 2056, but in other instances the federal government will gain tax revenue by recognizing same-sex marriage. *See* Amicus Curiae Br. of the Center for Fair Administration of Taxes 12–13 (discussing Code §§ 267(c) and 4975, regarding prohibited interspousal transfers to avoid taxation).

In sum, we hold that sexual orientation classifications, like gender and sex classifications, are subject to intermediate scrutiny under equal protection doctrine, requiring at least that the challenged classification serves important governmental interests and that the means employed are substantially related to the achievement of those interests. We further hold that Section 3 of DOMA prohibiting federal recognition of valid same-sex marriages is not substantially related to any important government interests, and therefore Section 3 of DOMA violates the equal protection component of the Fifth Amendment.

IV

It can seem axiomatic that marriage and family law are within the province of states rather than the federal government and that such an arrangement is "guaranteed" by the Tenth Amendment. Section 3 of DOMA and the federal tax laws belie such an assertion. Section 3 of DOMA altered the federal Dictionary Act's definition of marriage and thereby affected more than 1,000 federal laws and thousands more federal regulations. The federal tax laws and regulations are far from marriage neutral, but contain numerous provisions that not only rest on marital definitions but that reify assumptions about marriage and that seek to achieve social policy choices through the tax system. For example, the present treatment of married couples for income tax purposes requiring a "joint return" or its equivalent is a congressional response to decisions from this Court regarding tax consequences relative to community property and common law marital regimes. *See Lucas v. Earl,* 282 U.S. 101

(1930); *Poe v. Seaborn*, 281 U.S. 111 (1930). Perhaps predictably, the 1948 congressional compromise rendered essentially irrebuttable the fiction of marital unity and reified the breadwinner-dependent model of marriage, penalizing other marital realities. Less explicably, unlike most other nations, we have not abandoned this outdated filing method, despite cogent critiques and discussions from tax scholars, *see, e.g.*, Patricia A. Cain, *Taxing Families Fairly*, 48 Santa Clara L. Rev. 805 (2008); Anthony C. Infanti, *Decentralizing Family: An Inclusive Proposal for Individual Tax Filing in the United States*, 2010 Utah L. Rev. 605; Lily Kahng, *One Is the Loneliest Number: The Single Taxpayer in A Joint Return World*, 61 Hastings L.J. 651 (2010); Nancy J. Knauer, *Heteronormativity and Federal Tax Policy*, 101 W. Va. L. Rev. 129 (1998); Marjorie E. Kornhauser, *Love, Money, and the IRS: Family, Income-Sharing, and the Joint Income Tax Return*, 45 Hastings L.J. 63 (1993). There remain important questions about how and why Windsor's (or anyone's) marriage, whether it be to a same-sex partner or a different-sex partner, should be a litmus test for her treatment under the federal tax laws.

Windsor's equality challenge to the government's refusal to allow her the estate tax marital deduction implicitly raises widespread equality concerns for the entire tax regime based upon the extant marital status and family classifications that assume heteronormativity, as well as upon the gendered, racial, and socioeconomic class–based disparate effects of these classifications. State laws that might similarly raise equal protection concerns do not then insulate federal laws, including tax laws, from constitutional scrutiny. Instead, tax laws like all other laws, must comply with mandates of equal protection. Moreover, tax laws, like all other laws, should have as their mandate progress toward equality.

The judgment of the Court of Appeals for the Second Circuit is affirmed.

It is so ordered.

Index